CARDINAL WOLSEY

CARDINAL WOLSEY
Church, state and art

❋

Edited by S. J. GUNN
Fellow and Tutor in Modern History, Merton College, Oxford

and P. G. LINDLEY
Post-doctoral Research Fellow, The British Academy

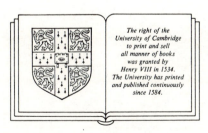

The right of the
University of Cambridge
to print and sell
all manner of books
was granted by
Henry VIII in 1534.
The University has printed
and published continuously
since 1584.

CAMBRIDGE UNIVERSITY PRESS
Cambridge
New York   Port Chester   Melbourne   Sydney

Published by the Press Syndicate of the University of Cambridge
The Pitt Building, Trumpington Street, Cambridge CB2 1RP
40 West 20th Street, New York, NY 10011, USA
10 Stamford Road, Oakleigh, Melbourne 3166, Australia

First published 1991

Printed in Great Britain by the Bath Press, Avon

British Library cataloguing in publication data

Cardinal Wolsey: Church, state and art.
1. England. Wolsey, Thomas, 1475?–1530
I. Gunn, S. J. (Steven J.) II. Lindley, P. G. 942.052092

Library of Congress cataloguing in publication data

Cardinal Wolsey: Church, state and art / edited by S. J. Gunn and P. G. Lindley.
p.   cm.
Includes index.
ISBN 0 521 37568 1
1. Wolsey, Thomas, 1475?–1530.
2. Great Britain – History – Henry VIII, 1509–1547.
3. Statesmen – Great Britain – Biography.
4. Art patrons – England – Biography.
5. Cardinals – England – Biography.
I. Gunn, S. J. (Steven J.) II. Lindley, P. G.
DA334.W8C29 1991
942.05'2'092–dc20   [B]90–37890   CIP

ISBN 0 521 37568 1 hardback

Thomas Wolsey was England's leading statesman, churchman and patron of the arts for a period of over fourteen years. In that time England played a greater role in European politics than she had done for a century or more; there were bold initiatives in domestic government; the church faced the call for reform and the challenge of heresy; and the influence of the Renaissance was felt strongly in many areas of English culture. In this fully illustrated volume, eleven expert contributors assess Wolsey's role in all these developments, from his patronage of music, sculpture, stained glass, goldsmiths' work and domestic and collegiate architecture, through his handling of the church and the criticism it evoked, to his management of politics, central and local government, and foreign affairs. A general introduction sets the individual chapters in context by evaluating the whole range of Wolsey's ministerial responsibilities and achievements, and his part in the early English Renaissance. It also sets him in his proper context by comparing him in detail with other cardinal–ministers active in the European states of the day.

In examining Wolsey's career in all its aspects – not least the cultivation of artistic magnificence which so struck his contemporaries – this volume provides a fuller and more balanced understanding of Wolsey's impact on early Tudor England and of his significance in a dramatic and controversial period of history.

Contents

Plates

Figures

Preface

This book developed out of a conference on Cardinal Wolsey held at St Catharine's College, Cambridge, in 1988. It was apparent to everyone at the conference that a good deal of new research on Wolsey was taking place simultaneously in many different fields, and that the fruits of this research, which profoundly affected the picture of the cardinal provided in A. F. Pollard's *Wolsey*, should be brought together in print. It is symptomatic of the diversity of Wolsey's interests that a team of specialists from a wide range of historical disciplines has provided the best means of reassessing his importance.

Our thanks are due to the Master and Fellows of St Catharine's College, and to Professor G. D. S. Henderson, of the History of Art Department at Cambridge, for their hospitality to the conference. A number of friends and colleagues have read drafts of the introduction and we particularly wish to thank Cliff Davies, Eric Ives, Paul Joannides, Simon Thurley, Sandy Heslop, Richard Morris, Tom Campbell, John Blatchly, Hilary Wayment and Susan Foister. Finally, the editors wish to record their gratitude to the Warden and Fellows of Merton College, Oxford and the Master and Fellows of St Catharine's College, Cambridge, the President and Fellows of the British Academy and the University of Newcastle upon Tyne for the research fellowships which enabled them to write their essays and edit the text.

S. J. Gunn
P. G. Lindley

Abbreviations

BL	British Library
Bodl.	Bodleian Library, Oxford
Cavendish	G. Cavendish, *The Life and Death of Cardinal Wolsey*, ed. R. S. Sylvester (Early English Text Society, 243, 1959)
CSPM	*Calendar of State Papers, Milan*, ed. A. B. Hinds (London, 1912)
CSPS	*Calendar of State Papers, Spanish*, ed. G. A. Bergenroth et al., 15 vols. (London, 1862–1954)
CSPV	*Calendar of State Papers, Venetian*, ed. R. Brown et al., 9 vols. (London, 1864–98)
CVMA	*Corpus Vitrearum Medii Aevi*
Hall	E. Hall, *Hall's Chronicle* (London, 1809 edition)
HKW	*History of the King's Works*, ed. H. M. Colvin, 6 vols. (London, 1963–82)
LP	*Letters and Papers, Foreign and Domestic of the Reign of Henry VIII*, ed. J. F. Brewer et al., 22 vols. in 35 (London, 1862–1932)
Pollard	A. F. Pollard, *Wolsey* (London, 1929 edition)
PRO	Public Record Office, Chancery Lane
RCHM	*Royal Commission on Historical Monuments*
Skelton	*John Skelton: The Complete English Poems*, ed. J. Scattergood (Harmondsworth, 1983)
StP	*State Papers, Henry VIII* (Record Commission) 11 vols. (London, 1830–52)
VCH	*Victoria County History*

Introduction

S. J. GUNN and P. G. LINDLEY

Thomas Wolsey's contemporaries could not doubt his importance. For fourteen years he was Henry VIII's lord chancellor and chief minister, and for eleven of those years he controlled the national church as the pope's legate *a latere*, as though sent specially from Rome. He was the most powerful man in England bar the king. But for all Wolsey's prominence, it has never been easy to form a balanced assessment of his career. Even before his fall from power in 1529, protestants began to vilify him as the archetype of a proud popish prelate. Soon afterwards, catholics started to decry his failure to strengthen the church, stand by Catherine of Aragon, and prevent the Reformation. By 1724, Richard Fiddes felt that Wolsey's repute had sunk so low that a primary aim of his biography of the cardinal should be to do 'justice to his injured memory'.[1] More recent historians have also tried to restore Wolsey's reputation, but less often as an individual than as the representative of some abstract type: the balance-of-power diplomat, the 'national statesman' of 'far-reaching patriotism', or the 'balanced, cynical, efficient administrator and power-politician' with no time for dangerous fanaticism.[2] Others have used him as a convenient antithesis to the real object of their interest, presenting a 'truly medieval' chancellor whose 'moderately inspired amateurishness' contrasts with the modern administrative genius of Thomas Cromwell, or a corrupt cardinal, against whom 'no charge . . . was too gross to be impossible', quite unrepresentative of the popular and exemplary English clergy of his day.[3] Even Wolsey's greatest biographer valued the cardinal largely as the political educator of Henry VIII.[4]

[1] R. Fiddes, *The Life of Cardinal Wolsey* (London, 1724), p. ii.

[2] Pollard, pp. 3–4; M. Creighton, *Cardinal Wolsey* (London, 1888), p. 213; J. Ridley, *The Statesman and the Fanatic: Thomas Wolsey and Sir Thomas More* (London, 1982), p. 293.

[3] G. R. Elton, *The Tudor Revolution in Government. Administrative Changes in the Reign of Henry VIII* (Cambridge, 1953), p. 65; Elton, 'Cardinal Wolsey', in his *Studies in Tudor and Stuart Politics and Government*, 3 vols. (Cambridge, 1974–83), I, p. 120; C. A. Haigh, 'Anticlericalism in the English Reformation', *History*, 68 (1983), 394.

[4] Pollard, pp. 340–73. An important new biography of Wolsey by P. J. Gwyn is in press at the time of writing. As will be evident, the contributors to this volume differ from Mr Gwyn's interpretation of Wolsey's career at a number of points, but we are very grateful to him for his frequent, helpful and generous discussions of the cardinal.

1

It is important, then, to evaluate Cardinal Wolsey in his own right, as churchman, statesman, and patron of the arts, and that is what this volume sets out to do. But the state of the evidence makes it a difficult task, because Wolsey's contemporaries found it more than usually hard to take a detached view of him. His authority as Henry's chief minister was so great, and his apparent responsibility for all areas of government policy so sweeping, that politicians and political commentators alike had to be either entirely for Wolsey, or entirely against him. In a monarchy where no one conceived of a loyal opposition, noblemen and councillors had to work with the cardinal if they wished to serve the king, but it is hard to judge how willingly they did so. Once he had fallen from power, on the other hand, it was convenient never to have been his friend. At a court where Wolsey alone seemed to obstruct the schemes of foreign ambassadors, they blamed their failures on his perversity or corruption. And in a culture where fulsome praise and biting satire were the two best means of attracting attention, literary evidence about Wolsey's contemporary image demands very careful handling.

Three of Wolsey's contemporaries – clerics and schoolmasters like him, but aspirants to fame as authors not statesmen – illustrate the problem. In 1519 Robert Whittinton published several pieces of verse and prose in extravagant praise of Wolsey, wonder of the age and father of the nation, while in 1521–2 John Skelton wrote three poems filled with increasingly vitriolic abuse of the tyrannical cardinal who was doing his best to ruin church, state and people.[5] Neither Whittinton nor Skelton can be taken at face value, the more so since Skelton was soon dedicating to Wolsey poems which supported king and cardinal against the Scots and the Lutherans.[6] The third writer, John Palsgrave, encapsulated the problem of interpreting such works when he composed a comprehensive and sarcastic list of national achievements during Wolsey's ministry. He accompanied it with a letter to a friend in Wolsey's service, promising to do the only sensible thing, to join him without delay and 'dance attendance', if he could be persuaded that the cardinal's direction of England's affairs was anything but disastrous.[7] Palsgrave and Skelton had private reasons to resent Wolsey, and so too did the Italian historian Polydore Vergil, whose entire account of Wolsey's period of power is shot through with denigration of the minister's motives.[8] Yet we cannot dismiss all this evidence out of hand, nor that of the exiled English protestants

---

[5] R. Whittinton, *Libellus Epygrammaton* (London, 1519), sigs. Aiiir–cir; Skelton, 'Speke Parrot', 'Collyn Clout', 'Why come ye nat to courte?'.

[6] G. Walker, *John Skelton and the Politics of the 1520s* (Cambridge, 1988), pp. 188–217.

[7] *LP*, IV (ii) 5750 (iii).

[8] P. L. Carver (ed.), *The Comedy of Acolastus, Translated from the Latin of Fullonius by John Palsgrave*, Early English Text Society, 202 (London, 1937), pp. xiv–xxxviii; Walker, *John Skelton*, pp. 35–67; D. Hay, *Polydore Vergil, Renaissance Historian and Man of Letters* (Oxford, 1952), pp. 10–14, 154; Hay (ed.), *The Anglica Historia of Polydore Vergil, A.D. 1485–1537*, Camden Society 3rd Series, 74 (London, 1950), pp. 225–333.

Tyndale, Barlow and Roy, who attacked Wolsey venomously as the symbol of England's continued adherence to Roman orthodoxy.[9] The issues which Wolsey's enemies chose to play on in order to blacken his name are as instructive as those for which Whittinton, or the equally adulatory Henry Bullock of Cambridge University, thought Wolsey would like to be praised.[10] Both sides of contemporary opinion can be complemented by the image which Wolsey himself chose to project to society through his patronage of learning and the arts.

Thomas Wolsey's English contemporaries found it hard to be objective about him because he had no equals in their experience. But there is a context in which we can place him, for he was one among many cardinal–ministers who governed the monarchies of western Europe between the mid fifteenth and mid sixteenth century.[11] In France there were Cardinals Jean Balue (d. 1491), Georges d'Amboise (d. 1510), Antoine Duprat (d. 1535), François de Tournon (d. 1562), and Charles de Guise (d. 1574); in Spain, Cardinals Joan Margarit i Pau (d. 1484), Pedro González de Mendoza (d. 1495), Francisco Jiménez de Cisneros (d. 1517), and Antoine Perrenot de Granvelle (d. 1586), who also served as chief minister in the Netherlands from 1559 to 1564. In the Holy Roman Empire there were Cardinals Melchior von Meckau (d. 1509), Matthäus Lang (d. 1540), and Mercurino de Gattinara (d. 1530); in Scotland there was David Beaton (d. 1546); and in England there were Henry Beaufort (d. 1447) and John Morton (d. 1500). Other cardinals from each of these countries were responsible councillors, reliable diplomats and powerful churchmen, as John Kemp (d. 1454), Thomas Bourchier (d. 1486), Christopher Bainbridge (d. 1514) and Reginald Pole (d. 1558) were in England, but none combined prominence in domestic, international and ecclesiastical politics quite like these fifteen: they were truly Wolsey's peers.

Yet even in their company, Wolsey stood out. His rise to power was very rapid. He was a cardinal within twenty months of his first appointment to a bishopric: only Beaton and Gattinara moved faster, but the first had been a commendatory abbot for thirteen years before he became a bishop, and the second collected his ecclesiastical dignities towards the end of a distinguished career as a layman.[12] Wolsey was the son of an Ipswich tradesman, reputedly a butcher, and this humble birth made his social and political position very different from that of great noblemen such as Beaufort, Bourchier, Mendoza and Guise, who worked

---

[9] W. Tyndale, 'The practice of prelates', in H. Walter (ed.), *Expositions and Notes on Sundry Portions of the Holy Scriptures, together with The Practice of Prelates*, Parker Society (Cambridge, 1849), pp. 237–344; W. Roy, J. Barlow, *Rede me and be nott wrothe, For I say no thinge but trothe (The Burying of the Mass)*, ed. E. Arber (London, 1871).

[10] H. Bullock, *Doctissimi Viri H. Bulloci Oratio ad Thomam Cardinalem, Archiepiscopum Eboracensem* (Cambridge, 1521).

[11] Brief biographies of many of those mentioned can be found in W. J. McDonald et al. (eds.), *The New Catholic Encyclopedia*, 15 vols. (New York, 1967).

[12] M. H. B. Sanderson, *Cardinal of Scotland: David Beaton, c. 1494–1546* (Edinburgh, 1986), pp. 19, 67; J. M. Headley, *The Emperor and his Chancellor. A Study of the Imperial Chancellery under Gattinara* (Cambridge, 1983), p. 137.

closely with their lay relatives, or even from that of the numerous cardinal–ministers who were members of well-established ecclesiastical or administrative dynasties.[13] Wolsey held the leading position in English government and politics for fourteen years, and exercised delegated papal power over the church for eleven. In contrast Balue was Louis XI's most powerful adviser for four years at most, Lang obtained the legateship only months before the death of his master Maximilian, and Gattinara became a cardinal less than a year before his own death.[14] A number of others endured erratic careers in which interludes of disgrace separated periods of dominance, and Gattinara's relations with Charles V were so bad at one stage that he compared his sovereign unfavourably with Attila the Hun.[15] Only Amboise, minister for twelve years and legate for ten, could really parallel Wolsey.[16]

Wolsey's range of activity was astoundingly wide. Cisneros did manage the entire government of Spain as regent in 1516–17, but he was hampered at every turn by instructions from his new king in the Netherlands, and his administration proved disastrous.[17] About half of Wolsey's fellow cardinal–ministers coordinated their nation's foreign policy rather as he did, though rarely for such a sustained period.[18] A similar proportion shared Wolsey's commitment to financial administration and the organization of military effort, but several of these largely delegated the details of finance to expert colleagues.[19] Eight served as

---

[13] G. L. Harriss, *Cardinal Beaufort. A Study of Lancastrian Ascendancy and Decline* (Oxford, 1988), *passim*; R. L. Storey, 'Episcopal king-makers in the fifteenth century', in R. B. Dobson (ed.), *The Church, Politics and Patronage in the Fifteenth Century* (Gloucester, 1984), pp. 82–98; H. Nader, *The Mendoza Family in the Spanish Renaissance, 1350 to 1550* (New Brunswick, 1979), pp. 118–23; N. M. Sutherland, *The Huguenot Struggle for Recognition* (New Haven and London, 1980), pp. 73–174; R. B. Tate, *Joan Margarit i Pau, Cardinal-Bishop of Gerona, a Biographical Study* (Manchester, 1955), pp. 2–3, 45, 60–1; *Dictionnaire de biographie française*, in progress (Paris, 1933–), II, pp. 491–522 (Amboise); A. Buisson, *Le Chancelier Antoine Duprat* (Paris, 1935), pp. 17–40; M. François, *Le Cardinal François de Tournon, homme d'état, diplomate, mécène et humaniste* (Paris, 1951), pp. 4–9; M. Van Durme, *El Cardenal Granvela (1517–1586). Imperio y revolución bajo Carlos V y Felipe II*, 2nd edn (Barcelona, 1957), pp. 27–110; Sanderson, *Cardinal of Scotland*, pp. 8–9, 45–53.

[14] *Dictionnaire de biographie française*, V, pp. 16–19; H. Wiesflecker, *Kaiser Maximilian I*, 5 vols. (Vienna, 1971–86), IV, p. 387; Headley, *Emperor and his Chancellor*, p. 137.

[15] Harriss, *Beaufort*, *passim*; Sanderson, *Cardinal of Scotland*, pp. 153–228; François, *Tournon*, *passim*; Sutherland, *Huguenot Struggle*, pp. 73–211; Van Durme, *Granvela*, pp. 121–379; Headley, *Emperor and his Chancellor*, p. 50.

[16] B. Quilliet, *Louis XII, père du peuple* (Paris, 1986), pp. 186–91, 259.

[17] S. Haliczer, *The Comuneros of Castile. The Forging of a Revolution, 1475–1521* (Madison, 1981), pp. 129–54.

[18] Wiesflecker, *Maximilian*, V, pp. 230–6, 484–5; J. S. C. Bridge, *A History of France from the Death of Louis XI*, 5 vols. (Oxford, 1900–36), III, pp. 209–93, IV, pp. 8–66; Buisson, *Duprat*, pp. 131–215; Headley, *Emperor and his Chancellor*, pp. 33–9; D. L. Potter, 'Foreign policy in the age of the reformation: French involvement in the Schmalkaldic war, 1544–1547', *Historical Journal*, 20 (1977), 529–31, 542; Van Durme, *Granvela*, pp. 228, 343–8; Sutherland, *Huguenot Struggle*, pp. 73–5.

[19] Harriss, *Beaufort*, pp. 58, 78–9, 115–33, 138, 192–5, 202–8, 211–12, 234–6, 258–60, 277–91; Tate, *Margarit*, pp. 65–85; Wiesflecker, *Maximilian*, V, pp. 224–8, 231, 248–51; Buisson, *Duprat*, pp. 216–78; François, *Tournon*, pp. 478–87; H. O. Evennett, *The Cardinal of Lorraine and the Council of*

chancellors, and Amboise, though never chancellor, played a similar part to Wolsey in devising legislation: but for some of these the chancellorship was an honorific position, for others held only briefly or intermittently, and none carried a judicial workload as heavy as Wolsey's.[20] Perhaps seven exercised similar leadership to Wolsey in their national churches (though only Amboise, Duprat and Beaton were legates *a latere*), but for many of the others ecclesiastical duties came a poor second to matters of state.[21] Nearly all were patrons of education, literature, music, architecture and the visual arts in some measure, but few if any could match Wolsey's enterprises for scale, significance, and concentration of effort.[22] When Wolsey's achievements in church, state and art are put together, he appears remarkable even among his equals.

Later generations have judged Wolsey's churchmanship harshly, taking their lead from the tendentious application by Skelton and the Lutheran exiles of apostolic standards to the measurement of the cardinal's ministry, and their use of traditional criticisms of clerical faults to catalogue his failings.[23] Yet in some ways Wolsey emerges rather well from comparison with his European contemporaries.[24] The most conspicuous instance of his failure to meet the moral and procedural standards which his age expected senior clerics to observe (in theory though often not in practice) was his comprehensive use of ecclesiastical patronage to support Thomas Wynter, his illegitimate son.[25] Yet he could not

Trent, a Study in the Counter-Reformation (Cambridge, 1930), pp. 67–8; Quilliet, *Louis XII*, pp. 192–3, 261; Van Durme, *Granvela*, pp. 226–9.

[20] Harriss, *Beaufort*, pp. 18, 70–6, 133; Tate, *Margarit*, pp. 45, 64, 85–7; *New Catholic Encyclopedia*, IX, p. 650 (Mendoza); B. Hall, 'The trilingual college of San Ildefonso and the making of the Complutensian polyglot bible', in G. J. Cuming (ed.), *Studies in Church History*, 5 (1969), 124 (Cisneros); N. Pronay, 'The chancellor, the chancery, and the council at the end of the fifteenth century', in H. Hearder, H. R. Loyn (eds.), *British Government and Administration. Studies presented to S. B. Chrimes* (Cardiff, 1974), p. 92 (Morton); Buisson, *Duprat*, pp. 98–102; Headley, *Emperor and his Chancellor*, pp. 20–5; Sanderson, *Cardinal of Scotland*, pp. 153–76; Quilliet, *Louis XII*, pp. 336–42.

[21] C. Harper-Bill, 'Archbishop John Morton and the province of Canterbury, 1486–1500', *Journal of Ecclesiastical History*, 29 (1978), 1–21; A. Renaudet, *Préréforme et humanisme à Paris pendant les premières guerres d'Italie (1494–1517)*, 2nd edn (Paris, 1953), pp. 323–64, 437–62 (Amboise); Sanderson, *Cardinal of Scotland*, pp. 114–19; Van Durme, *Granvela*, pp. 231–40; J. Garcia Oró, *Cisneros y la reforma del clero español en tiempo de los reyes católicos* (Madrid, 1971), *passim*; Buisson, *Duprat*, pp. 198, 279–308; Evennett, *Cardinal of Lorraine*, *passim*

[22] Harriss, *Beaufort*, pp. 8, 369–75; *Dictionnaire de biographie française*, v, p. 17 (Balue); Tate, *Margarit*, p. 16; C. Harper-Bill (ed.), *The Register of John Morton, Archbishop of Canterbury, 1486–1500, volume I*, Canterbury and York Society, 75 (Woodbridge, 1987), p. x; Nader, *Mendoza Family*, pp. 143, 182, 184–5, 190; Hall, 'Trilingual college of San Ildefonso', pp. 114–46; J. de Contreras, *Historia del arte hispánico*, 5 vols. (Barcelona, 1931–49), II, pp. 30, 529, III, pp. 162, 169–70, 189, 194–7, 322, 391–2; Quilliet, *Louis XII*, pp. 368, 372, 398; Wiesflecker, *Maximilian*, v, pp. 224–8, 232, 397; Buisson, *Duprat*, pp. 322–44, 355; Headley, *Emperor and his Chancellor*, pp. 79–82; François, *Tournon*, pp. 491–524; Sanderson, *Cardinal of Scotland*, pp. 122, 140–1; Van Durme, *Granvela*, pp. 287–308; Evennett, *Cardinal of Lorraine*, pp. 12–13, 21–2; *Dictionnaire de biographie française*, XVII, pp. 324–5 (Guise).

[23] Walker, *John Skelton*, pp. 124–52.

[24] G. R. Elton, *Reform and Reformation: England 1509–1558* (London, 1977), p. 93.

[25] Pollard, pp. 308–12.

compete with Beaton's tally of eight illegitimate offspring, nor with the marqui-
sate and landed income to match with which Mendoza set up his eldest
bastard; Beaufort, Guise, Granvelle, and almost certainly Wolsey's contemporary Archbishop Warham of Canterbury all had illegitimate children, and
Lang's philandering was notorious.[26] The last cultivated a secular image so
devotedly that he insisted on wearing layman's clothes and a sword to meet the
pope, and, like several other future cardinal–ministers, began collecting benefices some time before his ordination to the priesthood.[27] Wolsey's pluralism –
by 1529 he held the archbishopric of York, the bishopric of Winchester and the
abbey of St Albans – looks pale beside the two Italian bishoprics and twenty-
seven abbeys and priories held (though not all at once) by Tournon, in plurality
with his four successive archbishoprics.[28] Similarly, none of Wolsey's sees
could match the revenues Mendoza or Cisneros drew from the archbishopric of
Toledo.[29] Yet Wolsey's combination of benefices, political office and a very
profitable exploitation of his legatine jurisdiction gave him a total income
which, at conceivably more than £30,000 a year, probably only Guise (after
several decades of inflation) clearly outstripped; and both Wolsey's wealth, and
the pluralism that sustained it, were previously unheard-of in the English
church.[30]

Wolsey certainly sought to extract the maximum profit from ecclesiastical
office, as indeed did almost all these cardinal–ministers: the one glaring exception
was Cisneros, who lived the life of a friar within his archiepiscopal palaces, and
reputedly received orders from two popes to conduct himself less austerely and
with more becoming grandeur.[31] Wolsey's attempts to secure the bishopric of
Tournai after Henry's conquest of the city gave the impression that it was above
all the see's revenues that interested him, and he kept close watch on the
administrators of his English dioceses as they implemented his sometimes
over-ambitious plans to increase income from the episcopal estates.[32] At Rome,
his agents were for ever haggling for reductions on the taxes he owed each time
he received a new appointment, and both there and in England he laid hands on

---

[26] Sanderson, *Cardinal of Scotland*, pp. 30–42; Nader, *Mendoza Family*, p. 120; Harriss, *Beaufort*, p. 16;
Evennett, *Cardinal of Lorraine*, p. 4; Van Durme, *Granvela*, pp. 267–8; Walker, *John Skelton*, p. 145;
Wiesflecker, *Maximilian*, v, p. 233.

[27] Wiesflecker, *Maximilian*, IV, p. 109, v, p. 233; *Dictionnaire de biographie française*, II, pp. 491–2
(Amboise); Sanderson, *Cardinal of Scotland*, pp. 13–67; Van Durme, *Granvela*, p. 34.

[28] François, *Tournon*, pp. 427–44.   [29] Nader, *Mendoza Family*, p. 120.

[30] Evennett, *Cardinal of Lorraine*, pp. 9–10; Pollard, pp. 173–4, 320–5; F. Heal, *Of Prelates and Princes. A
Study of the Economic and Social Position of the Tudor Episcopate* (Cambridge, 1980), p. 65; W. E. Wilkie,
The Cardinal Protectors of England. Rome and the Tudors before the Reformation (Cambridge, 1974), p. 58.

[31] R. Merton, *Cardinal Ximenes and the Making of Spain* (London, 1934), pp. 65–6, 257.

[32] C. G. Cruickshank, *The English Occupation of Tournai, 1513–1519* (Oxford, 1971), pp. 143–87; Heal,
Of Prelates and Princes, pp. 27–8, 34, 45–9; J. L. Drury, 'More stout than wise: tenant right in
Weardale in the Tudor period', in D. Marcombe (ed.), *The Last Principality. Politics, Religion and
Society in the Bishopric of Durham, 1494–1660* (Nottingham, 1987), pp. 79–80.

the goods of deceased episcopal colleagues with rather unseemly haste.[33] He capitalized on his powers as legate, which overrode the normal rights of bishops to hold church courts, to prove the wills of those resident in their dioceses and to visit and reform the clergy of their sees, by establishing his own profitable probate court, by exacting what amounted to protection money from other bishops and lesser dignitaries in return for allowing them to exercise their jurisdiction, and by holding visitations to collect the standard fees.[34] Meanwhile he took from Rome most of the profits of the sale of dispensations from the canon law (especially marriage licences) in England.[35] Such behaviour was by no means extraordinary among the English bishops, and both Morton and Warham as archbishops of Canterbury had fought long and hard to maximize their control of probate jurisdiction and other prerogatives across the southern province.[36] But Wolsey was more thoroughgoing, more successful and, as a result, considerably richer. Such success easily bred resentment, and many of the cardinal's critics hit on the link between his lavish income and his forcefully asserted legatine jurisdiction.[37]

Wolsey did not hide his wealth, indeed his enemies frequently accused him of flaunting it. Flaunting is a difficult activity to measure, but, as we shall see, Wolsey's artistic patronage did reveal a talent for spending large sums on projects calculated to impress. The size and splendour of his household, though attributable to its role as the centre of his ministerial and legatine activities (and paralleled on a smaller scale by Morton and by several of their European contemporaries), made it easy to charge him with pomp and pride, and may well have irritated the nobility, the size of whose liveried retinues Wolsey stringently limited.[38] The cardinal's splendid appearance and stately demeanour at such diplomatic encounters as the Field of Cloth of Gold were denounced by Palsgrave as 'manifest tokens of vainglory'.[39] Above all, the sight of his daily procession to Westminster Hall, dressed in crimson satin robes and jewelled shoes, surrounded by a glittering retinue of noblemen and servants, preceded by the great seal, cardinal's hat, crosses and silver pillars which were the symbols of

---

[33] Wilkie, *Cardinal Protectors*, pp. 153–5; D. S. Chambers, *Cardinal Bainbridge in the Court of Rome, 1509 to 1514* (Oxford, 1965), p. 140; Pollard, p. 197 n. 3.

[34] Pollard, pp. 192–200; M. J. Kelly, 'Canterbury jurisdiction and influence during the episcopate of William Warham, 1503–32' (Cambridge University PhD thesis, 1963), pp. 176–94.

[35] Ibid., pp. 194–5.

[36] Harper-Bill, 'John Morton and the province of Canterbury', pp. 12–19; Kelly, 'Canterbury jurisdiction', pp. 55–93.

[37] Roy, Barlow, *Rede me and be nott wrothe*, p. 57; F. J. Furnivall (ed.), *Ballads from Manuscripts*, 1 (ii), Ballad Society (London, 1872), p. 354; Walker, *John Skelton*, pp. 144–6.

[38] Wolsey's household is currently under study by Mr L. R. Gardiner of the University of Melbourne. C. Harper-Bill, 'The *familia*, administrators and patronage of Archbishop John Morton', *Journal of Religious History*, 10 (1979), 247–8, 252; Nader, *Mendoza Family*, pp. 184–5; François, *Tournon*, pp. 491–8; Sanderson, *Cardinal of Scotland*, pp. 131–41; A. Fox, *Politics and Literature in the Reigns of Henry VII and Henry VIII* (Oxford, 1989), pp. 143–7.

[39] *LP*, IV (iii) 5750 (ii); J. G. Russell, *The Field of Cloth of Gold. Men and Manners in 1520* (London, 1969), pp. 43, 50, 86–7, 171–6.

his authority, epitomized his magnificence. For the satirists it served as a powerful demonstration of Wolsey's pride; for the cardinal's gentleman usher, George Cavendish, looking back philosophically on his late master's career, it provided a panorama of transient worldly glory.[40]

Such display was an accepted means to command respect for oneself, one's office, or the king or pope one represented, and for that reason Wolsey had licence for a good deal of pomp. As papal legate he was entitled to all the ceremonial honour due to the pope, and Beaufort, Wolsey's forerunner as an English prelate sent as legate to England, had claimed at least some of this right, while Amboise, Wolsey's model as a permanently resident legate *a latere*, had set a splendid example by his legatine entries into French cities.[41] As Henry's lieutenant in diplomatic encounters, Wolsey could and did claim the respect due to the king, as Lang and Amboise did when representing their sovereigns: Lang even demanded the right to remain seated and keep his hat on to meet the pope.[42] As an archbishop, Wolsey could deploy ordinary ecclesiastical pomp, as even the proverbially ascetic Cisneros did at his stately first entry into Toledo as primate of Castile.[43] Yet such magnificence was a double-edged weapon in the hands of any churchman, laying him open to charges of ungodly and tyrannous pride. Balue's pompous reception of his cardinal's hat brought upon him withering satire of the sort which afflicted Wolsey, Granvelle was pilloried for his pride and other enormities in a torrent of bitter propaganda, and Guise was hanged and burned in splendid effigy on the hostile streets of Paris.[44] We need not believe that all Wolsey's contemporaries reacted to his pomp in the same way. Many were probably genuinely impressed by his authority, and even his critics divided into those who stressed the moral faults he revealed in his ritual self-glorification and those who emphasized the waste of money and effort involved.[45] But when Wolsey, merely the king's almoner, provided himself with tents for the invasion of France in 1513 half as large again as those occupied by Lord Lisle, second-in-command of the army, and when foreigners with no critical axe to grind found Wolsey's splendour excessive and presumptuous, we would do well not to discount the arrogance implied by, and the dangers inherent in, the cardinal's visual presentation of his own importance.[46]

[40] Roy, Barlow, *Rede me and be nott wrothe*, pp. 56–7; *Ballads from Manuscripts*, I (ii), p. 360; Skelton, 'Speke Parrott', l. 517, 'Collyn Clout', ll. 308–20; Cavendish, pp. 22–4.

[41] F. Wasner, 'Fifteenth-century texts on the ceremonial of the papal "Legatus a latere"', *Traditio*, 14 (1958), 300; Harriss, *Beaufort*, p. 178; *Dictionnaire de biographie française*, II, pp. 497–8.

[42] Wiesflecker, *Maximilian*, IV, pp. 108–12; Bridge, *History of France* , III, p. 209; Walker, *John Skelton*, pp. 146–50.

[43] Garcia Oró, *Cisneros*, p. 335; Heal, *Of Prelates and Princes*, p. 76.

[44] P. R. Gaussin, *Louis XI, un roi entre deux mondes* (Paris, 1976), pp. 78, 140–1; Van Durme, *Granvela*, pp. 230–1, 247; Evennett, *Cardinal of Lorraine*, p. 113.

[45] Skelton, 'Collyn Clout', ll. 308–20; *LP*, IV (iii) 5750 (ii).

[46] C. G. Cruickshank, *Army Royal. Henry VIII's Invasion of France 1513* (Oxford, 1969), p. 45; see below, pp. 156–7.

That visual presentation was the complement to a campaign of rhetorical propaganda on his own behalf. Wolsey has been perceptively characterized as a rhetorical politician, and as leader and putative reformer of the English church no less than in other areas of his activity, he made large claims for the benefits which would accrue from his exercise of authority.[47] His legatine powers were granted, renewed and extended to enable him to impose reform on the church, and to obtain them he had to paint a picture of English clerical morality so unflattering that his words still rankled in 1529.[48] They rankled all the more because Wolsey's critics believed that his interest in ecclesiastical reform was a sham, aimed only to increase his own power and wealth.

These are a number of ways we can test Wolsey's reformist credentials. His career as a diocesan bishop was unimpressive, perhaps unavoidably so because his duties in government kept him at court. He never visited his sees of Lincoln (1514), Bath and Wells (1518–23) and Durham (1523–9), and retired to the diocese of York only reluctantly after his fall.[49] This set him apart not only from the bulk of the English episcopate, who resided with reasonable frequency, but also from Morton, who ordained clergy in person at Canterbury once a year, and a number of other cardinal–ministers who managed to combine activity in central politics with commitment to their sees.[50] Wolsey's consequent reliance on suffragan bishops and diocesan administrators was not unusual among ecclesiastical statesmen, but Amboise and Tournon, for instance, had at least involved themselves in diocesan affairs before matters of state began to take up too much of their time.[51] Both residents and absentees – Morton, Mendoza, Cisneros, Duprat, Tournon, Guise – held reforming provincial or diocesan councils.[52] Wolsey did so too, but the York convocation of 1518, like other elements of his ecclesiastical policy that year, was too closely related to his campaign for the legateship to serve as convincing evidence of his reforming intentions.[53] The convocation put York on a par with Canterbury by codifying its canon law, but

---

[47] D. R. Starkey, *The Reign of Henry VIII, Personalities and Politics* (London, 1985), pp. 61–3.

[48] Pollard, pp. 179–83.

[49] M. Bowker, *The Secular Clergy in the Diocese of Lincoln, 1495–1520* (Cambridge, 1968), p. 7; P. M. Hembry, *The Bishops of Bath and Wells, 1540–1640: Social and Economic Problems* (London, 1967), p. 6; Pollard, p. 271.

[50] S. Thompson, 'The bishop in his diocese', in B. Bradshaw, E. Duffy (eds.), *Humanism, Reform and the Reformation. The Career of Bishop John Fisher* (Cambridge, 1989), pp. 67–80, 250, 253; *Register of John Morton*, p. xiii; *New Catholic Encyclopedia*, IX, p. 650; Garcia Oró, *Cisneros*, pp. 311–39; Sanderson, *Cardinal of Scotland*, pp. 103–4; Evennett, *Cardinal of Lorraine*, pp. 15–20.

[51] François, *Tournon*, pp. 437–43; Van Durme, *Granvela*, p.392; Kelly, 'Canterbury jurisdiction', p. 20; Renaudet, *Préréforme et humanisme*, pp. 291–2.

[52] Harper-Bill, 'John Morton and the province of Canterbury', pp. 11–12; J. M. Revuelta Somalo, 'Renovación de la vida espiritual', in L. Suárez Fernández (ed.), *Los Trastamara y la Unidad Española (1369–1517)*, Historia General de España y América, 5 (Madrid, 1981), pp. 233–4, 263–4; Garcia Oró, *Cisneros*, pp. 336–9; Buisson, *Duprat*, pp. 293–8; François, *Tournon*, pp. 439, 448–9; Evennett, *Cardinal of Lorraine*, pp. 15–20.

[53] Wilkie, *Cardinal Protectors*, p. 113.

the regulations it promulgated against absenteeism and clerical concubinage, and for the better instruction of the laity, were merely repetitions of decrees several centuries old.[54] The same was true of much of Cisneros's synodal legislation, but the clergy of Toledo were probably more in need of such basic improvement than those of York, and Cisneros accompanied his reforms with a personal activity and a range of initiatives, such as the printing of catechisms and mystical works, which were quite alien to Wolsey.[55] As an archbishop, Wolsey professed affection for the inhabitants of his diocese, but he seems to have expressed it more in helping to meet the political and economic needs of the city of York than in local spiritual leadership.[56]

Wolsey's personal qualities were important indicators for contemporaries of his fitness to reform the church. While his enemies suggested that his sins led the entire clergy astray, his friends were keen to stress his virtues.[57] Cavendish countered the accusation of Roy and Barlow that Wolsey got up in the morning too late to say his prayers with the evidence of the cardinal's chaplain that he conscientiously said every prescribed service, and Whittinton praised Wolsey's temperance in living abstinently among the temptations of the court.[58] As a potential reformer, Wolsey lacked the moral authority of Cisneros or even of Amboise, but if Mendoza or Granvelle could present themselves as agents of improvement, Wolsey could not be disqualified; and at least none of his self-advancement was achieved so spectacularly at the cost of reform as was Lang's election as coadjutor to the archbishop of Salzburg, which was secured (against the will of the archbishop) by a promise that on his appointment the canons would be released from their observation of the Augustinian rule.[59] There were also moral themes in Wolsey's statesmanship which were not inappropriate for a clerical minister. He devised the only known English proclamation regulating food consumption, and put into stringent effect the sumptuary statutes against gluttony and socially subversive over-dressing.[60] He waged an increasingly sharp campaign against dicing, gambling and other activities which

54 R. M. Woolley (ed.), *The York Provinciale put forth by Thomas Wolsey Archbishop of York in the year 1518* (London, 1931); P. Heath, *The English Parish Clergy on the Eve of the Reformation* (London, 1969), pp. 59, 93, 108.

55 J. N. Hillgarth, *The Spanish Kingdoms, 1250–1516*, 2 vols. (Oxford, 1976–8), II, pp. 403–4; Garcia Oró, *Cisneros*, pp. 336–9; P. Saínz Rodríguez, *La siembra mistica del cardenal Cisneros y las reformas en la iglesia* (Madrid, 1979), pp. 42–56; F. Fernández-Armesto, 'Cardinal Cisneros as a patron of printing', in D. W. Lomax, D. Mackenzie (eds.), *God and Man in Medieval Spain. Essays in Honour of J. R. L. Highfield* (Warminster, 1989), pp. 149–68; C. Harper-Bill, 'Dean Colet's convocation sermon and the pre-reformation church in England', *History*, 73 (1988), 204–5.

56 D. M. Palliser, *Tudor York* (Oxford, 1979), pp. 46–7.

57 Skelton, 'Collyn Clout'; Hall, pp. 593, 703.

58 Roy and Barlow, *Rede me and be nott wrothe*, p. 59; Cavendish, pp. 22–3; Whittinton, *Libellus Epygrammaton*, sigs. Bivr–v.

59 Garcia Oró, *Cisneros*, p. 185; *Dictionnaire de biographie française*, II, p. 502; *New Catholic Encyclopedia*, IX, p. 650; Van Durme, *Granvela*, p. 387; Wiesflecker, *Maximilian*, v, p. 235.

60 R. W. Heinze, *The Proclamations of the Tudor Kings* (Cambridge, 1976), p. 104; Hall, p. 583.

diverted the yeomen of England from the healthy and militarily vital pursuit of archery.[61] In 1526 he tried to restrain the pilfering and destruction which accompanied the court's visits to the houses of gentlemen and nobles, and he may have been behind the campaign for decency at court which resulted in the temporary expulsion of a number of the king's young companions in 1519.[62] Unfortunately it was rather easy to contrast all this with his legatine ritual and his artistic magnificence, and to conclude that he was a hypocrite who grudged everyone's pleasure save his own.[63] At any rate, as Keith Brown argues in chapter 8, Wolsey's grandiose style of churchmanship seems to have hindered his efforts to convince the austere and respected Franciscan Observants of his reforming bona fides.

Wolsey's reform of the English church was intensely centralized, and in that unlike the French and Spanish developments with which it is often compared. Amboise used his legatine authority in parallel with the efforts of the Paris *parlement* to strengthen reforming bishops, and to support movements originating within regular orders for the better observance of monastic rules; similarly Cisneros, though autocratic at times, forced reform on only within a limited range of regular movements, never made use of his powers to meddle with the secular clergy of dioceses other than his own, and never really dominated the royally inspired and royally controlled wave of reform which spread throughout the Spanish church.[64] In contrast, Wolsey's chosen instruments were a legatine council of bishops, a legatine synod of the clergy of both English provinces, and legatine visitations of monastic houses, colleges of secular priests, cathedral chapters and vacant dioceses. The legatine council published measures of reform along traditional lines and tried to improve their implementation, but the legatine synod apparently discussed nothing but taxation.[65] Wolsey had more sweeping plans for change, and by the end of his career he was aiming to improve ecclesiastical administration by using his powers to establish new bishoprics based on dissolved monasteries.[66] Meanwhile he took steps to reform the religious orders. His officers visited many monastic houses and often made constructive criticisms, he prescribed a more rigorous observance of the monastic lifestyle for the Benedictines and the Augustinian canons, and a number of abbots and priors were deprived and replaced by his nominees, who were

[61] Heinze, *Proclamations of the Tudor Kings*, pp. 89–94.
[62] D. M. Loades, *The Tudor Court* (London, 1986), pp. 94–5; Starkey, *Reign of Henry VIII*, p. 78; G. Walker, 'The "expulsion of the minions" of 1519 reconsidered', *Historical Journal*, 32 (1989), 1–16.
[63] Hall, p. 712; *Ballads from Manuscripts*, I (ii), p. 357.
[64] Renaudet, *Préréforme et humanisme*, pp. 327–53, 437–61; Hillgarth, *Spanish Kingdoms*, II, p. 409; Garcia Oró, *Cisneros, passim*; Revuelta Somalo, 'Renovación de la vida espiritual', pp. 230–69.
[65] Kelly, 'Canterbury jurisdiction', pp. 161–8, 174–6; Bowker, *Secular Clergy*, pp. 124–6; Pollard, pp. 187–91.
[66] D. Knowles, *The Religious Orders in England*, 3 vols. (Cambridge, 1948–59), III, p. 164.

usually upright and competent.[67] As in his reform of the secular clergy, his achievements were real though modest. What aroused opposition, from many clergy from Archbishop Warham downwards, was the ruthless assertion of authority which accompanied his reforms. Much of the opposition was a self-interested defence of privilege, and, as Greg Walker shows in chapter 9, in the immediate aftermath of Wolsey's fall the easiest way to defend the church was to decry the cardinal's assault on its liberties.[68] But the mark of the true reformer was to override privilege only when it obstructed internal reform, as Amboise and Cisneros did. In this respect, Wolsey's dealings with the Franciscan Observants, described in chapter 8, form an important test case, for he set out to humiliate the best examples of reforming religion in England not to improve them, but to demonstrate and extend his own power.

Wolsey upset defenders of the monasteries above all by the dissolutions which provided the endowment for the colleges he established at Oxford and Ipswich.[69] The majority of English bishops made some sort of educational benefaction, for improvement of the education available to the clergy was an obvious service to the church, and at Cardinal College, Oxford, Wolsey drew on the models of previous episcopal foundations, as John Newman shows in chapter 3.[70] Yet he set himself to surpass all his predecessors in scale and in quality. Those who wished to praise him stressed his beneficence to the 'magnificent throng of studious people' that frequented his household, and his commitment to 'pure humanite'; and in the number of its scholars, the size of its buildings and revenues, the audacity of its founder's search for talented foreign and domestic teaching staff, and its cultivation of humanist studies alongside the traditional curriculum, Cardinal College and its forerunners, Wolsey's public lectureships at Oxford, amply upheld the cardinal's reputation.[71] Their deliberate magnificence suggests that to uphold that reputation was one of their greatest aims, and it is characteristic of Wolsey that he named his college not after a feast of the church or a saint, nor even after his diocese, but after his dignity and, effectively, himself. His unfulfilled scheme for a system of feeder schools in fifteen of the seventeen English dioceses might have carried him as a patron of education beyond all his fellow cardinal–ministers except Cisneros, who founded a complete university at

---

[67] Ibid., pp. 82–3, 159–61.
[68] Bowker, *Secular Clergy*, pp. 124–6; Knowles, *Religious Orders*, III, pp. 82–3, 159; Kelly, 'Canterbury jurisdiction', pp. 161–7, 181–8.
[69] Knowles, *Religious Orders*, III, pp. 161–3.
[70] H. Jewell, 'English bishops as educational benefactors in the later fifteenth century', in *The Church, Patronage and Politics*, pp. 147–61.
[71] Whittinton, *Libellus Epygrammaton*, sig. cir; *Ballads from Manuscripts*, I (ii), p. 338; J. McConica, 'The rise of the undergraduate college', in McConica (ed.), *The History of the University of Oxford, III, the Collegiate University* (Oxford, 1986), pp. 29–32; G. D. Duncan, 'Public lectures and professorial chairs', ibid., pp. 337–41; T. F. Mayer, *Thomas Starkey and the Commonweal. Humanist Politics and Religion in the Reign of Henry VIII* (Cambridge, 1989), p. 85.

Alcalá, and within it the first college in Europe to teach Greek and Hebrew on a par with Latin.[72] Yet despite his close personal oversight of these projects – he even composed the grammar textbook for use at Ipswich – Wolsey never displayed humanist learning on his own account to the extent of Mendoza, Cisneros, Lang, Gattinara, Tournon or Granvelle.[73] His patronage of humanism was to a greater extent than theirs a question of mere fashion, yet it was not without significance, not only in Oxford but also in his promotion of the performance of classical Latin drama, and in his support for such initiatives as the establishment of the College of Physicians.[74]

Wolsey's plans for Oxford extended beyond his own college. He effectively supplanted Archbishop Warham as chancellor, obtaining a new charter to confirm the university's liberties, intervening in university elections and proposing a thorough revision of the statutes of the arts faculty.[75] Oxford also played a part in his struggle against heresy, both in a scheme for a collective assault by the university's scholars on Luther's theology, and in the need to purge Cardinal College of embarrassingly Lutheran tendencies.[76] In Oxford as in Cambridge, Wolsey's officers forced unorthodoxy underground, but in the universities and elsewhere the cardinal was less rigorous than he might have been in suppressing heresy, or so his enemies claimed.[77] He might, it is true, have ordered the burning of one or more of the preachers whom he investigated with considerable personal attention, but it is far from clear that their martyrdom would have hindered their cause more than their abjuration or exile.[78] Wolsey coordinated an impressive anti-Lutheran campaign by English theological polemicists, took rapid, though not always effective, steps to prevent the spread of Lutheran books, especially William Tyndale's English New Testament, and allowed other bishops to continue their persecution of the old-established indigenous heresy,

[72] M. Dowling, *Humanism in the Age of Henry VIII* (London, 1986), pp. 119–22; Hall, 'Trilingual college of San Ildefonso', pp. 114–46.

[73] Dowling, *Humanism*, p. 121; *New Catholic Encyclopedia*, IX, p. 650; Wiesflecker, *Maximilian*, V, pp. 232, 236; Headley, *Emperor and his Chancellor*, pp. 79–82; François, *Tournon*, pp. 500–15; Van Durme, *Granvela*, pp. 287–308.

[74] S. Anglo, *Spectacle, Pageantry, and Early Tudor Policy* (Oxford, 1969), p. 235; Anglo, 'The evolution of the early Tudor disguising, pageant, and mask', *Renaissance Drama*, new series 1 (1968), 35–7; C. Webster, 'Thomas Linacre and the foundation of the College of Physicians', in F. Maddison, M. Pelling, C. Webster (eds.), *Essays on the Life and Work of Thomas Linacre c.1460–1524* (Oxford, 1977), pp. 198–222.

[75] C. I. Hammer, 'Oxford town and Oxford university', in McConica (ed.), *History of the University of Oxford*, III, pp. 88–9; C. Cross, 'Oxford and the Tudor state from the accession of Henry VIII to the death of Mary', ibid., pp. 119–22.

[76] Ibid., pp. 123–4.

[77] H. C. Porter, *Reformation and Reaction in Tudor Cambridge* (Cambridge, 1958), pp. 48–9; E. Lord Herbert of Cherbury, *The Life and Raigne of King Henry the Eighth* (London, 1649), pp. 273–4.

[78] W. A. Clebsch, *England's Earliest Protestants, 1520–1535* (New Haven and London, 1964), pp. 47, 206–7, 277; J. F. Davis, *Heresy and Reformation in the South-East of England, 1520–1559* (London, 1983), pp. 52, 68.

Lollardy.[79] At a time when over-enthusiastic but fundamentally orthodox reformers were hard to distinguish from potential leaders of national Lutheran movements, Wolsey's mixture of vigour and circumspection was not inappropriate – and not unlike the policy of Duprat in France.[80] It was not until the generation of Beaton, Tournon, Granvelle and Guise that cardinal–ministers would regard the destruction of protestant movements as an integral part of their calling.[81]

For Wolsey a more important function of his dual status was the management of relations between church and state. In practice that meant submitting the English church to the will of Henry VIII, as Wolsey learned as early as 1515 when the king cut short his attempts to refer to Rome the vexed issue of what sort of immunities the clergy should enjoy in the English courts.[82] In 1519 he was rather more successful in defending the right of sanctuary – a problem which Amboise had had to tackle in France – against the aggressive attacks of the common-law judges, but even then he was quick to stress that sanctuaries existed only by royal creation.[83] In one sense, as Keith Brown suggests, Wolsey the reformer was also a royal agent, implementing the programme of christian kingship adumbrated by Henry VII. In matters of high ecclesiastical patronage, Wolsey certainly had to follow the king's line: though one or two of his friends received bishoprics, so did one or two of his early opponents.[84] By the use or threat of legatine preventions, his influence over lesser appointments was far greater, and both Thomas Wynter and Thomas Larke, the brother of the cardinal's mistress, were well provided for; yet he proved a less thoroughgoing nepotist than most of his fellow cardinal–ministers, and he gave his relations a far smaller part in the administration of his dioceses than did a number of his contemporaries among the English episcopate.[85] As long as Wolsey rewarded the king's servants as well as his own – which

---

[79] R. Rex, 'The English campaign against Luther in the 1520s', *Transactions of the Royal Historical Society*, 5th ser. 39 (1989), 85–106; Davis, *Heresy and Reformation*, pp. 9, 45–6, 57–65.

[80] Buisson, *Duprat*, pp. 286–307.

[81] Sanderson, *Cardinal of Scotland*, pp. 119–22, 188–94, 210–11; François, *Tournon*, pp. 205–21; G. Parker, *The Dutch Revolt* (London, 1977), pp. 47–8, 62–4; Sutherland, *Huguenot Struggle*, pp. 54–7, 81–2, 103, 122–3, 151–2.

[82] J. D. M. Derrett, 'The affairs of Richard Hunne and Friar Standish', in J. B. Trapp (ed.), *The Complete Works of Sir Thomas More, volume IX, The Apology* (New Haven and London, 1979), pp. 225–36; J. G. Bellamy, *Criminal Law and Society in Late Medieval and Tudor England* (Gloucester, 1984), pp. 133–9.

[83] E. W. Ives, 'Crime, sanctuary and royal authority under Henry VIII: the exemplary sufferings of the Savage family', in M. S. Arnold, T. A. Green, S. A. Scully, S. D. White (eds.), *On the Laws and Customs of England. Essays in Honour of Samuel E. Thorne* (Chapel Hill, 1981), pp. 297–303; *Dictionnaire de biographie française*, II, p. 496.

[84] Wilkie, *Cardinal Protectors*, pp. 157–9.

[85] Pollard, pp. 204–8, 306–12; Kelly, 'Canterbury jurisdiction', pp. 195–8; *Dictionnaire de biographie française*, II, pp. 487–522 (Amboise), V, pp. 16, 19 (Balue); Merton, *Ximenes*, pp. 69–71, 185–7; Nader, *Mendoza Family*, p. 121; Buisson, *Duprat*, p. 357; François, *Tournon*, pp. 164, 173–4, 517–22; Van Durme, *Granvela*, pp. 87–8; Sanderson, *Cardinal of Scotland*, pp. 39–40, 51–3, 132–4; University

he did – the niceties of his ecclesiastical patronage network probably concerned Henry little. What did concern him, as it concerned the royal masters of Cardinals Morton, Mendoza, Cisneros, Amboise and Duprat, was royal taxation of the church; and though he failed in his promise to tax the English clergy on the pope's behalf, Wolsey succeeded in taxing the church for the king considerably harder than even the rapacious Henry VII had done.[86]

It was not only the clergy whom Wolsey taxed, and those who wished to stir up resentment against him repeatedly cited the heavy extraordinary levies of the 1520s as the cause of national poverty and the greatest sign of the cardinal's tyranny.[87] Wolsey alone was not to blame for such taxation, for king and council had resolved on war with France, and Wolsey was left to fund it. But the cardinal's conspicuous role as manager of the nation's finances, and as a very aggressive negotiator with the London authorities in 1516, 1522 and 1525 and with the house of commons in 1523, made him the king's 'lightning conductor' for opposition to fiscal demands.[88] In contrast, the apparent popularity of Georges d'Amboise may well reflect the comparatively light burden of taxation in Louis XII's France, even though it was not demonstrably the minister's doing.[89] Earlier in his ministry, Wolsey had proved himself an effective financier, cutting the king's expenses, clawing back his revenues, and cajoling parliament into helping repair the damage done by Henry's first war.[90] In the 1520s he continued to save money where he could, and to improve the exploitation of the crown's estates.[91] But in search of the cash to support renewed warfare he proved himself too competent for comfort. The assessments for the forced loans and subsidies of 1522–6 tapped the wealth of individuals and of the nation remarkably effectively: the result was that the very impressive yield of the loans (which were never repaid) was followed by non-cooperation in the levies of 1522–3 in some parts of the North, resolute and successful opposition in the commons in the parliament of 1523 to the size of subsidy demanded by Wolsey, and a total defeat for the

---

of Durham, Department of Palaeography, Durham Priory Register v, fol. 204 (grant of the keepership of Durham Place, London, to one John Wolsey); Heal, *Of Prelates and Princes*, p. 44.

[86] Harper-Bill, 'John Morton and the province of Canterbury', pp. 3–4; Haliczer, *Comuneros of Castile*, p. 133; Garcia Oró, *Cisneros*, pp. 322–4; Renaudet, *Préréforme et humanisme*, pp. 333–7; Buisson, *Duprat*, pp. 260–5; Kelly, 'Canterbury jurisdiction', pp. 168–74, 292–317.

[87] Walker, *John Skelton*, pp. 100–23; *Ballads from Manuscripts*, I (ii), p. 353.

[88] Walker, *John Skelton*, pp. 104–7; S. E. Brigden, *London and the Reformation* (Oxford, 1989), pp. 27, 163–6; G. W. Bernard, *War, Taxation and Rebellion in Early Tudor England. Henry VIII, Wolsey and the Amicable Grant of 1525* (Brighton, 1986), p. 67; J. A. Guy, 'Wolsey and the parliament of 1523', in M. C. Cross, D. M. Loades, J. J. Scarisbrick (eds.), *Law and Government under the Tudors. Essays presented to Sir Geoffrey Elton on his Retirement* (Cambridge, 1988), pp. 2–4.

[89] *Dictionnaire de biographie française*, II, p. 501; Quilliet, *Louis XII*, pp. 345–6.

[90] S. J. Gunn, 'The act of resumption of 1515', in D. T. Williams (ed.), *Early Tudor England. Proceedings of the 1987 Harlaxton Symposium* (Woodbridge, 1989), pp. 87–106.

[91] A. P. Newton, 'Tudor reforms in the royal household', in R. W. Seton-Watson (ed.), *Tudor Studies presented . . . to Albert Frederick Pollard* (London, 1924), pp. 237–56; W. C. Richardson, *Tudor Chamber Administration 1485–1547* (Baton Rouge, 1952), pp. 259–66, 269.

attempt to raise an even more ambitious 'Amicable Grant' in 1525, which provoked widespread refusals and a rebellion in East Anglia.[92] Wolsey failed, but he was right to think that direct taxation was the best way to fund expensive and protracted warfare, as Henry unwittingly confirmed when he paid for his next French war by debasement of the coinage (which damaged the economy) and the sale of confiscated church lands (which weakened the crown).

In the administration of the crown's finances Wolsey made no very great changes. He kept close personal charge of expenditure, improved auditing procedures, and seems to have deployed with care the skilled financial personnel who had served Henry VII, especially those who supervised most aspects of crown finance as the general surveyors.[93] Wolsey, like his successor Cromwell, directed in person a system made up of 'an assembly of autonomous and semi-autonomous financial agencies', and his institutional management was more a matter of encouraging internally generated improvements in working practices, and restraining the budget of potentially irresponsible spending departments (above all the king's privy purse), than of any sweeping reorganization.[94] Characteristically, while his actions amounted to pragmatic tinkering, his rhetoric went much further, with the result that historians have blamed him for failing to execute the thoroughgoing reform of a moribund exchequer which he unnecessarily trumpeted in 1519.[95]

Finance interested Wolsey less than justice, as everyone who praised him knew: Robert Whittinton not only placed justice first among the four cardinal virtues under which he rather heavy-handedly organized his panegyric, but added a separate treatise on the great difficulties of doing good justice and the glory of Wolsey's triumph over them.[96] In reply, the cardinal's critics could only accuse him of ranting in court and prosecution for profit, cite occasional instances of favouritism or procedural waywardness, or more realistically suggest that

---

[92] J. J. Goring, 'The general proscription of 1522', *English Historical Review*, 86 (1971), 700–5; R. S. Schofield, 'Taxation and the political limits of the Tudor state', in *Law and Government under the Tudors*, pp. 231–3, 243, 252–3; H. Miller, 'Subsidy assessments of the peerage in the sixteenth century', *Bulletin of the Institute of Historical Research*, 28 (1955), 24–31; R. W. Hoyle (ed.), *Early Tudor Craven. Subsidies and Assessments 1510–47*, Yorkshire Archaeological Society Record Series, 145 (Leeds, 1987), pp. xiv–xxvii; Guy, 'Wolsey and the parliament of 1523', pp. 1–18; Bernard, *War, Taxation and Rebellion*, pp. 54–148.

[93] Richardson, *Tudor Chamber Administration*, pp. 231–9, 256–7, 274–7; B. P. Wolffe, *The Crown Lands, 1461–1536* (London, 1970), pp. 79–80.

[94] J. D. Alsop, 'The structure of early Tudor finance, c.1509–1558', in C. Coleman, D. R. Starkey (eds.), *Revolution Reassessed. Revisions in the History of Tudor Government and Administration* (Oxford, 1986), p. 160; D. R. Starkey, 'Court and government', ibid., pp. 39–41; Richardson, *Tudor Chamber Administration*, pp. 284–8; J. D. Alsop, 'The exchequer in late medieval government, c.1485–1530', in J. G. Rowe (ed.), *Aspects of Late Medieval Government and Society. Essays Presented to J. R. Lander* (Toronto, 1987), pp. 179–212.

[95] Elton, *Tudor Revolution in Government*, pp. 37–8; Starkey, *Reign of Henry VIII*, pp. 79–80.

[96] Whittinton, *Libellus Epygrammaton*, sig. Aiiiv–Bvr; Bullock, *Oratio*, sig. Biv; *Ballads from Manuscripts*, I (ii), p. 338; Cavendish, p. 4; Knowles, *Religious Orders*, III, p. 36 n. 3; Walker, *John Skelton*, p. 188.

justice was a good thing but that the king should take more personal interest in it.[97] From the early days of his chancellorship, Wolsey made the provision of unbiased justice and the enforcement of the law policies uniquely his own, and the subject of important orations before the king and the council.[98] Sitting as judge in the court of chancery, he set no limits on the role of conscience in correcting the decisions of the common-law courts, and this, together with the recognition by common-lawyers of chancery's superior facilities for devising and enforcing settlements, encouraged a boom in chancery litigation over real property, even though Wolsey never broke the rule that only the common-law courts could finally decide title to land.[99] Wolsey also greatly expanded the judicial role of the king's council, laying the basis by his 'vision and originality' for the fully developed court of star chamber.[100] There too he found that litigation over land soon swamped the council in response to the effective mechanisms he had provided for bringing parties to court, settling their differences and enforcing the result.[101] None the less, he recorded significant successes against retaining, riots and abuses of the local judicial system, and through the council in star chamber he exercised tightening control over the crown's officers in the localities, the sheriffs and justices of the peace.[102]

Local government attracted Wolsey's attention in other ways, as John Guy shows in chapter 1. He managed with skill the vital relationship between the crown and the leaders of county society, buying the loyalty of the gentry elites with appointments at court, but where necessary purging rogue justices from the commissions of the peace and replacing them with reliable outsiders, including members of his own household. Such work was important to the establishment of the stable relations between court and country which would carry the Tudor regime through the troubled decades after his fall. In Wales and the North, Wolsey reconstructed regional government in 1525, establishing councils attached to the households of Princess Mary and the king's bastard son Henry, duke of Richmond. These councils, their methods and in some cases even their personnel dated back to Henry VII's reign and before, but Wolsey revived them with new powers and a clear role in his system of justice and administration centred on the star chamber; though they certainly did not solve every problem that faced them, they pointed the way forward to the success of the later councils

---

[97] Skelton, 'Why come ye nat to courte?', ll. 314–45; *Ballads from Manuscripts*, I (ii), pp. 353–4; Herbert, *Henry VIII*, pp. 269–73; see below, p. 256.

[98] J. A. Guy, *The Cardinal's Court. The Impact of Thomas Wolsey in Star Chamber* (Hassocks, 1977), pp. 30–2.

[99] F. Metzger, 'The last phase of the medieval chancery', in A. Harding (ed.), *Law-Making and Law-Makers in British History* (London, 1980), pp. 79–90; J. A. Guy, 'The development of equitable jurisdictions, 1450–1550', in E. W. Ives, A. H. Manchester (eds.), *Law. Litigants and the Legal Profession* (London, 1983), pp. 80–6.

[100] Guy, *Cardinal's Court*, pp. 132–9.   [101] Ibid., pp. 36–40, 51–9, 83–4, 97–108, 115–17.

[102] Ibid., pp. 27, 31–4, 60–7, 72–4, 119–24.

of the North and of the Marches.[103] Yet Wolsey's work to increase the power of central government did have its limits. His challenges to local judicial franchises were tactical measures in specific disputes rather than part of a general policy.[104] At times his interventions in peripheral areas seemed to admit the indispensability of strong individuals such as Sir William Griffith in North Wales or Sir Hugh Vaughan in Jersey, though his careful investigations of their alleged abuses must have done something to restrain their autocracy.[105] In Ireland he did not even succeed to that extent, for, despite many experiments in government and the introduction of characteristic conciliar methods, the strength of the earl of Kildare made him unwilling to be bridled and his followers unwilling to serve under any alternative deputy or lieutenant.[106]

Overworked as he always was, Wolsey can be forgiven for devoting more attention to equally intractable problems closer to home. His enemies suggested ironically that he should have stopped the rainstorms of 1527 by his 'poletyck wysdom' and thus averted the famine of 1528, but he did the next best thing, sending commissioners to identify stocks of grain and regulate their use.[107] In 1518 he initiated quarantine arrangements to inhibit the spread of plague in London and Oxford, and he made several attempts to regulate the vagrant poor.[108] He sought to prepare the nation for the wars of the 1520s by organizing an innovative military survey of able-bodied men, available arms and armour, and the relations of tenure and service through which captains assembled their retinues: the results were conveniently applicable to the assessment of the forced loans, but they also facilitated improvements in the way armies were raised and equipped.[109] The unerring flattery of Whittinton and Bullock hit on a still more important scheme, which in Whittinton's classicizing idiom became 'the most holy decree of the senate ... for the opening of enclosed fields'.[110] In 1517–18, Wolsey instituted vigorous and wide-ranging surveys of the conversion of land

---

103 C. A. J. Skeel, *The Council in the Marches of Wales* (London, 1904), pp. 49–55, 217–19; S. J. Gunn, 'The regime of Charles, duke of Suffolk in North Wales and the reform of Welsh government, 1509–25', *Welsh History Review*, 12 (1985), 461–94; R. B. Smith, *Land and Politics in the England of Henry VIII. The West Riding of Yorkshire: 1530–46* (Oxford, 1970), p. 155; R. R. Reid, *The King's Council in the North* (London, 1921), pp. 84–5, 92–112. The continued existence of 'the most honorable counsell of Yorkshire' beyond the death of its president Archbishop Savage in 1507 is demonstrated by Durham Priory Reg. Parv. IV, fols. 171v–2r.

104 H. Garrett-Goodyear, 'The Tudor revival of quo warranto and local contributions to state building', in *On the Laws and Customs of England*, pp. 249–55.

105 Gunn, 'North Wales', pp. 474–8; A. J. Eagleston, *The Channel Islands under Tudor Government, 1485–1642* (Cambridge, 1949), pp. 18–25.

106 S. G. Ellis, *Tudor Ireland. Crown, Community and the Conflict of Cultures 1470–1603* (London, 1985), pp. 85–122.

107 *Ballads from Manuscripts*, I (ii), p. 356; Heinze, *Proclamations of the Tudor Kings*, pp. 99–103.

108 P. A. Slack, *Poverty and Policy in Tudor and Stuart England* (London, 1988), pp. 116–17.

109 Goring, 'General proscription', pp. 681–705.

110 Whittinton, *Libellus Epygrammaton*, sig. Bvv; Bullock, *Oratio*, sig. Biv.

from arable to pasture and the associated destruction of husbandmen's houses, and between 1518 and 1529 he proceeded against at least 264 offending landlords, pressing the great majority of cases to a decision.[111] Wolsey could not reverse economic and social change single-handed, but he could, he felt, do justice to the poor, as he also sought to do by his organization of committees of councillors to hear poor men's suits, and of the embryonic court of requests.[112] The abbot of Fountains called Wolsey in about 1520 (in a letter to a third party abroad) 'the especial helper of the poor and oppressed', and more recently he has been dubbed 'the inventor of Tudor paternalism'.[113] It is to the cardinal's credit that he played such a fitting role for a clerical statesman in his public life, even if he does not seem to have matched the private generosity to the poor of Amboise, Mendoza or Cisneros.[114]

Skelton was joking when he compared Wolsey to Robin Hood.[115] Yet some noblemen at least thought that the cardinal had no love for them, whatever his affection for the poor. Edward, duke of Buckingham complained that Wolsey 'would undo all noble men if he could', and Buckingham himself was indeed undone – executed for treason in 1521 – though it is hard to pin the real responsibility for his end on anything but the duke's unrealistically inflexible sense of his own natural importance.[116] There was, however, plenty of evidence for Buckingham's view of the cardinal. Leading noblemen fell foul of Wolsey's law-and-order drive, of his attempts to recover crown debts, of his regulation of local government in the Welsh Marches, and of his enclosure policy.[117] Wolsey's measures smacked of the repressive ways of Henry VII, and so did the men who helped him to execute those measures, survivors of the old king's council such as Sir Thomas Lovell and Sir Henry Marney.[118] Wolsey's policies for the regions involved humiliating exclusion from office for a number of peers, one of whom, Thomas, Lord Darcy, especially resented his subordination to the clergymen who sat as Wolsey's clients on the duke of Richmond's council, and became an

---

[111] J. J. Scarisbrick, 'Cardinal Wolsey and the common weal', in E. W. Ives, R. J. Knecht, J. J. Scarisbrick (eds.), *Wealth and Power in Tudor England. Essays presented to S. T. Bindoff* (London, 1978), pp. 45–67.

[112] Guy, *Cardinal's Court*, pp. 40–5.

[113] Knowles, *Religious Orders*, III, p. 36 n. 3; Slack, *Poverty and Policy*, p. 116.

[114] Bridge, *History of France*, III, p. 29; Revuelta Somalo, 'Renovación de la vida espiritual', pp. 233, 268–9.

[115] Skelton, 'Why come ye nat to courte?', l. 197.

[116] B. J. Harris, *Edward Stafford, Third Duke of Buckingham, 1478–1521* (Stanford, 1986), pp. 171, 203–14. Eric Ives would place more stress on the contemporary accusations that Wolsey contrived the duke's downfall: see p. 289.

[117] H. Miller, *Henry VIII and the English Nobility* (Oxford, 1986), pp. 107–10; Gunn, 'Act of resumption of 1515', pp. 93–4; Harris, *Buckingham*, pp. 172–5; Scarisbrick, 'Cardinal Wolsey and the common weal', pp. 63, 65–6.

[118] J. R. Lander, 'Bonds, coercion and fear: Henry VII and the peerage', in his *Crown and Nobility, 1450–1509* (London, 1976), pp. 267–300; Miller, *English Nobility*, pp. 108–9; Harris, *Buckingham*, p. 183.

embittered critic of the cardinal as a result.[119] On the other hand, new peers continued to be elevated, restricted grants of crown land were still distributed to noblemen, they were almost universally named to the commissions of the peace, and selected individuals were entrusted with senior military commands, an important role in diplomacy, and great responsibilities in local government.[120]

The result was ideal for the crown, since presumptuous noblemen were chastened and all had to compete to serve the king and win his favour. In one way it was also ideal for Wolsey, since peers worked hard to gain his confidence and his assistance in their dealings with the king.[121] But it was easy for those who felt unrewarded or aggrieved to foist the blame on the chief minister, and in the long term many noblemen probably resented the need for subservience to the son of a butcher, as the cardinal's critics expected them to do.[122] It was a subservience made gallingly public. Noblemen were accessories to Wolsey's legatine ritual, holding bowls and towels while he washed his hands, and young peers taken into his household for their education served as ornaments to his daily splendour.[123] Englishmen were used to bishops who were, on average, slightly richer than noblemen, and they were more used than the French to bishops of comparatively humble origins.[124] But cardinal–ministers everywhere (unless they were themselves of high noble birth) tended to enjoy uneasy relations with lay nobles. Cisneros had to make dangerous concessions to the local power of the Castilian magnates in order to maintain their support for his regency, Lang had to fight off noble opposition to his appointment as provost of Augsburg, Tournon made a virtue of standing aside from the power-struggles of the great noble houses, and Beaton in Scotland and Granvelle in the Netherlands ruled only in the teeth of consistent noble opposition.[125] Wolsey was no exception. As long as he retained the king's confidence, noblemen had to work with him, as they did

[119] M. E. James, 'A Tudor magnate and the Tudor state: Henry fifth earl of Northumberland', in his *Society, Politics and Culture. Studies in Early Modern England* (London, 1986), pp. 48–90; Gunn, 'North Wales', p. 491; Miller, *English Nobility*, pp. 78–9, 187–8; Reid, *King's Council in the North*, pp. 103–12.

[120] Miller, *English Nobility*, pp. 14–22, 145–8, 204, 214–17; R. W. Hoyle, 'The first earl of Cumberland: a reputation reassessed', *Northern History*, 22 (1986), 91–2; M. J. Tucker, *The Life of Thomas Howard, Earl of Surrey and second Duke of Norfolk* (The Hague, 1964), pp. 125–40; S. J. Gunn, *Charles Brandon, Duke of Suffolk c.1484–1545* (Oxford, 1988), pp. 38–54, 78–83.

[121] Miller, *English Nobility*, pp. 90, 174–5, 216; Tucker, *Norfolk*, p. 139; Bernard, *War, Taxation and Rebellion*, pp. 88–90; Gunn, *Charles Brandon*, pp. 35–7, 56–62, 66, 71–3, 98.

[122] Miller, *English Nobility*, p. 79; *Ballads from Manuscripts*, I (ii), pp. 333–5; Skelton, 'Why come ye nat to courte?', ll. 292–313, 480–1, 615–24; Roy and Barlow, *Rede me and be nott wrothe*, pp. 58–9; LP, IV (iii) 5750 (ii).

[123] Russell, *Field of Cloth of Gold*, p. 174; Miller, *English Nobility*, p. 82; Gunn, *Charles Brandon*, p. 110; Cavendish, p. 20.

[124] Heal, *Of Prelates and Princes*, pp. 72, 173–4; M. M. Edelstein, 'The social origins of the episcopacy in the reign of Francis I', *French Historical Studies*, 8 (1973–4), 377–92.

[125] Haliczer, *Comuneros of Castile*, pp. 92, 105, 124–5, 151–2; Wiesflecker, *Maximilian*, V, p. 232; François, *Tournon*, p. 489; Sanderson, *Cardinal of Scotland*, pp. 153–230; Van Durme, *Granvela*, pp. 225–61.

with dedication even in the crisis over the Amicable Grant.[126] However, as Eric Ives shows in chapter 11, when the opportunity presented itself the leaders of the nobility were at the forefront of those prepared to cry Wolsey down.

Wolsey's relations with the nobility were one aspect of the system of political management by which he maintained himself in power. His most important relationship was that with the king, a close and effective working partnership from which all his authority ultimately sprang. So close was the partnership, so great the authority, that some suggested that Wolsey was the real king, just as they claimed that Amboise was 'the true king of France', Mendoza 'the third king of Spain' and Lang 'the other emperor'.[127] But such ministers could not simply arrogate to themselves the monarch's authority, as perhaps Beaufort, Beaton and Guise, who governed during royal minorities, came close to doing.[128] Not only did these men have to work hard to maintain their masters' favour – the aim of Wolsey's grand orations as well as of his splendid gifts to the king – they had to work out that favour in council and at court.

As lord chancellor from December 1515, Wolsey occupied the office from which Cardinal Morton had chaired the king's council and played a central role in government.[129] Yet Morton had never been a chief minister like Wolsey, not least because Henry VII was a more active monarch than Henry VIII: foreign ambassadors realized the fact, and never treated Morton as they did Wolsey.[130] As chancellor Warham too had chaired the council, but never really dominated it.[131] Wolsey, on the contrary, made the council in star chamber the centrepiece of his own ministerial supremacy, not only as a judicial organ but also in the control of heresy, the discussion and public announcement of initiatives in foreign affairs, and the execution of policy of every kind.[132] Unfortunately, the council's burgeoning judicial business increasingly obstructed its executive role. Wolsey moved towards the obvious solution, the division of the council into two branches, one judicial and the other executive, but, as John Guy suggests in chapter 1, his political needs frustrated this rationalization. Wolsey could not be simultaneously at court to lead an executive council in counselling the king, and at Westminster to lead a judicial council in dispensing good justice, so he resolved not to separate the two.

In the council Wolsey faced dissent, especially over foreign policy, but never defeat. Only days before his fall he was still presiding over council meetings, and

---

[126] Bernard, *War, Taxation and Rebellion*, pp. 76–87.

[127] Walker, *John Skelton*, pp. 168–80; *Dictionnarie de biographie française*, II, p. 500; *New Catholic Encyclopedia*, IX, p. 650; Wiesflecker, *Maximilian*, V, p. 232.

[128] Harriss, *Beaufort*, p. 133; Sanderson, *Cardinal of Scotland*, pp. 153–76; Sutherland, *Huguenot Struggle*, pp. 73–5.

[129] Pronay, 'The chancellor, the chancery, and the council', pp. 87–103.

[130] *CSPS*, I, 21, 27, 30, 41, 98, 136, 197, 202–5, 221, 239–40, 268, 279, 292; *CSPV*, I, 509, 535, 550, 590, 741, 754, 776, 794.

[131] Guy, *Cardinal's Court*, pp. 23–6.

[132] J. A. Guy, *The Public Career of Sir Thomas More* (Brighton, 1980), p. 108; Hall, pp. 644, 733, 742–4.

he tried to sit in the star chamber on the very day he was charged with offences against the king's authority over the English church under the statute of praemunire.[133] He had been undermined in the king's confidence and at court. Cooperative and confidential though his relationship with Henry was, king and cardinal did not operate in a vacuum. Henry's retention of the final power to decide on questions of policy and of the distribution of patronage made the court a political centre which Wolsey could not neglect, however much his own dominance of the execution of policy made York Place and Hampton Court, in Skelton's jibe, pre-eminent over the king's court.[134] For most of Wolsey's ministry, his greatest problem was the practical one of securing Henry's comments and reluctant signature on the documents he prepared during his long separations from the king. He needed to place a reliable and efficient intermediary among the king's closest attendants, and the task was complicated by his own tendency to suspect that successive candidates were not doing the job properly.[135] Difficulties in communication with the king were an irritation to the cardinal, who needed to discuss matters with Henry in detail even when they were apart, in order to be sure that he might be seen to be presenting and executing the king's policy, and not merely his own. Until the later 1520s, however, king and minister were remarkably unanimous on great questions of state, and in the making of high policy Wolsey had little to fear from the court.

The state of the evidence makes it hard to judge whether Wolsey's control in matters of patronage was ever so complete, though his combination of intimacy with the king and control of the great seal as lord chancellor certainly made him an important element in all calculations concerning royal bounty in the years of his dominance.[136] Like his fellow cardinal–ministers, he aspired to a prominent place in the patronage system centred on the monarch. Balue, Lang, Amboise, Granvelle and Guise were particularly noted for their ability to promote their clients and friends, and obtain grateful loyalty and generous presents in return.[137] On the one hand, Wolsey had to fulfil his responsibility to the king by suggesting suitable candidates for important offices, or pointing out crown servants worthy of reward. On the other, he had to demonstrate to the political nation his continuing influence with Henry (and thus facilitate the exercise of his authority), by visibly assisting those who sought his help to obtain the king's favour. Wolsey's role as a patronage broker proved very profitable, for candidates for royal bounty or mercy sought to buy his services with gifts to him or to his

133 Pollard, pp. 241–2.
134 Starkey, *Reign of Henry VIII*, pp. 16–17; Skelton, 'Why come ye nat to courte?', ll. 406–11.
135 Starkey, 'Court and government', pp. 48–52; Guy, *Public Career of Sir Thomas More*, pp. 16–17.
136 Loades, *The Tudor Court*, p. 134; Gunn, *Charles Brandon*, p. 73; E. W. Ives (ed.), *Letters and Accounts of William Brereton of Malpas*, Record Society of Lancashire and Cheshire, 116 (1976), pp. 22–8.
137 T. Basin, *Apologie ou plaidoyer pour moi-même*, ed. C. Samaran, C. de Groër (Paris, 1974), pp. 79, 113, 115; Wiesflecker, *Maximilian*, v, p. 232; Buisson, *Duprat*, pp. 67–8; Van Durme, *Granvela*, pp. 228–9; Sutherland, *Huguenot Struggle*, pp. 73–4.

colleges of cash, plate, furnishings, lands and annual pensions; others could offer him practical favours in return for his goodwill, as Lord Dacre did in disciplining some of the unrulier tenants of the see of York.[138] Despite these benefits, Wolsey demonstrably did not let considerations of personal power and profit override his duty to the king: in 1515, for instance, he spurned the financial inducements proffered by superfluous office-holders deprived by the Act of Resumption, and refused to back their reinstatement.[139]

Anyone who could speak to the king could petition him for favour, and the attendants who served him day and night in his privy chamber were better placed than most. The phenomenal self-advancement of William Compton, groom of the king's close stool and head of the privy chamber staff, tailed off after 1515 as Wolsey urged constraints on the king's liberality, but Compton continued to be used by others as an intermediary with the king.[140] Wolsey showed consistent concern that the privy chamber staff should not exploit their intimacy with the monarch to sustain large clientage networks of their own, and in 1525–6 and perhaps 1519 he oversaw major reconstructions of the privy chamber which seems to have been intended to prevent excessive intervention with the king by the gentlemen and grooms in matters of patronage and perhaps even of policy.[141] The cause was a hopeless one. Supplicants for royal favour would use every avenue available, simultaneously or successively petitioning Wolsey, other leading councillors, the relevant regional or departmental authorities, and members of the privy chamber.[142] Wolsey could not rationalize and dominate the processes of lobbying and royal grant as he sought to rationalize and dominate so much else, because to do so he would have had to deprive Henry of the fundamental authority of personal kingship, the very authority by which he himself was maintained in power. Even his control of the great seal gave him no veto over grants made under lesser seals, and the real value even of his tenure of the great seal was limited, since to refuse to make grants unequivocally approved by Henry was to oppose the king's will and court his wrath, as Wolsey found to his cost in slightly different but analogous circumstances when he fell foul of Anne Boleyn over the nomination of the abbess of Wilton in 1528.[143] It doubtless irked him when his policies of financial retrenchment, local government reform

---

[138] Cavendish, p. 13; *LP*, IV (ii) 4452; C. H. Cooper, *Memoir of Margaret, Countess of Richmond and Derby* (Cambridge, 1874), pp. 205–6, 209, 211; Gunn, 'Act of resumption of 1515', pp. 104–5; Gunn, *Charles Brandon*, pp. 20, 73, 103; S. M. Harrison, *The Pilgrimage of Grace in the Lake Counties, 1536–7* (London, 1981), p. 32.

[139] Gunn, 'Act of resumption of 1515', pp. 105–6.

[140] G. W. Bernard, 'The rise of Sir William Compton, early Tudor courtier', *English Historical Review*, 96 (1981), 754–77; PRO, C1/917/27.

[141] Starkey, *Reign of Henry VIII*, pp. 77–81, 88–9; Walker, 'Expulsion of the minions', pp. 1–16.

[142] E. W. Ives, 'Patronage at the court of Henry VIII: the case of Sir Ralph Egerton of Ridley', *Bulletin of the John Rylands Library*, 52 (1969–70), 366–9; Gunn, *Charles Brandon*, pp. 96–100.

[143] *Letters and Accounts of William Brereton*, pp. 27–8; E. W. Ives, *Anne Boleyn* (Oxford, 1986), pp. 121–2.

and the imposition of law and order were partly undone by courtiers able to persuade the king to make exceptions for themselves and their friends, as it irked him to find that choice rewards he had earmarked for his own servants had been snapped up by gentlemen of the privy chamber.[144] But none of these developments at court represented a coherent and thoroughgoing challenge to his position with the king. Indeed, it was a mark of Wolsey's very special relationship with Henry and of the political skill with which he maintained it that for most of his career he did not need to engage in the sort of grand political manoeuvring against challengers for his ministerial status which punctuated the lives of other cardinal–ministers. The rivalries of Beaufort and Gloucester, Balue and Charles de Melun, Lang and Paul von Liechtenstein, Amboise and the Maréchal de Gié, Gattinara and Lalemand, Beaton and Arran, Granvelle, Orange, and Egmont, and Guise, Condé and Coligny, could be paralleled from Wolsey's experience only by a brief period of competition with the Howard clan in the years before 1515.[145] Thereafter Wolsey could not be shaken except by some profound alteration in his place in the king's trust, a place so remarkable that many contemporaries could attribute it only to sorcery.[146]

By 1529 that alteration had arrived, as Henry's determination to divorce Catherine of Aragon and marry Anne Boleyn brought about a comprehensive breakdown in Wolsey's political system. Anne became a rival for the 'lovyng fantzy' which Henry felt towards Wolsey, and used her position to contest his influence over crown patronage, forcing him to place ever more trusted allies in the privy chamber to negate her effect on the king, and hence maintain general confidence in his own political strength.[147] In the management of the divorce, Henry, egged on by Anne, also began to take a more independent role in policy-making, at times working behind his minister's back.[148] As chapter 1 recounts, Wolsey's management of the undivided council was outflanked as prominent councillors began to meet at court to advise the king. From January 1529, as Eric Ives shows in chapter 11, a campaign of increasingly open opposition to Wolsey gathered support from individuals and groups who either resented his authority or saw in its end a chance to advance themselves: the prospective queen Anne Boleyn and her ambitious family, leading councillors

---

[144] Gunn, 'Act of resumption of 1515', pp. 99–104; Gunn, 'North Wales', pp. 489–92; Herbert, *Henry VIII*, p. 272; Starkey, *Reign of Henry VIII*, pp. 73–4.

[145] Harriss, *Beaufort*, pp. 134–66, 214–28, 308–13; Gaussin, *Louis XI*, p. 141; Wiesflecker, *Maximilian*, v, pp. 232, 248–51; Quilliet, *Louis XII*, pp. 295–324; Headley, *Emperor and his Chancellor*, pp. 119–30; Sanderson, *Cardinal of Scotland*, pp. 153–8; Parker, *Dutch Revolt*, pp. 50–4; Sutherland, *Huguenot Struggle*, pp. 75–120; Gunn, *Charles Brandon*, pp. 27, 33, 36; Tucker, *Thomas Howard*, pp. 98–103, 125–33.

[146] Tyndale, 'Practice of prelates', p. 308; Walker, *John Skelton*, p. 171; Gunn, *Charles Brandon*, pp. 36, 74; PRO, E314/82/5.

[147] Cavendish, p. 11; Ives, *Anne Boleyn*, pp. 121–2, 126–8; Starkey, *Reign of Henry VIII*, pp. 97–9.

[148] Ives, *Anne Boleyn*, pp. 116–21; E. Surtz, V. Murphy (eds.), *The Divorce Tracts of Henry VIII* (Angers, 1988), pp. vi–xx; H. A. Kelly, *The Matrimonial Trials of Henry VIII* (Stanford, 1976), pp. 38–53.

such as the dukes of Norfolk and Suffolk, and disgruntled individuals on the margin of politics such as Lord Darcy.[149] Wolsey bent all his powers as a diplomat, as papal legate, and as the pope's appointed judge at the Blackfriars trial of summer 1529, to obtain Henry's divorce; but he could not overcome the fateful combination of the weakness of Henry's case in canon law, the stubbornness of Henry's insistence that his marriage to Catherine was plainly invalid by the law of God, and the difficulty of placing political pressure on the recalcitrant pope to provide a solution.[150]

In July 1529, immediately the legatine court at Blackfriars failed and Henry's case was revoked to Rome, Wolsey's rivals staged a coup against him, but it stalled. Only in October was the cardinal indicted for praemunire and dismissed from the chancellorship; only in December were charges against him exhibited in parliament; and only in April 1530 did he leave the environs of London for his diocese of York. As Greg Walker points out in chapter 9, the interpretation of Wolsey's fate is complicated by the fact that his status as a cardinal made him a potential pawn in Henry's deteriorating relations with the pope, just as the disgraced Balue had been for Louis XI.[151] But the chronology of his long-drawn-out humiliation, as chapter 11 argues, can most plausibly be explained by the successive waves of pressure on the king from Wolsey's enemies (who increased in numbers steadily as he sank), determined as they were to eliminate any possibility that he might recover his authority and turn on them. The very intimacy of the working relationship between king and cardinal makes it difficult to analyse the breakdown of confidence between them, and the stress necessarily placed in official pronouncements in the wake of Wolsey's fall on the king's dissatisfaction with him further obscures the dynamics of that breakdown. We cannot enter Henry's mind at the moment of Wolsey's dismissal to discover conclusively whether it was the king's own frustration at the faltering divorce campaign or the urgings of Wolsey's rivals that contributed more to Henry's decision to break with his minister; but Eric Ives argues strongly that key details of the events of 1529 and even some of the king's own words and actions firmly indicate the latter.

The Blackfriars fiasco was not the only signal for Wolsey's enemies to strike in July 1529. The conclusion of peace at Cambrai between Francis I of France and Charles V of Spain and the Holy Roman Empire, without significant English involvement, marked the failure of Wolsey's preferred route to the solution of the divorce problem, the manipulation of the European conflict to force the pope to

---

[149] The degree of Anne's influence over Henry and of her hostility to Wolsey was unclear to contemporaries and remains debatable: Ives, *Anne Boleyn*, pp. 131–52; R. M. Warnicke, *The Rise and Fall of Anne Boleyn* (Cambridge, 1989), pp. 73–95.

[150] *Divorce Tracts*, pp. ii–iii, xvii–xviii; Kelly, *Matrimonial Trials*, pp. 21–129; Wilkie, *Cardinal Protectors*, pp. 179–99; G. de C. Parmiter, *The King's Great Matter, a Study of Anglo-Papal Relations 1527–1534* (London, 1967), pp. 11–112.

[151] *Dictionnaire de biographie française*, v, pp. 18–19.

satisfy the king. Wolsey always placed foreign affairs high on his list of ministerial priorities, a reflection both of their importance to Henry and of the traditionally large diplomatic role of clerical statesmen. In August 1529, as he
struggled for survival, he sought to demonstrate to the king the indispensability
of his diplomatic skill, and in his last desperate manoeuvres to regain power in
1530, he seems to have commenced simultaneous intrigues with Francis I,
Charles V and the pope, to drive England into a disastrous isolation from which
only he could rescue her.[152] Wolsey evidently thought that diplomacy was his
strongest suit, and he had good grounds to do so, even though his critics pointed
out that his management of Henry's foreign affairs had involved a great deal of
expenditure for no very solid gains.[153]

The outlines of Wolsey's diplomacy are clear, but its aims are not readily com-
prehensible. In 1514, 1518 and 1525–7 he negotiated a series of treaties of peace
and marriage alliance with France; but in 1516–17 he tried (without much success)
to coordinate international opposition to Francis I, and from 1521 to 1525 he maintained an offensive alliance against the French king with the Emperor Charles V.
From 1527 until the peace of Cambrai he tried to exploit his alliance with France to
impose peace on Francis and Charles on English terms which would include a
settlement of the king's divorce. Commentators have always sought some grand
design behind these manoeuvres, but none has been found which fully explains
them. A. F. Pollard believed that Wolsey courted first one continental power,
then the other, in the hope that one or both would secure his election to the
papacy; but he never seems to have taken his own candidacy for the tiara very
seriously.[154] He certainly did not pursue it with the assiduity of Amboise, who
marched a French army almost to the gates of Rome for the election of 1503.[155]
The Lutheran William Tyndale claimed that Wolsey bent English policy to serve
successive occupants of the papal throne as part of an international clerical conspiracy.[156] The cardinal was indeed prepared to fall in with papal peace initiatives
or changes of side in the European conflict, and to speak up for the political
independence of the papacy; but only, it seems, when it suited his broader diplomatic purposes or his requests for ever greater legatine powers.[157]

Rather more of the cardinal's contemporary critics attributed his fondness
alternately for Francis and Charles to the size of the pensions each ruler paid
him.[158] It is true that he collected gifts and promises of reward from a number of

152 See below, p. 177; L. R. Gardiner, 'Further news of Cardinal Wolsey's end, November–December
1530', *Bulletin of the Institute of Historical Research*, 57 (1984), 99–107.
153 *LP*, IV (iii) 5750 (ii); Skelton, 'Why come ye nat to courte?', ll. 70–183, 921–5. For a brief narrative of
Wolsey's foreign policy, see chapter 6.
154 Pollard, pp. 121–64; D. S. Chambers, 'Cardinal Wolsey and the papal tiara', *Bulletin of the Institute
of Historical Research*, 38 (1965), 20–30.
155 Quilliet, *Louis XII*, pp. 287–8.   156 Tyndale, 'Practice of prelates', pp. 310–19.
157 Wilkie, *Cardinal Protectors, passim*; Russell, *Field of Cloth of Gold*, pp. 83–5.
158 *Anglica Historia of Polydore Vergil*, pp. 267, 287; Roy, Barlow, *Rede me and be nott wrothe*, p. 54;
Skelton, 'Why come ye nat to courte?', ll. 169–83.

states, and that he was in the pay of both Francis and Charles from 1517, drawing at the apogee some £10,000 a year from them, the larger part from France.[159] But his ability to bleed both the rivals should presumably have encouraged him to hold Henry to neutrality rather than to commit him first one way, then the other (thus cutting off his own pensions from each side in turn); and it was only the size of the sums involved that distinguished Wolsey's annuities and gifts from those given to many other English councillors, and indeed to Amboise and Lang.[160] A more honourable justification of Wolsey's policy is that it reflected the humanist quest for peace.[161] The cardinal did often try to arbitrate general peace in Europe – in 1518, in 1521, in 1527–9 – but his ulterior motives were all too often apparent, and he was not shy to organize and revel in war when the king wished it.[162] For Henry took a more active part in the formation of foreign policy, and at times a more exasperating part in its execution, than in any other area of Wolsey's responsibility.[163] In advising the king, Wolsey must have been affected by his own interests – the expansion of the legacy (though this was also an aspect of the king's control over the national church), the size of his foreign pensions, and the wholehearted praise with which scholars like Whittinton and Bullock could extol his prudence in joining together all the princes of Europe in perpetual amity.[164] But Wolsey's policy had to serve the king's will first and foremost.

One of Henry's pressing concerns was to provide for the succession, and Wolsey's diplomacy certainly bore the problem in mind.[165] Between 1518 and 1527 the king's only legitimate child, Princess Mary, was promised in marriage to the royal houses of France and Spain alternately, with appropriate provisions for her dowry and upbringing. Then Wolsey turned his efforts to the more intractable task of re-marrying his sovereign to produce a male heir. The advent of the divorce, as chapter 6 argues, did force Wolsey into extreme measures in the conduct of foreign affairs, but before that there is little sign that the succession problem was of pre-eminent importance. Instead, the twin criteria which Wolsey sought to meet were the assertion and maintenance of the king's honour, and the continuing security of a kingdom whose crown had at times in the previous seventy years been the plaything of the rulers of France and the Netherlands.[166] This made his policy fluid, enabling him to exploit war or peace to glorify the king, but also to draw back if danger threatened, as it did conspicuously in the revolts of 1525 and the economic crisis of 1528. The potential threat from Scotland

---

[159] Pollard, pp. 116–17, 148–9, 323–4; Russell, *Field of Cloth of Gold*, pp. 82, 120.

[160] *Dictionnaire de biographie française*, II, p. 501; Wiesflecker, *Maximilian*, V, p. 486.

[161] J. J. Scarisbrick, *Henry VIII* (London, 1968), pp. 46–50.

[162] P. J. Gwyn, 'Wolsey's foreign policy: the conferences at Calais and Bruges reconsidered', *Historical Journal*, 23 (1980), 755–72; Bernard, *War Taxation and Rebellion*, pp. 43–5.

[163] Ibid., pp. 40–5; Walker, *John Skelton*, pp. 168–80.

[164] Whittinton, *Libellus Epygrammaton*, sig. Bvr; Bullock, *Oratio*, sigs. Biv–iiir.

[165] R. B. Wernham, *Before the Armada. The Growth of English Foreign Policy 1485–1588* (London, 1966), pp. 98–121.

[166] Gwyn, 'Wolsey's foreign policy', p. 772; Bernard, *War, Taxation and Rebellion*, pp. 3–45.

Fig. 1a Conjectural reconstruction drawing of Cardinal College, Oxford, by Daphne
Hart, from Howard Colvin's *Unbuilt Oxford* (Yale, 1983), figure 7, by kind permission of
Mr Colvin. Certain details, notably the form of the tower at the south-east corner,
beyond the hall, and of the ante-chapel, may need to be revised in the light of Martin
Biddle's essay, 'Wolsey's Bell-Tower', *Oxoniensia*, 53 (1988), 205–10, and John Newman's
chapter, below.

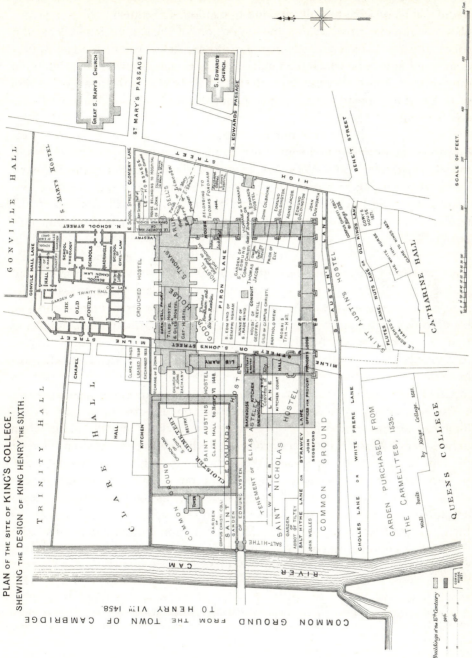

Fig. 1b Plan of site of King's College, Cambridge, showing King Henry VI's design, from Willis and Clark: *Architectural History of the University of Cambridge*, Volume IV (1886)

had also to be considered, and Wolsey made continual efforts to neutralize the traditional Franco-Scottish alliance and to manipulate Scottish politics in favour of the anglophile party among the councillors of the young James V.[167] But controlling Scotland remained secondary to the achievement for Henry of a dominance in Europe which the military and financial resources of his kingdom did not merit. This was Wolsey's greatest aim and, briefly, in the treaty of London of 1518 and the construction of the imperial alliance in 1520–1, his most visible achievement.

Such a foreign policy was not just a matter of empty show, for to assert England's importance convincingly was to make that importance concrete and thus deter aggression; but Wolsey's splendid façade was dented by the discovery in 1523 that even under propitious circumstances, England and the Netherlands could make little lasting military impact on France, and still more so by the realization in 1528 that even coercion of the Netherlands lay beyond England's power.[168] At this point, chapter 6 suggests, the cardinal fell foul of the problem that foreign affairs were never in reality what diplomatic historians often make them, a princely chess-match, isolated from other concerns of government and politics. The charges of Wolsey's enemies in 1529 laid great stress on the independence and secrecy of his diplomacy, and by that year his intense personal identification with a policy, conducted in the face of opposition from a number of leading councillors, which not only failed to secure the king's divorce but also threatened England's internal stability, helped to ruin him.[169] In foreign affairs as in so much else, Wolsey's schemes were so grand that they were incapable of modest achievement: the cardinal's failure was as magnificent as his successes.

Wolsey's artistic patronage was conceived on as striking a scale as his diplomacy. In this sphere, however, it was not so much the unrealizable ambition of his schemes as the consequences of his fall which prevented the achievement of some of his greatest projects. Wolsey's major architectural works were, perhaps revealingly, collegiate and domestic rather than specifically ecclesiastical: unlike Cardinals Cisneros or Balue he commissioned no great work for any cathedral church, nor did Wolsey pay for a hospital or church cloister as Mendoza did.[170] He did, however, build on a grand scale, comparable with Cardinals Mendoza, Amboise or, indeed, any of his continental counterparts and, more importantly, outstripping any English precursors.

---

[167] R. G. Eaves, *Henry VIII's Scottish Diplomacy, 1513–1524* (New York, 1971); Eaves, *Henry VIII and James V's Regency 1524–1528. A Study in Anglo-Scottish Diplomacy* (Lanham, 1987).

[168] S. J. Gunn, 'The duke of Suffolk's march on Paris in 1523', *English Historical Review*, 101 (1986), 596–634.

[169] Herbert, *Henry VIII*, pp. 266–7.

[170] For Cisneros's patronage of the Toledo cathedral screen, see Contreras, *Historia del Arte Hispánico*, III, pp. 195–7 and for Mendoza's foundation of the hospital of Santa Cruz (he also paid for the stalls of Toledo cathedral) pp. 169–70 and 189; J. M. de Azcárate, *La Arquitectura Gótica Toledana del Siglo XV* (Madrid, 1958), pp. 29–30 (for the post-1504 building of the hospital) and Nader, *Mendoza*

Wolsey's great architectural enterprise, Cardinal College, Oxford (plate 1) could be assessed in the context of Cisneros's, Guise's or Tournon's foundations but it is more important to recall that Cardinal College numbered among its immediate models the foundations of three other bishops of Winchester: William of Wykeham's New College, William Waynflete's Magdalen and, most recently, Richard Fox's Corpus Christi. Wolsey, a former bursar, had an intimate knowledge of Magdalen, which in view of its planning, scale, materials and style is the most relevant model. It is characteristic of Wolsey that his foundation was to surpass it and all previous Oxford colleges in size, numbers of fellows (or, in this case, canons), scholars and architectural magnificence (fig. 1a).[171] His college's endowment, derived from no less than twenty monasteries, and bringing in about £2,000 p.a., was over double that of its nearest rival.[172] In terms of sheer scale, the only English architectural precedent for Wolsey's college was, significantly enough, not the Oxford foundation of a bishop, but that of a king, at Cambridge. In 1448, the 'Wille and entent' of King Henry VI laid out the plans for his college on a scale enormously enlarged from that which he had already started to build in 1441. The huge chapel of King's College was intended to occupy the north side of a courtyard with chambers on the east and south sides, with a hall and library to the west and with a detached cloister and gigantic belltower to the west of the chapel (fig. 1b).[173] At the time of Henry VI's death, King's chapel was far from completion and almost nothing had been achieved towards the erection of the other buildings. It was not until Henry VIII's reign that the chapel's structure was completed (plate 2), and the fittings, furniture and stained glass were not finished until 1544. It is clear, since Henry VII and his son were responsible for financing the completion of the chapel, and since this was, during Wolsey's lifetime, their only large-scale involvement in college-building at either university, that Wolsey will have known a good deal about King's;[174] it seems to have been

---

Family, p. 115. For Balue, see *Dictionnaire de biographie française*, s.v. and G. Bonnenfant, *La Cathédrale d'Evreux* (Paris, 1925), pp. 18–19.

[171] See John Newman's chapter.

[172] *LP*, IV (i) 649, 650, 989, 990, 1001, 1137, 1138, 1499, 1695, 1728, 1833, 1834, 1845, 1913, 1961, 2014, 2024, 2059, 2137, 2138, 2151, 2152, 2167, 2193, 2217, 2379; *LP*, IV (ii) 2396, 2538, 2969, 3141, 3190, 3536, 3537, 3538, 3736, 4230, 4308, 4364, 4365, 4475, 4496, 4794, 5112, 5117; C. Cross, 'Oxford and the Tudor state', in McConica (ed.), *History of the University of Oxford*, III, p. 122.

[173] R. Willis and J. W. Clark, *The Architectural History of the University of Cambridge, and of the Colleges of Cambridge and Eton* (Cambridge, 1886, repr. 1988), pp. 312ff. (and fig. 3); *VCH Cambridge and the Isle of Ely*, III (London, 1959), pp. 376ff.; *RCHM City of Cambridge*, I (London, 1959), pp. 98ff.; *HKW*, III, pp. 187–195; F. Woodman, *The Architectural History of King's College Chapel and its place in the Development of Late Gothic Architecture in England and France* (London, 1986).

[174] Clement VII granted Wolsey the faculty of suppressing certain religious houses for the benefit of Eton and King's in a bull of November 1528; *LP*, IV (ii) 4902. In September 1528, the Fellows wrote to Wolsey recognizing with what 'zeal and energy you exhort our most serene King to complete and embellish our College' (King's College, Muniments, Ledger Book, 1451–1558 fol. 280v, translated in H. G. Wayment, *The Windows of King's College Chapel, Cambridge* (London, 1972), p. 3). There were also numerous personnel in common at King's and Cardinal College (see below for the glaziers).

his ambition to surpass not only the latter's newly completed chapel, as John Newman points out, but even the, still unrealized, intentions of its founder.[175] By the time of his fall, Wolsey had spent between £20,000 and £25,000 on the buildings of Cardinal College, which was still far from complete.[176]

In layout and in scale, Cardinal College drew from but exceeded its models, as it did in its projected complement of fifteen feeder schools where King's and New College had one each and Magdalen two.[177] Of these schools, the Cardinal's College of St Mary at his birthplace, Ipswich, combining the roles of a college of secular priests, a school for boys and an almshouse for poor men (just as Henry VI's first plan for King's feeder, Eton, had done) must always have been intended to be *primus inter pares*, with an income of £1,000 p.a.[178] Wolsey's personal involvement even in some of the minutiae of the college is attested no less by his ensuring that high quality building stone from Caen in Normandy was provided for the buildings (the surviving brick built gateway (plate 3) can only have been a side entrance to the college, whose site can be traced on Ogilby's map of Ipswich: fig. 2), than by his compilation of the grammar textbook for the boys.[179]

Letters to the cardinal from Sir Nicholas Vaux during the erection of the English temporary palace at the Field of Cloth of Gold indicate that on this earlier occasion too Wolsey was intimately concerned not just with the broad specifications but also with certain of the details of planning during the hectic rush to complete work: he was, for instance, asked to arrange for the loan of terracotta arms and beasts from the duke of Suffolk, whose Southwark town-house extensively featured terracotta decoration with Renaissance motifs.[180] By the

[175] If the drawing for the bell-tower to join the freestanding cloister at King's College actually dates from the early sixteenth century (Willis & Clark, *Cambridge*, I, p. 554; cf. *HKW*, I, p. 272n.) rather than the mid (J. Harvey, *The Perpendicular Style* (London, 1978), p. 229) or late fifteenth century (Woodman, *King's*, pp. 132–4), it provides evidence that thought was given in the early Tudor period to the continuation of Henry VI's scheme for the college.

[176] J. H. Harvey, 'The building works and architects of Cardinal Wolsey', *Journal of the British Archaeological Association*, 8 (1943), 50–9 (54). See also J. Newman, 'The physical setting: new building and adaptation', in McConica (ed.), *History of Oxford*, III, pp. 611–15 and Mr Newman's essay in this volume.

[177] Dowling, *Humanism*, pp. 119–20.

[178] Archbishop Chichele's college at Higham Ferrers, founded in 1422, also housed a bedehouse for twelve poor men: *VCH Northants*, II (London, 1906), pp. 177–9; *Archaeological Journal*, 69 (1912), 477–81.

[179] J. Grove, *Two Dialogues in the Elysian Fields beetween Cardinal Wolsey and Cardinal Ximenes* (London, 1761), Appendix B; N. F. Layard, 'Remarks on Wolsey's college and the priory of St Peter and Paul, Ipswich', *Archaeological Journal*, 56 (1899), 211–15; W. M. Morfey, 'Wolsey's gateway', *Archaeological Journal*, 108 (1952), 141. We are indebted to Dr John Blatchly for guidance on the extent of Wolsey's college and for the material on which fig. 2 is based. For the Caen stone see *LP*, IV (ii) 4778. For the grammar book, see J. Simon, *Education and Society in Tudor England* (Cambridge, 1967), pp. 143–4 and above p. 13.

[180] J. G. Nichols (ed.), *The Chronicle of Calais in the reigns of Henry VII and Henry VIII to the year 1540*, Camden Society 1846, pp. 84–5. See also *LP*, III (i) 825 (where it is erroneously claimed that the letter is also printed in Nichols (ed.), *Chronicle*, p. 82). For the duke of Suffolk's Southwark house, see M. Howard, *The Early Tudor Country House: Architecture and Politics 1490–1550* (London, 1987),

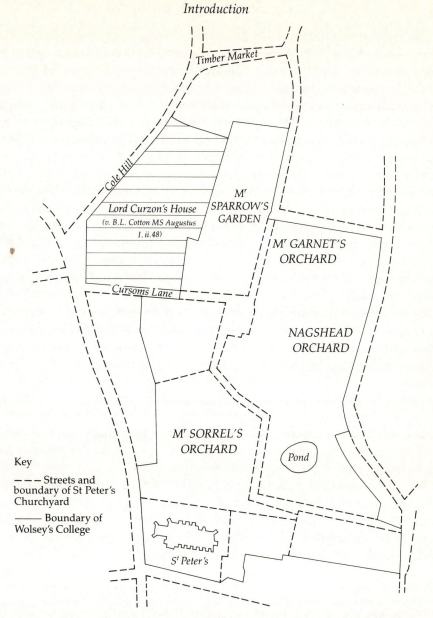

Key

- - - Streets and
boundary of St Peter's
Churchyard

——— Boundary of
Wolsey's College

Fig. 2 Plan of the site of Cardinal College, Ipswich, and Lord Curzon's house, based on
Ogilby's Map of Ipswich (information from Dr John Blatchly)

time of the construction of the English palace at Guines, with its cornice
decorated *à l'antique*, scalloped pediment, and two Renaissance style fountains,
such motifs were becoming increasingly popular in England. Indeed, recent
excavations at Hampton Court have suggested that Wolsey's earliest building
works there featured terracotta decoration designed and produced by the same

workshop that was responsible for the still-surviving decoration at Sutton Place, Surrey, in the 1520s.[181] This specific type of terra-cotta decoration appears to have been abandoned for the extant buildings from Wolsey's period at Hampton Court, but quite why this should have happened, especially since their popularity in court circles continued up to Wolsey's fall, is unclear.[182] John Newman suggests in chapter 3 that terracottas were used at Ipswich College, for which the foundation licence was obtained late in June 1528; it would be interesting to know the range of terracotta ornament the college would have featured.

At Hampton Court, the earlier decorative reliefs, employed to stress major architectural features, seem to have given way to the reliefs of Hercules and roundels of Emperors produced by the Florentine sculptor Giovanni da Maiano, and set into towers and wall surfaces. The chief function of all such decoration was to render fashionable what was essentially a traditional architectural structure. Renaissance ideas on planning or proportion cannot be said to have determined the design of Wolsey's house: 'antique' forms were simply applied or added onto the surface. Nor is the striking search for symmetry which distinguishes Sutton Place evident at Hampton Court. Indeed, Simon Thurley argues in chapter 2 that important features of the design of Wolsey's Hampton Court were developed from ideas current in Henry VII's reign and so, in this sense, the house was far from innovative.[183] Such considerations help to put into proper perspective the rather inflated claims that have been made for Wolsey as an innovator in the reception of Italian Renaissance art into England.[184] Hampton Court is in no sense a stylistic parallel for Cardinal Mendoza's Guadalajara palace, the first Renaissance palace in Spain, any more than Cardinal College, Oxford could be said to be an architectural counterpart to the University of Alcalá de Henares founded by Cardinal Cisneros in 1508.[185]

It was the scale and multiplicity rather than the style of Wolsey's domestic building programmes which attracted the attention of his English contemporaries. Besides the well-known satire of the magnificence of Hampton Court and York Place contained in John Skelton's 'Why come ye nat to courte', Wolsey's architectural patronage was condemned by the anonymous author of critical

35 and fig. 15; see also S. J. Gunn and P. G. Lindley, 'Charles Brandon's Westhorpe: an early Tudor courtyard house in Suffolk', *Archaeological Journal*, 145 (1988), 272–89.

[181] D. Batchelor, 'Excavations at Hampton Court Palace', *Post-Medieval Archaeology*, 11 (1977), 36–49; R. K. Morris, 'Windows in early Tudor country houses', in Williams (ed.), *Early Tudor England*, pp. 125–38; Morris, 'Architectural terracotta at Sutton Place and Hampton Court Palace', *British Brick Society Information*, 44 (March 1988), 3–8.

[182] Excavations currently underway at Hampton Court may help to clarify this problem.

[183] See also Harvey, 'Building works', 50–9.

[184] E. Auerbach, *Tudor Artists* (London, 1954), p. 38, describes the Maiano roundels and the tomb-project as the 'first major manifestations of renaissance art in this country', adding, 'it was probably Wolsey's influence that induced his master to call foreign artists to court ...'

[185] Cf. Azcárate, *Arquitectura*, pp. 19–20 and Nader, p. 115. The famous façade of the university dates, of course, only from 1543.

verses on the cardinal recorded in British Library Harleian MS 2252, and by Roy and Barlow who, not perhaps without grudging admiration, comment on his

> grett palaces with out compareson,
> most glorious of outwarde sight
> And with in decked poynt device
> More lyke unto a paradice
> Than an erthely habitacion.[186]

In the 'Metrical Visions', a poem which continues the moralizing on the theme of the fickleness of fortune which marks his 'Life' of Wolsey (and also implicitly recants some of the more eulogistic passages in that work), George Cavendish has Wolsey describe his buildings in a very similar vein

> My buyldyngs somptious, the roffes with gold and byse
> Shone lyke the sone in mydday spere,
> Craftely entaylled as connyng could devise,
> With images embossed, most lively did appere;
> Expertest artificers that ware both farre and nere,
> To beautyfie my howssys, I had them at my will:
> Thus I wanted nought my pleasures to fulfill.

Wolsey goes on to say

> My galleries ware fayer; both large and long
> To walke in them whan that it lyked me best.[187]

It is significant that Cavendish represents Wolsey as celebrating his galleries for, as chapter 2 reveals, their distinctive form was the most innovative design feature of his domestic buildings.

Wolsey's best known domestic architecture is at Hampton Court Palace. He had leased the site from Sir Thomas Docwra, Prior of the Knights of St John, in 1514 and building was so rapid that the king and queen were able to dine there by May 1516.[188] At the same time that work was underway at Hampton Court, extensive alterations were also being undertaken at York Place, the London residence of the archbishops of York, which Wolsey had acquired on his promotion to the see in 1514.[189] In the early 1520s, when work was underway at both sites, the cardinal had also embarked on major rebuilding and enlargement works at The More – which Du Bellay thought more splendid than Hampton

---

[186] Skelton, 'Why come ye nat to courte', ll. 401–15; see also 'Collyn Clout', ll. 934–59; E. Arber (ed.), *Rede me and be nott wrothe, For I saye no thinge but trothe*, (London, 1871), p. 57; Furnivall, *Ballads*, p. 352, printing BL, MS Harley 2252 fol. 158: 'with Abbayes good thy Colage thou byldeste;/with pore mens good thy place thou gyldeste'.

[187] S. W. Singer (ed.), *The Life of Cardinal Wolsey* (London, 1825), II, 'Metrical visions', p. 10.

[188] *LP*, II (i) 1935; E. Law, *The History of Hampton Court Palace* (London, 1885), I, p. 30. For Hampton Court, see also C. Peers in *VCH Middlesex*, II, 327–87; *RCHM Middlesex*, pp. 30ff; *HKW*, IV, pp. 126–35.

[189] *LP*, II (ii) 4662; J. G. Milne and J. H. Harvey, 'The building of Cardinal College, Oxford', *Oxoniensia*, 8 & 9 (1943–4), 137–53 (147).

Court[190] – and Tyttenhanger, which fell to him as titular abbot of St Alban's; Henry VIII liked Tyttenhanger so much that he had Thomas Heritage design additions for him and, after Wolsey's fall, considered appropriating the manor to himself.[191] In 1527, work was still underway at both Hampton Court and York Place and in 1529, when Wolsey became bishop of Winchester, he also started to improve the episcopal palace at Esher.[192] At the time of his fall, Wolsey was running a domestic works organization which was larger than the king's. Even after his fall, Wolsey engaged in repair work at Southwell, employing London craftsmen,[193] and despite Cromwell's earnest entreaties to 'refraygne your self, for a season, from al maner byldyngges, more than mere necessite requireth',[194] he rebuilt and repaired Cawood castle, apparently employing a workforce of over 300 artificers.[195]

It is stressed in chapter 2 that Wolsey was not alone, or even unusual, in being an episcopal patron of domestic architecture in late medieval England. Indeed, almost a sixth of all the nearly 200 medieval episcopal palaces were being improved in the period 1470–1535.[196] Many of Wolsey's predecessors also built on a lavish scale. Bishop Waynflete of Winchester (d.1486) built at Eton, Tattershall and Winchester, Farnham, Esher and Wainfleet, besides founding Magdalen College, Oxford; Bishop Alcock of Ely (d.1500) rebuilt Downham and Ely palaces as well as founding Jesus College, Cambridge, on the site of the dissolved convent of St Radegund, and he also constructed a magnificent chantry chapel for himself at the east end of his cathedral church (plate 4). Alcock's predecessor at Ely, Cardinal Morton (d.1500), had rebuilt the episcopal palace at Hatfield and the castle at Wisbech; as archbishop of Canterbury, he engaged in building work at Canterbury, Lambeth, Croydon, Maidstone, Aldington-Park, Charing and Ford.[197] Morton was the most recent English cardinal resident in this country

---

[190] Pollard, p. 325; *HKW*, IV, pp. 164–7.   [191] *LP*, IV (ii) 4463; *LP*, IV (ii) 4497; *HKW*, IV, p. 282.

[192] *LP*, IV (ii) 3334 (for building in progress on 6 August 1527 at Hampton Court and York Place). Bishop Fox wrote to Gardiner on 11 May 1528 that Wolsey was then residing at Durham Place, 'the hall of York Place, with other buildings there being now in building, my Lord's Grace intending most sumptuously to repair and furnish the same' (*LP*, IV (ii) 4251). For work at Esher, see Law, *Hampton Court*, p. 34. Wolsey used Esher before becoming bishop of Winchester: see Bishop Fox's (d.1528) letter to him in P. S. and H. M. Allen (eds.), *Letters of Richard Fox 1486–1527* (Oxford, 1929), pp. 121–2. See also Simon Thurley's chapter.

[193] *LP*, IV (iii) 6329, 6447.   [194] *LP*, IV (iii) 6751; *StP*, I, p. 366.

[195] Pollard, p. 274; Cavendish, p. 144.

[196] P. Hembry, 'Episcopal palaces, 1535 to 1660' in E. W. Ives, R. J. Knecht and J. J. Scarisbrick (eds.), *Wealth and Power in Tudor England* (London, 1978), pp. 146–66 (152).

[197] For Waynflete, see M. W. Thompson, 'The date of "Fox's Tower", Farnham Castle, Surrey', *Surrey Archaeological Collections*, 59 (1960), 85–92. At Eton, his building-work was a consequence of his being one of Henry VI's executors; see Thompson, *The Decline of the Castle* (Cambridge, 1987), p. 98 for his erection of Tattershall parish church and college as Lord Cromwell's principal executor. For Alcock, see J. Bentham, *The History and Antiquities of the Conventual and Cathedral Church of Ely* (Cambridge, 1771), pp. 179–83; Hembry, 'Episcopal palaces', p. 153. Morton's arms also appear on the church tower at Wisbech, indicating that he may have had a hand in its construction.

before Wolsey, and his example was evidently an important one. Just as relevant, perhaps, was the example of Bishop Fox (d.1528), the founder of Corpus Christi College, Oxford, who as bishop of Durham undertook extensive building at Norham and Durham and who began a large-scale rebuilding of Winchester Cathedral shortly after his translation to the see.[198] Archbishop Warham of Canterbury (d.1530) claimed to have spent as much as £30,000, mainly on a grand new palace at Otford, though it was only three miles away from the palace at Knole erected by Cardinal Bourchier (d.1486).[199] The loss of all but a fragment of the accounts for Wolsey's domestic buildings unfortunately precludes detailed cost-comparisons, but Wolsey's expenditure on Hampton Court alone probably exceeded Warham's total, and given that the cardinal also engaged in huge building programmes at York Place, The More, Tyttenhanger, as well as at his Oxford and Ipswich colleges and, further, that he intended to rebuild the university schools at Oxford and, at the time of his fall was apparently intending to turn Lord Curzon's Ipswich town house (fig. 2) into his palace there,[200] it emerges that his actual and intended architectural patronage far surpassed that of English ecclesiastics of the recent past.

Indeed, the scale of Wolsey's building enterprises is only really comparable with that of Kings Henry VII and Henry VIII. Henry VII spent over £28,000 between 1494 and his death on a new palace at Richmond, extensive works at Greenwich, and substantial additions to older buildings at Woodstock and Langley, Windsor, Woking and Hanworth. Richmond Friary and the king's almshouses at Westminster were completed by 1502, whilst construction of his chantry chapel at Westminster (plate 5), and the completion of the fifteenth-century fabric of King's College Chapel, Cambridge, were all underway at his death and funded by his executors. Henry VIII spent some £39,000 on his first new palaces, Bridewell in London and New Hall in Essex, between 1515 and 1522, and engaged in extensive alterations at Hunsdon in 1525–34, but it was not until the cardinal's death that the latter's great buildings were dwarfed by the

---

[198] Christopher Bainbridge was promoted to the cardinalate whilst at the court of Rome, where he was murdered in 1514. For Fox, see A. J. Smith, 'The life and building activity of Richard Fox c.1448–1528', unpublished PhD thesis, University of London, 1988.

[199] For Warham, see J. G. Nichols and J. Bruce (eds.), *Wills from Doctors' Commons*, Camden Society 1863, p. 22; C. P. Ward, 'Emergency excavations at Otford Palace, 1974', *Archaeologia Cantiana*, 87 (1974), 199–203; A. D. Stoyel, 'The lost buildings of Otford Palace', *Archaeologia Cantiana*, 100 (1984), 259–80. For a revised plan, see R. Coope, 'The "Long Gallery": its origins, development, use and decoration', *Architectural History*, 29 (1986), 43–72, fig. 4. For Bourchier, see F. R. H. du Boulay, 'A note on the rebuilding of Knole by Archbishop Bourgchier', *Archaeologia Cantiana*, 63 (1950), 135–9. See also P. A. Faulkner, 'Some medieval archiepiscopal palaces', *Archaeological Journal*, 127 (1970), 130–46.

[200] Simon, *Education and Society*, p. 138, for Wolsey's intention of rebuilding the university schools. For Ipswich, see D. MacCulloch, *Suffolk and the Tudors: Politics and Religion in an English County 1500–1600* (Oxford, 1986), p. 152.

king's works.[201] Wolsey's buildings were, in short, the most expensive and most magnificent of his time.

Wolsey's projected tomb is also distinguished by its scale and cost. The cardinal's commissioning of the distinguished Florentine sculptor, Benedetto da Rovezzano, to produce his monument, should be seen in the context of the two most prestigious previous tomb contracts of the preceding decade – those for Margaret Beaufort's monument and the double tomb of King Henry VII and Queen Elizabeth – both of which had also been awarded to a Florentine sculptor, Pietro Torrigiano, who had subsequently left England for Spain.[202] Benedetto was the obvious successor to Torrigiano in a milieu in which, as in courts from Poland to France, Italian sculptors were widely perceived as superior to natives.[203] If Wolsey's monument would have been the first purely Renaissance tomb on a grand scale in England, this is because the patrons of the earlier royal monuments had been manifestly concerned with ensuring a visual continuity with the earlier royal tombs in Westminster Abbey and therefore allowed Torrigiano less freedom than Wolsey evidently permitted Benedetto.[204] Where Torrigiano had been given a freer rein, in the monument for Dr Yonge, now in the museum of the Public Record Office, he had produced a work which marked a radical departure from earlier English wall-tombs and drew close to Florentine practice.[205] His high altar for Henry VII's chapel and other works, such as the terracotta busts of King Henry VII, Bishop Fisher and Henry VIII, also constitute major innovations in English art.[206] Benedetto's work on Wolsey's monument represented another significant advance in the direction of a purer Florentine Renaissance style (though the freestanding format is difficult to parallel in Italy)

[201] *HKW*, III, pp. 1, 187–90, 196–201, 206–10, 210–13, 308–11; *HKW*, IV, pp. 1, 97–9, 147–8, 160, 223, 344, 349–51. Greenwich £3,000; Richmond c.£20,000; Hanworth at least £700; Woking c.£1,400; Woodstock over £4,000; Westminster Abbey Chapel c.£20,000; Savoy Hospital c.£10,000; King's c.£7,000; Westminster Almshouses c.£500; Windsor, c.£4,000. He also paid for the construction of the friary of Franciscan Observants at Richmond at a cost of about £1,500 (*HKW*, III, pp. 195–6). Wolsey also built at Richmond (Cavendish, p. 123).

[202] For Torrigiano, see A. Higgins, 'On the work of Florentine sculptors in England in the early part of the sixteenth century; with special reference to the tombs of Cardinal Wolsey and King Henry VII', *Archaeological Journal*, 51 (1894), 129–220; A. P. Darr, 'Pietro Torrigiano and his sculpture for the Henry VII Chapel, Westminster Abbey', unpublished PhD dissertation, New York University, 1980; P. G. Lindley, '"Una grande opera al mio Re": Gilt-bronze effigies in England from the Middle Ages to the Renaissance', *Journal of the British Archaeological Association*, 143 (1990), 112–30.

[203] For Poland, see J. Bialostocki, 'Renaissance sculpture in Poland in its European context: some selected problems', in S. Fizman (ed.), *The Polish Renaissance in its European Context* (Indiana, 1988), pp. 281–90; a useful bibliography on French Renaissance sculpture, now in need of updating, is provided by M. Beaulieu, *Description raisonée des sculptures du Musée du Louvre, II, Renaissance Française* (Paris, 1978).

[204] Lindley, 'Gilt-bronze effigies', p. 123.

[205] C. Galvin and P. G. Lindley, 'Pietro Torrigiano's tomb for Dr Yonge', *Church Monuments*, 3 (1988), 42–60. Wolsey purchased hangings from Yonge's executors (*LP*, IV (iii) 6184).

[206] C. Galvin and P. G. Lindley, 'Pietro Torrigiano's portrait bust of King Henry VII', *Burlington Magazine*, 130 (1988), 892–902.

and, had it been completed, the tomb would have constituted an influential contribution to the increasingly widespread taste for Renaissance art. In the English context, however, its style would probably have attracted less attention than its magnificence of materials, its grandiloquent iconography, and its sheer size. These features were undoubtedly specified by Wolsey himself and, as chapter 10 demonstrates, we have Benedetto's own testimony that the cardinal had verbally contracted with the sculptor for a tomb to surpass Torrigiano's recently completed double monument to Henry VII and Queen Elizabeth.

Wolsey's sensitivity to the latest artistic fashions is clearly illustrated in his seal designs; he was himself constantly in receipt of documents emanating from the papal chancery and sealed with Renaissance seals and, as chancellor, received letters patent from the king directing him to redesign the great seal in 1525.[207] This lends weight to Erna Auerbach's argument that Wolsey was personally concerned with the design of the gold seal attached in September 1527 to the treaty of perpetual peace with France.[208] This seal is the first ostentatious Renaissance example to be produced in England, and features a shell-topped, arched throne, flanked by pillars and pilasters receding into depth in three layers, and with a Tudor rose supported by two cherubs at the base. The impetus to use Italianate designs may also have been stimulated by the display on Francis I's seals of an advanced Renaissance idiom: indeed, copying the widespread employment of Italian artists and designers at the French court was undoubtedly an important factor in the patronage Wolsey and the English court themselves gave to Italians. The seal used by Wolsey as archbishop of York has Renaissance architectural features, and such influences are also evident in the Ipswich college seal (plate 6), which shows the ascending Virgin between cherubs and angels, and standing on a crescent moon overlapped by the cardinal's hat and with his coat of arms below; she is crowned by Christ and God the Father, with the dove of the Holy Spirit above.[209] The seal of Cardinal College Oxford (plate 7), shows the Trinity (sheltering saints and ecclesiastics) in a Renaissance architectural structure flanked by the Madonna and Child and St Frideswide. Below, the cardinal's hat and arms are flanked by griffins holding pillars (this last feature can be paralleled in sculpture in Wolsey's work at Hampton Court). The dolphins and

---

[207] *LP*, IV (i) 1859. A. B. and A. Wyon, *The Great Seals of England* (London, 1887), pp. 67–71, state that the first usage of the second seal was only in October 1532. The instructions given to Wolsey correspond very closely to the features of this seal.

[208] Auerbach, *Tudor Artists*, pp. 38ff. remains the fundamental study of Wolsey's seals. For the French seal, see J. B. Trapp and H. S. Herbrüggen, *'The King's Good Servant': Sir Thomas More 1477/8–1535*, Catalogue of an exhibition at the National Portrait Gallery (London, 1977), pp. 99–100 and for the golden seal of Henry VIII, Wyon, pl.XIX and p. 71. The editors are indebted to Dr T. A. Heslop for advice on this understudied subject and for the information that two other members of Wolsey's circle, John Clerk, bishop of Bath and Wells, and John Kite, bishop of Carlisle, also had Renaissance seals in the early 1520s.

[209] PRO, E24/23/15; E24/23/16.

ornament are strongly reminiscent of the East Anglian terracotta tombs studied by Tony Baggs.[210] Such sophisticated design features argue for their creation by an artist of considerable stature. The usual practice seems to have been for a painter to furnish the design for a seal matrix to the goldsmith responsible for its facture – as in the documented case of Morgan Wolff's third great seal of Henry VIII (1542) – and it is likely that a specialist painter supplied the designs for the seals supplied to Wolsey by Robert Amadas and Cornelius Hayes in 1525, 1526 and 1528.[211]

Dr Auerbach connected Wolsey's seals with the seventy or so letters patent relating to the colleges, now preserved in the Public Record Office.[212] They are generally written on very high quality vellum and have the initial letter and top margin illuminated, often in monochrome but occasionally with additions of colour. Some are decorated simply with floral patterns or with the cardinal's arms and supporters, while others have the king's portrait and arms. The portraits of the king on letters patent are intimately related to the development in England of the independent portrait miniature: this can be highlighted by a patent of 1524 exhibiting a portrait of Henry VIII which is very close in style to the Fitzwilliam Museum miniature of 1525–6, a key work in reconstructing the oeuvre of Lucas Horenbout.[213] Clearly, their decoration could be the province of major artists. Auerbach has examined three of the Wolsey patents in detail: one dated 5 May 1526 (PRO, E24/6/1) (plate 8), on letters patent confirming the possessions granted by the King to Cardinal College; and two others dating from 25 and 26 May 1529 (PRO, E24/20/1 (plate 9) and E24/2/1). She connects the first of the patents with Holbein, but the artist was only certainly in England by 18 December 1526 and is very unlikely to have reached the country before September at the earliest.[214] Moreover, Holbein had returned to Basle by August 1528. It seems possible that the illumination should instead be attributed to the Ghent artist Gerard Horen-

[210] PRO, E322/188. Cf. A. P. Baggs, 'Sixteenth century terracotta tombs in East Anglia', *Archaeological Journal*, 125 (1968), 296–301. See also the ornament from Charles Brandon's Suffolk Place, published in P. G. Lindley's review of Howard, *Early Tudor Country House*, in *Oxford Art Journal*, 11 (1988), 64–7, fig. 1.

[211] R. Strong, *Artists of the Tudor Court: The Portrait Miniature Rediscovered 1520–1620*, Exhibition Catalogue of the Victoria and Albert Museum (London, 1983), pp. 41–2 suggests Lucas Horenbout as the designer of the third great seal of King Henry VIII. In the Middle Ages too, miniaturists and painters were sometimes responsible for seal designs. See, for example, F. Baron, 'Enlumineurs, peintres et sculpteurs parisiens des XIVᵉ et XVᵉ siècles, d'après les archives de l'Hôpital Saint-Jacques-aux-Pèlerins', *Bulletin Archéologique du Comité des Travaux Historiques et Scientifiques*, 6 (1970), 77–115 (112 for Jean Pucelle's design of the fraternity's great seal). For Wolsey's seals, see *LP*, IV (iii) 6748, items 7, 9 and 11.

[212] Auerbach, *Tudor Artists*, p. 39.

[213] For the letters patent of 1524, see S. Foister, review of Strong, *Artists*, *Burlington Magazine*, 125 (1983), 635–6, fig. 62 and R. Bayne-Powell, *Catalogue of Portrait Miniatures in the Fitzwilliam Museum, Cambridge* (Cambridge, 1985), p. 130; but see also J. Backhouse, 'Illuminated manuscripts and the early development of the portrait miniature', in *Early Tudor England*, p. 11.

[214] S. M. Foister, 'Holbein and his English patrons' (unpublished PhD thesis, University of London 1981), pp. 30–1.

bout, who was certainly in royal service by October 1528, and may well have worked for Henry VIII in previous years,[215] and the other two may be either his work or that of his son, Lucas, who was in royal service by September 1525 or Gerard's daughter Susanna, both of whom he probably trained.[216] Given the close connection between these designs and those of Wolsey's seals, it is likely that the designs for some of the stylistically advanced seal matrices were furnished by the same workshop.

Hugh Paget has credited Gerard Horenbout with other work for Cardinal Wolsey: the Christ Church Epistolary (MS 101) of 1528 (plates 10 and 11) and the Magdalen College Gospel Lectionary (MS Lat 223), probably dating to 1529.[217] These two manuscripts alone would suffice to demonstrate the cardinal's patronage of one of the finest humanist scribes in Northern Europe, Peter Meghen, and the best manuscript illuminators then working in England.[218] Wolsey, cannot, of course, be ascribed a place in the introduction of humanism into England comparable with Cardinal Mendoza in Spain, who himself translated Homer, Vergil and Ovid into the vernacular, but Wolsey's patronage of Meghen, as well as of Thomas Lupset and Linacre, Richard Pace, Thomas Clement and Vives,[219] no less than his personal involvement in the compilation of the Ipswich grammar book, stresses that he was committed to the new learning. Wolsey's manuscripts, like Cardinal Cisneros's 'Rich Missal', reinforced the dominance of Netherlandish illumination in England; Netherlandish manuscripts had been purchased on a grand scale by Edward IV, and this taste was

[215] There is no record of Gerard Horenbout's whereabouts between January 1522 and October 1528. Given the gaps in the documentation, it is far from safe to assume, simply because he is not recorded in the royal account of September 1525, that he had not already come to England, and worked for the king, prior to that date. The fundamental study of the documentary evidence for the Horenbouts is by L. Campbell and S. Foister, 'Gerard, Lucas and Susanna Horenbout', *Burlington Magazine*, 128 (1986), 719–27.

[216] The 5 May 1526 patent (PRO, E24/6/1) is attributed by Strong, *Artists*, p. 35 to Gerard Horenbout, to whom he also gives the other two patents discussed by Auerbach; the latter does not, however, suggest the attribution of all three to Gerard as Strong implies; the argument is, instead, advanced by H. Paget, 'Gerard and Lucas Hornebolt in England', *Burlington Magazine*, 101 (1959), 396–402. See also J. Murdoch, J. Murrell, P. J. Noon and R. Strong, *The English Miniature* (New Haven and London, 1981), pp. 29–33. E101/518/14 fol. 5, which Auerbach, *Tudor Artists*, p. 42, quotes, implies that an artist named Hert wrote (not illustrated) the initial letters.

[217] Paget, 'Gerard and Lucas Hornebolt', p. 400 (also ascribing the obituary roll of Abbot John Islip (ob.1532) to Gerard). See also Trapp and Herbrüggen, p. 37 and J. J. G. Alexander and E. Temple, *Illuminated Manuscripts in Oxford College Libraries, the University Archives and the Taylor Institution* (Oxford, 1985), p. 83. S. M. Hardie, 'Cardinal Wolsey's patronage of the arts' (unpublished M.Litt thesis, University of Bristol, 1982), contains much new information on Wolsey's manuscripts and underlines the debts of the miniaturists to Dürer's *Small Passion* woodcuts. It is to be hoped that some of this material will soon be published.

[218] For Meghen see, most recently, J. B. Trapp, 'Pieter Meghen, yet again', in J. B. Trapp (ed.), *Manuscripts in the Fifty Years after the Invention of Printing* (London, 1983), pp. 23–8.

[219] A. J. Slavin, 'Profitable studies: humanists and government in early Tudor England', *Viator*, I (1970), 307–25. See also Pace's fulsome flattery of Wolsey in F. Manley and R. S. Sylvester (eds. and transl.), *De fructu qui ex doctrina percipitur* (New York, 1967), pp. 140–1.

inherited by his successors.[220] Indeed, the admiration at the English court for Burgundian literature and manuscripts and the employment of large numbers of Netherlandish artists in England form part of the background against which the introduction of Italian Renaissance art into this country should be seen. Frequently, it was contact not so much with Italian art and artists at first hand, but through the mediation of art from the Burgundian Netherlands that English patrons came into contact with the Renaissance;[221] unlike their French counterparts, English patrons, apart from scholars who had been trained at Padua and elsewhere, generally had little first-hand experience of Italy and will probably only have seen Italian art in France or the Low Countries. Wolsey himself conforms to this pattern, for though he had travelled fairly extensively in northern France and the Netherlands, he never saw Italy. By the 1520s, Netherlandish artists, like so many of their French contemporaries, had mastered a wide variety of 'antique' decorative motives and an elementary grasp of the new perspective (although this was often the area in which they were weakest) and had acquired a vocabulary of classical architectural detail. It is possible, therefore, that the artist to whom Dr Auerbach ascribes the Trinity Roll of 1529 with a naked boy holding a scroll inscribed 'Bonenfaunte', was not Italian but Netherlandish.[222] Comparable naked putti, supporting the Cardinal's arms, appear in the Wolsey manuscripts, which are amongst the finest products of the Ghent-Bruges school.

A number of manuscript-painters in this period, Gerard Horenbout among them, made designs for ecclesiastical vestments, tapestries and stained glass windows. No such designs have yet been attributed to Gerard's son, though one of Lucas's closest associates was the French glazier William de la Hay, to whom work at King's College Chapel, Cambridge, has been attributed.[223] William may not have come to England before Wolsey's fall but the cardinal certainly employed some of the finest glaziers to work in the early sixteenth century. No building of any importance was complete without a display of stained glass, whether heraldic or figural, and Wolsey was fully aware of its importance. In 1515 an artist originally from the Duke of Burgundy's dominions, Barnard Flower, king's glazier from 1497, is documented as working at York Place, and in 1529 and 1530 James Nicholson, a Netherlander who is one of the finest glaziers of the period, worked for Wolsey at his Oxford college and at Southwell, Scrooby and

[220] J. Backhouse, 'Founders of the Royal Library: Edward IV and Henry VII as collectors of illuminated manuscripts', in D. Williams (ed.), *England in the Fifteenth Century*, pp. 23–41; C. M. Meale, 'Patrons, buyers and owners: book production and social status', in J. Griffiths and D. Pearsall (eds.), *Book Production and Publishing in Britain 1375–1475* (Cambridge, 1989), pp. 201–38.

[221] There is no doubt, however, that there was an interest in Italian architecture: in 1482, for instance, Sir Robert Chamberlayne intended to visit Milan and its surrounding area explicitly 'to see its marvels and princely palaces' (*CSPV*, I (1202–1509) 482).

[222] Auerbach, *Tudor Artists*, p. 34.

[223] Paget, 'Gerard and Lucas Hornebolt in England', 402; Wayment, *Windows of King's College Chapel*, p. 127.

Cawood.[224] Some of Nicholson's heraldic work survives at Christ Church and it is argued by Hilary Wayment that *vidimuses*[225] at Edinburgh and Brussels with annotations in Nicholson's hand can be related to the lost glazing of Wolsey's chapel at Hampton Court. Today, Nicholson's oeuvre has to be reconstructed around his work in the chapel of King's College, where he contracted in 1526, along with Galyon Hone, Flower's successor as king's glazier, and two native English master-glaziers, Richard Bond and Thomas Reve, to glaze eighteen windows:[226] it may, in fact, be possible to trace Nicholson's contributions to the work in King's chapel from the window north of the screen, which is arguably the first in this country to exhibit the flowering of the new Renaissance style (1517), to its majestic culmination in the east window which was probably completed in 1541, not long before he died. The vidimuses suggest that Wolsey's lost schemes must have rivalled the outstanding achievements in glass from the 1520s: the glass of the middle period (1526–31) in King's, the glazing of the chapel of The Vyne, Hampshire, and the Crucifixion of St Margaret's, Westminster.[227] But some of Nicholson's other work for Wolsey may still survive, as Hilary Wayment argues, taking up R. H. C. Davis's suggestion that the Passion scenes in the east window of Balliol College Chapel, Oxford, dated 1529, were originally intended for Cardinal College's great, unbuilt, chapel. It is, therefore, possible to argue that although little of Nicholson's work for Wolsey is conventionally thought to have survived, a plausible picture can be formed of his work for the cardinal at Oxford and Hampton Court.

By contrast, it is very difficult to picture the appearance of the goldsmiths' work which was employed by Cardinal Wolsey to embellish his colleges, domestic buildings and chapels: not a single piece of the huge quantity of metalwork which he ordered survives today. Yet the inventories of Wolsey's possessions, periodically updated, reveal something of the splendour, and range of these lost objects and their value.[228] Their style and origin are frequently indicated, as in the case of the 'gilt layer of Spanish work, pounced with naked children and beasts' or the 'salt with a gilt cover with scallop shells, antics in the feet, and a boy with a serpent on the cover' from York Place or, again, the 'six candlesticks with leopards' heads and cardinals' hats, made at Bruges, 297 ounces, with a leather

---

[224] *LP*, IV (iii) 6329 and 6748 item 15.

[225] H. G. Wayment, 'The great windows of King's College Chapel and the meaning of the word *vidimus*', *Proceedings of the Cambridge Antiquarian Society*, 69 (1979), 53–60. See below, pp. 117–18.

[226] Wayment, *Windows of King's College Chapel*, Appendix D.1.

[227] H. G. Wayment, 'The stained glass in the Chapel of The Vyne', *National Trust Studies 1980*, (London, 1979), pp. 35–47; 'The stained glass of the Chapel of The Vyne and the Chapel of the Holy Ghost, Basingstoke', *Archaeologia*, 107 (1982), 141–52; 'The east window of St Margaret's Westminster', *Antiquaries Journal*, 61 (1981), 292–301.

[228] *LP*, IV (iii) 6184, 6784. One object which should perhaps be included in this category, however, is the portable sundial made for the cardinal by Nicholas Kratzer, the German astronomer who received Wolsey's patronage: see L. Evans, 'On a portable sundial of gilt brass made for Cardinal Wolsey', *Archaeologia*, 57 (1901), 331–4.

case', and one can occasionally discern the importance of imported works such as the high cross of Cardinal Campeggio, which was carefully copied for Wolsey.[229] Philippa Glanville argues in chapter 5 that Wolsey's taste for 'antique' work in his goldsmiths' work distinguishes it from that of Henry VIII: a large proportion of the antique works listed in the inventory made of the Jewel House on the death of Robert Amadas in 1532 seem to have been acquired by the king from Wolsey. The cardinal's specific predilection for the newest, Renaissance, style of work is highlighted in Cavendish's 'Metrical Visions', where Wolsey recalls his

> Plate of all sorts most curiously wrought,
> Of facions new, I past not of the old.

Just as Wolsey's seals seem to have embraced the new Renaissance styles long before those of the king exhibited them, so too did his metalwork. The massive sums disbursed by Wolsey on plate – he still owed Robert Amadas £1,690 7s on his death – were spent with the specific purpose, as Cavendish makes clear, of indicating his status to contemporaries.[230] As chapter 5 demonstrates, gold-smiths' work played a vital part in every ceremonial occasion, and constituted an instantly measurable index of the wealth and power of its possessors. The great silver crosses and pillars borne before Wolsey in procession or the 'gilt plate very somptious and of the newest facions' exhibited at Hampton Court in 1527 to the admiring eyes of the French embassy, were an integral part of Wolsey's display. On that occasion, the Venetian ambassador, Marco Antonio Venier, reported that Wolsey's gold and silver plate at Hampton Court were estimated to be worth 300,000 golden ducats, or about £150,000: this puts Wolsey's expenditure on architecture and manuscripts into perspective.[231] The carefully graduated gifts to the French ambassadors on that occasion were as much part of the diplomacy as the golden chalice and paten, image of the Virgin and altar service which Wolsey received from Francis I in 1527 or the sixty carpets which the Venetian signory sent him in 1521.[232]

The total loss of the most costly of all Wolsey's effects irreparably damages our understanding of this aspect of his patronage, but it is clear from a variety of sources that the cardinal's employment of tapestries and hangings, some of which do survive, could play an analogous role in impressing the viewer with the cardinal's wealth, power and glory.[233] Giustinian describes how one had to

[229] *LP*, IV (iii) 6184; *LP*, IV (iii) 6784, item 5.   [230] *LP*, IV (iii) 6784, item 15.

[231] Law, *Hampton Court*, pp. 80–1, quoting *CSPV*, IV (1527–33), 205.

[232] *CSPV*, III (1520–26), 94, IV (1527–33), 168; R. Brown (ed.), *Four Years at the Court of Henry VIII*, (London, 1854), II, pp. 241 and 315; Law, *Hampton Court*, p. 71; E. G. Salter, *Tudor England through Venetian Eyes* (London, 1930), p. 45. See also Philippa Glanville's chapter.

[233] The editors are deeply indebted to Mr Tom Campbell for much information and advice on Wolsey's tapestry collections, on which he lectured at the Wolsey conference, and which he is currently researching. For the impression made by the silk and gold tapestries hung inside the temporary palace at the Field of Cloth of Gold, see M. Mitchell, 'Works of art from Rome for Henry VIII', *Journal of the Warburg and Courtauld Institutes*, 34 (1971), 198.

traverse eight rooms hung with tapestry, changed every week, before one reached Wolsey's audience chamber:[234] in 1527, for the reception of the French ambassadors at Hampton Court, the waiting-chambers were each hung with fine tapestries, in ascending quality up to the chamber of presence in which Wolsey's finest plate was also on display, untouched during the meal 'for ther was sufficient besides'.[235] Every one of the ambassadors' rooms was hung with costly hangings and furnished with silver or parcel gilt plate. There could hardly be a more effective way to demonstrate the cardinal's wealth.

The taste for tapestries, manufactured generally in Bruges, Tournai or Brussels, was well established in England, but Wolsey purchased them on an enormous scale, unprecedented in England for any other than a royal patron. In 1520 Richard Gresham visited Wolsey to take the measure of eighteen chambers for tapestries, taking a 1,000 mark down payment; in December 1522 Wolsey obtained twenty-two complete sets of tapestries, consisting of no less than 132 pieces, from him.[236] These were to furnish the rooms in and around the great base court gate-house of Hampton Court. In the larger room on the south side of the gate on the first floor, for instance, were hung 'six peces of the Story of Ester', whilst that of the Prodigal Son, comprising seven pieces, was placed in the second chamber over the porters' lodge. The great chamber over the gateway was supplied in the following April with 'nine peces of the nine Worthys' and at the same time five other sets were acquired.[237] A considerable number of Wolsey's purchases were made from the executors of Thomas Ruthal and Richard Fitzjames, the bishops of Durham and London, who seem to have been, on the evidence of Wolsey's own inventories, considerable patrons of tapestry, and he also purchased on a smaller scale, as for instance from the executors of Dr Yonge, former master of the rolls.[238] As bishop of Tournai, Wolsey had direct access to one of the major areas of production and employed the provost, Jehan le Sellier, to search out for him tapestries of varying quality, cost and subject.[239] In 1527, Francis I reportedly gave Wolsey tapestries worth 30,000 ducats.[240] Some of Wolsey's tapestries were set with 'new borders of my Lord Cardinal's arms', either to trumpet their ownership, or to make them fit a space exactly, or for both reasons. As many as 140 of them could still be seen in the royal collection at the time of Henry VIII's death.[241] The extremely varied subject matter of the tapestries emerges from Wolsey's inventories: besides many biblical or sacred

[234] *Four Years at the Court of Henry VIII*, II, p. 314.

[235] Cavendish, p. 70. In this way, Wolsey surpassed even the magnificence of the reception in 1518 of the English ambassadors by the bishop of Paris, on which occasion they dined at a 'stately banquet served solely on gold plate' (*LP*, II (ii) 4661).

[236] *LP*, III (i) 1021; Law, *Hampton Court*, p. 58.

[237] Law, *Hampton Court*, p. 59. We are indebted to Mr Campbell for the dating of this entry.

[238] *LP*, IV (iii) 6184.   [239] *LP*, II (ii) 3206; Hardie, 'Wolsey's patronage of the Arts', p. 113.

[240] *CSPV*, IV (1527–33), 168.

[241] W. G. Thomson, *A History of Tapestry* (Wakefield, 1973), p. 187.

subjects, he obtained from the executors of the bishop of Durham sets of Priam, Paris and Achilles, Jupiter, Pluto and Ceres, Hannibal, Virtue and hunting subjects, and his collections also featured subjects from the most popular of medieval love allegories, the Romance of the Rose. Besides these, there were also numerous pieces of 'Hangings of Verdures', and other unidentified subjects such as 'a fountain and a lady, in her hair, standing by it'. In 1523, Wolsey obtained one of his sets of Petrarch's Triumphs, comprising eight pieces (Time, Death, Chastity, Eternity, Cupid and Venus, Renown or Julius Caesar and two duplicates), some of which still remain at Hampton Court. Skelton seems to have possessed a considerable knowledge of Wolsey's tapestry collections, explicitly listing some of the subjects in 'Collyn Cloute' in a passage condemning the 'Arayse of ryche aray' displayed by ecclesiastics:

> With tryumphes of Cesar
> And of his Pompeyus warre,
> Of renowne and of fame
> By them to gette a name.
>
> Howe all the worlde stares
> Howe they ryde in goodly chares,
> Conveyde by olyfauntes
> With lauryat garlantes,
> And by unycornes
> With theyr semely hornes;
> Upon these beestes rydynge,
> Naked boyes strydynge,
> With wanton wenches wynkyng![242]

The inventory of Cawood Castle, after Wolsey's fall, indicates that he still owned a number of tapestries, some of which presumably included those purchased for £83 12s from 'Sir John Alen, alderman of London ... sold to my Lord at his departure northwards', a bill which Wolsey left unpaid at his death.[243] The Cawood inventory, however, reveals in simple numerical terms just how much Wolsey had lost.

Apart from the tapestries, very little survives of the internal fittings of Wolsey's domestic buildings. Ernest Law, writing in 1885, thought that the so-called Wolsey closet at Hampton Court 'preserves in many essentials its pristine state'.[244] This seems doubtful. The ceiling (plate 12), which is perhaps the chief point of interest from the architectural point of view, is divided into octagonal panels, each subdivided into five panels, the central one being square in shape. The ribs are of wood, with lead balls or leaves at the intersections. Each panel contains dolphins, torches or other antique work filling the space surrounding a

---

[242] Skelton, 'Collyn Clout', ll. 956–68, and notes p. 477. Wolsey owned three sets of the Triumphs, see *LP*, IV (iii) 6184.

[243] *LP*, IV (iii) 6748.   [244] Law, *Hampton Court*, p. 53.

central roundel. Some of the roundels contain the three ostrich feathers of the Prince of Wales, and this feature suggests that the ceiling may considerably postdate Wolsey's ownership of the palace, and belong to a period subsequent to the birth of the future Edward VI.[245] The same objection may be made to the frieze below, but it appears to be contradicted by the cardinal's motto beneath, set out with lead letters (plate 13). Certainly, aside from the Prince of Wales's feathers, there are no features of the decorative repertoire which predicate a date after Wolsey's fall: most of the motifs were commonplace by the late 1520s. The frieze shows badges of Tudor roses or the Prince of Wales's feathers alternating with rectangular panels or grotesque fish-like creatures flanking elaborate vases out of which their tails protrude with, in the centre, armoured mermen and mermaids. The reliefs are moulded from boiled leather and brick dust and form an important connection between the decoration of temporary structures such as those erected for the Banqueting House of the Greenwich Revels in 1527 and permanent buildings such as this one. At Greenwich, the Italian sculptor Giovanni da Maiano headed a workshop which produced antique heads and candlesticks and made extensive use of cast lead ornament; in view of the fact that Giovanni is documented as working for Wolsey in the early 1520s, it is tempting to believe that one of his designs underlies the Hampton Court relief panels. It is possible that his workshop even produced them, though whether this work should be dated to Wolsey's ownership of the house or to Henry VIII's must remain doubtful.

If the date of such features is doubtful, the famous panel paintings in the same room are even more controversial. The present surfaces, painted in oil on wooden panels, exhibit a series of scenes from the Passion of Christ, in a slightly clumsy mannerist style, evidently influenced by the late Raphael workshop, and adapting models by Raphael and Penni, but also employing designs by Dürer.[246] The present scenes comprise a fragment of an Entry into Jerusalem, the Last Supper (plate 14), the Flagellation, Christ carrying the cross, the Resurrection (plate 15), a fragment of a *Noli me Tangere*, and three Apostles. Underneath some of these scenes, though, are remains of much higher quality, apparently Netherlandish, painting (plate 16). These panels appear to have been sawn up and re-employed by later artists of inferior talent working in a markedly different style, reminiscent of the late Raphael workshop. The repainting of earlier panels in this way is well documented: in 1530, for instance, Toto del Nunziata was paid 13s 4d 'for sundrye Colours by hym employd and spent uppon the olde payntyd tablis in the King's prevy closet'.[247] It is probable that

---

[245] Hardie, 'Wolsey's patronage of the Arts', p. 18. Dr Lindley is grateful to Simon Thurley for his comments on the ceiling. The ceilings in the 'Wolsey suite', much less elaborate than those of the closet, seem more reliably linked to the cardinal's patronage.

[246] Hardie, 'Wolsey's patronage of the Arts', p. 21. Dr Lindley is grateful to Mr P. Keevil for advice on the paintings and for showing the x-ray photographs of the panels to him.

[247] Auerbach, *Tudor Artists*, pp. 17 and 145.

only the earlier paintings (if any) are the remains of works commissioned by Cardinal Wolsey, although his patronage of Raphaelesque art would be of considerable interest if, as Shelagh Hardie has argued, a set of tapestries woven at Brussels before 1528 from Raphael's cartoons was actually ordered by Wolsey.[248] There is no direct evidence to support such speculation but it is clear that, through his agents, Wolsey was supplied with the best works available on the market: in 1515, for instance, he was sent from Antwerp 'a table for an awter, which was made by the best master of all this land', and the inventories of his goods reveal that he possessed a number of panel paintings for the altars of his chapels.[249]

The physical fabrics and furniture of Wolsey's domestic chapels were designed to provide an impressive setting for the liturgical services and for the cardinal's household chapel, the body of personnel and its equipment which formed his musical establishment. As Roger Bowers shows in chapter 7, Wolsey's household chapel was of a size and status commensurate with the other manifestations of his political and religious importance: Cavendish's list of the chapel's personnel reveals that at one time it was larger than the Chapel Royal itself. Chapter 7 shows that its quality was as remarkable as its numbers and that its composers included Richard Pygott, Avery Burnett and John Mason. Even at a date when the choir was smaller than that of the Chapel Royal, its quality surpassed it. Or so Henry VIII felt. Even the master of the Chapel Royal choristers was unable to deny that Wolsey's chapel would handle a piece of music unknown to both choirs better than his own. Subsequently Wolsey was forced to send the king one of the ablest of his singing boys.[250] Clearly, the singing of such a household chapel was a matter which reflected directly on the prestige of its patron. The importance of the quality of the singers is highlighted by the strenuous endeavours of Wolsey's agents to secure the best available men to fill his new chapels at Oxford and Ipswich: the reason is clearly expressed by William Capon, dean of the Ipswich foundation, who wrote to Wolsey 'in our quere standith the honnor of your graces collage'.[251] The short-lived Ipswich college was, indeed, to have a choir which ranked in numbers with the collegiate churches of the second rank, while that at Oxford had only two less personnel than Wolsey's own household chapel; the quality of the Oxford college's choir is illustrated by the fact that John Taverner, the outstanding composer of a fertile period of English musical history, was employed as master of the choristers.

It is difficult to know how far Wolsey's personal taste is reflected in the polyphonic pieces composed for his household and collegiate chapels: Roger

[248] Hardie, 'Wolsey's patronage of the Arts', pp. 108ff.

[249] LP, II (i) 1013: the artist is generally identified as Quentin Massys (c.1465–1530). LP, IV (iii) 6184 for the altar panels.

[250] LP, II (ii) 4024, 4025, 4043, 4044, 4053, 4055. Cornysh, of course, may have conceded the point simply in order to obtain the chorister he wanted.

[251] See Roger Bowers' paper, p. 196.

Bowers argues that the cardinal favoured a luxuriant and grandiose musical style, but an essentially traditional one which failed to respond to contemporary innovations in England or the Continent. Although it is not easy to assess Wolsey's artistic tastes, the effort is rewarding, for he was indisputably one of the greatest patrons of the arts in English history. The cardinal's architecture is his most important surviving legacy in this sphere, but Wolsey's place in deciding the general design of his buildings is complicated and may have varied from project to project. However, he does seem always to have been closely concerned with his buildings and the suggestion that he took no detailed part in the design of his Oxford college seems extremely unlikely to be correct.[252] Wolsey was not, of course, a master mason, with specific technical skills, but his involvement in and control of the project should not be underestimated. Early in 1529, Lee and Barbour, the master masons of the Ipswich College, took Wolsey 'the whole platte of the college, to know his pleasure therein', and it is almost certain that the same procedure would have been adopted by Redman, Lebons and Johnson, the master masons at Oxford.[253] Again, the fact that Wolsey did not intervene directly in the construction of his own tomb cannot be interpreted to imply his indifference to its appearance. Much more probably, the sculptor, Benedetto da Rovezzano, had already agreed with him the general outlines of the design.

Although Wolsey did not, indeed could not, endlessly concern himself with all the minutiae of every one of his artistic projects, he was prepared, on occasion, to intervene at a detailed level – he evaluated, for instance, the estimates of the king's painter, Clement Urmeston for painting the roofs of the English palace at the Field of Cloth of Gold, and was regularly consulted by the commissioners on various aspects of the building.[254] At first sight it seems rather more surprising that Wolsey should bother to write to Silvestro Gigli in Rome solely to ensure that his cardinal's habit and cap were of the same material, fashion and colour as those used in Rome.[255] However, the social and political implications of clothing were extremely sensitively perceived in the early sixteenth century and Wolsey may additionally have had a parvenu's fastidiousness about such matters, for he put into stringent effect the sumptuary statutes against dressing above one's degree.[256] The prestige attached to the maintenance of a good choir at Ipswich explains why he himself took the trouble to hear four singing boys at Hampton Court, in order to select two for the college.[257] He also took great care to obtain

[252] Harvey, 'Building works', *Oxoniensia*, pp. 145–6: 'it is to be noted that there is no suggestion that either Wolsey himself or the administrative chief, Dr Higden, took part in the design'. But see also *LP*, IV (i) 1499, which seems to contradict this.

[253] *LP*, IV (ii) 5077. For all these masons, see J. H. Harvey, *English Medieval Architects* (Gloucester, 1984) s.v.

[254] *LP*, III (i) 825, 826; Nichols, *Chronicle of Calais*, pp. 77–85.   [255] *LP*, II (i) 894.

[256] See above, p. 10.

[257] See Roger Bowers' paper, p. 200.

the best scholars for his Oxford college, importing Cambridge men for that purpose, and as early as 1525 was concerned with forming the college library.[258]

Cavendish implies that Wolsey took a personal interest in the 'antique' style of the goldsmiths' work he purchased, but it may well have been more important to him that his plate was in the latest, most fashionable style, than that this style happened to be Renaissance: the same point applies to his seal designs. His manuscripts evince, for all their humanist script, a conventional preference for illuminations in the Ghent-Bruges style which continued to dominate the taste of the English court, although that style was itself being affected by the impact of the Renaissance. It would be anachronistic to expect Wolsey to have had a clear preference for a pure Florentine Renaissance style: in general, his works did not constitute a radical break with the immediate past but rather a continuation and acceleration of existing developments. If in some fields, as for example in sculpture or metalwork, his patronage favoured the development of Italianate art, in others, as in music or architecture, it may actually have hindered innovation. In April 1528, Thomas Cromwell wrote to Wolsey of Cardinal College that 'the like was never seen for largeness, beauty, sumptuous, curious and substantial building', thus highlighting precisely those qualities which were important to Wolsey.[259] Grandeur of scale, luxuriousness and opulence were the effects which his artistic patronage was designed to achieve. Wolsey's patronage is important not because it redirected the patterns of art in England but because it was conceived and funded on a grand scale, making full use of the cardinal's gigantic revenues[260] to impress the viewer with his wealth and power.

Wolsey's visible magnificence and the greatness it proclaimed made his fall an object-lesson for contemporaries. The theme found its fullest expression in Cavendish's life of his master, which bent historical fact and adjusted the timescale of its narrative to present the cardinal as a classic victim of fortune's propensity to raise men to worldly grandeur and then to cast them down.[261] But it had struck the French ambassador as early as October 1529, when he described Wolsey as 'the greatest example of fortune that one could think to see'; and it provided authors of the later sixteenth and seventeenth centuries with a tragic Wolsey to balance the tyrant of protestant or catholic polemic.[262] At a more practical level, Wolsey's readiness to promise Henry and his subjects remarkable

[258] CSPV, III (1520–26), 1187; LP, IV (ii) 2181, 2188; LP, IV (ii) 3536.   [259] LP, IV (ii) 4135.

[260] By comparison, the Valor of 1535 puts the annual taxable revenue of the lands of the archbishop of Canterbury at no more than £3,224; Heal, Of Prelates and Princes, p. 54.

[261] R. S. Sylvester, 'Cavendish's Life of Wolsey: the artistry of a Tudor biographer', Studies in Philology, 57 (1960), 44–71; see also W. W. Wooden, 'The art of partisan biography: George Cavendish's Life of Wolsey', Renaissance and Reformation, n.s. 1 (1977), 24–35.

[262] R. Scheurer, 'Les relations franco-anglaises pendant la négociation de la paix des Dames (juillet 1528–août 1529)', in P. M. Smith, I. D. McFarlane (eds.), Literature and the Arts in the Reign of Francis I. Essays presented to C. A. Mayer, French Forum Monographs, 56 (Lexington, 1985), p. 160; P. L. Wiley, 'Renaissance exploitation of Cavendish's Life of Wolsey', Studies in Philology, 43 (1946), 121–46.

results from the large powers entrusted to him made him vulnerable to criticism when his policies were less than triumphantly successful. Even Thomas Cromwell noted Wolsey's 'many words without deeds', and Skelton was quick to remind his readers that

> whan he toke first his hat
> He said he knew what was what.
> All justyce he pretended:
> All thynges sholde be amended,
> All wronges he wolde redresse,

yet the cardinal was demonstrably not the panacea for the nation's ills.[263] In the views formed of him by his own contemporaries, Wolsey was probably the victim of his own flamboyant self-propaganda; certainly he has been so in the assessments of historians. And while he retained power, the assiduity with which he repressed criticism of his failings seems only to have done further damage to his public image.[264]

The cardinal's contemporary reputation must also have suffered from his ready identification with the policies of Henry VII and of the ministers whose execution had propitiated public resentment at the old king's rapacity, Empson and Dudley.[265] In his determination to enforce the king's laws and augment the king's revenues, his confrontations with noblemen, Londoners, reluctant taxpayers and even defenders of clerical privilege – all victims of Henry VII – stirred up widespread enmity, in which literary attacks like Skelton's could hope to catch the public mood just as Thomas More's discreet but biting indictment of Henry VII's government or the various lampoons on Empson had tried to do.[266] The completeness of his executive control over the king's affairs opened Wolsey to more general hostility, not only from those who felt themselves excluded from power, but also from all those who conveniently failed to recognize the royal will behind the cardinal's often painful imposition of the crown's authority; his role was potentially fatal should Henry decide – as monarchs had done before and would do again – to buy popularity by sacrificing his minister. Meanwhile the satirists' task was made all the easier by the various aspects of Wolsey's personality and political style that lent themselves readily to caricature or hostile interpretation: the tendency to bully his way past objections which backfired so badly in the parliament of 1523, the ritual self-glorification of his daily processions and diplomatic protocol, the truly grandiose scale of his artistic enterprises,

---

263 Pollard, p. 266; Skelton, 'Why come ye nat to courte?', ll. 1108–12.

264 *LP*, IV (iii) 5750 (ii); Skelton, 'Collyn Clout', ll. 1145–226, 'Why come ye nat to courte?', ll. 1048–77; Fox, *Politics and Literature*, pp. 134, 234–5; Hay, *Polydore Vergil*, pp. 10–14; Gunn, *Charles Brandon*, p. 103; see below, p. 169.

265 Tyndale, 'Practice of prelates', p. 342.

266 C. H. Miller et al. (eds.), *The Complete Works of St Thomas More, volume 3, part ii, Latin Poems* (New Haven and London, 1984), pp. 100–7; A. H. Thomas, I. D. Thornley (eds.), *The Great Chronicle of London* (London, 1938), pp. 344–7.

and so on.[267] Indeed, for those who claimed that he sought to 'play checke mate / With ryall majeste', the uniqueness in recent English and arguably even European terms of his clear supremacy among the king's ministers was all of a piece with his college to rival King's, his tomb to rival Henry VII's and his palaces to rival Richmond.[268]

Contemporaries were well able to compare Wolsey with other ecclesiastical statesmen. Skelton characteristically picked out Balue as a man disgraced by his royal master, just as Wolsey ought to be.[269] Tyndale bracketed Morton with Wolsey as men who twisted Tudor foreign policy to serve the pope, and taxed the English commons to fund their schemes.[270] On a more positive note, the papal nuncio at the French court in 1527 reported that he had seen no one since Pope Alexander VI who upheld his ecclesiastical rank with more majesty and gravity than Wolsey did, and that the English cardinal was in addition 'most religious' in comparison with the Borgia pope.[271] Yet such commentators could never find an exact parallel for Wolsey's career among his European contemporaries: Amboise came closest, but even his dominance in political, administrative and ecclesiastical affairs was not so comprehensive as Wolsey's. What was unusual in degree in continental terms was startlingly new in Wolsey's English context. His power in the state, his pluralism, his wealth and his centralized legatine authority were remarkable even to contemporaries used to a rich, powerful and worldly church. Wolsey, while no paragon of ecclesiastical propriety, had fewer vices than many contemporary clerical politicians, paid at least lip service to the ideals of reform, and gave some sort of moral tone to Henry's social and foreign policies. Yet at a time when the theological convulsions of the continent threatened to engulf England and the judgement of senior churchmen by apostolic standards became a matter of serious religious polemic, the cardinal provided a ready symbol for all that was wrong with the Roman church in England. When forced to decide, his loyalty was to Henry rather than to Rome, and in his desperation to win the divorce he threatened to lead the English church into schism; but there were those at court in 1529 who added pressure for the disendowment of the church to their criticism of the cardinal, and by 1530–1 the clergy's acquiescence in Wolsey's legatine regime had been redefined as an offence against royal authority, the punishment of which Henry used as a threat to browbeat the entire church.[272]

As a churchman Wolsey found himself out of step with his rapidly changing

[267] Guy, 'Wolsey and the parliament of 1523', pp. 1–4; Skelton, 'Why come ye nat to courte?', ll. 202–5, 329–35, 591–624, 647–54; see above, pp. 7–8, 50.

[268] Skelton, 'Why come ye nat to courte?', ll. 588–9.

[269] Skelton, 'Why come ye nat to courte?', ll. 722–49.

[270] Tyndale, 'Practice of prelates', pp. 305–19.

[271] A. Desjardins (ed.), *Négociations diplomatiques de la France avec la Toscane*, II, Collection des documents inedits sur l'histoire de France (Paris, 1861), p. 982.

[272] Wilkie, *Cardinal Protectors*, p. 187; Guy, *Public Career of Sir Thomas More*, pp. 106–11, 136–8, 147–50.

·times: he was not cut out to lead a reformation or a counter-reformation, though he might perhaps have accompanied Henry further along the road to a doctrinally conservative but jurisdictionally independent Anglican settlement, the sort the king seems later to have wanted and the sort the cardinal had in effect constructed. In ecclesiastical affairs Wolsey perhaps lacked the vision displayed in so many of his initiatives in government and diplomacy, from the enclosure commissions and the treaty of London to the general proscription and his sponsorship of an expedition to find the North-West Passage.[273] Yet the sheer scale of his enterprises, and the vigour, skill and personal attention to detail with which he pursued them, were common to Wolsey's activities in the church, the state and the arts. They made him a leading promoter of the English Renaissance in education and in a number of the decorative arts, an important architect of England's re-emergence as a European power, and a significant agent of the strengthening of English royal government initiated by Edward IV and Henry VII and continued by the cardinal's servant Thomas Cromwell. These qualities were tempered by a realism which made him compromise when faced by insoluble difficulties like the Kildare ascendancy in Ireland or the foreign policy crises of 1525 and 1528, while the execution of his schemes was facilitated by the exercise of a political skill so great that William Tyndale thought his fall from power was just a clever trick to escape from a tight corner.[274] Wolsey's dramatic impact on his contemporaries testified to an importance which only a rounded examination of his activities in the church, the state and the arts can properly reconstruct, and it is just such a three-dimensional portrait that this book hopes to present.

---

[273] Scarisbrick, *Henry VIII*, pp. 123–5.   [274] Tyndale, 'Practice of prelates', pp. 334–8.

CHAPTER 1

Wolsey and the Tudor Polity

JOHN GUY

> . . . in the Chambre of Sterres
> All maters there he marres,
> Clappying his rod on the borde.
> No man dare speke a worde,
> For he hathe all the sayenge
> Without any renayenge.
> He rolleth in his recordes,
> He sayth, 'How saye ye, my lordes?
> Is nat my reason good?'[1]

For centuries the wit and wisdom of John Skelton underpinned debate upon the achievements of Cardinal Wolsey even though his criticisms were calumnies. This fact was acknowledged by Richard Fiddes as early as 1724.[2] George Cavendish, Wolsey's gentleman-usher, himself made the essential point when he completed his *Life and Death of Cardinal Wolsey* in the summer of 1558. He protested: 'And synce his [Wolsey's] deathe I haue hard dyuers sondry surmysis & imagyned tales made of his procedynges & doynges, w[hi]che I my selfe haue perfightly knowen to be most vntrewe'.[3]

Historians have been wary of Skelton during the past decade, and in a major new study his satires have been systematically debunked.[4] But if they are still allowed to dictate the historical agenda, it is insufficient to show that they are calumnies.[5] Whatever emerges from the current process of revisionism, Tudor propaganda should be recognized for what it was: opinion of Wolsey was moulded by his opponents. The ballads of the London citizens mirrored Skelton's satires in the early 1520s.[6] When Wolsey silenced Skelton with a promise of lucrative patronage, John Palsgrave continued where the poet had left off, overstepping the mark by April 1528, when he was hauled before the council for

---

[1] Skelton, 'Why come ye nat to courte?', ll. 188–96.
[2] R. Fiddes, *The Life of Cardinal Wolsey* (London, 1724).
[3] Cavendish, p. 4.   [4] G. Walker, *John Skelton and the Politics of the 1520s* (Cambridge, 1988).
[5] In some respects the satires do still dictate the agenda. The offending work here is A. F. Pollard, *Wolsey* (London, 1929; reprinted in the Fontana Library with a critical introduction by Sir Geoffrey Elton, 1965).
[6] A. G. Fox, *Early Tudor Literature: Politics and the Literary Imagination* (Oxford, 1989).

writing his thundering 'remembrances'.[7] When Wolsey's fall was imminent in the summer of 1529, Lord Darcy experimented with draft accusations which have survived.[8] When the cardinal's dismissal looked irrevocable, articles of attainder were formulated by members of the Reformation Parliament.[9] Although unashamedly manufactured to condemn Wolsey, the forty-four articles were signed by Thomas More, which enhanced their credibility. It is true that Richard Moryson paid a gracious tribute to Wolsey in his *Remedy for Sedition*, published in 1536.[10] His compliment is usually dismissed as a piece of special pleading by a client on behalf of his former patron. Yet the same conventions permit indiscriminate citation of Edward Hall's chronicle, a work blatantly hostile to Wolsey by an anticlerical lawyer who in May 1539 supervised the destruction of St Thomas Becket's window in Gray's Inn chapel.[11] Lastly, the smear spread by catholics and protestants alike in the sixteenth century that Wolsey was the instigator of Henry VIII's first divorce proved highly tenacious.[12]

Historians have scrutinized the primary sources over the past thirty years: Wolsey's correspondence and the records of chancery, star chamber and the exchequer.[13] More accurate impressions have been obtained, but the verdict is mixed. On the one hand, writers applaud Wolsey's zeal for better law enforcement, justice for the poor, the restraint of illegal enclosures and efficient taxation.

[7] PRO, sp1/54, fols. 244–52; *LP*, iv (iii) 5750; PRO, c54/396, m. 31.

[8] sp1/54, fols. 234–43 (*LP*, iv (iii) 5749).

[9] Fiddes, *Life of Wolsey*, Collections no. 101 (pp. 215–23).

[10] The passage concerns Wolsey's brief diocesan career. It begins 'Who was less beloved in the North than my lord cardinal (God have his soul) before he was amongst them? Who better beloved after he had been there a while?' It is reprinted in D. S. Berkowitz, *Humanist Scholarship and Public Order* (Folger Books: Washington DC, 1984), pp. 134–5.

[11] *The Union of the two Noble and Illustrate Famelies of Lancastre and Yorke* (London, 1548), STC² 12721; S. T. Bindoff (ed.), *The House of Commons, 1509–1558*, 3 vols. (London, 1982), II, pp. 279–82; R. J. Fletcher (ed.), *The Pension Book of Gray's Inn*, 2 vols. (London, 1901–10), I, p. 496.

[12] That Wolsey first proposed the idea of Catherine of Aragon's divorce to Henry VIII was variously asserted by Polydore Vergil, Edward Hall, William Tyndale, Nicholas Sander, and Nicholas Harpsfield.

[13] G. R. Elton, *The Tudor Constitution* (Cambridge, 1960; 2nd edn 1982); J. J. Scarisbrick, *Henry VIII* (London, 1968); Scarisbrick, 'Cardinal Wolsey and the common weal' in E. W. Ives, R. J. Knecht, and Scarisbrick (eds.), *Wealth and Power in Tudor England* (London, 1978), pp. 45–67; F. Metzger, 'Das Englische Kanzleigericht unter Kardinal Wolsey, 1515–1529', unpublished Erlangen PhD dissertation (1976); J. A. Guy, *The Cardinal's Court: The Impact of Thomas Wolsey in Star Chamber* (Hassocks, 1977); Guy, 'Thomas More as successor to Wolsey', *Thought: Fordham University Quarterly*, 52 (1977), 275–92; Guy, 'Wolsey and the parliament of 1523' in C. Cross, D. Loades, and J. J. Scarisbrick (eds.), *Law and Government under the Tudors* (Cambridge, 1988), pp. 1–18; R. S. Schofield, 'Taxation and the political limits of the Tudor state', ibid., pp. 227–55; P. J. Gwyn, 'Wolsey's foreign policy: the conferences at Calais and Bruges reconsidered', *Historical Journal*, 23 (1980), 755–72; G. W. Bernard, *War, Taxation, and Rebellion in Early Tudor England: Henry VIII, Wolsey, and the Amicable Grant of 1525* (Brighton, 1986); Walker, *Skelton and the Politics of the 1520s*; S. J. Gunn, *Charles Brandon, Duke of Suffolk, c. 1484–1545* (Oxford, 1988). A new biography of Wolsey is in preparation by Mr Peter Gwyn. See also H. Miller, *Henry VIII and the English Nobility* (Oxford, 1986); B. J. Harris, *Edward Stafford, Third Duke of Buckingham, 1478–1521* (Stanford, 1986).

On the other, they acknowledge that he overreached himself, notably in the parliament of 1523, and especially two years later over the Amicable Grant, when he attempted to levy taxation without parliamentary consent and sparked a regional revolt. In this chapter I shall revisit and reassess Wolsey's contribution to the two most central aspects of Tudor political life: the king's council and local government. What emerges is less the 'case for the defence' than a perspective on Wolsey's career which is more sharply focused and yet more favourable than previous synoptic assessments.

I

Despite the controversy that currently rages over the reconstruction of the privy council in the 1530s, no one would dispute that the council was the matrix of Tudor government.[14] Under Henry VII it met regularly in star chamber, but these assemblies were large and unwieldy and the king rarely attended them in the second half of his reign. Moreover, fiscal and enforcement decisions were at first taken by Henry VII and his council attendant at court; then, after the deaths of Archbishop Morton and Sir Reynold Bray, they were vested in the hands of the king and the members of the council learned in the law. Under Wolsey the main forum of activity was star chamber, but this position was reversed immediately upon his fall, when Henry VIII's 'political' councillors raced to serve the king at court.[15] By 1540 the privy council had been reconstructed as an executive board acting corporately under the crown. Policy-making at the highest level was subsumed within the court, and it remained so throughout Elizabeth's long reign.[16]

The creative vigour of Wolsey's management of star chamber is unchallenged. His first policy was his law-enforcement plan, unveiled in Henry VIII's presence

[14] C. G. Bayne and W. H. Dunham (eds.), *Select Cases in the Council of Henry VII*, Selden Society (London, 1958); M. M. Condon, 'Ruling elites in the reign of Henry VII', in C. Ross (ed.), *Patronage, Pedigree and Power* (Gloucester, 1979), pp. 109–42; Guy, *Cardinal's Court*, pp. 9–21; G. R. Elton, *The Tudor Revolution in Government: Administrative Changes in the Reign of Henry VIII* (Cambridge, 1953); Elton, 'Tudor government', *Historical Journal*, 31 (1988), 425–34; D. R. Starkey (ed.), *The English Court: From the Wars of the Roses to the Civil War* (London, 1987); D. R. Starkey, 'Tudor government: the facts?', *Historical Journal*, 31 (1988), 921–31; Starkey, 'Court, council and nobility in Tudor England' (forthcoming); Starkey, 'The lords of the council: aristocracy, ideology, and the formation of the Tudor privy council', paper read to the 101st Annual Meeting of the American Historical Association, December 27–30, 1986; S. L. Adams, 'Eliza enthroned? The court and its politics', in C. Haigh (ed.), *The Reign of Elizabeth I* (London, 1984), pp. 55–77; J. A. Guy, *Tudor England* (Oxford, 1988). Dr Starkey's 'Court, council and nobility' will become the starting point for an understanding of the inter-relationship of Henry VIII's council and court. I am heavily indebted to him for permission to cite his paper in advance of publication.

[15] J. A. Guy, 'The privy council: revolution or evolution', in C. Coleman and D. R. Starkey (eds.), *Revolution Reassessed: Revisions in the History of Tudor Government and Administration* (Oxford, 1986), pp. 68–74.

[16] Adams, 'Eliza enthroned?'; M. B. Pulman, *The Elizabethan Privy Council in the Fifteen-Seventies* (Berkeley, 1971); Guy, *Tudor England*, pp. 266, 309–19.

on 2 May 1516 and reiterated in May 1517 and October 1519. This was a two-tiered strategy emphasizing law enforcement and the impartial administration of justice irrespective of social status. Wolsey's second policy was to publicize the merits of the justice of star chamber and chancery for private parties. I have discussed these keynote policies elsewhere, and will not repeat myself here.[17] I want instead to look at the dynamics of the council, which are more difficult to reconstruct.[18] The best place to begin is Cavendish's *Life*, which paints its canvas with bold brush strokes. Cavendish reports that Wolsey rode in state each weekday morning during the four legal terms from York Place to Westminster Hall. When he had arrived and exchanged words with the judges, he went into the court of chancery, where he sat until eleven o'clock hearing suits. 'And frome thence he wold dyuers tymes goo in to the sterrechamber, as occasion dyd serue, where he spared nother highe nor lowe, but iuged euery estate accordyng to ther merites and desertes.'[19]

Wolsey sat in star chamber between three and five days a week.[20] He was therefore absent from Henry VIII's court, which settled itself during term at Greenwich or Windsor, or sometimes Eltham, Richmond or Bridewell.[21] Westminster had been abandoned as a royal residence in 1512 after a disastrous fire, and it was not until Wolsey's own York Place became Henry's property upon the cardinal's conviction for praemunire in 1529 that the king acquired a suitable replacement.[22] So a problem of communications arose. Wolsey wrote regularly to Henry VIII, and on Sundays during term he travelled to court to clear the week's business in person with the king. This Cavendish confirms, and he adds the information that on Sundays the court was much better attended than during the week, since others followed Wolsey there. 'And after dynner among the lordes, hauyng some consultacion w[ith] the kyng or w[ith] the councell', Wolsey returned home. This arrangement, Cavendish says, his master 'vsed contynually as opportunyte dyd serue'.[23]

Henry and Wolsey might therefore consult members of the council on Sundays. Nor is this the only instance of counselling outside star chamber, since urgent business could arise in vacation. At Whitsuntide 1523, to take just one example, Henry and Wolsey were immersed in two highly important debates. The first concerned a proposal that the Anglo-Habsburg 'Great Enterprise'

---

[17] Guy, *Cardinal's Court*, pp. 23–78, 119–31; Guy, 'Thomas More as successor to Wolsey'.

[18] The problem is the huge gaps in the sources; see J. A. Guy, *The Court of Star Chamber and its Records to the Reign of Elizabeth I* (London, 1985).

[19] Cavendish, p. 24.

[20] See especially PRO, STAC10/4, Pt 2 (bundle of unlisted papers including notes, drafts and minutes of the clerk of the Council); Henry E. Huntington Library, San Marino, California, Ellesmere MSS. 2652, 2654, 2655. Manuscripts in the Huntington Library are cited by kind permission of the Librarian.

[21] PRO, OBS1419 (Henry VIII's itinerary).

[22] *HKW*, IV, pp. 286–8; Starkey (ed.), *The English Court*, p. 18.

[23] Cavendish, p. 24; Starkey, 'Court, council and nobility'.

against France should be abandoned in favour of an invasion of Scotland.[24] By the 2nd or 3rd of June the earl of Surrey, the king's lieutenant in the North, had been summoned to court. Surrey replied that he hoped to be with Henry and Wolsey on the 9th, and thereafter Wolsey wrote to Lord Dacre of the North, whom Surrey had appointed his deputy, informing him why Surrey had been summoned and what had subsequently passed in the council.[25]

The scheme for the invasion of Scotland was dropped when Charles, duke of Bourbon, constable of France, agreed to commit treason, a prospect which made the 'Great Enterprise' suddenly seem feasible. This was the second great issue over Whitsuntide: the earliest hints that Bourbon might prove a realistic ally reached Wolsey's ears at the end of May. So Wolsey provisionally agreed with Charles V's ambassador that the English would invade France with an army of 15,000 foot under the duke of Suffolk in the summer. And throughout he involved the council. The duke of Suffolk, the earl of Shrewsbury, Sir Robert Wingfield and three bishops were among those consulted. Moreover, these consultations were begun and completed during the vacation.[26]

It is often remarked that Henry VIII felt himself ill-attended by his council.[27] His actual words were that he lacked 'some personages about him, as well to receive strangers that shall chance to come, as also that the same strangers shall not find him so bare without some noble and wise sage personages about him'.[28] Earlier he had complained that he had 'but few to give attendance'.[29] Neither statement supports the view that Henry was uncounselled; he seems to have been demanding that Wolsey supply him with some noble attendants. The conventional picture of an uncounselled king sulking at court while Wolsey ruled the roost in star chamber is heavily overdrawn. True, the king's 'continual' council was virtually extinguished: councillors attending Henry VIII daily at court were reduced by the spring of 1518 to Thomas More, John Clerk and Richard Pace, who were joined at Easter by the dukes of Buckingham and Suffolk, Sir Thomas Lovell, and Sir Henry Marney.[30] Nor, on at least this occasion, were these councillors kept properly informed. Wolsey was secretly negotiating a *rapprochement* with France in a tense atmosphere, and Henry VIII told Clerk 'that in no wise he should make mention of London matters before his

24 Guy, 'Wolsey and the parliament of 1523', p. 15.   25 *LP*, III (ii) 3071–2, 3114–15.
26 *LP*, III (ii) 3064; *Further supplement to letters, despatches and state papers ... preserved in the archives at Vienna and elsewhere*, ed. G. Mattingly (London, 1940), pp. 233–6; Bernard, *War, Taxation and Rebellion*, p. 12. For the approximate dates of the legal terms, see *Appendix to the Twenty-Eighth Report of the Deputy Keeper of the Public Records* (London, 1867), no. 12; *Handbook of Dates for Students of English History*, ed. C. R. Cheney (Royal Historical Society: London, repr. 1970), pp. 65–8. The Scottish debate is likely to have taken place at court: Surrey was told to attend on Henry VIII, and the king spent the entire month of June at Greenwich. By contrast, the consultations leading to the agreement with Louis de Praet were probably held at York Place. Cavendish, p. 37.
27 Cf. Elton, *Tudor Revolution in Government*, p. 64.
28 *LP*, III (ii) 2317; Starkey, 'Court, council and nobility'; Guy, *Cardinal's Court*, pp. 23–50.
29 *LP*, II (ii) 4355.   30 *LP*, II (ii) 3885, 4025, 4055, 4124–5.

lords'.[31] But the council attendant still functioned when necessary. In 1521 More was authorized, on appointment as under-treasurer of the exchequer, to reimburse the costs of the diets of the lords of the council for their meetings in star chamber and at 'other places'. These meetings debated 'matters concerning as well the common weal and politic rule and order of this our Realm . . . as also our own particular matters and causes'.[32] Although the phrase 'other places' is elliptical, it suggests that the council had held some meetings at court, or at the very least somewhere outside star chamber.

If Henry VIII believed that he was ill-served, he was probably thinking of weekdays during term, or more likely of the lengthy vacations between the legal terms when Wolsey retired to The More, Hampton Court or Tyttenhanger instead of following the royal progress. By withdrawing to his own houses in vacations Wolsey was taking a risk. Richard Fox, his former mentor and patron, had warned him in April 1516, 'And, good my lord, when the term is done, keep the council with the King's grace wheresoever he be.'[33] Wolsey sometimes celebrated the great religious festivals at court, but mostly spent the festivals of the 1520s at his own houses. His lengthy absences from court exposed him to a series of whispering campaigns and attacks which explain his various swoops on the privy chamber and efforts to manipulate the king's secretaries.[34] Yet the bonds of Wolsey's personal friendship with Henry VIII were so secure until the summer of 1527 that he could *afford* to risk long separations from the king. It cannot seriously be maintained that Henry would have tolerated Wolsey's frustration of his consistently expressed wishes on such a vital matter as political counselling over a period of a decade had the king *really* sought a genuine council attendant meeting daily at court before 1525.

It is well known that from the beginning it was Henry VIII's special relationship with Wolsey which underpinned the latter's ascendancy: the overriding issue was Wolsey's ministerial status.[35] This is not to deny that he consulted the council, but rather to acknowledge that the inner circle of Henry VIII's advisers during his chancellorship was reduced to one. Whereas Henry VII, and Elizabeth before the Cecil-Essex feud, opened the inner circle to five or six leading councillors and courtiers, who thrashed out policies at court before presenting

---

[31] *LP*, ii (ii) 4124; Gunn, *Charles Brandon*, p. 58.

[32] PRO, e404/93 (privy seal dated 23 July 1521). Spelling here and in other quotations from manuscripts has been modernized. I am grateful to Margaret Condon for this reference. For the difficulties faced by attendant councillors in obtaining their subsistence allowances, see *LP*, ii (ii) 4055.

[33] *LP*, ii (i) 1814; Starkey, 'Court, council and nobility'.

[34] Starkey (ed.), *The English Court*, pp. 101–8; Starkey, 'Court, council and nobility'; J. A. Guy, *The Public Career of Sir Thomas More* (Brighton, 1980), pp. 15–18; J. J. Scarisbrick, 'Thomas More: the king's good servant', *Thought: Fordham University Quarterly*, 52 (1977), 251–6.

[35] Pollard, *Wolsey*, pp. 99–164; G. R. Elton, *Reform and Reformation: England 1509–1558* (London, 1977), pp. 42–114; Scarisbrick, *Henry VIII*, pp. 41–162; Guy, *Cardinal's Court*, passim; Starkey, 'Court, council and nobility'.

them for wider discussion in the council, Henry VIII and Wolsey first decided policy between themselves, and only then consulted the council. Cavendish describes the process when discussing the decision of 1523 to treat with Bourbon. He says that Wolsey first 'move[d] the kyng in this matter', whereupon Henry 'dremed' of it more and more, 'vntill at the last it came in question among the Councell in consultacion'.[36] Moreover, Wolsey in 1524 clarified that this was indeed the way things worked when overruling the suggestions of Pace, Henry's ambassador with Bourbon during the siege of Marseilles. He wrote: 'All which matters by the King's Highness and me first apart, and after with the most sad and discreet Lords of his most honourable council, substantially digested, and profoundly debated, it hath been finally, by good deliberation determined ...'[37]

Wolsey's ministerial status marked a dramatic turnabout from earlier practice under Henry VIII. Between 1509 and 1513 the council had worked as a corporate board. Councillors who counter-signed documents included Archbishop Warham (lord chancellor), Bishop Fox (lord privy seal), the earls of Shrewsbury and Surrey, Sir Edward Howard (lord admiral), Lord Herbert, Thomas Ruthal (bishop of Durham), Sir Henry Marney and Sir Thomas Lovell. They exercised control over policy as well as patronage, and generally ran the country while the young king found his feet.[38] Of course, the council liked this arrangement and tried to protract it. Henry VIII disliked it and turned to Wolsey, who liberated him by combining the roles of councillor and courtier at once.[39] As Cavendish explains, he was 'most earnest and redyest among all the Councell to avaunce the kynges oonly wyll & pleasure w[ith]out any respect to the case. The kyng therfore perceyved hyme to be a mete instrume[n]t for the accomplyssheme[n]t of his devysed wyll & pleasure'.[40] Wolsey started to break the mould in May 1511, when he delivered in person a signed bill to Warham in chancery, and told him by the king's command to seal the letters patent without counter-signature.[41] It took two more years finally to overthrow the embargo on signed bills, but Henry and Wolsey had their way over this as over everything else.[42] By February 1514 the corporate board was a dead letter, and by the end of 1515 Wolsey was unchallenged as the king's minister.[43] Wolsey was in his element, for Henry

[36] Cavendish, p. 37.   [37] StP, VI, p. 334.

[38] PRO, c82/335, 338, 341, 355, 364, 365, 374; Elton, Tudor Revolution in Government, pp. 62–5; Starkey, 'Court, council and nobility'; Guy, Cardinal's Court, pp. 23–4. Henry VIII was only seventeen years and ten months old when he succeeded to the throne, and therefore technically not of age as king until he was eighteen. I argued that the Council at this point was functioning almost as a council of regency in 'The privy council: revolution or evolution', p. 63. The significance of the contrast between 'conciliarist' and 'ministerial' approaches to Tudor government was first discussed by Dr Starkey. See also T. F. Mayer, 'Thomas Starkey: an unknown conciliarist at the court of Henry VIII', Journal of the History of Ideas, 49 (1988), 207–27; Guy, Tudor England, pp. 159–64, 189.

[39] Starkey, 'Court, council and nobility'.

[40] Cavendish, pp. 11–12; Starkey, 'Court, council and nobility'.

[41] LP, I (i) 784 (44); Starkey, 'Court, council and nobility'.

[42] Starkey, 'Court, council and nobility'.

[43] Elton, Tudor Revolution in Government, p. 63.

esteemed him so highly 'that his estymacion and fauour put all other auncyent councellours owt of ther accustumed fauour'.[44]

When Wolsey subverted the council's standing as a corporate board, he acted unilaterally and this was his offence. It was why he rarely got any credit later for his attempts to consult the council: he was seen to be ministerial, even when his efforts to involve the council were sincere. It was why he was said to have arrogated power to himself, depriving the king of attendant councillors at court. In particular, it was why he was charged with saying and writing, 'The King and I would ye should do thus: the King and I do give unto you our hearty thanks.'[45] For fourteen years Henry and Wolsey worked as a partnership.[46] The king needed a minister to accomplish his 'will and pleasure' and in general Wolsey succeeded. True, there were tensions in their relationship, especially in the field of ecclesiastical politics.[47] Only rarely did Henry and Wolsey disagree, however, as in the summer of 1521, when Wolsey was at Calais and unable to ride to court, or in the spring of 1522, when he urged a combined attack on the French navy at anchor in various ports, but Henry thought the plan too dangerous.[48]

Although Wolsey became notorious for his pomp and circumstance as papal legate, he seems genuinely to have tried not to flaunt his relationship with the king. Only once does he seem to have been observed strolling arm in arm with Henry.[49] On the contrary, Wolsey consistently maintained the posture of the king's loyal executive, which was not simply a matter of tact or presentation, it was strictly true.[50] By definition Henry was the senior partner in any relationship with a subject, and he occasionally fumed that he 'would ... be obeyed, whosoever spake to the contrary'.[51] But although he alone was in charge of *overall* policy, only in the broadest sense was he taking independent decisions whilst Wolsey's career was at its height. Until the summer of 1527 it was Wolsey who almost invariably calculated the available options and ranked them for royal consideration; who established the parameters of each successive debate; who controlled the flow of official information; who edited correspondence from Europe by summarizing it in his own letters to Henry; who selected the king's secretaries; and who promulgated decisions he himself had largely shaped, if not strictly taken. In foreign affairs, although Henry's overall responsibility for policy is not in doubt, more than mere details were left to Wolsey. To ambassadors

[44] Cavendish, p. 12.   [45] *LP*, IV (iii) 5750; Fiddes, *Life of Wolsey*, Collections no. 101 (p. 216).

[46] Scarisbrick, *Henry VIII*, pp. 43–6; Bernard, *War, Taxation and Rebellion*, pp. 3–45.

[47] Wolsey's request at Baynard's Castle in 1515 that Convocation might refer the matter of clerical immunities to Rome for a 'solution' following the Hunne and Standish debates was refused by Henry VIII. J. D. M. Derrett, 'The affairs of Richard Hunne and Friar Standish', in J. B. Trapp (ed.), *The Complete Works of St Thomas More, IX, The Apology* (New Haven and London, 1979), pp. 215–37.

[48] Scarisbrick, *Henry VIII*, pp. 90–2; *Further supplement to letters, despatches and state papers ... preserved in the archives at Vienna*, p. xvi.

[49] R. S. Sylvester, D. P. Harding (eds.), *Two Early Tudor Lives* (New Haven and London, 1962), p. 208.

[50] Walker, *Skelton and the Politics of the 1520s*, pp. 154–87.   [51] *StP*, I, p. 79.

Henry seemed largely consistent: he was bent on conquering new territory in France, an objective which in principle Wolsey shared, but about which in practice he reserved judgement. Wolsey always saw ambassadors first, replying to them *extempore*, and what he said was normally repeated unchanged by Henry at a later interview.[52]

Did the council in these circumstances steadily abdicate its executive role to Wolsey and concentrate instead on the mass of judicial business that his keynote policies created? A mass of evidence has survived to show that judicial business was increasingly important, justifying the frequency of council meetings in star chamber as well as spawning new conciliar sub-committees or 'under-courts'.[53] But I have always stressed that Wolsey's council remained a real governing institution. It supervised the swearing-in of sheriffs and JPs, made arrangements for the redistribution of grain stocks following bad harvests, fixed and enforced the prices of many basic commodities, attacked racketeering in essential food-stuffs, debated projected legislation, attempted to relieve poverty in London and its suburbs, and enforced the statutes against vagrancy and unlawful games. The council was especially active in the socio-economic sphere in the latter half of the 1520s, and was engaged in debates throughout Wolsey's chancellorship that were far removed from the set-piece formalities satirized by Skelton.[54] Moreover, the council was consulted about strategic foreign policy options, even if Henry and Wolsey had already discussed or settled in principle the policies they proposed to adopt.

The name of the game was politics. As Henry's partner, Wolsey enjoyed the king's special trust and confidence, but the council was far from eclipsed. The minister had continually to earn his place and keep ahead of the field: this is the context of his Eltham Ordinance, published in January 1526. The *débâcle* of the Amicable Grant in the spring of 1525 was followed by the Anglo-French peace in the summer. The French alliance was a diplomatic *volte-face* and therefore controversial; within two years it had become the mainspring of a foreign policy crisis and of a public breach between Wolsey and the duke of Norfolk, who criticized it continually in the king's presence.[55] In addition, the peace brought about the return of the magnates to domestic routine at a time when Wolsey was weakened by the uproar over the East Anglian revolt.[56] Writing to Wolsey in May 1525, the day after receiving the submission of the rebels of Lavenham, the dukes of Norfolk and Suffolk insisted that 'all things well considered ... we think we never saw the time so needful for the king's highness to call his Council unto him

---

[52] *StP*, i, p. 165; *Further supplement to letters, despatches and state papers ... preserved in the archives at Vienna*, pp. xv–xvi; Bernard, *War, Taxation and Rebellion*, pp. 60–3; Guy, *Cardinal's Court*.

[53] Guy, *Cardinal's Court*, pp. 29–50.

[54] Henry E. Huntington Library, San Marino, California, Ellesmere MSS 2652, 2654, 2655; Guy, *Cardinal's Court*, pp. 23–35, 119–24.

[55] *LP*, iv (ii) 3105 (pp. 1410–11), 3663.   [56] Starkey (ed.), *The English Court*, pp. 105–7.

to debate and determine what is best to be done'.[57] Whether this appeal should be linked to the gestation of the Eltham Ordinance is unclear. But the final text of that document and Wolsey's preparatory drafts signal his intentions, which were to satisfy Henry VIII's demand by the end of 1525 to have 'an honourable presence of councillors about his Grace', and to reconstruct the royal household, and in particular the privy chamber, in such a way as to limit the access to the king enjoyed by Wolsey's political rivals.[58]

The Eltham Ordinance instructed twenty 'honourable, virtuous, sad, wise, expert, and discreet' councillors to give 'their attendance upon [the king's] most royal person', and to perform the council's full range of advisory, administrative and judicial duties. The councillors named included Wolsey, the dukes of Norfolk and Suffolk, the marquises of Dorset and Exeter, the earls of Shrewsbury and Worcester, Bishop Tunstall, Lord Sandys, Sir William Fitzwilliam, Sir Henry Guildford, Sir Henry Wyatt and Thomas More. They were the leading office-holders of court and state; had the proposed council come into effect and acted as a corporate board, it would have been in size, function and place of meeting the close equivalent of the privy council of nineteen which declared its hand in August 1540.[59] It would have been a powerful counterbalance to the ministerial status of Wolsey, who was obliged by his official duties as lord chancellor to keep the legal terms in chancery and star chamber at Westminster. Moreover, the Eltham Ordinance would be implemented when signed by the king's hand and published.[60] The earl of Worcester even felt obliged to obtain a licence, signed by the king, excusing his daily attendance in the council as specified by the Ordinance on account of age and ill-health, and providing that Lord Sandys should undertake his duties in his absence, but without assuming his style of lord chamberlain.[61]

If the Eltham Ordinance was implemented, however, the plan for the council of twenty was not. Wolsey immediately devised that 'by reason of their attendance at the [legal] terms for administration of justice' and other duties, the lords of the council 'shall many seasons fortune to be absent from the king's court, and specially in the term times'.[62] This was written into the Ordinance itself, whereupon Wolsey reduced the twenty councillors to a committee of ten

[57] SP1/34, fol. 196 (*LP*, IV (i) 1329); Starkey, 'Court, council and nobility'; Bernard, *War, Taxation and Rebellion*, p. 85.

[58] Bodl. Library, Oxford, MS Laud Misc. 597; SP1/37, fols. 65–103; BL, Cotton MS Vespasian C XIV, fols. 287–94ᵛ; *A collection of ordinances and regulations for the government of the royal household* (Society of Antiquaries: London, 1790), pp. 159–60; Starkey, 'Court, council and nobility'; Starkey (ed.), *The English Court*, pp. 105–7; Guy, *Cardinal's Court*, pp. 45–6.

[59] MS Laud Misc. 597, fols. 30–1.

[60] PRO, LC5/178 is the later copy used for official reference in the royal household, and it refers to a lost 'Liber Vetus'. See also *LP*, IV (iii) App. 65; *LP*, XIV (ii) 3.

[61] BL, Cotton MS Vespasian C XIV, fos. 295–7. Elton, *Tudor Constitution*, pp. 94–5 creates confusion by muddling Worcester's office with that of the earl of Oxford, and glossing Sandys as chamberlain. Worcester was lord chamberlain of the household; Oxford was lord great chamberlain; Sandys was not appointed lord chamberlain of the household until April 1526.

[62] MS Laud Misc. 597, fol. 31.

and then to a sub-committee of four, it being finally provided that two councillors from among those resident at court should always be present to advise the king and dispatch matters of justice unless Henry otherwise gave them leave. The councillors 'so appointed for continual attendance' were to meet at 10 a.m. and 2 p.m. daily in the king's dining chamber 'or in such other place as shall fortune to be appointed for the Council chamber'. 'Which direction well observed', concluded Wolsey in a final ironic flourish, 'the king's highness shall always be well furnished of an honourable presence of councillors'.[63]

What Wolsey did in 1526, then, was to offer his fellow-councillors on paper the corporate political role he had denied them since February 1514, but in reality to thwart exactly that. The conciliar chapters of the Eltham Ordinance were designed to reinforce Wolsey's ministerial status. For eighteen months, moreover, the ploy worked. Until the summer of 1527, when the twin crises of the king's divorce and foreign policy interacted to sap the minister's power, the councillors daily attendant at court were still only the royal secretaries. True, the marquis of Exeter, nominated to the titular headship of the privy chamber by the Eltham Ordinance, probably became more active.[64] He was on Wolsey's list of twenty councillors, and as Henry VIII's kinsman had long been close to the king. His exact role in 1526 is, however, hard to interpret, for he was barely active as a councillor and was probably chosen for that reason.[65] Certainly the gentlemen of the privy chamber appointed by the Ordinance were selected expressly because they were not councillors.[66] Even then they were warned not to approach the king unless summoned, and Wolsey's working papers reveal his nagging concern that privy chamber staff should not follow the king into 'secret places' to play politics.[67]

Many historians, myself among them, have at various times criticized Wolsey for failing to disentangle and reconstruct the council's executive and judicial components in the 1520s. Wolsey's system in star chamber almost collapsed under the bulk of litigation that his keynote policies created. He was forced to remit the vast majority of suits either to the regional councils or *ad hoc* commissioners, or else to abandon them to the common law.[68] Of course, Wolsey was hamstrung politically. Had he reconstructed the council in the interests of bureaucratic efficiency, the end result would most likely have been a council of lords at court and a council of lawyers in star chamber.[69] Indeed, when Wolsey

---

[63] MS Laud Misc. 597, fol. 31.   [64] MS Laud Misc. 597, fol. 24.

[65] He did not attend a single documented meeting in star chamber under Wolsey. He also opposed the French alliance. For Henry's insistence on retaining Exeter in the privy chamber and Wolsey's counterbalancing action, see Starkey (ed.), *The English Court*, p. 107.

[66] MS Laud Misc. 597, fols. 24–9; Starkey, 'Court, council and nobility'.

[67] BL, Cotton MS Vespasian c xiv, fol. 290v; Starkey, 'Court, council and nobility'.

[68] Guy, *Cardinal's Court*, pp. 46–50.

[69] This was especially so at a time when the king did not reside at Westminster and did not attend star chamber.

experimented with drafts to streamline the council in February 1525, this was precisely the impasse he reached. 'An order taken for the division of such matters as shall be treated by the King's Council' projected reform by differentiation of function, and was intended to relieve leading office-holders of routine judicial work.[70] Twenty-eight lesser councillors, the judges, king's serjeants and the attorney-general were deputed to deal with 'matter in law'. Inevitably the plan was dropped. It released the lords of the council from the very tasks for which the Eltham Ordinance would demand their presence. In the face of Henry VIII's increasingly insistent demands for 'an honourable presence of councillors about his Grace' by the end of 1525, it would have enabled the lords themselves to reconstruct the council attendant at court – the threat Wolsey always sought to avert.

Within two years the council attendant was in any case in process of reconstruction. Wolsey could not maintain his supremacy when confronted by a European situation that forced him to develop the French alliance at ever-increasing cost in order to obtain progress on the divorce. The dukes of Norfolk and Suffolk and Viscount Rochford, Anne Boleyn's father, were prominent among the unusually large group of lords resident at court in the summer of 1527 and dining with Henry in the privy chamber.[71] Already the king had started to show Wolsey's letters to Norfolk and Rochford, and by the following Easter Norfolk and Rochford were being directly consulted on matters of policy without reference to Wolsey.[72] By March 1529 Henry was showing all his European correspondence to Suffolk as well as Norfolk and Rochford.[73] For Wolsey it was the beginning of the end. When Henry began openly to criticize his minister and the nobles returned to court to attend the king daily, Wolsey had to work by different rules to those he had previously sustained. The lesson was not lost on Thomas Cromwell, who avoided the office of lord chancellor with its heavy legal responsibilities at Westminster. Moreover, in January 1537, when his own career was on the line, Cromwell resolved to 'keep the court ordinarily'.[74] That was the option Wolsey had denied himself, and he paid the price.

II

If, however, court and council were the hub of national politics, relations between court and country were the key to political stability. Central government

---

[70] SP1/59, fol. 77 (*LP*, IV (iii) App. 67); SP1/235 (Pt. 1), fol. 37 (*LP*, *Add.* 481). The documents are dated 5 February. The year is established from internal evidence, in particular from the fact that Fyneux C. J. K. B. died in November 1525. I owe the date of Fyneux's death and therefore that of these documents to Dr Amanda Bevan and Professor John Baker.

[71] *LP*, IV (ii) 3318; Gunn, *Charles Brandon*, p. 102.   [72] *LP*, IV (ii) 3360, 3992–3; *StP*, I, p. 261.

[73] *StP*, I, p. 332; Gunn, *Charles Brandon*, pp. 106–14.

[74] M. St Clare Byrne (ed.), *The Lisle Letters*, 6 vols. (Chicago and London, 1981), IV, p. 242. I am grateful to Dr Starkey for this reference.

was effective only when it enjoyed the support of local magistrates. Henry VIII 'was far from omnipotent, and the real measure of his power was his ability to have his decisions executed at the level of the county and village'.[75] Judged in these terms, his reign was successful. The ability to tax efficiently is a valid measure of the strength of an early-modern European state, and Roger Schofield has argued that Henry VIII created such strong bonds of political cohesion between the leaders of provincial society and the crown that 'the former displayed an unparalleled willingness to operate a system of taxation, which ... was several centuries ahead of its time'.[76] Certainly Henry's government was stable despite war and taxation, the break with Rome, the Pilgrimage of Grace, the steep rise of population after 1520, and social distress caused by inflation and unemployment.

Henry and Wolsey built bridges between court and country by constructing an affinity in the provinces. This was a long-established crown policy. Beginning with Richard II during his last years, the crown had attempted to split entrenched noble and gentry affinities and to create networks of royal power instead. Some 300 to 400 knights and esquires were invited to court for reasons which were local rather than military, conciliar or diplomatic. They were not given salaried court appointments, but they often received annuities and robes. Richard II realized that he needed to cultivate local landowners in order to widen his power-base and win the support of their own retainers and followers.[77] Political security was the key to his plan, which failed because he was vindictive to persons he suspected, and because he moved too quickly and ended up by dividing the counties. But the essential step was taken: the value to the crown of a governing elite more broadly based than in the past was recognized.[78]

Henry IV followed Richard's example. In 1400 his council advised him 'that in each county of the kingdom a certain number of the more sufficient men of good fame should be retained ... and charged also carefully and diligently to save the estate of the king and his people in their localities'.[79] Again, Edward IV managed his household appointments so as to create an interlocking system of territorial lordship centred on the court and the Yorkist dynasty. It was said that 'the names and circumstances of almost all men, scattered over the counties of the kingdom, were known to him just as if they were daily within his sight'.[80] The ultimate weapons of political discipline were acts of attainder and penal bonds or

[75] R. B. Smith, *Land and Politics in the England of Henry VIII: the West Riding of Yorkshire, 1530–46* (Oxford, 1970), p. 123; P. Williams, *The Tudor Regime* (Oxford, 1979).

[76] Schofield, 'Taxation and the political limits of the Tudor state', in Cross, Loades, and Scarisbrick (eds.), *Law and Government under the Tudors*, p. 255.

[77] Cf. *The Governance of England*, ed. C. Plummer, 2nd edn (Oxford, 1926), p. 129.

[78] C. Given-Wilson, *The Royal Household and the King's Affinity: Service, Politics and Finance in England, 1360–1413* (New Haven and London, 1986), pp. 203–57.

[79] Cited in ibid. p. 219.

[80] D. A. L. Morgan, 'The house of policy: the political role of the late Plantagenet household, 1422–1485', in Starkey (ed.), *The English Court*, pp. 64–7.

recognizances, but strategic deployment of crown patronage was essential. Between 1461 and 1515 grants of lands, salaried offices and annuities on the one hand, and parliamentary acts of resumption on the other, were wielded in a judicious combination of carrot and stick.[81]

The crown's resources, were, however, limited before the dissolution of the religious houses. Only a small minority of local magnates or JPs could receive a grant; a wider mechanism for court-country cohesion was needed. That mechanism under Henry VIII was furnished through the chamber, the main ceremonial department of the royal household where the king sat under a canopied throne on days of estate and performed such formal duties as the reception of ambassadors. Between April 1509 and the fall of Wolsey at least 400 chamber officials were appointed at court, including forty-five knights of the body, fifty-four esquires of the body, forty-one sewers, fifty-nine gentlemen-ushers, forty-seven yeomen-ushers, thirty-six pages, thirty yeomen and fifty-nine grooms.[82] Some of these posts were salaried, but most were supernumerary. The exact ratio of salaried to supernumerary appointments is impossible to compute owing to imperfect sources, but of the forty-one sewers appointed only six were paid, of the fifty-nine gentlemen-ushers only twelve were paid, and of the thirty-six pages only eight were paid. Although the knights and esquires of the body had already surrendered their duties as intimate royal body servants to the gentlemen of the privy chamber, their posts were not abolished, and several incumbents were later advanced to the privy chamber or the council.

Despite the rise of the privy chamber by 1518, Henry and Wolsey continued to recruit supernumeraries from the counties. In 1519 Wolsey made a 'privy remembrance' for Henry 'to put himself in strength with his most trusty servants in every shire for the surety of his royal person and succession' – Edward IV's policy by another name.[83] Soon a special book recorded the names 'of the king's servants in all the shires of England sworn to the king', listing knights, esquires, carvers, cupbearers, sewers and gentlemen-ushers in order of their counties.[84] All thirty-eight English counties were represented, as were South Wales, North Wales, Calais, Ireland and Jersey. Although the book is severely damaged by water, the names of 184 knights, 148 esquires, five carvers, thirteen cupbearers, 107 sewers and 138 gentlemen-ushers can still be read.[85] This was the roll-call of Henry's local men in the 1520s, and like Edward IV he must have known their names 'as if they were daily within his sight'. Some 200 county landowners or

---

[81] B. P. Wolffe, *The Crown Lands, 1461–1536* (London, 1970); Wolffe, *The Royal Demesne in English History* (London, 1971); S. J. Gunn, 'The act of resumption of 1515', in D. Williams (ed.), *Early Tudor England* (Woodbridge, 1989).

[82] Compiled from *LP*. These figures are provisional, and derive from my current research.

[83] BL, Cotton MS Titus B I, fol. 192 (formerly fol. 184) (*LP* III (i) 576 (3)).

[84] PRO, E36/130, fols. 165–231 (*LP*, III (i) 578). This document can be read only under ultra-violet light.

[85] The book concludes with a consolidated list of 74 grooms. My figures exclude chaplains and a handful of foreigners on the lists.

their sons were listed as unsalaried supernumeraries at court by 1525.[86] What proportion of these 'king's servants' ever set foot in a royal palace is a question for which evidence is lacking, but the opportunity to do so when they had business at court must have added to the attraction of their appointments. An obvious fiction was in play; supernumeraries did not receive 'bouge of court',[87] therefore their attendance was likely to have been occasional. Yet their loyalty was assured once they were 'sworn' and their names entered in the register. What happened to a 'king's servant' who did not abide by the rules is amply demonstrated by the misfortunes of Sir William Bulmer, whom Wolsey hauled into star chamber in a show trial for wearing the duke of Buckingham's livery in the king's presence.[88]

This approach to local government was consistently bilateral. Not only were county landowners or their sons sworn as the 'king's servants' and given supernumerary positions at court. In addition, a direct if admittedly fluctuating relationship existed in many counties between the king's affinity and the commissions of the peace. By 1500 the expanded role of JPs as the crown's unsalaried agents in the provinces had been cemented. Their judicial and administrative duties had been defined by innumerable statutes and proclamations as well as by the commissions themselves. It was axiomatic that the roll-call of the 'king's servants' should be consulted when appointments to the commissions were pending. It was equally important that the crown augment its influence by recruiting to its affinity established 'men of worship' or their dependants in the localities. With hindsight it might be supposed that the membership of the king's affinity and the commissions should ideally have coincided. One might even expect a majority of JPs to be listed on the roll-call of the affinity, but this is vastly to overestimate the crown's regional power. The exact relationship between the affinity and the commissions was complex, and varied considerably in individual counties.

Some preliminary conclusions emerge if the composition of the affinity by the early 1520s is compared with that of the commissions. I shall here attempt this exercise for a sample of fourteen counties: Buckinghamshire, Cumberland, Devon, Kent, Norfolk, Northumberland, Oxfordshire, Shropshire, Somerset, Suffolk, Surrey, Sussex, Warwickshire and Yorkshire.[89] It is immediately clear that the greatest correspondence between the membership of the affinity and the commissions was at the highest social level. A majority of peers and knights of

---

[86] *LP*, IV (i) 1939 (8).   [87] i.e. free food and accommodation.

[88] Guy, *Cardinal's Court*, pp. 32, 74.

[89] I am here comparing the roll-call of the 'king's servants' in E36/130 with the commissions in force during Wolsey's chancellorship. All material concerning the composition of the commissions is taken from my computerized database of JPs appointed in the reign of Henry VIII. This database draws on commissions recorded on the Patent Rolls and in Crown Office books (as calendared in *LP*), supplemented by unpublished commissions enrolled on the Originalia Rolls of the Exchequer at the PRO. The lists in E36/130 were compiled over several years, and the exact date of this document is unknown. Some entries must have been made before 1523 while others were made after 1522, but internal evidence suggests it is safest to think in terms of *c*. 1520–5.

the affinity also served as JPs in their counties. Generally, however, the degree of correspondence is lower. Only in Suffolk, Surrey, Kent and Norfolk were more than one-third of the affinity named as JPs in their counties. In Suffolk twelve out of twenty-five members of the affinity were JPs; in Surrey six out of thirteen; in Kent ten out of twenty-three; and in Norfolk nine out of twenty-four. Counties where one-fifth or fewer of the affinity were named JPs included Somerset, Buckinghamshire and Oxfordshire. Moreover, in the north the correspondence between the affinity and commissions was almost negligible. In Yorkshire (all Ridings) only eight out of fifty-two sworn 'king's servants' were appointed JPs; in Northumberland the figure was three out of ten; and in Cumberland none.

If, however, membership of the king's affinity seems to have complemented rather than duplicated that of the commissions of the peace, the direction of flow between the two is fairly clear where correlation of membership exists. Henry and Wolsey almost invariably augmented the affinity from the ranks of established 'men of worship' in the shires, and not *vice-versa*. Counties where at least half the JPs among the affinity were existing members of the commissions who were thereafter sworn the 'king's servants' included all those sampled except Cumberland, Shropshire, Somerset and Yorkshire. Only in Kent, Norfolk and Suffolk is there additional evidence to suggest that new JPs were selected from the roll-call of the affinity, and even then the numbers involved are very small.

On the other hand, the king's or Wolsey's own servants seem to have numbered consistently among those JPs placed as 'outsiders' on the commissions of the peace for other counties. Wolsey is known to have made several attempts to reconstruct certain county benches, for instance those of Kent and Gloucestershire, where the proportion as well as the number of resident JPs was reduced.[90] He deployed his power most obviously in the north, appointing JPs who were prepared to implement crown policy at the expense of local vested interests. In Yorkshire the number of local gentry in the commissions was significantly reduced during the 1520s, and the number of 'outsiders' correspondingly increased. Six clerical JPs with close ties to Wolsey (of whom five were appointed to the duke of Richmond's council in the North) were placed on the commissions for Cumberland, Westmorland, Northumberland and Yorkshire.[91] In the West

---

[90] M. L. Zell, 'Early Tudor JPs at work', *Archaeologia Cantiana*, 93 (1977), 126–7.

[91] The dispositions were as follows. Thomas Dalby (archdeacon of Richmond), JP Westm 1525; JP Northumb 1525; JP Yorks East Riding 1525; JP Yorks North Riding 1525; JP Yorks West Riding 1525. William Franklin (chancellor of Durham), JP Cumb 1525; JP Westm 1525; JP Northumb 1525; JP Yorks East Riding 1525, 1529; JP Yorks North Riding 1525, 1528; JP Yorks West Riding 1525, 1528. Brian Higdon (archdeacon and dean of York), JP Cumb 1525; JP Westm 1525; JP Northumb 1525; JP Yorks East Riding 1525, 1529; JP Yorks North Riding 1525, 1528; JP Yorks West Riding 1525, 1528. William Holgill (Wolsey's steward as archbishop of York), JP Yorks East Riding 1525, 1529; JP Yorks North Riding 1525, 1528; JP Yorks West Riding 1525, 1528. Thomas Magnus (archdeacon of East Riding, Wolsey's secretary as archbishop of York), JP Yorks North Riding 1528; JP Yorks West Riding 1528; JP Yorks East Riding 1529. William Tate (almoner to the duke of Richmond), JP Cumb 1525; JP Westm 1525; JP Northumb 1525; JP Yorks East Riding 1525, 1529; JP Yorks North Riding

Riding of Yorkshire the reconstruction of the bench was undeniably systematic. Although some former JPs had died, the exclusion of so many leading local gentry from the commissions can only have been the result of deliberate planning.[92]

Wolsey's household was noted as a training-ground for agents in central and local government. He named his dependants to offices and commissions, and some two dozen were placed on the county benches.[93] They included Sir William Gascoigne of Cardington, Bedfordshire (treasurer of Wolsey's household 1523–9), Richard Page, Thomas Heneage, Ralph Pexsall (clerk of the crown in chancery from 1522) and Sir Thomas Tempest (comptroller of the duke of Richmond's household). Gascoigne was appointed as an 'outsider' in Berkshire, Buckinghamshire, Hertfordshire, Oxfordshire, Surrey and Yorkshire.[94] Page was named in Surrey, Cumberland, Westmorland, Northumberland and Yorkshire.[95] Heneage and Pexsall between them covered Surrey, Berkshire and Devon.[96] Lastly, Sir Thomas Tempest was appointed in Cumberland, Westmorland, Northumberland and Yorkshire.[97]

Wolsey turned his attention to local government as soon as his law-enforcement policy was promulgated. Between 1516 and 1519 he orchestrated a series of exemplary cases in star chamber and king's bench for 'negligence', corruption or maladministration in local government. Those accused of aiding and abetting homicide in their counties included Sir John Savage, Sir John

1525, 1528; JP Yorks West Riding 1525, 1528. All except Holgill were members of the northern council appointed in 1525. R. R. Reid, *The King's Council in the North* (London, 1921; repr. 1975), pp. 103–4.

[92] Smith, *Land and Politics*, pp. 153–5, and table 15.

[93] They were Sir Edward Aston, Sir John Aston, Thomas Audley, Sir Christopher Conyers (Lord Conyers), Sir Thomas Denys, William Drury, Sir William Gascoigne of Cardington, John Hales, Anthony Hansard, Thomas Heneage, Richard Lee, Thomas Lisle, Walter Luke, John More, Richard Page, Ralph Pexsall, John St Clere, Henry Savile, John Skewes, Thomas Stanley, Thomas Straunge, Sir Thomas Tempest, Henry Torrell, and Edmund Wyndham. Names of members of Wolsey's household were obtained from the Subsidy Rolls, PRO E179/69/8–10. The extent to which Wolsey's dependants were active JPs is a subject for further research.

[94] Sir William Gascoigne of Cardington, Bedfordshire. JP Beds 1510, 1512, 1514, 1515, 1521, 1524, 1525, 1529; JP Northants 1512, 1514, 1515, 1523, 1524, 1526, 1528; JP Hunts 1510, 1513, 1514, 1524, 1525, 1528; JP Berks 1525, 1526; JP Bucks 1525; JP Herts 1525, 1526, 1528; JP Middx 1524, 1526, 1528; JP Oxon 1525, 1526; JP Surrey 1525, 1526, 1528; JP Yorks North Riding 1525, 1528; JP Yorks West Riding 1525, 1528; JP Yorks East Riding 1525, 1529.

[95] Richard Page of Flamstead, Hertfordshire, JP Cumb 1525; JP Westm 1525; JP Northumb 1525; JP Surrey 1522, 1524, 1525, 1526, 1528; JP Middx 1524, 1526; JP Yorks East Riding 1525; JP Yorks North Riding 1525; JP Yorks West Riding 1525.

[96] Thomas Heneage of Lincolnshire, JP Lincs Lindsey 1520, 1522, 1524, 1526, 1528; JP Middx 1523, 1524, 1526, 1528; JP Berks 1526; JP Surrey 1525, 1526, 1528. Ralph Pexsall of Hampshire, JP Hants 1513, 1514, 1515, 1518, 1523, 1524, 1525, 1526, 1529; JP Surrey 1514, 1528; JP Devon 1522, 1524, 1526; JP Middx 1528.

[97] Sir Thomas Tempest of Holmside, co. Durham, JP Yorks North Riding, 1511, 1512, 1514, 1528; JP Cumb 1525; JP Westm 1525; JP Northumb 1525; JP Yorks East Riding 1525, 1529; JP Yorks West Riding 1525, 1528.

Hussey, Sir Robert Sheffield and Sir William Brereton of Brereton. Savage, whose family had increasingly monopolized crown appointments in Worcestershire and Gloucestershire after 1488, was imprisoned in the Tower, indicted in king's bench and dismissed in favour of Sir William Compton.[98] Hussey, a courtier and king's councillor as well as a JP in Lincolnshire and Huntingdonshire, was bound over to avoid treason, felony, robbery, murder or other acts of violence following a private complaint.[99] The proceedings against him collapsed and he was discharged, unlike Sheffield, a former councillor, speaker of the house of commons and JP in Lincolnshire and Nottinghamshire, whom Wolsey convicted in a star chamber show trial before sending him to the Tower, where he died.[100] Lastly, Brereton, who became increasingly involved in power-struggles in the palatinate of Chester, was compelled to attend daily in star chamber for almost a year while the allegations against him were investigated by Wolsey's own local commissioners.[101]

Wolsey ordered the assize judges to file reports about the 'misdemeanours' they encountered on their circuits: 'that is to say, who be retainers or oppressors, or maintainers of wrongful causes, or otherwise misbehaved persons'.[102] These inquiries increasingly extended to the localities, and the JPs of Norfolk and Suffolk were among those compelled to appear in star chamber to answer complaints about their conduct.[103] Wolsey also tackled the endemic factionalism among the JPs of Surrey which had led to violence, corruption and perversion of justice in the shire. Lord Edmund Howard, Sir John Legh and Sir Matthew Browne were prosecuted in the summer of 1519 for 'maintenance, embracery and bearing'. At least eight Surrey JPs were examined, and Wolsey obtained from Sir William Fitzwilliam a long list of 'misdemeanours contrary to the king's laws and statutes' committed in the shire since Henry VIII's coronation.[104]

---

[98] Henry E. Huntington Library, Ellesmere MS 2652, fol. 3; PRO, KB29/148, *roti* 37d–38d, 44, 50–5; R. Keilwey, *Relationes quorundam casuum selectorum ex libris oberti Keilwey* (London, 1602), fos. 188–96; E. W. Ives, 'Crime, sanctuary and royal authority under Henry VIII: the exemplary sufferings of the Savage family', in M. S. Arnold, T. A. Green, S. A. Scully, and S. D. White (eds.), *Of the Laws and Customs of England* (Chapel Hill, 1981), pp. 296–320.

[99] STAC10/18 (recognizance dated 20 Oct. 1516 among bundle of unlisted documents from Exchequer K. R. Miscellanea B/2), STAC2/30/23.

[100] STAC10/4, Pt 2 (unlisted bundle), fols. [127–32]; SP1/16, fols. 141–3ᵛ (*LP* II (ii) 3951); STAC2/17/227; C54/386; E36/216, fol. 176; Guy, *Cardinal's Court*, pp. 76–8.

[101] STAC2/3/311; 2/17/185, 227; 2/18/162, 2/19/81, 2/20/175; 2/22/113, 2/24/434; 2/26/370. For further references to Brereton, see Guy, *Cardinal's Court*, p. 116; E. W. Ives (ed.), *Letters and accounts of William Brereton of Malpas*, Lancashire and Cheshire Record Society, 116 (1976) pp. 6, 31, 33, 55. In addition, Lord Ogle was punished in star chamber in July 1519 after admitting to the 'supportation' of a murderer. Henry E. Huntington Library, Ellesmere MS 2652, fol. 6ᵛ.

[102] Henry E. Huntington Library, Ellesmere MS 2655, fol. 13.

[103] PRO, STAC2/26/395; STAC2/17/347; STAC2/32/fragment (bundles of unlisted papers and fragments); Henry E. Huntington Library, Ellesmere MS 2655, fol. 15ᵛ.

[104] STAC2/2/163, 178–82, 194–7; 2/6/183–4; 2/18/246; 2/22/50; 2/26/252, 355; STAC10/4, Pt 5 (unlisted bundle); Guy, *Cardinal's Court*, pp. 72–4; W. B. Robison, 'The justices of the peace of Surrey in

Later the same year Wolsey issued revised instructions for use at the annual swearing-in of sheriffs, which explained more precisely than before how sheriffs were to exercise their offices. They were to prevent their subordinates from embezzling royal writs and perverting the crown's directions. Juries were to be composed of honest and impartial residents of the county 'most near to the place where the matter or cause is alleged'. Sheriffs were not to accept money or favours for naming a corrupt jury or otherwise obstructing the course of justice, and they were to demand the highest standards of conduct from their under-sheriffs and clerks, who were to be sworn. Lastly, the oath sworn by sheriffs in star chamber upon their admission into office was tightened and printed alongside the new instructions.[105]

At the same time Wolsey insisted that as many JPs as possible should attend star chamber to be 'new sworn' immediately before the swearing-in of sheriffs.[106] This enabled him to deliver a homily driving home the duties of JPs and stressing the links between central and local government. Such occasions could also be used to collect information. As many JPs and other commissioners as could conveniently be crammed into star chamber were assembled in July 1526 to hear a speech from Wolsey, whereupon one hundred and ten JPs were required to supply written answers to a twenty-one section questionnaire concerning the state of the realm.[107] Although a majority of JPs plainly could not be expected to attend personally in star chamber to be sworn, absentees were subsequently sworn in their localities by commissioners led by the assize judges.[108]

Wolsey also taught some two dozen delinquent sheriffs and JPs the 'new law of the star chamber'. Most offenders were dealt with summarily by the council or appeared in star chamber as defendants in private suits, but Wolsey seized the initiative by urging litigants frustrated by corruption or malfeasance in their counties to travel to star chamber 'where the complainants shall not dread to show the truth of their grief'.[109] Moreover, his policy was sustained for a decade, especially in the north. Thus the bailiffs of Beverley were threatened for failing to report riots and unlawful assemblies to the nearest JPs; the mayor of York was deposed for offences against justice; and Wolsey kept a list in star chamber of 'misdemeanours, enormities, injuries and wrongs' committed in Yorkshire

national and county politics, 1483–1570', unpublished Louisiana State University PhD dissertation (1983), pp. 100–43.

[105] SP1/14, fols. 108–13 (*LP*, II (i) 2579*); the date is established by Henry E. Huntington Library, Ellesmere MS 2652, fol. 7. See also Ellesmere MS 2655, fol. 15ᵛ.

[106] Henry E. Huntington Library, Ellesmere MS 2655, fol. 15ᵛ.

[107] Ellesmere MS 2652, fol. 12; P. L. Hughes, J. F. Larkin (eds.), *Tudor Royal Proclamations*, 3 vols. (New Haven and London, 1964–9), I, pp. 153–4.

[108] PRO, C254/161/25–6.

[109] *StP*, IV, p. 155. A full summary of Wolsey's law enforcement policy in star chamber may be found in Guy, *Cardinal's Court*, pp. 30–5, 72–8, 119–131.

which remained 'unreformed'.[110] In the summer of 1524 he appointed special commissioners to inquire into the administration of justice and to reform 'enormities' in Yorkshire and Northumberland.[111] The duke of Norfolk, sent to the region for the second time in two years, sat at York and Newcastle upon Tyne and duly reported to Wolsey, who promptly summoned Lord Dacre of the North into star chamber to answer corruption charges. Dacre compounded in the sum of 5,000 marks to re-appear in star chamber at any time upon twenty days' notice. He was also required to compensate those he had injured, but died within two months following a riding accident.[112]

Of course, Wolsey's impact on local government should not be exaggerated. If he aimed at centralized administration and a crown-controlled magistracy, the balance of power in the counties still remained with local landowners. A plethora of local networks bisected central ones, and the limited extent to which Wolsey or (later) Cromwell might purge the commissions of the peace exemplified this fact. In 1524 the numbers appointed to the commissions began to swell in almost every county. True, the crown needed active JPs to implement its policies, but the root cause of the expansion was that new appointments could not be offset by the removal of unworthy JPs. Almost all those dropped from the Kent commission in 1521 had crept back within three years. Again, the 'outsiders' Wolsey appointed in Surrey had only a marginal impact. Local power remained in the hands of the resident gentry and it was difficult to purge even serious offenders from the commissions. Lord Edmund Howard, Sir John Legh and Sir Matthew Browne remained on the Surrey commissions despite Wolsey's star chamber proceedings. All that resulted from his disciplinary action was that gentry feuding in Surrey went underground.[113] Cromwell encountered identical problems during the break with Rome, when only active opponents of the regime were purged from the benches. Passive opponents were ignored, and critics of the divorce continued to be recruited as supernumeraries at court. It was therefore recognized that good relations between court and country depended on the willingness of each to respect the other's interests.

III

'We have put about the King and Queen such as we listed.' 'We have wearied and put away, both out of the King's council and out of his house, all such officers and

---

[110] SP1/51, fols. 288–92 (*LP*, IV (ii) 5107); *LP*, IV (i) 1218; Pollard, p. 319; STAC2/24/79. The manuscript 'correction' inserted into the Kraus reprint of the official PRO list which re-dates this last document to the reign of Henry VII is itself incorrect. Several of the offences in the document pertained to the activities of the fifth earl of Northumberland, whom Wolsey had humbled in star chamber in 1516.

[111] *Tudor Royal Proclamations*, I, pp. 143–4.

[112] Henry E. Huntington Library, Ellesmere MS 2652, fol. 6; BL, Lansdowne MS I, fol. 105; PRO, c244/168/15A; *LP*, IV (ii) 3022; Guy, *Cardinal's Court*, pp. 122–3.

[113] Robison, 'The justices of the peace of Surrey', pp. 143–53, Zell, 'Early Tudor JPs at work', p. 127.

councillors as would do or say anything freely, and retained such as would never contrary us.' 'We have begun to make learned men sheriffs of the shire.'[114] These accusations, levelled by Palsgrave, are as superficial and distorted as Skelton's satires. The partnership between Henry VIII and Wolsey was acrimoniously dissolved in October 1529, but it proved a resounding political success until the summer of 1527. True, Wolsey's status was ministerial, but the issue of 'ministerial' *versus* 'conciliar' methods of government was not finally resolved until 1558–9. It is especially misleading to claim that Wolsey did not involve the council. He usually settled policy first with Henry in outline, and then consulted councillors. The Amicable Grant may prove to be the crucial exception, but the facts there as yet remain uncertain.[115] At the level of central government Wolsey worked on a broad front; his sweep was wider than I have had space to describe. In particular, his achievements should not be measured against the criteria laid down by his opponents. Palsgrave was himself equivocal, supporting in principle many of Wolsey's ideas. He wrote: 'Every of these enterprises were great, and the least of them to our commonwealth much expedient ... but that they have been begun, and brought to no good end.'[116]

In local government Wolsey was less dominant than at the centre, but he still played a significant role. Taken together, his efforts to cement the king's affinity in the provinces, to appoint the king's servants or his own to key positions in local administration, and to place 'outsiders' in the commissions of the peace in particular shires, contributed to the stability of Henry VIII's regime. True, it was difficult to make more than marginal inroads on county government. Nor were Henry's and Wolsey's techniques intrinsically new. Only in the fourteenth and early fifteenth centuries had the crown limited itself when selecting JPs to landowners resident in the shire. Edward IV and Henry VII had each nominated 'outsiders'. They had also recognized the need to appoint JPs who would serve regularly in quarter sessions at a time when perhaps less than half the bench of justices in any shire was normally active at sessions. It is possible that Wolsey was the first administrator to appreciate the potential of assigning JPs to the task of policing the parishes, but this is among several questions that require further research.

[114] *LP*, IV (iii) 5750 (pp. 2557, 2560).
[115] Cf. Bernard, *War, Taxation, and Rebellion*, p. 155. I largely accept Bernard's argument that councillors did their best to implement Wolsey's policy in difficult circumstances, but I doubt that the proposal for the Amicable Grant was backed in council on 10 March 1525. The document cited by Dr Bernard is not a minute of a council meeting, but a diplomatic report to Margaret of Savoy by her London representatives. They called on Wolsey after dinner (probably at York Place) and 'were introduced into the council chamber' where, in the presence of some councillors, Wolsey 'asked them their advice'. But it was the envoys and Wolsey alone who then spoke. So even supposing this was a formal meeting of the king's council rather than a *rendezvous* of diplomats, it is unlikely that the English councillors could have aired their true opinions. See *Calendar of State Papers, Spanish*, 13 vols. in 20 pts (London, 1862–1954), III (i) 39 (p. 86).
[116] *LP*, IV (iii) 5750 (p. 2562).

When reaching historical assessments, the context is decisive. Too often historians have brought prejudiced or anachronistic assumptions to their evaluations of Wolsey's career, for which Palsgrave bears as much of the blame as Skelton. His laconic litany 'We have begun . . .' has led generations of students to believe that Wolsey rushed out a superfluity of ill-considered reforms which he inevitably dropped or failed to sustain. Wolsey was far from perfect, and he certainly began some ambitious projects which he was unable to finish.[117] Particularly damaging is that his concern to defend his own ministerial status prevented him from completing the organization of the 'court of star chamber', the one institution that his policy had almost single-handedly created.[118] Yet to launch initiatives that subsequently collapse is not uncommon among politicians; a more realistic standard of assessment is required. From the standpoint of 1558, Cavendish wrote: 'I neuer sawe thys realme in better order, quyotnes & obedyence than it was in the tyme of his [Wolsey's] auctoryte & rule; ne iustice better [ad]mynestred w[ith] indifferencye'.[119] His words were exactly what Wolsey had always liked to hear, but his judgement is still one that historians ought to consider.

---

[117] For instance, the military reorganization that should have followed from the surveys of 1522; the crack-down on crime, prostitution, and vagrancy in London and its suburbs; the prosecution of graziers and butchers reported for racketeering in the meat trade; and the attack on fraudulent recoveries. See J. J. Goring, 'The general proscription of 1522', *English Historical Review*, 86 (1971), 681–705; Guy, *Tudor England*, pp. 94–5; Guy, 'Wolsey and the parliament of 1523', pp. 7–10.

[118] Guy, *Cardinal's Court*, pp. 119–39.   [119] Cavendish, p. 4.

CHAPTER 2

The domestic building works of Cardinal Wolsey

SIMON THURLEY

In size and magnificence, Thomas Wolsey's domestic buildings outclassed those of his contemporary competitors with the possible exceptions of Archbishop Warham and Edward, duke of Buckingham. In one short essay these buildings cannot be given comprehensive treatment and the discussion below will consider them under three heads. First, a 'History of the cardinal's works' will outline the scope of his domestic building activity; secondly, a more detailed discussion of some of the larger works will highlight certain features common to all his buildings. Finally an assessment of the significance of these building projects will attempt to place Wolsey in the context of his age.

I

The first suggestion of Wolsey's future building megalomania was seen in his Oxford days. Here, from 1497, he was supervising works at Magdalen College and, from 1518, at Frewin Hall. It is entirely unclear where he lived in this period but as college bursar, and later as a royal servant employed on embassies, he must have had lodging rights at first in college and later at court. A letter to Wolsey from Thomas, Lord Darcy in January 1514 states that while he was captain of the guard and vice-chamberlain late in Henry VII's reign the two men 'were bedfellows'. At the time Wolsey was a royal chaplain and must have shared lodgings with Darcy.[1] It is likely therefore that he had no separate private residence before 1510.

In that year Wolsey probably acquired his first private property; this was just outside the walls of the city of London at Bridewell. From the fourteenth century the Knights Hospitallers had owned property there and in 1507 they leased what was described as a garden to Henry VII's minister, Richard Empson.[2] Empson also took a lease on the adjoining rectory house of St Bride's, which he seems not to have used but let to his son. After his execution in 1510 the whole property passed to the crown and was granted by Henry VIII to Wolsey.[3]

[1] *LP*, I (ii) 2576.   [2] BL, Cotton MS Claudius E, VI, fol. 52.
[3] W. H. Godfrey, 'The Church of St Bride Fleet St', *Survey of London 15th Monograph* (London, 1944), p. 4.

The neighbourhood in which the property lay was an ecclesiastical quarter with inns belonging to the bishop of Salisbury and the abbots of Faversham and Tewkesbury. Wolsey, who was already Henry VIII's almoner, dean of Lincoln, prebendary of Hereford, and soon to be councillor, must have been pleased with the location, and eager to compete architecturally with the neighbouring ecclesiastical mansions. Yet it seems that Wolsey used the rectory, not as a private house, but as a lodging for his household[4] and evidence relating to the later royal building on the site strongly suggests that Wolsey began a house to the south of the rectory which he intended to use himself. Certainly in June 1513 Wolsey was able to write a letter dated at his house at Bridewell.[5]

In 1513 Wolsey accompanied Henry and much of the court to France and after Henry's victory at Tournai Pope Leo X awarded Wolsey the bishopric of that town. Although Wolsey never obtained possession of the see the state papers contain several references to his palace there. In 1515 the king's lieutenant was lodging in it and the following year William Pawne was writing to Wolsey requesting architectural advice about building at Tournai.[6]

Tournai can have been only a minor diversion and Bridewell remained Wolsey's primary building concern until 1514, when he became archbishop of York and acquired the see's two London properties, York Place in Westminster and Brigge Court in Battersea. At this point it seems as if Wolsey transferred the partially built house at Bridewell to the king who continued, under the supervision of Wolsey, and Wolsey's works organization, to extend it considerably.[7]

York Place was the prime Westminster property, especially as the king's palace of Westminster had burnt down in 1512 leaving Henry without a major London house. It was a large and relatively modern house on the Thames within a stone's throw of the legal and administrative centre of Westminster. Wolsey had been made archbishop on 5 August and two months later he borrowed £3,500 which was to be directed towards the embellishment of York Place and his new country house acquired at the same time, at Hampton Court.[8] Hampton Court, like Bridewell, had been leased from the Knights Hospitallers by a courtier of Henry VII. In this case it was Henry's chamberlain, Giles, Lord Daubeny, who between 1500 and his death in 1508 had enormously enlarged the tiny camera of the Hospitallers.[9] Wolsey took up the work here, as at York Place, with enormous enthusiasm and used the Battersea manor house, conveniently lying on the river between the two houses, as a centre for his building organization.

[4] Cavendish states that Bridewell was where Wolsey 'kept howsse for his ffamely', Cavendish, p. 11.
[5] Wolsey to Thomas, Lord Howard, *LP*, I (ii) 1969. The evidence for Wolsey's building is related at length in S. Thurley, 'English Royal Palaces 1450–1550', unpublished University of London PhD thesis, 1989, pp. 94–107.
[6] *LP*, II (i) 29, 1403.   [7] S. Thurley, 'English Royal Palaces', pp. 94–107. Below p. 83.
[8] S. Thurley *et al.*, 'Excavations on the east side of Whitehall 1938–1978', (forthcoming).
[9] S. Thurley and D. Hart with contributions by D. Batchelor, R. Morris and S. Nelson, *Hampton Court 1100–1530* (English Heritage Archaeological Monograph, forthcoming).

Both York Place and Hampton Court underwent a preliminary transformation between 1514 and 1522, but after 1522 Wolsey was building at two other houses as well. It was as the titular abbot of St Albans that Wolsey acquired The More near Rickmansworth and Tyttenhanger near St Albans. At both of these houses work immediately began on improvements and extensions and Wolsey's works organization was forced to expand to cope.

The following year Wolsey, as bishop of Durham, acquired Durham Place, the London seat of that see. He seems not to have used the house himself at first, allowing Henry Fitzroy, the duke of Richmond, to occupy it but in 1528 he briefly took up residence while a major building campaign at York Place rendered that house uninhabitable.[10] In 1529, Wolsey swapped the bishopric of Durham for that of Winchester, thus losing Durham Place but gaining the bishop of Winchester's house at Esher which he had been using on and off since 1515 at the invitation of his former patron Bishop Fox. Work immediately began on extending and improving Esher, and on Wolsey's fall he stayed there for over three months.[11]

In 1525, the king allowed Wolsey to occupy Richmond Palace, supposedly in exchange for Hampton Court. The evidence of his itinerary shows that Wolsey occupied the palace on and off and, on his removal from Esher in February 1530, he stayed at first in the keeper's lodge in the great park and later at the Carthusian Charterhouse there.[12]

By 1529 Wolsey's building operations were at a peak. He was running a domestic works organization bigger and busier than the king's. Not only this, he was also building two colleges, one at Oxford and one at Ipswich. Work was also underway on what a contemporary described as 'a more costly mausoleum than any royal or papal monument',[13] and perhaps most onerous of all he was supervising the King's own building operations at Beaulieu and Bridewell.[14] In August 1529 Lawrence Stubbs, Wolsey's almoner and building co-ordinator, could write 'Your beldinges at Yorke place, Hampton Courte, The Moore and Tyttynhangre be in such forwardness as may appere unto your grace by bills therof herin enclosed.'[15] Unfortunately few of these bills survive, but the evidence of those that do, of archaeology, and of secondary accounts of Wolsey's activities, bears out a picture of the cardinal's building on a scale no less than royal.

In the heyday of Wolsey's power, Skelton's jibes had publicly condemned the scale and magnificence of the cardinal's building projects.[16] On his fall it was left

[10] *Survey of London*, XVIII (St Martin-in-the-fields, Vol. II), p. 86; Guildhall Library MS 231.
[11] *LP*, III (i) 412, 414, III (ii) p. 1537. Wolsey would have also have gained the episcopal properties at Farnham Castle and Bishops Waltham as bishop of Winchester. But he seems neither to have built nor resided at these houses.
[12] Cavendish, p. 127; *CSPS*, IV (i) p. 486.   [13] *CPSM*, IV, 637.
[14] S. Thurley, 'English Royal Palaces', pp. 94–111.
[15] H. Ellis, (ed.), *Original Letters Illustrative of English History*, ser. 3., (1846), II, pp. 62–6.
[16] Skelton, pp. 269–70.

to those nearer to him to warn him of the effects of his prodigality. Thomas Cromwell, employed by Wolsey on many matters concerning his buildings could write warning 'Sir, sum therbe that doth alledge that your grace doth kepe to grete a house and famylye, and that ye are contynually buylding; for the love of God, therefore, I eftesones, as I often tymys have done, most heartelye beseche your grace to have respecte to every thing, and consyderyng the tyme, to refraygne your self, for a season, from all maner of byldynggs more than mere necessite requireth; which I assure your grace shall sease and put to sylence, sum persons that moche spekyth of the same.'[17]

Certainly the vultures were hovering and when the fall came the pickings were extraordinarily rich. On Wolsey's retreat to Esher in 1529 it must have seemed to all that the history of the cardinal's building works was over. But not so, for on his partial rehabilitation, in Hall's words, 'he made great provision to go northward and aparelled his servants newly and bought many costly things for his household'[18] and, it may be added, he began to build again. Wolsey wrote to the king in April 1530 complaining that his houses in the north were by 'oversight, dispoile and evill behaveour of such as I dyd trust in such ruyn and decay, aswell in the roofes and flowres, which be almost redie to fall downe that a gret parti of the portyon assigned unto me to lyve with for one yere wooll scantly, in a veray basse and meane facyon, repare and made the same mete to be inhabited'.[19] He estimated to Gardiner that over 500 marks were needed to make the houses habitable and to remedy this deficiency a final series of building campaigns was undertaken at Southwell and Cawood.

There, despite Wolsey's protestations that his building was merely 'stopping of holes where it rained in', substantial new works were soon underway, once again arousing jealousy and suspicion.[20] Robert Smythe wrote to Wolsey in June 1530 'wold to god that your grace wold content yourself with that you have and ther yes no dot but that the king wyl be good and gracyus to your grace. Yet yes is sade that your grace makeyed moche mor beilding there than ye do bycawse that you will men from London, thou we say nay that sawyt yet we cannot be belewyd.'[21]

The warning came too late, for in November 1530 Wolsey died leaving behind him enormous building debts. To clear these the king had given £1,000 in 1529, but Lawrence Stubbs, Wolsey's almoner, was writing to Wolsey in May 1530 saying that although he had paid the painter, smith and glazier at Esher and York Place the carpenter, James Nedeham, was not satisfied and that the king would have to pay him separately. Stubbs also feared that no payment had been made for the other unpaid workmen at York Place, Esher, Tyttenhanger or at The More.[22]

---

[17] PRO, sp1/57 fols. 296–7.   [18] Hall, p. 769.

[19] PRO, sp1/57 fols. 78–9, (*LP*, iv (iii) 6344), also see 6224.

[20] *LP*, iv (iii) 6545, p. 3048; R. Phillips Shilton, *The History of Southwell* (Newark, 1818), p. 72; N. Summers, *A Prospect of Southwell* (London, 1974), p. 54; For Cawood see Cavendish, p. 144.

[21] PRO, sp1/57 fol. 163 (*LP*, iv (iii) 6447).   [22] *LP*, iv (iii) 6390.

Wolsey, throughout the period of his ascendancy, was not only building for himself, but was also supervising the king's building operations. As described above, Henry took over Wolsey's partially built house at Bridewell, but more importantly the king's works there continued to be supervised by Wolsey's organization. Thomas Larke, Wolsey's confessor and close friend, who had formerly supervised works at King's College Chapel, Cambridge, and who had responsibilities at Cardinal College, was the royal comptroller of works.[23] At Beaulieu (now New Hall, in Essex) the king's other early house, William Boulton, prior of St Bartholomews and Wolsey's paymaster at Hampton Court, was supervising the king's extensions.[24] More obviously, Wolsey appears to have been entirely responsible for the design and erection of the temporary palace built outside Guines for The Field of Cloth of Gold.[25]

To manage these extensive and diverse building operations Wolsey had created a works organization which rivalled that of the crown. In the early years, Robert Cromwell, cousin of the more famous Thomas, headed this but Lawrence Stubbs replaced him sometime after 1516. Stubbs, a clerk in holy orders like most of Wolsey's aides, was formerly in the service of the duke of Buckingham at Thornbury castle near Bristol. It is unclear how he made the transfer to Wolsey's service, but when he joined Wolsey's household he was clearly an experienced building administrator who had worked on one of the most important houses of the first part of Henry VIII's reign. As Wolsey's receiver general he paid out money for all of the cardinal's building operations, and his name actually heads the surviving Hampton Court accounts. After Wolsey's fall he was responsible for paying Wolsey's debts and subsequently became vicar of Kingston upon Thames, where he set up as a supplier of bricks for the king's buildings at Whitehall.[26]

The cardinal's works organization conveniently falls into three main divisions, each under Stubbs's watchful eye. There was the central office at Battersea which dealt with Hampton Court and York Place. Then, under Thomas Cromwell there was the collegiate division dealing with Ipswich and Oxford.[27] There was a certain amount of common ground in men and materials between Oxford, Hampton Court and York Place, but this did not, it seems, extend to Ipswich. At least seven masons from Oxford also worked at York Place; John Lebons who was drawing plans for the first phase of alterations at Hampton Court had an important role at Oxford as well, and Cromwell spent much time commuting

---

[23] Pollard, pp. 306–8, p. 307n; *HKW*, III, p. 189; L. F. Salzman, *Building in England to 1540* (Oxford, 1967) appendix A, pp. 411–12; PRO, E101/517/23.

[24] PRO, E36/235 p. 738; E36/215 fols. 125v, 254v; E36/216 fols. 123, 131, 132.   [25] See below, p. 94.

[26] For Robert Cromwell, J. G. Taylor, *Our Lady of Battersea* (Chelsea, 1925), pp. 401–2; For Stubbs see PRO, SP1/22, ff. 65, 69, 83; *LP*, V, 386, IV (iii) 6390; PRO, E101/474/6.

[27] *LP*, IV (ii) 4229 (9), IV (iii) 5186, 5792.

between Oxford and Hampton Court on building errands.[28] The third group comprised the works at The More (possibly under Thomas Heritage) and those at Tyttenhanger and Esher of which we know little.[29] In 1529–30 a new northern organization was set up for which workmen were brought from London. This seems to have been under the control or supervision of John Forman, formerly in charge of the masons at Hampton Court.[30]

Unfortunately only a very few of the building accounts produced by this hierarchy have survived. Accounts for 1515–16 survive for York Place and Hampton Court but for the other buildings, except for Battersea, for which there are two accounts, nothing remains.[31] Yet through the accounts that do exist we learn a little about the everyday workmen who were employed at York Place and Hampton Court. The names of about 300 are known. They were mostly men who were local to the house upon which they worked, but John Forman, warden of the masons at Hampton Court, had a royal commission to impress workmen and many came from much further afield.

Many workmen who started their careers at Wolsey's Hampton Court and York Place continued to work on the same buildings under royal ownership. Indeed, 25 per cent of the names in Wolsey's 1515–16 accounts can be traced in the king's accounts of 1529–30. Several of Wolsey's workmen rose to attain high office in the king's works; John Russell, an apprentice carpenter at Wolsey's York Place, worked for the king as warden carpenter at Whitehall in 1530–31 and master carpenter at Greenwich in 1533–4.[32] John Ripley, a joiner at York Place, became Henry's master joiner at Whitehall and Richard Watchett, a mason at Hampton Court in Wolsey's earliest accounts, worked there continuously until 1537 as warden and then in 1538 transferred to the works at Nonsuch.[33]

II

Having given a brief history of Wolsey's houses and of the organization he created to build and maintain them some of his major works will now be

[28] R. H. C. Davis, 'A catalogue of Masons' Marks as an aid to architectural history', *Journal of the British Archaeological Association*, 3rd. ser., 17 (1954), pp. 48–9; J. H. Harvey, *English Medieval Architects, A Biographical Dictionary down to 1550*, revised edition (Gloucester, 1984), pp. 172–3; PRO, E101/518/14.

[29] In 1530 Henry took many of Wolsey's household into his own employment. Thomas Heritage had been a gentleman of Wolsey's privy chamber and was receiving payments from the king for work at The More in 1530 (*LP*, v, p. 750). This may signify that under Wolsey he was paymaster there. Certainly his household property was moved from The More to Whitehall by royal agents when he was appointed clerk of works there in 1531 (E36/251 p. 20).

[30] Harvey, *Dictionary*, p. 110.

[31] York Place: PRO, E36/236. Hampton Court: E36/235 pp. 683–836, E101/518/14, E101/474/8, SP11/17 fols. 212–3. Battersea: SP1/12 fol. 54–6, E101/474/6.

[32] PRO, E36/236 fol. 88v; E36/251 p. 126; Bodl. Rawl. MS D 775 fol. 22, 55; also see Harvey, *Dictionary*, pp. 260–2.

[33] PRO, E36/235 fol. 721; E36/237 p. 363.

Fig. 3 Bridewell palace (detail from
the   woodcut   *Civitas   Londinium,*
1561–79)

examined in greater detail. Only recently has more been found out about Wolsey's first house which later became Bridewell palace. The excavation of part of the site in 1978, although limited, answered some critical questions and recent documentary work has greatly helped to fill out the picture.[34] It seems that the king inherited from Wolsey a square courtyard house of brick with a gatehouse in the west, and a great hall in the east. Nothing is known about the disposition of the lodgings at this date but they presumably ranged around the outside of the court. In 1515 the king took possession of the house and work continued for seven months on the completion of the original structure. Connections between Bridewell and its former owner remained strong through this period. Entries relating to Bridewell appear in Wolsey's York Place accounts and the principal officer in charge was Wolsey's close friend Thomas Larke who lived nearby.[35]

In early 1516 there was a sudden change of direction. Someone, we do not know who, drew up a new plan for the house, which the king signed; the plan has not survived but the specification that accompanied it has.[36] From this we learn of an important new feature, a long gallery. This structure is described as being 'the long gallery from the great chamber wherof the foundacion is laid unto the Temmes'. Early views of the house clearly show this running from the main courtyard to the river. It was 230 feet long and ended in a watergate with a bay window and two towers facing the Thames (fig. 3).

It seems, from the fact that it was Wolsey who signed the bills, and that Wolsey's men managed the builders, that it was he, rather than the king, who was responsible for the house's form. Its principal features, when complete, were the long gallery and the stacked royal lodgings, disposed one on top of the other and not side by side as was the convention. Bridewell was, however, only a very minor forerunner of the major houses which Wolsey acquired in 1514–15.

York Place, unlike Bridewell, was a major house with a long building history beginning two hundred years before Wolsey started his enlargements. It was essentially the house built by Archbishop George Neville in the mid fifteenth century. There was a great hall separated from the principal residential block by a cloister. The main rooms comprised a great chamber, behind which was a withdrawing chamber and a series of three or four smaller rooms. To the east was the chapel with an ante-chapel which seems to have been separated from the main block (fig. 4).[37]

[34] D. Gadd and T. Dyson, 'Bridewell Palace excavations at 9–11 Bridewell Place and 1–3 Tudor Street, City of London 1978', *Post-Medieval Archaeology*, 15 (1981), 1–79; S. Thurley, 'English Royal Palaces', pp. 94–105; *HKW*, IV, pp. 53–5.

[35] PRO, E36/236 fols. 92, 108, 166v; Pollard, p. 307; E. G. O'Donoghue, *Bridewell Hospital* (London, 1923), p. 41.

[36] PRO, SP1/29 fols. 181–6.

[37] The discussion of York Place which follows is a condensed version of that which is to appear in S. Thurley et al., 'Excavations on the East Side of Whitehall 1938–1978' (forthcoming). Also see J. H. Harvey, 'The building works and architects of Cardinal Wolsey', *Journal of the British Archaeological Association*, 3rd ser., viii (1943), 50–3.

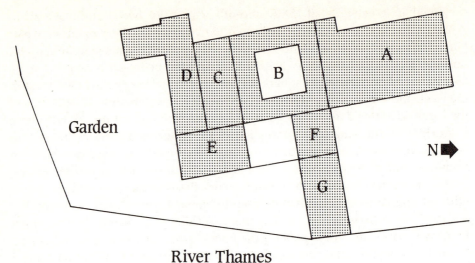

Garden

River Thames

Fig. 4   York Place, Westminster. Block plan of the house *c.*1500
A Great Hall
B Cloister
C Great Chamber
D Residential rooms in south range
E Withdrawing chamber
F Ante-chapel
G Chapel

Wolsey immediately identified the shortcomings of this plan, for his first building accounts, dated February 1515, indicate that a careful scheme to increase the number of main reception rooms was underway. The plan was to add a new great chamber to the west of the cloister and next to the great hall to provide three main reception rooms beyond the hall. When the site was excavated in 1939 the undercroft which supported this new room was revealed fully intact (plate 17). At the side of this, upon the top of the cloister, he built a gallery to link the great hall directly with the presence chamber (figs. 4, 5). These improvements meant that the house was habitable within six months, and Wolsey was able to entertain the king there for a day in July 1515.

The development of York Place, like that of other town houses such as Bridewell, was governed by the availability of land, and after 1517 further major expansion at York Place was not possible for lack of space. The first means by which Wolsey attempted to solve this problem was to obtain a grant from the king of the property to the north of the house called Scotland. This failed to solve the problem of expansion as the land lay behind the service end of the hall and not alongside the domestic quarters. This impasse was broken in 1520 when Wolsey was able to buy the land to the south of the house from the two tenants of

Westminster Abbey who held it.[38] This signalled a second phase of building in which the principal work was the building of a long gallery. To build this Wolsey had to reclaim 1,600 square yards of river upon which he constructed a gallery 250ft long facing east onto the Thames and west onto a garden (fig. 5).

Wolsey's final building campaign at York Place was partly facilitated by his ownership of Durham Place. In 1516 during his first building campaign he had borrowed the house from Thomas Ruthal, then bishop of Durham, while York Place was uninhabitable. In 1528 he was able to move his entire household and wardrobe there for eight months while his final and most ambitious building campaign began.[39] In it he replaced the two principal structures of the house, the great hall and the chapel. Also under construction was a new single storey gallery designed to run around the garden and a privy kitchen built on a new vaulted platform over the Thames (fig. 5). This last building campaign was not completed in Wolsey's lifetime and Henry VIII's first building accounts for York Place contain references to the completion of Wolsey's garden gallery and privy kitchen.[40]

By 1529 Wolsey had built himself a substantial town house the core of which was the medieval palace of the archbishops of York, but which had been much extended and modernized. Beyond the new great hall there were the great and presence chambers which led to his privy chamber. Connecting directly with this on the west were a further three rooms and on the south his bedchamber, beyond which was another room which opened onto his long gallery. Off the long gallery were two chambers, named, according to Cavendish, the rich chamber and the council chamber.[41] West of the long gallery was the cardinal's orchard, itself surrounded by a single storey gallery (fig. 5).

Hampton Court and The More were altogether different projects. York Place was essentially Wolsey's working town house; he stayed there during the legal term, riding in procession each day from the house to the law courts at Westminster.[42] York Place did not provide extensive accommodation either for visiting ambassadors or for the royal family. During the summer when the royal court was on progress and the legal term did not require his presence at Westminster, Wolsey stayed at one of his country houses.

The difference in function between York Place and Wolsey's other houses is borne out by the known movements of the king. Henry paid sixteen separate visits to Hampton Court between 1515 and 1528, staying there for a total of eighty-seven days. In the same period he visited Wolsey at The More at least eight times, a total of twenty-one days. Meanwhile there was not a single

---

[38] G. Rosser and S. Thurley, 'Whitehall Palace and King Street Westminster: the urban cost of princely magnificence', *London Topographical Record* (1990).
[39] *LP*, IV (ii) 4251; Guildhall Library MS 231.   [40] PRO, E36/251 pp. 17, 31.
[41] Cavendish, p. 99.
[42] Cavendish, pp. 40, 97; Hall, p. 760.

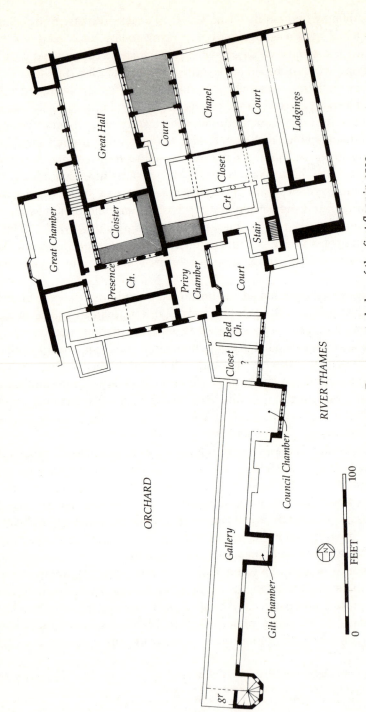

Fig. 5 York Place, Westminster. Reconstructed plan of the first floor in 1529

ORCHARD

RIVER THAMES

Great Chamber

Great Hall

Presence Ch.

Cloister

Court

Chapel

Court

Lodgings

Privy Chamber

Closet

Crt

Closet

Court

Stair

Closet

Bed Ch.

?

Gallery

Council Chamber

Gilt Chamber

gr

FEET

0   100

overnight visit to York Place and the king is only known to have paid two or three visits there.[43] Indeed, on the cardinal's fall, Henry visited York Place to survey what he had gained and his surprise at the quality of what he saw indicates his ignorance of the building.[44] Hampton Court and The More were both heavily used by Wolsey for ambassadorial and royal entertainments and much of each summer was spent at these houses. Hampton Court was a favoured location to spend Christmas; the Christmases of 1517, 1521–4 and 1526 were spent there.[45]

Recent research has shown that Wolsey's use of these country houses, and those of Tyttenhanger, and later Esher, was governed closely by the location of the court. It has been shown that while Henry was staying in the south Wolsey stayed at Hampton Court, but when the king moved west or north Wolsey moved to The More.[46] For example, during the progress of 1523 Wolsey was at Hampton Court while the king remained south of London, but when the royal court moved to Henley and then to Woodstock via Abingdon in early September, Wolsey transferred to The More. This was typical of the cardinal's movements during the summer months of progress when he struggled to keep as close to the king as possible.[47] Thus not only were Wolsey's country houses used for entertaining the king in person but they were used as bases for tracking the king when he went on progress.

The requirements of Wolsey's country houses were very different to those of York Place. More accommodation had to be provided both for foreign visitors and for the royal family. Whereas York Place made no provision for the queen's household, both these country houses did. The case of Hampton Court will be taken first.

The house that Wolsey inherited in 1514 was, like York Place, a substantial mansion. Its former owner, Giles, Lord Daubeny, had regularly entertained Henry VII there, and had between *c.* 1505 and *c.* 1508 built a moated brick courtyard house. It had a gatehouse in the south, possibly approached by an outer court and opposite this, across the court, was the great hall, which led up, at its eastern end, to a great chamber and a suite of rooms which ranged around the courtyard.[48] Wolsey's first building accounts (1514–15) specifically mention the king's dining chamber and his great chamber, indicating that from the start Wolsey intended the house to provide lodgings for the royal family.[49] These lodgings were overhauled during 1515 and 1516, in a crash programme of repairs. Beneath the king's lodging, on the ground floor, Wolsey set up a series of four parlours which were for his own use. In an inventory of Wolsey's goods these rooms are described in detail, and from this we know that his first parlour or great

[43] PRO, OBS1/1419; N. Samman, 'The Tudor Court During the Ascendancy of Cardinal Wolsey', unpublished University of Wales PhD thesis, 1989.

[44] *CSPS*, IV (i) pp. 303–4.   [45] N. Samman, 'The Tudor Court', appendix 1.

[46] Ibid., pp. 216–17.

[47] Ibid.   [48] S. Thurley et al., 'Hampton Court 1100–1530'.   [49] PRO, E36/235 p. 788.

chamber was behind the hall and his bed chamber (the legate's chamber) on the south front.[50]

Meanwhile, workmen were engaged on building what were described as 'the lodgings without the court', which can be identified with the existing base court.[51] To do this part of the moat was filled in and re-dug on the west side of the new court. In addition to the new lodgings Wolsey built a new range of kitchens to help feed his household and the large numbers of anticipated visitors.[52] The other major addition to the house in this phase was a long gallery which ran out 200 feet eastwards from the main range of lodgings.[53] It was connected to the main house by a short connecting gallery about which little is known (fig. 6). This first phase of building was over by late 1521 or early 1522, for it is known that large numbers of furnishings were bought for the house in that period.[54]

The first building campaign had not significantly improved the principal lodgings of the house, but these were tackled in a second phase of building in which Wolsey entirely rebuilt the south end of the east side of the inner courtyard, replacing the principal floor lodgings with a new two storey block.[55] This provided very grand accommodation on three levels approached by a processional staircase on the east. The other important addition of this phase was the new south range which was partially to replace Daubeny's original south range. This was linked to the end of the long gallery in the east and to the base court in the west (fig. 6). This second phase of building must have been over by 1528 when the hall and chapel at York Place were being rebuilt for we know that Wolsey stayed at Hampton Court for much of that summer. A final building campaign, interrupted by Wolsey's fall, and completed by Henry VIII, involved the rebuilding of the chapel and the construction of a cloister to its west between it and the guard chamber (fig. 6).

A brief description of the house by the Venetian ambassador, together with references in the building accounts, allow us to identify the various lodgings which existed in 1528.[56] Wolsey seems to have retained the original great hall on the ground floor; from this a staircase led up to the king's lodgings which comprised four principal rooms and a bedroom. Off the bedroom was a linking building which joined the east range with the long gallery and the south range. Above the king the queen had two state rooms (plate 18) and beneath the king there were lodgings for Princess Mary (plate 21).

---

[50] BL, Harleian MS 599.   [51] PRO, E36/235 p. 738.

[52] S. Thurley, 'The sixteenth-century kitchens at Hampton Court', *Journal of the British Archaeological Association*, 143 (1990), 1–28.

[53] The gallery is mentioned in the first building account (PRO, E36/235 p. 711) and was complete by May 1517 when it was measured for hangings (*LP*, II (ii) 3206). Much of the structure has been seen in recent excavation (Thurley et al., *Hampton Court 1100–1530*).

[54] *LP*, III (i) 1021, 1194; BL, Harl. MS 599.

[55] For the details of this see S. Thurley et al., *Hampton Court 1100–1530*.

[56] *CSPV*, IV, 682.

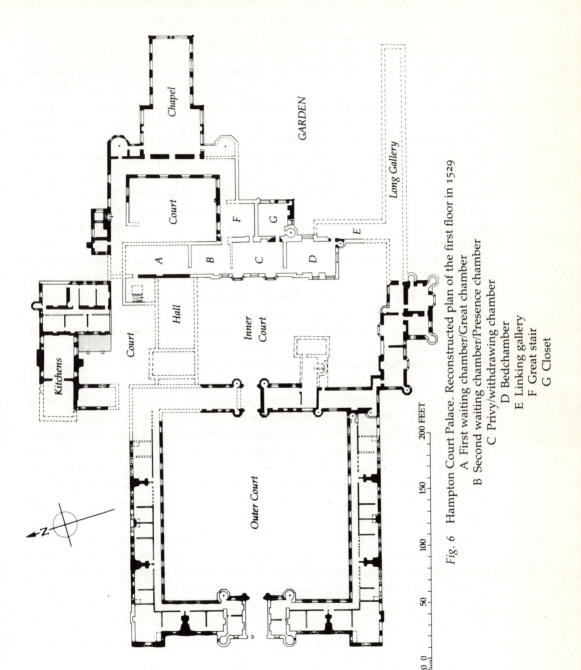

Fig. 6 Hampton Court Palace. Reconstructed plan of the first floor in 1529

A First waiting chamber/Great chamber
B Second waiting chamber/Presence chamber
C Privy/withdrawing chamber
D Bedchamber
E Linking gallery
F Great stair
G Closet

Every schoolboy knows that Wolsey gave Hampton Court to Henry VIII in 1525 to retain his master's favour.[57] But this version of history now seems increasingly unlikely. The principal reason for throwing doubt on tradition is that Henry VIII did not visit Hampton Court between June 1522 and March 1527, a four-year and three-month absence. In March 1527, when he did visit, he was the guest of Wolsey. After this stay, Henry's next overnight visit was not for a further eighteen months. Throughout this period Wolsey was using the house regularly, spending much of the summer there each year and four out of five Christmases.[58]

If the house had been Henry VIII's from 1525, he would have stayed there more than once. The real turning point in the ownership of Hampton Court came in September 1528. On the 23rd, Fitzwilliam wrote to Wolsey on the king's behalf demanding that he vacate the house for four days, so that the king could receive the papal legate there.[59] This was the first time that Henry had made any claim on the house, and from then on he and Catherine (not to mention Anne Boleyn) used the house regularly. As far as is known Wolsey visited the house only three times thereafter, and then as a refugee.[60] From this it seems that far from Wolsey's having given the house to the king, the king demanded it in September 1528 and failed to give it back. Significantly it was not included in the list of properties in Wolsey's inquisition post mortem taken in 1530.[61]

This leaves the problem of the episode in 1525 when several different reports mention a gift to the king, or a swap with the king for Richmond.[62] The answer to this lies in the nature of the house and the lodgings it provided. We have seen that as early as 1515 the building accounts mention *the king's lodgings* and that Wolsey made special provision in his second phase of building for the queen and Princess Mary. Clearly the whole house was orientated towards entertaining the royal family. Indeed Wolsey, in the Eltham Ordinances of 1526, snatched for himself, and his house, the ultimate accolade – he included Hampton Court amongst the list of houses at which, when visited by the king, hall should be kept.[63] In other words he ranked his own house as one of the five largest and most luxurious palaces in the kingdom, one of the few at which the king could stay with the entire court.

Wolsey's ostentatious provision for the king and queen at Hampton Court was not unique, for Sir Thomas Lovell, in the previous reign, had provided lodgings for Henry VII at his house at Enfield. This was an extreme version of the phenomenon whereby any great courtier would refer to his own house as 'your grace's' in correspondence. Wolsey, for instance, referred to The More as such in 1525 and there is no suggestion that this was given to the king.[64] Therefore the

[57] The classic exposition of this theory can be found in E. Law, *A History of Hampton Court Palace*, I (London, 1885), pp. 99–100.

[58] N. Samman, 'The Tudor Court', appendix 1; PRO, OBS1/1419.   [59] SP1/50 fol. 123 (*LP*, IV (ii) 4766).

[60] Ibid.   [61] *VCH Middlesex* II, p. 326.   [62] *CSPS*, III 119; Hall p. 703; Cavendish, p. 123.

[63] *A Collection of Household Ordinances*, p. 160.

[64] PRO, PROB2/199; *LP*, IV (i) 1646.

'gift' of 1525 can be seen in context. By 1525 the lodgings Wolsey had built for the king and queen at Hampton Court must have been nearly complete and Wolsey would have been in a position to offer them to the king for his exclusive use, meanwhile retaining the rest of the house for himself.

A similar re-appraisal can be taken of the gift of Richmond which has traditionally been seen as a swap for Hampton Court. The gift was in reality a licence to use the house for private occupation. Wolsey eagerly took up the offer and used the house several times, most famously at Christmas 1526 when the king was lying low at Eltham.

There are several parallels which would support this argument. The first is the case of Eltham. Early in the 1520s Henry made substantial alterations to the house there. The evidence for these comes from a surviving list of alterations and additions to be made. The list bears the mark of Wolsey in that the longest item in it is a series of adaptations to be made to his own extensive lodging. Indeed the hand of Wolsey was so apparent that, in 1521, the Venetian ambassador could report that the house actually belonged to him.[65] A second case is that of St James's palace which Henry VIII 'gave' to Thomas Cromwell in 1537. This is an exact parallel to the Richmond episode. The king had allowed his most favoured minister to use a royal house when he was not in residence. There was no question of a transfer in ownership but certainly there was a licensing for non-royal use.[66]

Thus Hampton Court was fully in Wolsey's possession until September 1528 when he was dispossessed. By March 1529 Henry was paying for his own alterations there, and, although Wolsey stayed overnight on 3 July, it is clear that he did so as a visitor and not as proprietor.

York Place and Hampton Court were substantial residences, but these were not Wolsey's only principal houses, for from 1522 he was also building at The More, near Rickmansworth in Hertfordshire. This building operation was no less spectacular than those at York Place or Hampton Court, and one contemporary report describes the house there as more magnificent than Hampton Court.[67] We have seen that Wolsey adopted different solutions to the expansion of York Place and Hampton Court. At York Place, once the principal rooms were modernized, he bought more land on which to build a long gallery and orchard. At Hampton Court the original moated platform was extended and new buildings set up east and west of the original courtyard, which Wolsey retained.

The problem at The More was dealt with differently. Here a small but relatively modern house already existed. This was the house begun in 1426, which had been modernized by George Neville, one of the builders of the fifteenth-century house at York Place. It was situated off centre on a large moated platform in such

[65] PRO, E101/497/1; *CSPV*, III 219; also see S. Thurley, 'English Royal Palaces', pp. 112–16.
[66] *LP*, XII (ii) Appendix 44, XIII (i) 855.
[67] Pollard, p. 325; *HKW*, IV, pp. 164–7.

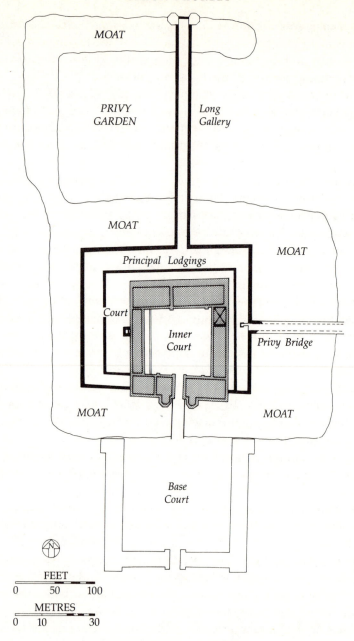

MOAT

PRIVY
GARDEN

Long
Gallery

MOAT

MOAT

Principal Lodgings

Court

Inner
Court

Privy Bridge

MOAT

MOAT

Base
Court

FEET
0   50   100

METRES
0   10   30

Fig. 7 The More, Hertfordshire. Reconstructed ground plan,
*c.*1529; (the shaded areas represent the pre-existing house).

a way that only its south front faced directly onto the moat and on the other three sides there was a gap of 34 feet and more between the house and the lip of the moat. There was a great hall opposite the gatehouse and a series of lodgings around the inner court (fig. 7).[68]

Unlike the pre-existent house at Hampton Court which was built directly out of the surrounding moat, The More had space within the moated platform for expansion. It was this space that Wolsey used to enlarge the house. He created a u-shaped block of buildings around the original house on the north, west and east sides, forming narrow courtyards between the two ranges. In addition to this he built a 253 feet long gallery off the north side of the house over the moat and through the privy garden, ending in two towers (fig. 7). Extra accommodation was provided here, as at Hampton Court, by a great base court which measured about 130 feet square internally – the exact proportions are not known but it was probably only a very little smaller than that at Hampton Court (figs. 6, 7).

Unfortunately little else is known about the detailed disposition of rooms within the house and little can be said about the planning of the house. Much the same is true of Wolsey's other properties. Nothing whatever is known about the house at Tyttenhanger but of the houses at Esher, Southwell and Cawood a little more is known.

The house at Esher was largely the mansion which Bishop William Waynflete had built in the mid fifteenth century. Today only one brick-built gateway survives, but a small-scale survey of the house drawn by Ralph Treswell in 1606 shows that it was a substantial mansion with a great hall and residential block in a tower.[69] Unfortunately it is not clear what Wolsey contributed to this group of buildings, but on his fall unused building materials were transported from his incomplete works to Hampton Court and Whitehall. Four tons of Caen stone, nineteen tons of plaster, fifteen tons of brick, and a further forty-eight loads of brick and tile were moved;[70] indicating the remains of, or the preparations for, a major building campaign. But, most important, we know that the long gallery which Wolsey was erecting at Esher was dismantled and carried to Whitehall for re-erection there.

The gallery was evidently timber framed, for 105 tons of framed timber was transported by river to the site at Whitehall. It was set up as the privy gallery of Whitehall Palace – the gallery which was to become the spine of the whole complex. It seems from the evidence of the Whitehall building accounts that the gallery was split into two parts, one either side of the gatehouse which has

[68] M. Biddle, L. Barfield and A. Millard, 'The excavation of the Manor of the More, Rickmansworth Hertfordshire', *Archaeological Journal*, 116 (1959), 136–99; S. Thurley, 'English royal palaces', pp. 180–5.

[69] J. K. Floyer, *Esher Place and its Associations with Cardinal Wolsey and the Spanish Armada* (Esher, 1913); J. Schofield (ed.), *The London Surveys of Ralph Treswell*, London Topographical Society Publication No. 135, (1987), p. 7.

[70] PRO, E36/251 pp. 20, 49, 54, 113, 114; E36/252 pp. 326, 430.

become known as the Holbein gate. Extrapolating these sections of gallery from the plan of Whitehall Palace, it can be seen that Wolsey's original gallery must have been about 200 feet long and probably ended in two small towers.[71]

The nature of Wolsey's works at the archbishop's palace at Southwell is only known through a letter sent to him by his agent Robert Brown. From this we learn that Brown had 'caused your [Wolsey's] mason, with other workmen under hyme to be working of the doores of your galary there as nere as can be devidsed according to your pleasre . . . also I have sent thider oon of the kings glasirers to glase your owne lodginge, your galary, and other places . . . as for castyng of your galery with lyme and heyre, according as mr. Holgik, your surveyor lately wrote to me, of truthe here be no workmene in this cuntrie to my knowledge that cane werke after any suche maner. Wherof yf your grace will have it so wrought, pleise hit you to command your surveyor to send doune in to the cuntrie some of your awne workmen.'[72] Despite this frenzy of activity, the house was still not ready for Wolsey on his arrival and he was forced to lodge temporarily in a prebendal house nearby.[73] In the buildings which remain today there is no trace left of the gallery or of any improvement which can be attributed to Wolsey. Yet it is clear that at Southwell Wolsey spared no less attention to modernizing his house than he had done in the south.

The case is similar with the archiepiscopal palace at Cawood where, according to Cavendish, Wolsey 'bylt and repayred the castell, which was then greatly dekayed, havyng a great multitude of artifycers and labourers, above the nomber of CCCth persons, dayly in wages'.[74] Even less is known of the nature of these works and the site today shows no trace of them.

All the works discussed above were extensions to existing buildings, for none of Wolsey's houses were built from scratch. However, here a short section should be devoted to a discussion of the temporary palace built at the Field of Cloth of Gold, for this, although built for the king, was entirely designed and supervised by Wolsey.

In the list of Wolsey's alleged 'prodigal and wasteful expenses', drawn up in 1529, he was accused of 'prodigal dispending of the king's treasure, as well in sumptious building made [at the Field of Cloth of Gold] only to that use, and not to endure'.[75] The letters which have survived relating to the construction of the palace, written by Sir Nicholas Vaux, are addressed to Wolsey and include one in April 1520 in which he was clearly asking for architectural advice.[76] Indeed Wolsey was the only one who was in a position to give that advice for he personally held the platt of the building.[77]

---

[71] Cavendish, p. 123; S. Thurley et al., 'Excavations on the east side of Whitehall'.
[72] Ellis (ed.), *Original Letters*, ser. 3, II, p. 179.
[73] Cavendish, p. 138.   [74] Cavendish, p. 144.   [75] *LP*, IV (iii) 5750 (p. 2559).
[76] J. G. Nichols (ed.), *Chronicle of Calais*, Camden Society, 1846, p. 82. Also see the letter of May 1520, PRO, SP1/20 fols. 77–8 (*LP*, III, 825).
[77] PRO, SP1/20 fol. 77 (*LP*, III, 825).

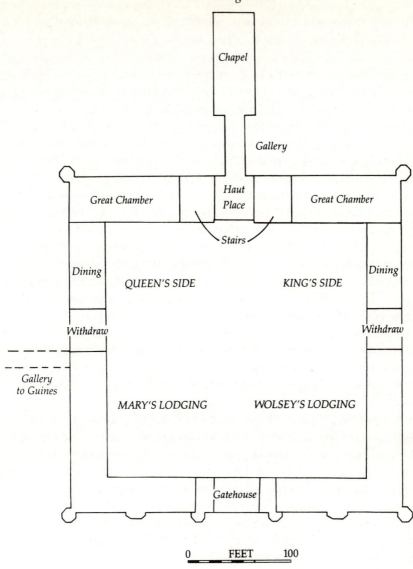

Chapel

Gallery

Great Chamber   Haut Place   Great Chamber

Stairs

Dining   QUEEN'S SIDE   KING'S SIDE   Dining

Withdraw   Withdraw

Gallery to Guines

MARY'S LODGING   WOLSEY'S LODGING

Gatehouse

0   FEET   100

Fig. 8 The temporary palace at the Field of Cloth of Gold, 1520. Conjectural first floor plan

There are several descriptions of the building erected outside Guines in 1520 and there have been various attempts at reconstructing its layout;[78] figure 8 is an

[78] Hall, pp. 605–6; *Chronicle of Calais*, pp. 79–83; *CSPV*, iii 50, 60, 69, 83, 88, 94; S. Anglo, *Spectacle, Pageantry and Early Tudor Policy* (Oxford, 1969) pp. 142–3; J. G. Russell, *The Field of Cloth of Gold* (London, 1969), pp. 37–47; My own full reconstruction can be found in 'English royal palaces', pp. 116–21.

attempt to put the evidence in plan form. The palace underwent a change in design halfway through its construction and here only the original plan will be discussed, as it, and not the altered scheme, represents Wolsey's original ideas. The overall dimensions of the building are given by Hall in his *Chronicle*; it was square, each side being 328 feet long.[79] The other dimensions are given in a letter sent to Wolsey during the building's construction.[80] It was entered by a gate-house measuring 38 feet by 34 feet, on one side of which Wolsey had three large chambers and on the other side of which the king's sister had three chambers. Beyond Wolsey's rooms were the king's and beyond the king's sister's were the queen's. The king's and queen's rooms were separated by a *haute place* 40 feet square, thus completing the quadrangle (fig. 8). The *haute place* was probably the 'halpace and stair' which Hall refers to as being 'directlye agaynst the gate'.[81] The halpace had, going out from it, a gallery 50 feet long and 22 feet wide, which led to a chapel with two closets measuring 100 feet by 42 feet.

The king's great chamber must have opened off the stair. It measured 124 feet by 42 feet which would leave an additional 20 feet for a staircase either side of the *haute place*. The king's dining chamber would have lain at right angles to the great chamber along the narrower side range; it measured 100 feet by 34 feet. The withdrawing chamber beyond it was 40 feet long and would have thus been exactly in the middle of the side range, leaving a full quadrant to Wolsey. The queen's chambers were arranged similarly and so each occupant had one quarter of the building. On the queen's side there was a gallery 400 paces long leading to the castle of Guines, where the king and queen slept (fig. 8).

The temporary palace at The Field of Cloth of Gold, as designed by Wolsey, displays many of the features which have already been observed in his domestic buildings. The compact, quadrangular plan is reminiscent of his first house at Bridewell (fig. 3), the gallery to the chapel can be closely compared to the long galleries at The More, Hampton Court and York Place (figs. 7, 6, 5). His use of a processional stair to approach the main lodgings is similar to the great stair at Hampton Court (fig. 6). In terms of accommodation Wolsey provided each occupant with three rooms, an outer chamber, a presence chamber and a withdrawing or bed chamber; in addition the king and queen had accommodation in the nearby castle.

III

The magnificence and ostentation of Wolsey's buildings are often cited as a cause of his downfall. It is claimed that his houses aroused jealousy amongst all, even the king, and that his efforts in the field of architecture outshone all before and after him. On closer examination all these claims appear overstated. Wolsey was in fact the last of a long line of English bishop-statesmen who had built on a scale

---

[79] Hall, p. 605.   [80] *Chronicle of Calais*, p. 191.   [81] Hall, p. 605.

no less than royal. For example, William Warham, archbishop of Canterbury (1503–32), and lord chancellor (1504–15), a contemporary of Wolsey, was also a building rival. His most important building was the palace at Otford which, in terms of area covered, was larger than Hampton Court (Hampton Court covering about 55,000 square yards and Otford 65,000 square yards). Warham was also building at Knole only a few miles away. In his will he claimed exemption from dilapidations as he had spent over £30,000 on rebuilding the see's houses.[82]

In the years before Warham, one of the greatest builders of the fifteenth century was at work; Cardinal John Morton, bishop of Ely (1479–86), archbishop of Canterbury (1486–1500) and lord chancellor (1487–1500). His building works were certainly as extensive as those of Wolsey, if not more so. While bishop of Ely he rebuilt Wisbech Castle, and from about 1480 rebuilt Hatfield on a lavish scale. As archbishop of Canterbury he made considerable improvements at Lambeth and constructed the great gateway there. He also further enlarged the house at Croydon, repaired the palaces at Maidstone and Aldington (both in Kent) and at Ford built a great five-storey guest tower.[83]

To these examples could be added many more,[84] but they serve to illustrate the point that there was little new about a great bishop-statesman who built on a royal scale. What was threatening to Wolsey's enemies was not the fact that his magnificence might surpass that of the king, for the king's wealth and magnificence far outstripped that of his minister; but the fact that Wolsey could be so close to the king that his principal country mansions were continually at his master's disposal. Equally presumptuous was his design for the Field of Cloth of Gold where he gave himself accommodation equal, and next to, the king's. Wolsey lived in a world where proximity to the king was the essence of political power and his architectural output reflected this fact. For the king, Wolsey's mansions were a luxury to be enjoyed, for Wolsey's enemies they were snares to entice the king further into the cardinal's grasp.

In terms of function, apart from the intimate connections with the king, Wolsey's houses can be seen as direct descendants of the houses of Warham and Morton. In terms of form, Wolsey's buildings can be compared with the royal and courtier buildings of the first part of the reign of Henry VIII.

Perhaps the most distinctive feature of Wolsey's houses was the form of his long galleries. In the first quarter of the sixteenth century in England there was a

---

[82] P. A. Faulkner, 'Some medieval archiepiscopal palaces', *Archaeological Journal*, 127 (1970), 144; A. D. Stoyel, 'The lost buildings of Otford Palace', *Archaeologia Cantiana*, 100 (1984), 259–81; *DNB* sub. Warham.

[83] N. Pevsner, *Hertfordshire*, The Buildings of England (Harmondsworth, 1978), pp. 164–5; D. Gardiner, *The Story of Lambeth Palace* (London, 1930) pp. 66–7; P. A. Faulkner, 'Some medieval archiepiscopal palaces', *Archaeological Journal*, 127 (1970), 135; A. Emery, 'Ralph, Lord Cromwell's manor at Wingfield: its construction, design and influence', *Archaeological Journal*, 142 (1985), 324; *DNB* sub. Morton.

[84] Including Bourchier, and the great secular lord, Ralph, Lord Cromwell.

group of long galleries of a particular and unusual form built for Wolsey or under his direction. These were at Hampton Court (fig. 6), York Place (fig. 5), The More (fig. 7), Esher, Guines (fig. 8), Beaulieu, Southwell and Bridewell (fig. 3), and six of these (for nothing is known about the galleries at Southwell and Beaulieu) exhibited identical characteristics. They were superficially built on the Richmond-type plan; that is to say they jutted out from the main house into the gardens. But there was an important difference. At Richmond the galleries formed part of a unified garden layout, they were not part of the house proper. From the main palace they ran out and around the gardens as did the galleries built by the duke of Buckingham at Thornbury.[85]

Wolsey's galleries were altogether different. They led nowhere (with the possible exception of that at Guines which led to the chapel). At Hampton Court, The More and Esher the gallery ended in two small towers, at York Place in a stair turret and at Bridewell in a watergate. It is clear that the gallery was nothing new in England in the early sixteenth century,[86] but the form which Wolsey's galleries took was. The distinguishing factor was that his galleries were free-standing, connected at one end to the house and at the other protruding into the gardens. Even the galleries at Richmond had been connected either to each other or back to the main house: none of them were dead ends.

The Wolsey gallery was, in this respect unique. At each house it was about 250 feet long, at each house it overlooked gardens, and at York Place (fig. 5), The More (fig. 7) and Esher the galleries were set off by running beside, or running over, water. Mario Savorgnano's well-known description of Wolsey's galleries as 'long porticoes or halls, without chambers, with windows on each side, looking on gardens or rivers' clearly refers to these houses.[87]

Only very few possible sources for the Wolsey gallery have been identified. At Eltham Edward IV built a gallery which jutted out from his lodgings, leading nowhere. It overlooked the moat on the west facing towards London with a splendid view, on the other side it probably overlooked a garden.[88] Wolsey had extensive lodgings at Eltham (above p. 91) and undoubtedly knew the gallery well.

Two further examples of such a gallery are known. The first is Sheffield Manor, the house of George, earl of Shrewsbury, where a free standing gallery projected beyond the entrance front of the house. Shrewsbury was lord steward to Henry VII from c. 1505, and he was therefore, like Lovell and Buckingham, one of the circle of Henry VII's courtiers building in a manner similar to that of Wolsey. In this gallery Wolsey himself lodged in 1530.[89] The other example is Fulham Palace,

[85] HKW, IV, fig. 22 pp. 226; S. Thurley, 'English royal palaces', pp. 65–77; A. D. Hawkyard, 'Thornbury Castle', Bristol and Gloucester Archaeological Society Transactions, 95 (1977), 51–8.
[86] R. Coope, 'The Long Gallery: its origins, development, use and decoration', Architectural History, 29 (1986), 43–50.
[87] CSPV, IV, 682.   [88] S. Thurley, 'English royal palaces', pp. 34–9.
[89] R. Coope, 'The long gallery', p. 48; Cavendish, p. 163.

the house of the bishops of London where there was a free-standing gallery running eastwards into the gardens. It is unclear who was responsible for this but it is suggested here that Cuthbert Tunstall (bishop 1522–30) may have been the builder.[90]

Clearly Wolsey's galleries were an innovation but otherwise there was little new or surprising about the plan of Bridewell, Guines or York Place. These houses relied on the standard formula of three grand outward chambers followed by a more private inner chamber. This arrangement could be found in most of Henry VII's palaces and many courtier houses of the period.[91]

This was not the case at Hampton Court for here, although Wolsey did not provide anything more than the standard three-room lodging, the disposition of the various sets of lodgings was startling. At York Place there was only space for one household, Wolsey's, but at the other buildings there was space for the households of the king and queen as well. At Guines they faced each other across a courtyard (fig. 8), likewise at Bridewell they were ranged round a court, but there is evidence that the king and queen were lodged on different levels connected by a stair, the king's lodgings being above the queen's and taller and grander than hers (fig. 3).[92]

At Hampton Court there is no doubt that this stacked arrangement existed. As outlined above, there were three tiers, the queen on the second floor, the king on the first and Mary on the ground floor (plate 21). This was no coincidence or accident. Other options had been open to Wolsey: he could have built lodgings on the same level to the east as Henry VIII was later to do. It would have been easier and cheaper than rebuilding the main range three storeys high and providing a grand staircase. The architectural possibilities of such an arrangement were, of course, greater than those provided by a plan all on the same level, for a staircase could be used to great effect. Certainly the stair tower at Hampton Court was; it contained, at its highest level, a prospect chamber facing the park and gardens to the east. Both the palace at Guines and that at Bridewell also had spectacular stairs.

Wolsey's Hampton Court was not the only house to adopt this arrangement. It was one of a group of houses built between 1500 and 1530 in which the lodgings were arranged vertically rather than horizontally. The builders of these were all men of Henry VII's and Wolsey's generation and not of Henry VIII's. At Thornbury Castle, Gloucestershire, built by the duke of Buckingham the lodgings were stacked (plate 19). The duchess of Buckingham was lodged beneath the

[90] *Fulham Palace Management Plan*: S. Thurley, 'History', pp. 22–3 (plan b and j and development plan iii); R. Rodwell, 'Archaeological appraisal and plan', fig. 20; for Tunstall's connections with Wolsey's and the king's works at Whitehall see Bodl. MS vet. E i,b 6 (back cover recto).

[91] S. Thurley, 'English royal palaces', pp. 57–86; M. Howard, *The Early Tudor Country House, Architecture and Politics 1490–1550* (London, 1987), pp. 73–83.

[92] S. Thurley, 'English royal palaces', pp. 94–107.

duke, who occupied the first floor rooms with hugely tall windows.[93] Thornbury was one of the most important houses built in the first years of Henry VIII's reign, and as we have seen, Lawrence Stubbs, a key man in Wolsey's works organization, had been closely involved in its construction.

Another important building to adopt the stacked lodging was the house of Sir Thomas Lovell at Enfield. Not only were Lovell and Wolsey colleagues at Henry VII's court but his house has already been closely compared to Hampton Court, as it also provided extensive lodgings for the king.[94] A third house, another belonging to a courtier of Wolsey's generation, was Kenninghall, the house of the duke of Norfolk. Here again the ducal rooms were situated on the second floor above those of the duchess.[95]

The earliest English example of the stacked lodging range so far identified is at Maxstoke Castle, Warwickshire, where Lady Margaret Beaufort built herself a new three storey timber-framed north range in the 1480s and 90s (plate 20).[96] However this is unlikely to have been the English model for the rash of important courtier houses with stacked lodgings. The model was almost certainly Richmond Palace, the core of which was the massive stone three-storey *donjon* containing the king's and queen's lodgings one above the other.[97] Richmond itself was heavily influenced by the Franco-Burgundian architecture of Northern Europe, and when some French examples are considered both Wolsey's work and that of Henry VII at Richmond can be seen as part of a wider European movement.

In the first part of his reign Francis I of France was building stacked lodgings. At Blois, where Francis built a new wing between 1515 and 1524, the king lodged above the queen, with a *grande vis* connecting their lodgings. This was also the case at Chambord (begun 1519) where the main lodgings were, as at Richmond, stacked in an enormous donjon. The arrangement was also in operation at St Germain en Laye, and the Château of Madrid (plate 22).[98] Indeed, Anthony Blunt observed 'All these buildings are of very singular design, unlike anything else in French architecture. They are of unusual height . . .'.[99] The king's later works at Fontainebleau do not share the same vertical accent but lie all on a level as do Henry VIII's palaces built after 1530.

The fashion for the stacked lodging was probably popularized by the Burgundian ducal palaces of the late fifteenth century such as Princenhof, the Codenberg

---

[93] See the survey in BL Stowe MS 795 fol. 60.   [94] See the inventory in PRO, PROB 2/199.

[95] See the survey in PRO, LR2/115 fols. 34, 40v.

[96] N. W. Alcock, P. A. Faulkner and S. R. Jones with a contribution by G. M. D. Booth, 'Maxstoke Castle', *Archaeological Journal*, 135 (1978), 216–18.

[97] *HKW*, IV, p. 225; S. Thurley, 'English royal palaces' pp. 71–2.

[98] F. Lesuer, *Le Château De Blois* (Paris, 1970) pp. 119–24; J. Guillaume, 'Comprendre Chambord', *Dossier Technique de Monuments Historiques*, 2 (1983); M. Chatenet, 'Une Demure royale au milieu du XVIe siècle: La distribution des espaces au château de Saint Germain-en-Laye', *Revue De L'Art*, 81 (1988), 25; M. Chatenet, *Le Château de Madrid au Bois de Boulogne* (Paris, 1987), pp. 99–105.

[99] A. Blunt, *Art and Architecture in France 1500–1700* (Harmondsworth, 1982), p. 51.

and Ghent. These buildings comprised three-storey ranges with processional staircases and tower lodgings for the dukes, built, as the urban palaces of northern Italy, upwards and not outwards. The architecture of both the English and French courts reflected these concerns and Wolsey, who had spent his political apprenticeship at the court of Henry VII, and had subsequently seen many of these buildings first hand, was surely likewise influenced.

Wolsey was better travelled than many of his contemporaries. Before 1509, he had been chaplain to Sir Richard Nanfan, deputy of Calais, and would presumably have travelled to the Low Countries; subsequently Henry VII had used him on embassies and he had visited Flanders and Calais several times. The most important house we know that he saw in this period was Margaret of Austria's palace at Mechelen where he stayed for four days in 1508.[100] In the early years of Henry VIII's reign he, together with the rest of the court, would have seen Tournai and Lille during the first French war. Later, on his magnificent embassy to Charles V in 1521, he was entertained at Bruges. The Emperor would have lodged at the ducal palace of Princenhof and Wolsey is certain to have seen this at close quarters. The importance of these visits would have been to reinforce his enthusiasm for the buildings of Henry VII, buildings themselves influenced by Franco-Burgundian models.

Wolsey's adoption of the stacked lodging at Hampton Court was part of a wider European movement, one which he had experienced directly in Burgundy and northern France and indirectly through the buildings of Henry VII and his courtiers. We know far less about the free-standing gallery but its adoption by Edward IV at Eltham and its adaptation by Henry VII at Richmond indicate that Wolsey was building in a well established tradition, if not in a well established form.

In the later part of Henry VIII's reign neither the stacked lodging nor the free-standing gallery continued in fashion. The free-standing gallery was entirely abandoned by Henry VIII and his courtiers. Of Wolsey's galleries only the one at The More survived until the reign of Elizabeth, the others were absorbed into an overall plan where they became a means of communication between various parts of the building rather than being a part in themselves.

The stacked lodging was likewise abandoned. At Hampton Court after 1529 it is known that the grand second floor rooms built by Wolsey were used by the queen and that Henry's first move was to replace them with new lodgings for the queen on the same level as his own, consigning the second floor rooms to courtiers.[101] This perhaps suggests that Henry disliked the stacked arrangement of Richmond, Bridewell and the continent. Perhaps, then, this dislike of

[100] J. Gairdner, (ed.), *Letters and Papers Illustrative of the Reigns of Richard III and Henry VII* (London, 1861), I p. 438.
[101] S. Thurley, 'Henry VIII and the building of Hampton Court: a reconstruction of the Tudor Palace', *Architectural History*, 31 (1988), 13–16.

up-and-down living explains why he rarely visited the house and why in 1530, when he took up residence, the building accounts indicate that he lived on the first floor.

Therefore in his use of the stacked lodging Wolsey continued a fashion which Henry VII had instituted, and which must have been reinforced during his many continental trips. It is significant that courtiers of Wolsey's generation, Buckingham, Lovell and Norfolk, should build in a similar manner. And equally significant that Henry, the figurehead of the next generation, should so dislike the arrangement that he lived on the first floor at Hampton Court and made Bridewell over to be the residence of the French ambassadors, who, he perhaps felt, would appreciate such an arrangement.

One element of the stacked lodging outlived Wolsey, and that was the processional staircase which inevitably accompanied the tall lodging ranges. Almost all royal and courtier houses of the later part of Henry's reign adopted a grand staircase as an entrance to the main lodgings and the fashion continued well into Elizabeth's reign and beyond.[102] Indeed, Wren's state staircases at Hampton Court and Kensington follow, not the baroque models of the continent, but the indigenous example of Wolsey's processional stairs.

To conclude, Wolsey used his buildings both as a display of his magnificence and for political advantage. York Place was a base for his legal power as lord chancellor, his country houses, especially Hampton Court, were expressly designed to entertain important political visitors and more crucially, the king. Once Wolsey was dead most of his architectural innovations were abandoned and so although the core of Henry VIII's collection of palaces was made up of those which he inherited from Wolsey, the final form of those important and influential buildings owed little to the influence of the cardinal. It was Wolsey's development of the fashions of the reign of Henry VII which consigned his architectural influence after 1530 to a mere footnote. Professor Scarisbrick writes in his life of Henry VIII that Wolsey was, to an extent, a creature of the previous reign. This is certainly true in terms of his architectural output, which according to the rules of Henry VII's reign may have been *avant garde* but to the court of Henry VIII was completely out of date.

---

[102] S. Thurley, 'English royal palaces', pp. 207–8; Howard, *The Early Tudor Country House*, pp. 82–5; M. Girouard, *Robert Smythson and the Elizabethan Country House* (London, 1983).

CHAPTER 3

Cardinal Wolsey's collegiate foundations

JOHN NEWMAN

Cardinal Wolsey is celebrated as the founder of Cardinal College, Oxford, the princely establishment which, although in existence for less than five years, 1525–9, bequeathed essential elements of its constitution and a substantial part of its buildings, to present-day Christ Church.[1] Less familiar, but integral to Wolsey's educational conception, was Cardinal College, Ipswich, a grammar school in the town of his birth, which was to act as a feeder for his college at Oxford. The licence to found this was not granted until June 1528, so its buildings were less far advanced at its founder's fall, and although pupils were already being taught by January 1529,[2] this junior foundation was easily suppressed and enjoyed no afterlife. The object of this paper is to set Wolsey's two colleges within the context of earlier dual foundations, to suggest that for Wolsey they formed only a part of wider academic ambitions, and to discuss their most notable features both academically and architecturally.[3]

Wolsey's ultimate model was William of Wykeham's pair of colleges at Oxford and Winchester. Wykeham, who had become bishop of Winchester in 1366, wanted to increase the supply of secular clergy after the Black Death, by providing educational opportunities for 'poor and indigent scholars'.[4] Grammar, as the 'foundation, door and spring of all other liberal arts and sciences', was to be taught at Winchester, while New College, Oxford, unlike earlier Oxford colleges, was to cater principally for scholars between the ages of fifteen and twenty following the arts course to the BA degree,[5] thus inaugurating what was eventually to become the norm for all Oxford and Cambridge colleges except All Souls. Wykeham built his college at Oxford first, in 1380–6, proceeding at once with his grammar school, on which work started in 1387.[6] Each foundation had seventy scholars or fellows, and together with the priests and choristers who served the chapel, and the butler, the cooks and others who ran daily life, each formed a community of a little over 100. The buildings at Oxford (fig. 9) and

---

[1] *VCH Oxfordshire*, III (1954), 228–38. [2] *VCH Suffolk*, II (1907), 142–3.
[3] For the academic aspects of this subject see J. McConica (ed.), *The History of the University of Oxford*, III (Oxford, 1986), pp. 29–32.
[4] *VCH Oxon*, III, 154. [5] Ibid. [6] Ibid., 114.

Winchester closely resembled each other, ranges forming a quadrangle with the hall and the chapel end-to-end on one side, a muniment tower linked to them, and on the other three sides an upper-floor library and chambers for the inmates, the warden's lodging being over the entrance gateway. Each had a cemetery cloister as well, that at New College supplied with a bell tower.[7]

In the mid fifteenth century Wykeham's foundations inspired the king himself to emulation. In 1440 Henry VI founded Eton College close to the royal castle at Windsor, and the next year King's College, Cambridge, for a rector and twelve scholars. Letters patent of 1443, however, refounded King's, Cambridge, on a much larger scale and the founder stated his determination that scholars of Eton, when sufficiently instructed in grammar, and after examination, should proceed to King's. By 1445 it was clear that the number of scholars at King's was to be seventy. The scholars at Eton were at first to number twenty-four, but here too they were soon raised to seventy.[8] At Eton the buildings took many decades to construct, and at Cambridge the great chapel represents Henry VI's later ideas (and then much modified). However, his so-called 'will' details with remarkable precision the way in which his colleges were to be laid out.[9] The proposed layout at King's (Introduction, fig. 1b) clearly shows the inspiration of New College, in particular the cemetery cloister and tower and the muniment tower over the hall porch. The major difference, of course, is the greatly enlarged chapel, intended to occupy one whole side of the main quadrangle.

Henry VI's deposition in 1461 put the future of his foundations at risk. That they survived seems to have been largely due to the care and determination of William Waynflete, whom the King appointed overseer of his will as far as it related to Eton and King's.[10] Waynflete's experience was highly relevant; he had taught at Winchester, had been the first provost of Eton, became bishop of Winchester and in 1456 chancellor of England. As early as 1448 Waynflete had founded an academic hall in Oxford, and in 1458 he founded Magdalen College. Construction of the college buildings did not begin until 1474 and the statutes date from 1480. Here too the foundation included seventy scholars: forty seniors, the fellows, studying for MA degrees, and thirty juniors, demies as they were called, studying for the BA. Educationally the major innovation at Magdalen was the establishment of three lectureships, one in theology and two in philosophy. One other feature of the college should be mentioned: part of its endowment was provided by suppressing a number of decayed monastic establishments.[11]

[7] J. H. Harvey, 'Winchester College', Journal of the British Archaeological Association, 28 (1965), 107–28 and J. H. Harvey, 'The buildings of Winchester College', in R. Custance (ed.), Winchester College Sixth-centenary Essays (Oxford, 1982), pp. 77–127; G. Jackson-Stops, 'The buildings of the medieval college', in J. Buxton and P. Williams (eds.), New College Oxford 1379–1979 (Oxford, 1979), pp. 147–92.

[8] VCH Cambridgeshire, III (1959), 376–9.

[9] R. Willis and J. W. Clark, The Architectural History of the University of Cambridge (1889), I, pp. 368–70. See also F. Woodman, The Architectural History of King's College Chapel (London, 1986), pp. 71–2.

[10] Ibid., 379.   [11] VCH Oxon, III, 193–5, 203.

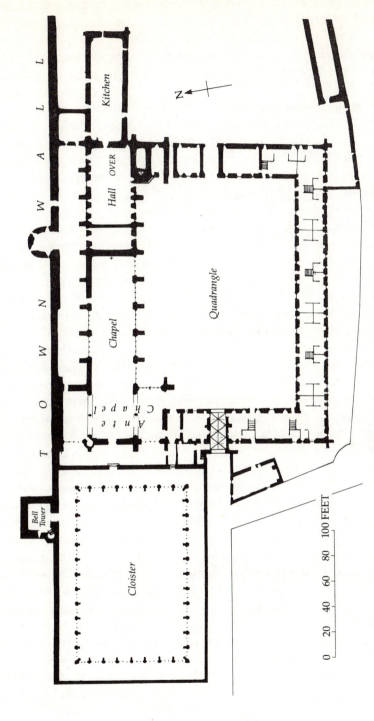

Fig. 9 Plan of New College, Oxford (adapted from *RCHM, Oxford*; chamber layout based on *VCH* schematic plan)

The buildings of Magdalen College were once again laid out along the lines of those at New College (plate 23). The main residential quadrangle has chapel and hall end-to-end in the south range, but the muniment tower is linked to the ante-chapel rather than the hall. A second, more prominent tower, the Founder's tower, stands over the entrance and housed the college head. Most prominent of all, in size and in position, is the bell tower, successor to the cemetery towers built at New College and planned for King's, Cambridge. The architectural novelty at Magdalen is the cloister which runs round all four ranges of the quadrangle and over which the upper chambers extend. This is an idea borrowed probably from Eton, where the Cloister Court begun in the mid fifteenth century is arranged in this way. It may also be seen as an integration of the cemetery cloister of New College with the residential ranges.

Waynflete founded not one but two feeder schools for his college. One was on a site adjoining the college, the predecessor of the present Magdalen College School; the other was established at Waynflete's birthplace, Wainfleet All Saints in Lincolnshire.[12] Wainfleet School was a very modest affair, to consist of a chapel and a school-house for just seven boys. The range erected in 1484 still survives, of brick measuring 70 feet by 20 feet, with the school-room above and the schoolmaster's lodging below. Only a two-towered entrance front gives it an air of some consequence. Magdalen College School had a more significant role to play. It seems to have provided a focus for the grammar teaching for which Oxford was well known throughout the Middle Ages. The college paid the salary of the grammar master, at the same high rate of £10 per annum as the lecturer in theology. However it was not strictly a feeder school, for there seems to have been no special mechanism to enable boys to pass from school to college.

Some of the innovations of Wykeham and Waynflete were picked up by a third bishop of Winchester, Richard Fox, whose foundation, Corpus Christi College, Oxford, was established by 1517.[13] This was a smaller institution, with only twenty fellows and twenty undergraduate 'discipuli' aged between twelve and seventeen, each of whom shared a chamber with and was under the academic direction of a fellow. Fox's mentor in this foundation and a major benefactor to it was Hugh Oldham, bishop of Exeter and founder of Manchester Grammar School; but Oldham's school was given no special preference in recruiting scholars for Corpus. Like Waynflete, Fox attached three public lecturers to his college, to teach theology, humanity and Greek. The authors they were to expound clearly indicate the intention to promote the new humanist curriculum.

The buildings of Corpus are modest in scale and pretension, though erected under the supervision of leading master-craftsmen of the day, the masons William Vertue and William East, and the carpenters Humfrey Cooke and Robert Carow.

Now at last we may turn to Wolsey. He became a fellow of Magdalen College, Oxford, in about 1491, and acted as college bursar in 1499–1500. His knowledge of

---

[12] *VCH Lincolnshire*, II (1906), 483–4.   [13] *VCH Oxon*, III, 219–28.

Magdalen and its ways coloured much of what he subsequently achieved. A first sign of this, as Dr John Blair has recently suggested, was to be found at the monastic St Mary's College, the completion of which Wolsey urged on in 1518. Excavation of the site of St Mary's has revealed a cloistered quadrangle of the Magdalen type. The chapel roof (reused in the 1650s in the chapel at Brasenose and thus the only part of the buildings of St Mary's to have survived) is structurally identical with the hall roof at Corpus, designed by Humfrey Cooke and constructed by Robert Carow in 1517–18.[14]

But this was a minor initiative. Far more revealing of his ambition was the offer which he made in an oration to the assembled University that same year, 1518, to found and maintain daily lectures and to revise the university statutes.[15] Though the university masters were keen to accept these offers, the last in particular cut across the jurisdiction of the chancellor, Warham, archbishop of Canterbury, who succeeded in preventing their acceptance.[16] Nevertheless there is evidence that between 1518 and 1523 Wolsey funded on a somewhat ad hoc basis four public lecturers, two of whom were resident at Corpus.[17] Their relationship to Fox's lecturers is not clear. Eight years later Wolsey offered to enlarge his benefaction to the University, promising to establish seven university lecturers at high salaries, in theology, canon law and the arts, to engage learned foreigners to teach, and to rebuild the Schools where lectures took place.[18] Once again, nothing directly came of this, but, as we shall see, the provision for public lecturers was rolled up in his new college.

In founding his college at Oxford Wolsey seems not to have had in mind such a constricted model as that provided by Winchester-and-New College or Eton-and-King's, but rather to have intended a broader and perhaps looser school–college relationship as suggested by Waynflete's foundations. At any rate, the statutes of Cardinal College, Oxford, refer to the election of the forty petty-canons (i.e. the undergraduate members) from the Founder's schools (in the plural): 'for we have it in mind to build and endow schools in several regions of this kingdom in order to train up youth in the study of grammar'.[19] The school at Ipswich then would have been only the first of a number founded to feed able boys to Wolsey's college at Oxford. Lack of time prevented the realization of this vision, not lack of money; for Wolsey's method of endowing his colleges at Oxford and Ipswich by suppressing monasteries and appropriating rectories could doubtless have been extended to fund other new schools.

---

[14] J. Blair, 'Frewin Hall, Oxford: a Norman mansion and a monastic college', *Oxoniensia*, 43 (1978), 90–4.

[15] W. T. Mitchell (ed.), *Epistolae Academicae, 1508–96* (Oxford Historical Society; new series 26, 1980), no. 63.

[16] E. Mullally, 'Wolsey's proposed reform of the Oxford University statutes: a recently discovered text', *Bodleian Library Record*, 10 (1978–82), 22–7.

[17] McConica (ed.), 338–9.   [18] Mitchell (ed.), no. 136.

[19] *Statutes of the Colleges of Oxford* (1853) ii, [11], 21.

Cardinal College, Oxford, was endowed with the site and revenues of St Frideswide's Priory, and with the revenues of twenty other monastic houses suppressed for the purpose, in various parts of the country, some as far away as Kent and Sussex. These, with the addition of several Oxfordshire rectories, raised an endowment worth £2,000 per annum.[20]

The first formal step to found Wolsey's college in Oxford was taken in April 1524, when he obtained a papal bull authorizing the suppression of St Frideswide's Priory. The statutes of the new college made provision for a dean, who was to be head of the college, a sub-dean, an academic establishment consisting of sixty canons, who were to be graduates, forty petty-canons studying for the BA, four censors or tutors chosen from among the canons, and most significantly, six public lecturers (in theology, humanity, canon law, civil law, philosophy and medicine), so the university lecturers whom Wolsey had funded for the past few years were now to be increased in number and attached to the new college; though their supra-collegiate responsibilities were indicated by the method of their election, by a committee consisting of most other college heads as well as senior members of their own college, and by the oath they were required to take not to interfere in the business of the college.[21]

In size therefore Wolsey's academic body outstripped all its models. In ethos it was to resemble Corpus, canon and petty-canon sharing chambers together. However, the fact that fellows and scholars were entitled 'canons' suggests Wolsey's aim to stress continuity with the suppressed St Frideswide's Priory. In the early days of the new college it is more than once officially referred to as St Frideswide's College, and Wolsey deferred the formal entry of the dean and first canons into the college in 1526 until St Frideswide's day.[22] The statutes of the new college defined its objectives as both the pursuit of learning and the 'perpetual observance of the worship of God', and to this end the college body included thirteen priests, twelve clerks, sixteen boy choristers and a music master.[23] So it would seem that in suppressing the Priory and building his new college on the site Wolsey did not mean to slight the patron saint of Oxford but to honour her more appropriately with his new nationally beneficial foundation. As Professor Scarisbrick has pointed out, Wolsey's redirection of monastic wealth into educational channels was a precedent which Henry VIII should have followed, but did not.[24]

The size of the whole community envisaged by its founder correlated closely with the £2,000 per annum which the appropriated revenues produced. Estimates among the state papers show that a total of 181 persons – from the dean down to the 'poor woman' who was to 'attend on the thirteen poor men daily

[20] LP, IV (i) 1137–8, 1499.   [21] Statutes of the Colleges of Oxford (1853), ii, [11], 12ff., 123.
[22] LP, IV (ii) 2457.
[23] Statutes of the Colleges of Oxford (1853), ii, [11], 13, 49–51.
[24] J. J. Scarisbrick, Henry VIII (Harmondsworth, 1971), p. 658.

attending upon the church' – were to receive stipends, liveries and commons at graduated rates which, together with extra stipends for teaching and bursarial duties and 'pittances' distributed on church festival days, amounted to an estimated total of £1,982.[25]

Erection of the new college buildings to house this great community began in January 1525, and continued for almost five years. The expense was prodigious, totalling £8,882 up to the end of December 1527, and from 1 November 1528 to 24 October 1529, when the last payments towards the unfinished building were made, a further £8,400. This leaves most of 1528 unaccounted for, and assuming expenditure of only a little over £5,000 during that period the total will have reached the colossal figure of £22,000.[26]

Wolsey's master craftsmen for this job were, not surprisingly, some of the most experienced men of the day. The three master-masons had worked for him for the past decade, Henry Redman as master mason at York Place, John Lebons and William Johnson at Hampton Court. It was they who in February 1525 produced the designs for the new building, Redman and Lebons viewing the site and 'devising the building' and Johnson making moulds. Redman was probably the principal designer, for he had already had considerable experience: in 1509 he had given advice over the completion of King's College Chapel, Cambridge, and in 1517 he helped to produce the design at Eton for the completion of the cloister court and for Lupton's Tower. It was also relevant that he, and his father before him, had been chief masons at Westminster Abbey for many years.[27]

The master carpenters on the other hand had already been active in Oxford. Humfrey Cooke had helped to design Corpus and acted as master carpenter there, with Robert Carow, an Oxford man, as executant carpenter. This partnership was repeated at Cardinal College, and, as we have seen, Wolsey may already have had experience of their workmanship at St Mary's College. On the other hand, Cooke was master carpenter to the crown and had been involved in design work at Eton.[28]

This meant that Wolsey's knowledge of Magdalen, combined with the experience of his craftsmen at Eton, at King's and at Corpus enabled the architectural design of Cardinal College to draw on all the recent colleges which we have seen were in academic terms particularly relevant. Through Redman and Cooke intimate knowledge of royal works could also be brought to bear. But it was clearly Wolsey's objective to outdo in scale and magnificence every relevant model. Though a great deal was achieved, at his fall much remained incomplete, and subsequent completion to a very different design has made it difficult to grasp much that he and his designers had in mind.

[25] PRO, sp1/35, fos. 81–90.
[26] PRO, e101/479/11 covers the earlier period, PRO, sp1/55 fos. 221–38 the later.
[27] J. H. Harvey, *English Medieval Architects* (revised ed. Gloucester, 1984), pp. 172–3, 246–7.
[28] Ibid., pp. 64–5.

The Christ Church familiar to us today is comprehensively depicted in David Loggan's engraving of 1675 (plate 24). However it shows the entrance gateway as left by Wolsey, without Wren's octagonal bell-stage; also absent, of course, is the C19 tower over the stair to the hall. Much that Loggan shows was then brand new; only three years previously had the great quadrangle finally been completed, by the erection of the north range and the north-west tower. The quadrangle thus enclosed was almost square, 276 ft by 271 ft, and it was all unified by continuous balustrading round the wall head within the quadrangle and on the west front. All this, therefore, must be discounted if we are to envisage the original design.

The original layout of the college is best described in a progress-report sent by Dr John London, warden of New College, to Thomas Larke, one of Wolsey's building administrators, at the end of 1526, when the footings of all four ranges of the quadrangle were in, the west range roofed, the kitchen already in use, and work going ahead vigorously on the south range including the hall.[29] Dr London reveals that the chapel was to be in the north range, on the opposite side of the quadrangle from the hall, not end-to-end with it as had been the case at New College and Magdalen. How long the chapel would have been is not known, for the footings were removed in 1671 and no one thought to record them. However John Aubrey did make a sketch of the decorated basement moulding, and it is interesting that he compares it with the moulding at King's chapel, Cambridge, pointing out the greater richness of the later work: 'The rich water-table tempore Henry 8. In Hen. 6. 'twas only plaine, as in the margent'.[30] Surely Wolsey will have wanted to outdo King's chapel in dimensions as well as in richness of decoration. It seems a fair presumption that foundations were laid for a chapel more than 289 feet long.

In the west range, according to Dr London's progress-report, there were lodgings, and the great tower over the gateway there was already built up as high as the roofs of the lodgings, i.e. in the state shown by Loggan. The almost free-standing sixteen-sided turrets flanking the gateway display richly panelled surfaces (plate 25) reminiscent of the exterior of Henry VII's chapel at Westminster Abbey (plate 5). The probable designer of the chapel, Robert Janyns, had earlier used strongly polygonal forms in domestic architecture on Henry VII's tower at Windsor (plate 26). Doubtless it was intended to raise the Christ Church gateway with a square outline and higher angle turrets, in the form familiar from contemporary Cambridge college gateways. At the south end of the entrance range stood what is also called by London a 'great tower', the lower two storeys of which had been completed. The south-west tower was never finished, though the seventeenth-century balustrade curtails it quite con-

[29] LP, IV (ii) 2734.
[30] H. M. Colvin, 'Aubrey's Chronologia Architectonica', pl. 4, in J. Summerson, (ed.), *Concerning Architecture, Essays . . . Presented to Nikolaus Pevsner* (London, 1968).

vincingly. The polygonal angle-turrets and oriel window belong to the original design, though the stonework is all refaced, and Wolsey's badges and cardinal's hat occur frequently. It is perhaps most likely that this tower was intended as a chamber tower associated with the dean's lodging, the rest of which would have been appropriately sited in the south range of the quadrangle west of the hall.

The hall itself, the foundations of which were only five or six feet high at the time of the progress-report, was finished just as Wolsey fell: its windows were glazed with his arms and motto in the autumn of 1529. The hall is raised on a high basement, like those at New College and Magdalen, but its length, 114 feet 6 inches, and breadth, 39 feet 9 inches, are twenty-five per cent greater than those of any earlier Oxford hall, reflecting the unprecedented size of the college community.

A sketch of the college in 1566 shows a further tower, over the site of the hall stairs; presumably this will have been for the college muniments, as at New College.[31] As for the east range Dr London refers to the foundations of lodgings here. The college library was presumably intended for the upper storey of this range. At this point the church of St Frideswide impinged and remained for the time being fully in use. London enthused about the quality of the college services 'both working day and holy day'. The first new building to be brought into use lay outside the quadrangle altogether. This was the kitchen, where Christmas dinner was prepared for the dean and canons in 1526.

It remains to mention the cloister. This was to run round the inner walls of the quadrangle. Its foundations were almost all in by the end of 1526. Wall-shafts and the springing of vaulting against the walls of the west and south ranges indicate the form the cloister would have taken. This too was an expansion of a feature introduced less obtrusively into other recent colleges, at Eton from the mid fifteenth century and at Queens', Cambridge, and, most relevantly, Magdalen, Oxford, in the 1490s (plate 23). But only at Cardinal College was the cloister to stand free in front of the ranges in the manner of a monastic cloister. And here too, as John Harvey has pointed out, there is a connection with Westminster, for St Stephen's cloister, arranged in the way envisaged at Cardinal College, but two-storeyed, dates from these same years, 1526–9.[32]

Cardinal College was clearly one of the most important late gothic buildings in England. What else can we say about its intended overall effect? The cloister would have tended to pull the quadrangle, surrounded by ranges of varied height and form, into a strongly unified whole. The most interesting question concerns the entrance front: was it conceived as a similarly unified composition? One can at least say that it was completely different from New College, which

31 Reproduced in *VCH Oxon*, III, 221.
32 J. G. Milne and J. H. Harvey, 'The building of Cardinal College, Oxford', *Oxoniensia*, 89 (1943–4), 149.

had no outward face at all, and from Magdalen, which was primarily inward-looking and had irregular frontages both towards the street and westwards toward a walled forecourt. By contrast Cardinal College makes a great deal of its entrance front. Here for the first time in Oxford was a gate-tower with boldly expansive angle turrets. And its decorative treatment, as already noted, allies it with the most up-to-date and prestigious of royal works. Another less obvious but equally effective innovation was the siting of the chimney-breasts of the west range, not as had been the universal practice on the outer wall but towards the quadrangle, where the cloister would mask them. This freed the outer wall for exceptionally large windows lighting the chambers and studies, and thus created an outward-looking character to the whole range.

This leads one on to ask the question, what overall composition was intended for the entrance front. In particular, would it have been symmetrical, designed in a way analogous to Thornbury Castle, Gloucestershire, which had been built, from c. 1511, with an overpoweringly symmetrical entrance front and irregular, if exquisitely detailed, inner ranges. Symmetry was soon to become an overriding aesthetic requirement, so it is important to determine what was intended at Cardinal College.

Howard Colvin, in his recent conjectural reconstruction of the original design (fig. 1a), comes down firmly against symmetry.[33] Strictly considered, he appears to be right; but there are two features of his reconstruction which fail to convince. First, while indicating a chapel like that at King's, Cambridge, he shows it extending only the length of the quadrangle within the cloister arcades; but this would make the chapel only 240 feet long, 50 feet shorter than the chapel at King's. This would hardly have satisfied Wolsey. It is much more likely that the chapel was to have extended eastwards to give it a freestanding east wall (as King's chapel has) and the extra 50 feet desired. Secondly, at the west end, such a low ante-chapel as Colvin suggests is quite contrary to Oxford practice, which went in for broad and lofty ante-chapels, as can be seen at all the grandest colleges, Merton, New College, All Souls, and Magdalen. A tall ante-chapel would also strengthen the design of the west front of the college, even though it would not make it symmetrical. John Aubrey's note under his sketch of the chapel basement decoration reads: 'This was the Water-table and basis of the magnificent chapell or Cathedral intended by Cardinal Wolsey, which did runne from the College to the Blew-bore-Inne.' The Blue Boar Inn stood to the north of the present Blue Boar Lane, so Aubrey's comment suggests that the chapel extended a considerable way further north than the present line of the quadrangle of Christ Church.[34] This would be compatible with a substantial north-south ante-chapel. And it is tempting to suggest that the moulding sketched by Aubrey may have been on this ante-chapel wall, the part nearest the Blue Boar Inn, not on the flank of the chapel within the quadrangle.

[33] H. M. Colvin, *Unbuilt Oxford* (New Haven and London, 1983), pl. 7.
[34] A. Clark (ed.), *Wood's City of Oxford*, Oxford Historical Society, 5 (1889), 155–6, 17 (1890), 56.

1   Christ Church, formerly Cardinal College, Oxford (photo: P. G. Lindley)

2   King's College Chapel, Cambridge (photo: Tim Rawle)

3 Brick Gateway, Cardinal College, Ipswich (photo: John Blatchly)

4 Bishop Alcock's chantry chapel, Ely Cathedral (photo: Royal Commission on the Historical Monuments of England)

5 Henry VII's Chapel, Westminster Abbey

6 Cardinal College, Ipswich, seal (appended to PRO,
E24/23/15, photo: Public Record Office, London)

7 Cardinal College, Oxford, seal (appended to PRO,
E322/188, photo: Public Record Office, London)

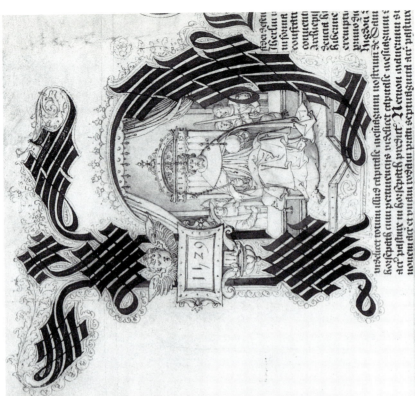

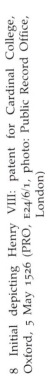

9 Initial depicting Henry VIII: patent for Cardinal College, Oxford, 25 May 1529 (PRO, E24/20/1, photo: Public Record Office, London)

8 Initial depicting Henry VIII: patent for Cardinal College, Oxford, 5 May 1526 (PRO, E24/6/1, photo: Public Record Office, London)

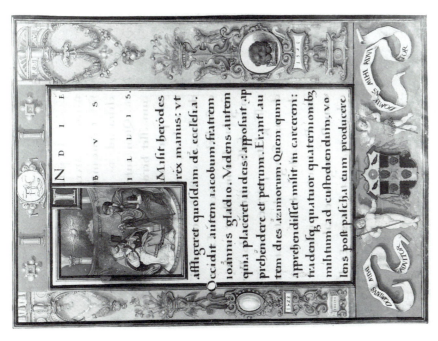

11 Christ Church, Oxford, MS 101, fol. 36 v (reproduced by permission of the Governing Body of Christ Church)

10 Christ Church, Oxford, MS 101, fol. 32 r (reproduced by permission of the Governing Body of Christ Church)

12   Ceiling of the 'Wolsey Closet', Hampton Court Palace, during conservation in 1961
(Crown copyright)

13   Detail of frieze below the ceiling of the 'Wolsey Closet', Hampton Court Palace
(Crown copyright)

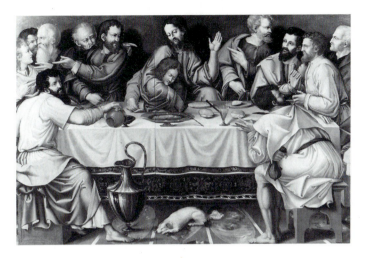

14   *The Last Supper*: panels from the 'Wolsey Closet', Hampton Court Palace (Crown copyright)

15   Detail of panels showing *The Resurrection*, with the appearance of Christ on the road to Emmaus (Crown copyright)

16   Detail of the same area as in 15, with all but a fragment of the overpainting removed to reveal the earlier painting on the reused panels (1962) (Crown copyright)

17 York Place, Westminster. View of the undercroft of Wolsey's great chamber as revealed in 1939 (photo: English Heritage)

18 Hampton Court Palace. Fireplace with Wolsey's motto in the spandrels, situated in the queen's second-floor lodgings (photo: English Heritage)

19 Thornbury Castle, Avon. South front showing the duke of Buckingham's 'stacked lodging' (photo: Simon Thurley)

20 Maxstoke Castle, Warwickshire. The stacked lodging built by Lady Margaret Beaufort can be seen on the right (Photo: *Country Life*)

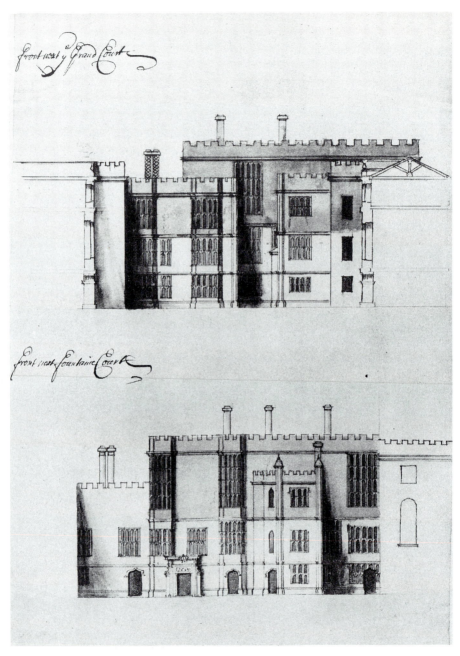

front west y Grand Court

front nest fountaine Covert

21 Hampton Court Palace. Western elevation of Wolsey's 'stacked lodging', early eighteenth-century drawing attributed to Hawksmoor (Wren Society VII, Pl. XXV)

22   The Château de Madrid, Bois de Boulogne, Paris. Southern elevation by J. A. du
Cerceau, 1576

23 D. Loggan, view of Magdalen College, Oxford (reproduced by permission of the Courtauld Institute of Art)

24 D. Loggan, view of Christ Church, Oxford (reproduced by permission of the Courtauld Institute of Art)

25   Christ Church, Oxford. Gate turret (detail) (photo: P. G. Lindley)

26   Henry VII's Tower, Windsor Castle, by J. Britton (reproduced by permission of the
Courtauld Institute of Art)

27 Christ Church hall, Oxford, bay window. Wolsey's personal badge, by J. Nicholson (photo: H. G. Wayment, by permission of the Governing Body of Christ Church)

28 National Gallery of Scotland, Edinburgh. Vidimus for a thirteen-light window.
Workshop of Erhard Schön

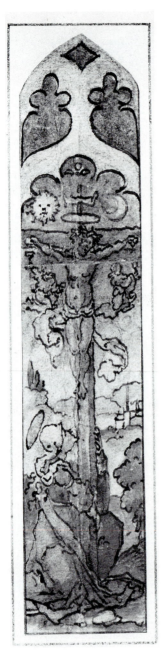

29 Musées Royaux des Beaux-Arts, Cabinet des Dessins, Brussels. *The Crucifixion with Mary Magdalene and angels*; vidimus attributed to the workshop of Erhard Schön (photo: copyright ACL-Bruxelles)

30 Musées Royaux des Beaux-Arts, Cabinet des Dessins, Brussels. *The Crucifixion with Mary Magdalene*; vidimus attributed to the workshop of Erhard Schön (photo: copyright ACL-Bruxelles)

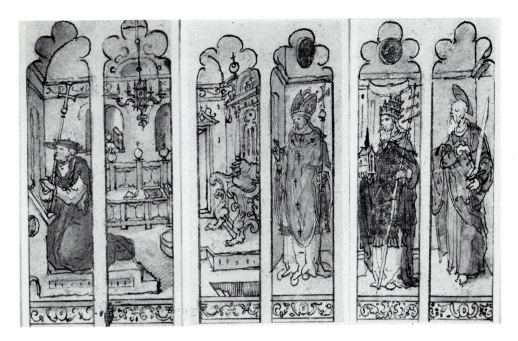

31 Musées Royaux des Beaux-Arts, Brussels. *Cardinal Wolsey, presented by SS Thomas of Canterbury, Peter and Paul*; vidimus attributed to the workshop of Erhard Schön (photo: copyright ACL-Bruxelles)

32 Musées Royaux des Beaux-Arts, Brussels. *Henry VIII, Catherine of Aragon and Princess Mary presented by SS George, Henry and Catherine*; vidimus attributed to the workshop of Erhard Schön (photo: copyright ACL-Bruxelles)

33 Musées Royaux des Beaux-Arts, Brussels. *Christ before the High Priest, Christ before Pilate, the Carrying of the Cross;* vidimus attributed to the workshop of Erhard Schön

34 Musées Royaux des Beaux-Arts, Brussels. *Deposition, Entombment* and *Resurrection of Christ;* vidimus attributed to the workshop of Erhard Schön (photo: copyright ACL-Bruxelles)

35 Musées Royaux des Beaux-Arts, Brussels. *The Adoration of the Magi* and the *Presentation*; vidimus attributed to Erhard Schön (photo: copyright ACL-Bruxelles)

36 Musées Royaux des Beaux-Arts, Brussels. *The Adoration of the Magi*; vidimus attributed to Erhard Schön (detail) (photo: copyright ACL-Bruxelles)

37 Musées Royaux des Beaux-Arts, Brussels. *SS John, James, Andrew and Peter*; vidimus attributed to the workshop of Erhard Schön (photo: copyright ACL-Bruxelles)

38 The British Library, London. Detail of *The Pope feeding gold to bears*, from Hans Sachs, *Eyn wunderliche Weyssagung von den Babstumb* (1527). Reproduced by permission of the British Library

39 The British Library, London. *The Pope feeding gold to bears*, from Hans Sachs, *Eyn wunderliche Weyssagung von den Babstumb* (photo: the British Library)

40 Balliol College Chapel, Oxford, east window. *The Agony in the Garden*; attributed to James Nicholson (photo: Royal Commission on the Historical Monuments of England)

41 *The Agony in the Garden*, from Dürer's engraved *Passion* (B4, 1508)

42 Balliol College Chapel, Oxford, east window. *The Ascension*; attributed to James Nicholson (photo: Royal Commission on the Historical Monuments of England)

43 Musées Royaux des Beaux-Arts, Brussels. *The Ascension*; vidimus attributed to the workshop of Erhard Schön (photo: copyright ACL-Bruxelles)

44 Balliol College Chapel, Oxford, east window. *Christ before Pilate*; attributed to James Nicholson (photo: H. G Wayment, reproduced by permission of the college)

45 King's College Chapel, Cambridge, east window. Pilate, from the *Ecce Homo*; here attributed to James Nicholson (photo: P. A. L. Brunney, by permission of the Provost and Fellows of King's College)

47 Bibliothèque, Arras. *Recueil d'Arras*: sketch from a portrait of Thomas Wolsey, 1508 (photo: Giraudon)

46 King's College Chapel, Cambridge, east window. The Impenitent Thief, from the *Crucifixion*; here attributed to James Nicholson (photo: P. A. L. Brunney, by permission of the Provost and Fellows of King's College)

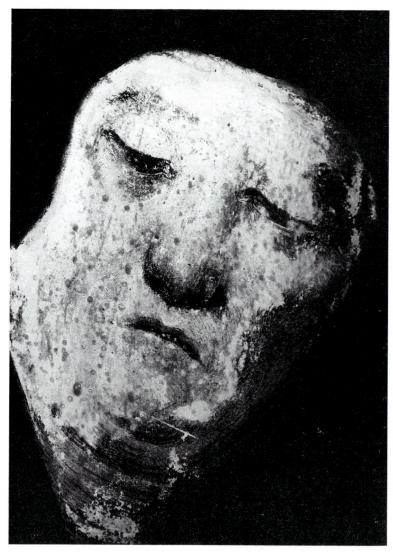

48   St Mary's, Fairford, Gloucestershire. A messenger above the *Judgement of Solomon* (detail); here attributed to Barnard Flower (photo: H. G. Wayment)

49 St Mary's, Fairford, Gloucestershire. St John at the Crucifixion, detail; here attributed to Barnard Flower (photo: H. G. Wayment)

50 St Mary's, Fairford, Gloucestershire. Attendant at the *Presentation of Christ*, here attributed to Barnard Flower (photo: H. G. Wayment)

51 Österreichische Nationalbibliothek, Vienna. *Hours of James IV* (Cod.1897, f. 243): Margaret Queen of Scotland (photo: Nationalbibliothek)

52   The Detroit Institute of Arts. *Catherine of Aragon as the Magdalen*, by Michiel Sittow: gift of Founder's Society, General Membership Donations Fund (photo: Detroit Institute of Arts)

53   St Mary's, Fairford, Gloucestershire. The Virgin Mary, from the *Nativity*; here attributed to Barnard Flower (photo: H. G. Wayment)

54   St Mary's, Fairford, Gloucestershire. Footsoldier from the *Crucifixion* (Sir John Savile) (photo: H. G. Wayment)

55 The Howard Grace Cup. Victoria and Albert Museum, London
(photo: Victoria and Albert Museum)

56 Tomb of Henry VII and Queen Elizabeth of York in Henry VII's Chapel, Westminster
Abbey (photo: Royal Commission on Historical Monuments of England)

57 Nelson's tomb, St Paul's Cathedral, London, re-using the sarcophagus and base from Wolsey's and Henry VIII's tomb projects (photo: P. G. Lindley)

58 Sernigi altar, Santa Trinità, Florence (detail) (photo: P. G. Lindley)

59 Fountain, Victoria and Albert Museum, London (photo: Victoria and Albert Museum)

60 Piero Soderini cenotaph, Santa Maria del Carmine, Florence (detail, showing sarcophagus) (photo: P. G. Lindley)

61 Altoviti tomb, SS Apostoli, Florence (detail, showing sarcophagus) (photo: P. G. Lindley)

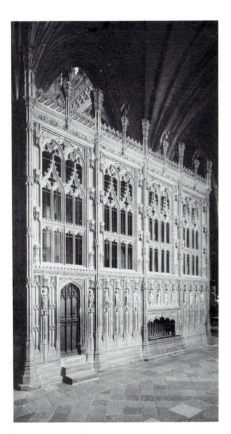

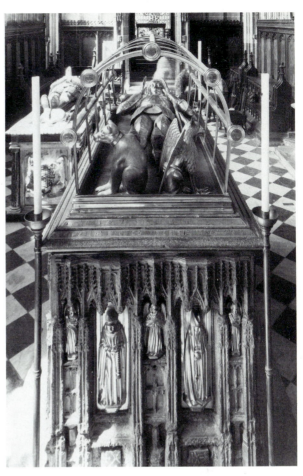

62　Chantry chapel of Bishop Fox, Winchester Cathedral (photo: John Crook)

63　Tomb of Richard Beauchamp, St Mary's, Warwick (photo: History of Art Department, University of Warwick)

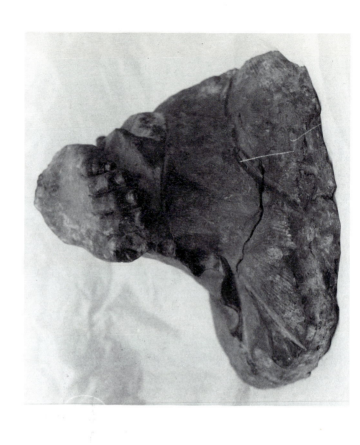

65   Terracotta fragment from Westminster Abbey (photo: J. Larson)

TOMBEAU *de marbre les figures se'l prie Dieu de Cuivre doré à gauche de l'autel*
dans le choeur de l'Eglise de l'Abbaye de S.t Denis. Il est de CHARLES VIII. *Roi de*
FRANCE *mort le 7. Avril veille de Pasques fleuries 1498.*

64   Tomb of Charles VIII, MS Gough Drawings Gaig-
nières 2, fol. 48 r (photo: Bodleian Library, Oxford)

69 Restored terracotta panel with winged *putti*, Wolsey's coat-of-arms, hat, archiepiscopal cross, and motto, Hampton Court Palace (Photo: P. G. Lindley)

66 Roundel with bust of Augustus, Hampton Court Palace (photo: P. G. Lindley)

67 Roundel with bust of an emperor, The Vyne (photo: P. G. Lindley)

68 *Putti* with royal coat of arms and roundels containing the Sandys arms and badge, The Vyne (photo: P. G. Lindley)

70 Angel from panels flanking the chapel entrance, Hampton Court Palace (photo: P. G. Lindley)

71 Oriel window, Christ Church, Oxford (detail, showing *putto*) (photo: P. G. Lindley)

72 Fragment of terracotta window-frame, from an excavation in Lady Mornington's garden, Hampton Court Palace (photo: P. G. Lindley)

73 Fragment of terracotta window-head, from an excavation in Clock Court, Hampton Court Palace (photo: P. G. Lindley)

74 Fragment of terracotta mullion, from an excavation in Clock Court, Hampton Court Palace (photo: P. G. Lindley)

So much for Wolsey's college at Oxford. We must now consider briefly Cardinal College, Ipswich, and in particular try to establish its scale and ambition. Was it a twin foundation, as Winchester was to New College and Eton to King's, or was it something much more modest, like Waynflete's grammar schools? First, its endowment: the annual value of the suppressed monastic houses and appropriated rectories for Ipswich was estimated at £1,000, half as much as the endowment of the Oxford college.[35] Second, its establishment: the college was to be a community of secular canons, headed by a dean, and consisting of twelve priests, eight clerks, eight singing boys and poor scholars.[36] This is about two-thirds of the chapel establishment at Oxford. At Ipswich, as at Oxford, there were to be in addition thirteen poor almsmen. All these were to pray for the good estate of the king and the cardinal, and for the souls of the cardinal's parents. This chantry college element allies Wolsey's foundation to the college founded by Archbishop Chichele at his birthplace, Higham Ferrers, Northants, in 1427, fifteen years before he founded All Souls College, Oxford.[37]

What about the educational aspects of the college? The first dean, William Capon, had previously been head of Jesus College, Cambridge. But otherwise the educational provision was almost wholly lacking. There were no scholars on the foundation apart from the eight singing boys. The undermaster in grammar was to teach them and 'others from any part of the realm coming to the college'. However, since the statutes for the college were never drawn up, these arrangements should be seen as representing a temporary scheme. It is only fair to point out that from the autumn of 1528 to the autumn of 1529, the period when the college was fully operational, teaching seems to have forged ahead. As early as January 1529, the schoolmaster sent Wolsey specimens of the handwriting of some of the boys, and expressed the hope that they would soon be speaking Latin in the modern (Italian) manner.[38] Numbers were increasing and three months later the dean referred to an usher as well as the schoolmaster and to the need to enlarge the school.[39]

So, finally, what of the buildings of Ipswich College? Clearly the community began by making use of pre-existing church and schoolroom. But the erection of new buildings soon went ahead. From the summer of 1528 building materials were being sought and stockpiled on site, in particular flints from the cliffs at Harwich and Caen stone from Normandy.[40] By the end of December the plans of the college were ready to be shown to Wolsey.[41] The names of its devisors are known: they were not royal craftsmen, as at Oxford, but two East Anglian master masons, Richard Lee, identified by John Harvey with the Richard Lee of Ely

---

[35] *LP*, IV (ii) 4435.   [36] Ibid.

[37] *VCH, Northamptonshire*, II (1906), 177–9. I am grateful to Dr M. W. Thompson for drawing my attention to Higham Ferrers College.

[38] *LP*, IV (iii) 5159. I am grateful to Dr. J. W. Binns for advice on the meaning of 'Italice' in this context.

[39] Ibid., 5458.   [40] *LP*, IV (ii) 4484, 4548, (iii) 5212 etc.   [41] Ibid., (ii) 5077.

whose only recorded work is the tomb, with renaissance detail, of Bishop John
Fisher, formerly at St John's College, Cambridge, and an even more shadowy
figure, Barbour by name.[42] In mid-1529 the report was that 'My Lord's college at
Ipswich is going on prosperously, and much of it above ground, which is very
curious work.'[43] 'Curious' would normally in the early sixteenth century have
meant 'richly decorated', but it is unfortunately impossible to get a sense of the
costliness of the building, since the one surviving building account, amounting to
£1,322, is lacking in detail and does not even specify what period of time it
covers.[44] Nor does much survive on the ground. After the dissolution of the
college, the exchequer accounts for 1531 record the removal to Westminster for
use in royal buildings of over 1,300 tons of Caen stone and 600 tons of flints.[45]
Some of the stone was already cut in various mouldings. But these will have been
stockpiled materials and it is not known what was the fate of the parts already
constructed. The earliest writer to discuss the college buildings is a certain J.
Grove of Richmond, who in 1761 published a small volume entitled *Two Dialogues
in the Elysian Fields, between Cardinal Wolsey and Cardinal Ximenes*, with an
appendix recording what was known of the college. By that date it was already
impossible to trace either the bounds of the site or the plan of the buildings; but
Grove does state that Wolsey 'designed to have had a noble front to his College,
and a handsome entrance to it' and refers to an entrance gateway 'built after the
Manner of that at Whitehall'. This gateway is also indicated in a vignette in the
border of the engraved town plan in the book and apparently had two broad
three-storeyed towers flanking an entrance arch. Where this gatetower stood is
unknown, as is its relationship to the only surviving fragment of the college, a
short stretch of the brick precinct wall forming an angle adjacent to St Peter's
churchyard. In it stands a handsome brick gateway (plate 3) giving pedestrian
access to what must have been one corner of the precinct. The gateway is wholly
gothic in character; but high up at the back, apparently part of the original fabric,
are two blocks which appear to be of terracotta. Do they provide a tantalizing link
with Wolsey's Hampton Court, where terracotta was used in rich Renaissance
decoration?[46] Perhaps we may sum up Ipswich College by saying that, had it
been completed, it would have formed a fine group of buildings, if not on the
scale or of the architectural quality of Wolsey's college at Oxford. However there
is the possibility that it would have been one of the small group of East Anglian
buildings which used Renaissance details before 1530.

In educational terms Ipswich College turns out to have been a relatively minor
element in Wolsey's overall strategy, and its main importance for him will

[42] J. H. Harvey, *English Medieval Architects*, pp. 13, 174.   [43] *LP*, IV (iii), 5792.

[44] PRO, SP1/53 fo. 99.

[45] Totals from figures in PRO, E36/251. Dr Simon Thurley kindly supplied the figures.

[46] M. Howard, *The Early Tudor Country House: Architecture and Politics 1490–1550* (London, 1987),
pp. 131–3. See also the paper by P. G. Lindley in the present volume.

probably have been as an expression of filial piety. The college at Oxford was a very different matter. Had it been allowed to develop and flourish it would undoubtedly have become the premier college at either of England's universities. As it was, Wolsey's public lectureships, inspired by Bishop Fox's, formed the model for the professorships which even today are one of the most characteristic features of British universities.

In the final year of his life Wolsey was desperately anxious about the fate of his colleges. By July 1530 Ipswich was clearly doomed. At Oxford things looked a little brighter, and in September Cromwell reported that the king wanted to reprieve the college but to make it smaller and less magnificent. What this meant transpired only after Wolsey's death, for when it was refounded in 1532 as King Henry VIII's College it lost all its educational establishment and dwindled into a mere ecclesiastical college of secular canons. This was a foretaste of the huge lost opportunity that the dissolution of the monasteries represented. Only at the end of his reign did Henry go some way to repair his omissions, with the establishment of five regius professorships and a second refoundation of the college in a way that realized most of Wolsey's educational aims.

CHAPTER 4

Wolsey and stained glass

HILARY WAYMENT

Stained glass, in the Middle Ages and the early Renaissance, was a major art, a luminous medium of the Word, and for the patron a striking index of power. Time, neglect, and iconoclasm have decimated the wealth of what must once have existed, but sufficient traces remain of Wolsey's activity in this field to make possible a general account of his work and to make clear what importance he attached to the medium. One measure of the value he set on it is the outstanding ability of the two master-glaziers whom he is known to have employed in putting windows into his buildings.

In 1515, the year after he became archbishop of York, Barnard Flower, who had been king's glazier since 1497, supplied Normandy glass (the finest and most expensive of such materials) enriched with heraldic shields and badges for the windows of York Place. These included the bay windows of the hall and great chamber, the gallery, the great staircase, 'my lord's closet', and the chapel chamber. The heraldic pieces comprised the king's and the queen's arms, as well as Wolsey's; in December eleven of these last were ensigned with the cardinal's hat.[1] None of this glass is known to survive. One most interesting fragment does survive, however, which in all probability was painted by Barnard Flower for Wolsey, though not at York Place; this will be described later on.

Barnard Flower died in the summer of 1517. The only other master-glazier whom Wolsey is known to have employed was James Nicholson, a Fleming by origin. He seems to have been recognized as the leading glazier of the time, alongside Galyon Hone, Flower's successor as king's glazier. It is now possible for the first time to group together a few examples of glass-painting which can confidently be diagnosed as his, and show him to have had outstanding flair and panache.

At Cardinal College, Oxford, between May and October 1529, Nicholson was paid a total of nearly £28 for forty-seven sets of Wolsey's arms at 6s 8d each, and

---

[1] A. Oswald, 'Barnard Flower, the King's Glazier', *Journal of the British Society of Master Glass Painters*, 11, 1 (1951–2), 15–17; A. Smith, 'Henry VII and the appointment of the King's Glazier', ibid., 18, 3 (1988), 259–61. The author wishes to thank the Revd D. Bell-Richards, Dr Eliane de Wilde, Michael Maclagan, Dr John Mason and John Prest for help of various kinds in connection with this paper.

246 'bends or poses called Dominus Mihi Adjutor' at 1s each; the prices are high, indeed on a regal scale.[2] At Christ Church a total of fifty-two pieces remains, which must have belonged to this group; most of them are in the south bay window and the high west gable window of the hall;[3] but there are no scrolls remaining with Wolsey's motto, which was no doubt written diagonally all over the backgrounds.[4] In all there are thirteen examples of Wolsey's arms in the gable window, either plain or impaled: some intact, some completed by intrusions. A few are only identifiable by the cardinal's hat, the ten red tassels depending from it, or the gold crosses of Wolsey's archbishopric and legacy set in saltire behind the shield.[5] Three are impaled by the pallium or crossed keys of York, one by the arms of Bath and Wells. More interesting are the wreathed badges, of which there are thirty-nine. Twenty-one show the columns or poleaxes of the legacy in saltire, with cross in pale;[6] five are devices of the archbishopric of York: *gules two keys in saltire argent and in chief a crown or*; one has T W within a love-knot. The most striking of all is Wolsey's own badge of a lion's head azure gorged with a coronet or, on a field or within a red rose: there are eleven of these (plate 27). The lion's head is excerpted from Wolsey's arms, and taken ultimately from the de la Poles, the earls and dukes of his native county; the red rose is of course the king's. A glazier's style can only with difficulty be gauged by his heraldic work, and many of these pieces must be from the hands of assistants; but the lion's head is painted with unmistakable dash and verve.

During the years 1526–9 Wolsey had been pressing on more vigorously than ever with the construction and decoration of his palaces and colleges. In August 1527 Lawrence Stubbs wrote to him as follows: 'Your buildings at York Place, Hampton Court etc. go forward, and I understand from Cromwell, who has come from Oxford, that he has certified you of the forwardness of the work there.' Then in May 1528 Edward Foxe writes to Gardiner: 'the hall of York Place with other edifices there being now in building, my lord's Grace intending most sumptuously and gorgeously to repair and furnish the same'.[7]

In the National Gallery of Scotland is a drawing or *vidimus* for a stained glass window of thirteen lights divided by a transom and rising into a lofty gable (plate 28).[8] The word 'vidimus' may require explanation.[9] *Vidimus* ('we have seen') is

---

[2] M. Maclagan in *VCH Oxford*, III (London, 1954), p. 231.

[3] Two are in the former Chapter House of St Frideswide's, now the Treasury. There is also a badge with columns in saltire and a cross in pale which is now in the hall of Trinity College; several royal coats of arms at Christ Church, and one at Trinity, seem also to belong to the group, though they are not mentioned in the account concerned (cf. York Place, as described above).

[4] Like the 'Dominus illuminatio mea' substituted by the nineteenth-century restorers, or the motto 'ffeyth fully serve' at Ockwells, Berks: C. Woodforde, *English Stained and Painted Glass* (Oxford, 1954), p. 28.

[5] Cavendish, p. 17.   [6] Cavendish, pp. 23–4.   [7] *LP*, IV, 3334 and 4251 p. 1872.

[8] There is a pair of large-scale reproductions, showing the two registers separately, in *Vasari Society Publications of Old Master Drawings*, ser. 1 pt 7 (1911), no. 25.

[9] H. G. Wayment, 'The great windows of King's College Chapel and the meaning of the word *vidimus*', *Proceedings of the Cambridge Antiquarian Society*, 69 (1979), 53–60.

originally a French equivalent of the word *inspeximus*, and comes to mean a certified copy. It was used, particularly in the Low Countries, to denote the two copies of a design for a stained glass window which was the subject of a contract between patron and glazier; on agreement each kept one, just as each would keep half an indenture. The design was not necessarily executed by the glazier himself, in fact it was more often by another artist, who would no doubt wish to keep his own original, in which case each of the three parties will have had a copy. So if a vidimus survives, it is on the whole more likely to be a workshop copy than the artist's original, though the copy might well be touched up by the master, and might sometimes be by his own hand.

The thirteen lights of the Edinburgh vidimus include four figures of saints, deployed at the extremities of each register. In between, at each level, are two scenes, each of three lights, flanking a central scene of five lights: above left, the *Carrying of the Cross*, centre, the *Crucifixion*, right, the *Deposition*; below left, the *Entombment*, centre, the *Resurrection*, and right, the *Ascension*. The attendant saints are: in the upper register, left, St Peter, right, St Paul; in the lower, left, St Thomas of Canterbury, right, St William of York. The drawing was first published in 1911 by Campbell Dodgson, who assigned it to a Nuremberg artist close to Dürer, and dated it, by watermark, about 1525–6.[10] He pointed out that the classicizing features filling in above and below the saints' figures were connected with the engraver Erhard Schön, though he gave no precise attribution for the authorship of the drawing or its destination. We must note that the vidimus is only a preliminary sketch; there are no master mullions indicated, and a window so built would speedily collapse. Above each register are notes suggesting an alternative arrangement of subjects, and these prove to be in James Nicholson's hand, as appears clearly from a comparison with his signatures to the contracts of 1526 for the great windows of King's College Chapel, Cambridge. The annotations strongly suggest, therefore, that the patron concerned was not William Warham, archbishop of Canterbury (which is theoretically possible), but Thomas Wolsey, archbishop of York and papal legate.

In 1983 a remarkable discovery was made in the Print Room of the Musées Royaux des Beaux-Arts at Brussels.[11] Tucked away in a safe, to which it had apparently been consigned long before, was an album of twenty-four drawings in pen, wash and watercolour. These proved to be a set of designs, almost complete, for an east window of thirteen lights and the north and south windows of four bays to the west (fig. 10). Just before this, in the last volume of the *History of the King's Works*, published in 1982, the results of excavations behind the east wall of Hampton Court Chapel were included; and in 1984 these were

---

[10] Above, n. 8; cf. K. P. Harrison, *The Windows of King's College Chapel, Cambridge* (Cambridge, 1952), pp. 63–4.

[11] H. G. Wayment, 'Twenty-four vidimuses for Cardinal Wolsey', *Master Drawings*, 23–4 (1985–6), IV, pp. 503–17.

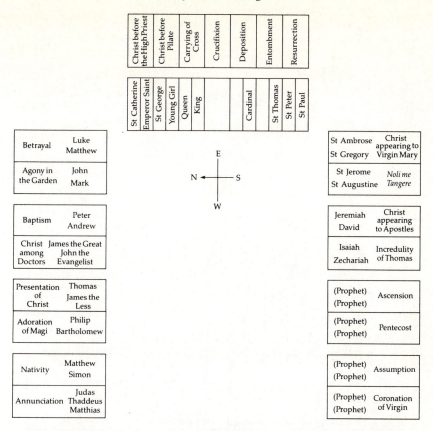

Fig. 10 Reconstruction of scheme for which the Brussels vidimuses were prepared

discussed in greater detail by Peter Curnow.[12] The window had been obscured from within by Grinling Gibbons' reredos, and outside to the east by other buildings; but it proved to consist of two windows of six lights each, in two registers, separated by a third, narrow window of a single light, making thirteen in all (figure 11). This arrangement, which must surely be unique, corresponds precisely with the nine (or ten) vidimuses from the Brussels set which make up a scheme for the east window. In the centre of the upper register comes the *Crucifixion* with Mary Magdalene at the foot of the Cross, for which there are two versions, one with angels collecting the blood of Christ (plate 29), and one without (plate 30). The designer clearly did not know, in an age racked by controversy about the Real Presence, which version the patron would favour. Below, on either side, kneel suppliants presented by their patron saints: on the right a cardinal with St Thomas of Canterbury, St Peter and St Paul: clearly

[12] *HKW*, IV (ii), fig. 23; P. Curnow, 'The east window of the chapel at Hampton Court Palace', *Architectural History*, 27 (1984), 1–10.

Fig. 11   Hampton Court Palace, east window of
chapel, reconstruction drawing from *Architectural
History* 27 (1984), courtesy of Mr Peter Curnow

Thomas Wolsey, papal legate (plate 31); on the left a king and queen, the king
presented by SS George and Henry, the queen by St Catherine (plate 32); the girl
must of course be the Princess Mary, and her name-saint is in the Crucifixion light
in the upper register. Left and right of the *Crucifixion*, and above the suppliants
and their saints, are six Passion scenes in two lights each: left, *Christ before the High*

Priest, *Christ before Pilate*, and the *Carrying of the Cross* (plate 33); right, the *Deposition*, *Entombment*, and *Resurrection* (plate 34).

Although no records of glazing at Hampton Court survive from Wolsey's time, there are accounts extant of repairs and alterations to the east window by Galyon Hone, Henry VIII's glazier, which prove that it had already been glazed with imagery in Wolsey's time. The alterations were consequent on Henry's marital ventures and his determination to eliminate any trace of the previous owner.[13] Between 30 October 1535 and 13 May 1536 a large number of Anne Boleyn's arms and badges were installed in different parts of the palace, including three badges in the east window of the chapel. In October–November 1535 sixteen feet of 'imagery' were set in the same window at a cost of 32s; a later entry, dating from the period 23 September to 21 October 1536, after Anne's execution, is more explicit:[14]

> *Itim for the translatynges and the remowfing off a ymagges of Saynt Anna and other off Saynt Tomas in the hye alter wyndwo off the chappell pryce le pyce* vis viiid = xiijs iiijd

The implication is that in November 1535 the figure of St Anne had replaced that of St Catherine, though it is only possible to guess what the other work involved. The figure of St Anne had lasted for less than a year, and no doubt Wolsey's figure had gone before his name-saint's.

A century later, in 1645, a Parliamentarian news-sheet records the recent destruction of the whole window:

> *Sir Robert Harlow gave order for the pulling down and demolishing of the popish and superstitious pictures at Hampton Court where, this day ... the popish pictures and superstitious images were also demolished, and order given for the new glazing of them with plain glass ... and among the rest, there was pulled down the picture of Christ nailed to the Cross, which was placed right over the high altar, and the pictures of Mary Magdalen and others weeping by the foot of the cross and some other such idolatrous pictures ...*[15]

The words 'and others' show that a central panel in the lower register must have contained the figures of the Virgin and St John (and perhaps others) standing underneath the Cross. This arrangement is found in the roughly contemporaneous *Crucifixion* now in St Margaret's, Westminster, which was probably given by Henry himself to Waltham Abbey.[16] The 'other such idolatrous pictures' mentioned in the news-sheet were probably, but not certainly, the six scenes sketched in the Brussels set.

The Brussels scheme starts with the *Annunciation* on the north side of the upper register, and seven more scenes down to the *Arrest of Christ*; on the south side come the *Appearances of Christ*, the *Ascension* and *Pentecost*, and finally the *Assumption* and *Coronation of the Virgin*. In n. iv, next to the north-west window,

---

[13] PRO, E36/243 and E36/299; Wayment, 'Twenty-four vidimuses', 508.
[14] PRO, E36/239.   [15] E. Law, *The History of Hampton Court Palace*, ii (London, 1838), p. 131.
[16] Wayment, 'The east window of St Margaret's, Westminster', *Antiquaries Journal*, 61 (1981), 292–301.

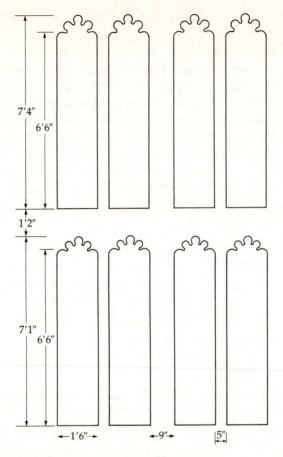

Fig. 12   Hampton Court Palace Chapel, elevation of south-east window, main
lights, courtesy of Mrs Juliet West

for instance, there were to be an *Adoration of the Magi* and a *Presentation of Christ*
(plate 35). Figures of Apostles, Prophets, Evangelists and Doctors of the Church
were to fill the lower register; the Apostles run from east to west, beginning with
SS Peter, Andrew, James Major and John the Evangelist (plate 37). Above these
lower designs, as in the Edinburgh vidimus, are notes in Nicholson's hand of
New Testament subjects which do not precisely correspond with those of the
scenes above. On the left, in the half-window illustrated, 'the mandaet' (i.e. the
Last Supper), which is crossed out, and above 'iii kynges' ; on the right 'the
monteyn of Olivet' crossed out, and 'the puryfycacion' above.

     None of these designs for north and south windows appears to have been used
at Hampton Court, although accounts of modifications in the 1530s indicate that
Wolsey did garnish them with armorials. One of them, the second on the south
side, was taken out to make room for an organ in 1535–6. Wren, at the end of the

seventeenth century, replaced the stonework of six more with contemporary designs, but one, the easternmost on the south side, was blocked up with its original stonework intact (figure 12). All eight windows can be assumed to have had the same dimensions. The four lights of the blocked window are 18 inches wide, and 7 feet 1 inches high in the lower register, 7 feet 4 inches in the upper, the variation being due to the different design of the cusping. The proportions of the vidimuses (which vary by up to ten per cent in parallel half-lights) suggest that the scenes would have covered about 5 feet in the lower register, and a little more in the upper, leaving about 2 feet in each for armorials. The seven remaining windows, three on the south side and four on the north, would then have had room, in the two registers, for 56 heraldic pieces. There are no records of glazing from Wolsey's time, but the accounts of 15 April to 13 May 1536, just before the execution of Anne Boleyn, give details of modifications to the heraldry. During the previous year the interior of the chapel had been completely refurbished, and above all the magnificent wooden vault, which still remains, had been installed in place of Wolsey's ceiling. Curnow points out that all this work must inevitably have involved damage to the glass, however efficient and careful the craftsmen may have been. The accounts of April–May 1536 record the installation of twenty-eight 'scrypters' at twelve pence each (i.e. one to each light), no doubt replacing DOMINVS MIHI ADJUTOR by DIEV ET MON DROIT, and eight arms and eight badges of the king and queen at four shillings each, presumably displacing Wolsey's and Catherine's. Three 'half arms' of the queen at two shillings each must have ousted Catherine's in three impaled coats, and (explicitly this time) three badges were 'set in the old garlands of the queen's' at eighteen pence each. The replacements add up to fifty pieces; Wolsey had no doubt, as later on at Oxford, included the king's arms (probably one to each of the seven windows), and of these six might well have remained undisturbed.

The same accounts go on to record the re-leading of 455 feet of glass at a cost of 2*d* a foot. The area corresponds with that left in the seven windows above the armorials in the foot of each light,[17] and the low cost shows that plain and not figured glass was involved. This fact, combined with the complete absence, in either these accounts or the news-sheet dating from 1645, of any reference to 'imagery' in the side-windows makes it pretty clear that there was none.

In the twenty-four vidimuses a number of different hands can be discerned;[18] but the first two in the historical series are clearly by Erhard Schön, whose name was mentioned by Dodgson in 1911. The simplest way to demonstrate this is to compare the detail of the Virgin's robe in the *Adoration of the Magi* (plate 36) with a similar passage (plate 38) in Schön's woodcut of the *Pope feeding Gold to Bears* for Hans Sachs' *Eyn wunderliche Weyssagung von den Babstumb* (plate 39).

[17] The designs sketched in the vidimuses would have covered about 420 sq. ft; the difference is accounted for by cusped areas unsuitable for figured work.

[18] For a full stylistic analysis see Wayment, 'Twenty-four vidimuses', pp. 510–12.

Returning now to the Edinburgh vidimus (plate 28), we must note that it is clearly from the same workshop as the Brussels set, though not in Erhard Schön's own hand. Moreover it carries annotations in the same handwriting as a number of the Brussels drawings, and this hand, as we have seen, is recognizably that of James Nicholson. Arthur Oswald thought it probably referred to the axial window at York Place (which actually faced north), and this is certainly a possibility, though the chapel there was not built until 1528, perhaps two years after the date of the drawing.[19] Peter Newton thought, for a long time at least, that the Edinburgh vidimus was a late design (presumably *c.* 1528) for the unbuilt chapel of Cardinal College, Oxford.[20] This it cannot have been, if, as is now believed, the existing flat vault of Hampton Court Chapel was formed from the timbers prepared at Sonning to fit the intended chapel at Oxford.[21] The elongated lights and the lofty arch of the Edinburgh vidimus must indicate a high gabled roof, similar to that known to have been built at York Place. At Hampton Court there are traces of the ceiling installed by Wolsey which suggest that, like the present vault, it was flat;[22] but there may well have been an earlier plan for a high gabled roof, and the Edinburgh vidimus may have nothing whatever to do with York Place, but simply represent a first draft (as the lack of master mullions also suggests) for a window which was modified, after Wolsey's assignment of a splendid set of lodgings to the king in 1525, so as to include the royal figures and their patron saints. The six Passion scenes of the Edinburgh drawing, covering each of them three or five lights, are replaced by six scenes in two lights each (four of these repeating the Edinburgh designs in an abridged form), so as to correspond with the figures in the lower register, while the *Crucifixion* is reduced to a single light covering both registers, and forming as it were a separate window on its own.

The annotations in James Nicholson's hand above the half-lights of the Edinburgh vidimus propose a rearrangement of subjects so as to include thirteen scenes in the two registers. These notes imply that Wolsey and Nicholson had in front of them at the same time both the Edinburgh vidimus and the six Brussels designs for the lower register of the side-windows, since the subjects suggested in them are complementary (figure 13). Those proposed on the north side designs run from the *Annunciation* to the *Baptism*, and those on the Edinburgh vidimus, for an axial window, from the *Last Supper* to the *Appearance to the three Marys*; the two surviving south side drawings continue with other Appearances and the *Incredulity of Thomas*. The annotations are obviously tentative, including as they

[19] See above, p. 85. For Oswald's view see ref. to Harrison in n. 10.

[20] Letters of August 1984 and Nov. 1986; I understand, however, that his *CVMA* volume *The City of Oxford*, when it eventually appears, will support Davis's conjecture, of which he seems to have been unaware. See below, p. 126.

[21] J. H. Harvey, 'The building works and architects of Cardinal Wolsey', *Journal of the British Archaeological Association*, 8 (1943), 55.

[22] Personal communication from Dr Thurley.

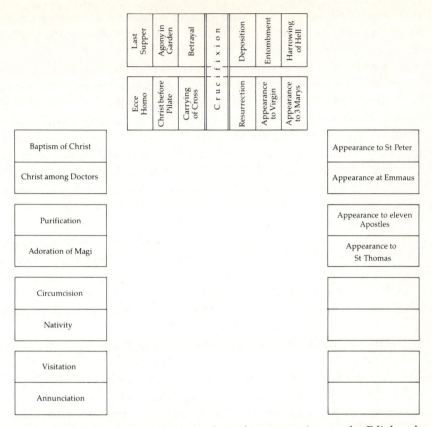

Fig. 13 Iconographical scheme adumbrated in annotations to the Edinburgh vidimus and on six drawings from the Brussels series, above figures of Apostles, Prophets, Evangelists and Doctors of the Church

do a number of erasures and changes of mind. They seem to mark a half-way stage to the series of subjects illustrated in the Brussels drawings for the upper register. The figures for the lower register may have been designed for York Place, but they may equally well have been intended for Hampton Court Chapel from the beginning. In either case the changes involved in the later scheme for the east window, as represented in the Brussels vidimuses, necessitated a concordant sequence of scenes in the upper register of the side windows. If there was a first draft of these scenes, either for York Place or Hampton Court, then it had to be superseded by a new scheme with a certain number of new designs. This view of the evolution of the Hampton Court scheme would explain why the designs for the four Doctors and the first four Prophets (the only ones remaining which refer to the lower register of the south side) were originally numbered 6 and 7, though the Resurrection scenes that fit above them are marked 7 and 8. The Edinburgh vidimus, for a single window of thirteen lights, is numbered 5, whereas the designs for the two linked six-light windows for Hampton Court are numbered 5 and 6; the numbering of each of the two registers on the south side continues accordingly, but out of step with the other.

From whatever glass was painted for the chapel of Hampton Court there now remain only a few minute fragments;[23] but there is glass in existence which is indirectly related to one or two of the scenes in the Brussels and Edinburgh vidimuses. It was R. H. C. Davis who first suggested, as long ago as 1954, that the Passion scenes in the east window of Balliol College Chapel may in fact have been painted by James Nicholson for Cardinal College, and passed on by Dean John Higdon, after Wolsey's fall, to Lawrence Stubbs.[24] Although the walls of Cardinal College Chapel were scarcely to rise above their foundations, Wolsey, as we have seen, had already ordered the wooden vault. The stained glass for the east window may equally have been commissioned in advance. Higdon was not to know, in 1529, when his world was tumbling about him, that he would return as dean three years later, after Henry's re-foundation of the college. Stubbs had been almoner of Cardinal College, and the date of the presentation to Balliol, 1529, as inscribed on the glass, is vouched for by Anthony à Wood.[25] In mid-October 1529 Wolsey fell. The Passion scenes, if already painted, could have been sold and installed at Balliol by the end of the year.

The Hampton Court windows seem to have been designed by Erhard Schön, a minor member of Albrecht Dürer's circle. At Balliol the Passion scenes are based, most of them, on Dürer's own prints. The *Crucifixion* itself covers two registers, as at Hampton Court and as in the scheme adumbrated in the notes on the Edinburgh vidimus; it is heavily restored, though the figures of the two Marys are original. The other scenes are limited to a single light and correspond to the proportions of an upright print. The *Agony in the Garden*, for instance (plate 40), reproduces the design in the engraved *Passion* (plate 41, reversed). In the *Ascension* (plate 42), however, it is clear that the designer is using the vidimus in the Hampton Court series, from the workshop of Erhard Schön (plate 43). The *Christ before Pilate* (plate 44), like many of the others, is based on a conflation of several prints by Dürer; the master-glazier clearly had a capacity for independent design, and never slavishly copied his models. Here Davis's attribution of these scenes to James Nicholson can be at least partially confirmed by a comparison of Pilate's figure with the same personage in the *Ecce Homo* from the east window of King's College Chapel, Cambridge (plate 45). In the 1526 contracts for the completion of the King's College windows Nicholson had signed directly after the king's glazier, Galyon Hone, and they both dined in college during the

---

[23] The fragments, apparently from a royal coat of arms, which were found in the east window at Hampton Court, may well date from the 1530s: Curnow, 'The east window', p. 9 n. 14.

[24] *VCH Oxford*, III (London, 1954), pp. 90–1.

[25] A. Wood, *The History and Antiquities of the Colleges and Halls in the University of Oxford*, ed. J. Gutch (London, 1786), pp. 99–102.

course of April 1535; the east window appears to date from 1541, probably the last year of Nicholson's life.[26] The evident correlation of the two images is not surprising, but in the east window at King's the panache which was traceable already at Cardinal College in 1529 has reached, particularly in the figure of the Impenitent Thief (plate 46), a quite stunning pitch of bravado.

Thus, although the collection of armorials at Christ Church is the only glass commissioned by Wolsey which is certainly known to have survived, it is possible to form a plausible if fragmentary picture of his more ambitious schemes for at least two of the three greatest of his chapels. There remains to be investigated, from the years of Wolsey's rise to power, a most interesting episode in which he seems to have been acting not as patron, but as agent for another.

At St Mary's, Fairford, Gloucestershire, the twenty-eight windows of painted glass must date from the beginning of the sixteenth century, but there is not a single document which so much as mentions them before 1630; we have to learn from the glass itself whatever it will tell us.[27]

The *Judgement of Solomon* in the west window of the north aisle was badly damaged in the great storm of November 1703, as Daniel Defoe records.[28] In the top left-hand corner, however, partially protected by the tower, is the demi-figure of a text-bearing Messenger which has all the marks of an actual portrait (plate 48). The face gives at once an unmistakable impression of ruthless power; and a comparison with the known portraits of Wolsey leaves little doubt whose it is. Apart from the various profile figures dating from his later years, after his right eyelid began to droop, the only other likeness of Wolsey is the drawing in the *Recueil d'Arras* from a lost painting which must once have been in the Scottish royal collection, showing him full-face (plate 47). This was presumably painted in March or April 1508, when Wolsey went on a mission from Henry VII to James IV. Apart from the multiple chins, the lips are the same in either case: rather thin, with decisive lines defining them both above and below, and turning downwards at the extremities. It is not so obvious at first sight, because of the shading on the glass, that the shape of the nostrils and the rounded tip of the nose are in each case the same; and if the eyes and eye-sockets have only a general similarity, this is because in the glass they follow the glazier's penchant for rather elongated eyelids, which in some cases seem to meet outside the eye-socket itself, as in the St John at the Crucifixion (plate 49).[29] In others they are too much rounded, even bunched up (plates 50 and 53). The glass-painter is, however, the most accomplished of all those who took part in the glazing of Fairford Church, and his influence can be traced on many of the others.[30] The name of Barnard Flower, the

---

[26] H. G. Wayment, *CVMA* Great Britain Suppl. vol. 1, *The Windows of King's College Chapel, Cambridge* (London, 1972), pp. 4, 82–4.

[27] H. G. Wayment, *The Stained Glass of the Church of St Mary, Fairford, Gloucestershire* (London, 1984), pp. 85–97.

[28] D. Defoe, *The Storm* (London, 1704), p. 97.   [29] Wayment, *Fairford*, pp. 31–2.

[30] Ibid., pp. 90 and 93, where he is called simply 'Glazier B'.

king's glazier from 1497 till his death in 1517, has all too often been taken in vain by writers on English glass; but after an intensive study of the Fairford windows I firmly believe this hand to be his. The judgement is based on a comparison of the pattern of relationships between the different glaziers whose hands can be traced there with the records of cooperation between various named glaziers, including Flower, in Westminster and London in 1501–2.[31] The head presumably dates from the years before March 1514, when Wolsey became a bishop, and certainly before November 1515, when he secured the cardinal's hat; after that he would scarcely have allowed himself to be portrayed without it.

The windows of a typical English church of the Middle Ages, as scores of examples make clear, must have been full of figures of donors, their wives and children, their ancestors and predecessors in office, together with their coats of arms and badges, not to mention explanatory inscriptions. Yet in almost the only remaining parish church which retains at least traces of medieval glass in every single window, and at least eighty per cent of the original glass as a whole, there are only two linked inscriptions, which long proved inscrutable, and one recognizable heraldic device, the Prince of Wales' feather with 'ich dene', seven times repeated.[32] The reason for the apparent anonymity of the glass is, I believe, that it is only apparent, and that in addition to their overt meaning the windows contain an elaborate series of impersonations, or portraits concealed under the guise of personages in the drama. The attendant in the *Presentation of Christ*, for instance (a character not infrequently distinguished by her fashionable dress),[33] bears the features of Princess Margaret (plate 50); this is clear from a comparison with her portrait in the *Hours of James IV* as queen of Scotland (plate 51).

Impersonation, or the representation of living persons in the guise of sacred characters, was common at this time in Netherlandish painting and tapestry, and had also spread to Spain. A notable example is the *Catherine of Aragon as the Magdalene*, now at Detroit (plate 52); this is attributed to Michiel Sittow, a painter born in Tallinn and trained in Bruges, who towards the end of the fifteenth century worked at the court of Isabella of Castile, Catherine's mother.[34] Jacqueline Folie argues that this portrait must have been painted about the end of the fifteenth century, that the two Cs facing each other on the knob of the vase cover are also initials, and that the rosettes below represent Tudor roses. In that case it must date from after Catherine's first proxy marriage to Prince Arthur, which

31 Oswald, 'Barnard Flower', pp. 10–12. The 'Adrian Andrew' who joined with Flower in hiring out glass to enliven the hall of the bishop of London's palace for the wedding feast was in all probability the designer and one of the chief painters of the early glass at Fairford, including the figure of Sir John Savile (see below). The surname must be a corruption of 'Adrian Vandenhoute', which was pronounced to rhyme with route.

32 In s.VI (two), s.VII (one), s.VIII (two), and s.X (two fragmented): Wayment, *Fairford*, pp. 95–6.

33 n.III: cf. Rogier van der Weyden's *Columba Altarpiece*, E. Panofsky, *Early Netherlandish Painting*, I (New York, 1971), p. 288, II, fig. 354.

34 Exh. cat. *Flanders in the Fifteenth Century: Art and Civilisation* (Detroit, 1960), pp. 197–200.

took place on 19 May 1499, and may well have been sent to Westminster before their actual marriage on 14 November 1501. This would explain the apparent dependence on it of the Virgin's figure in the Fairford *Nativity* (plate 53), which must be attributed, like the Messenger in the *Judgement of Solomon* (plate 48) and the attendant at the Presentation of Christ (plate 50), to Barnard Flower.[35]

It is against such a background that we should envisage the unexpected interposition of a Messenger in the guise of Thomas Wolsey. But in what capacity does he appear? The answer must depend on the identification of a character in the east window: that of a footsoldier staring up at Christ on the Cross, and bearing an inscription 'IOSXXELE' (plate 54).[36] This can only stand for John Savele, and must refer to the head, from 1482 to 1505, of the great Yorkshire family of Sayvile or Savile; this Sir John served Edward IV and Richard III at Westminster and elsewhere, and was a knight for the body to Henry VII.[37] After the death of his grandfather of the same name he had acted as 'overseer' of the Flemish glaziers who painted a *Resurrection of the Just* to his grandparents' memory in Thornhill Church, West Yorkshire, at his uncle's expense; he included his own and his wife's figures with theirs.[38] Henry VII in 1500 or so must have chosen him to 'oversee' the men who were to carry out the glazing of Fairford Church, no doubt in celebration of the forthcoming marriage of his elder son Arthur to Catherine of Aragon.

The manor of Fairford was one of the richest of the Warwick lands, which in 1478 had reverted to the crown owing to the minority of Edward Plantagenet, earl of Warwick; but on 28 November 1499 Edward was executed, on Henry's orders, at a time when Ferdinand, Catherine's father, was pressing for reassurance as to the stability of Henry's throne.[39] The administration of the manor seems to have been supervised by the council of Wales, which met either at Ludlow or at Westminster; and Robert Frost, chancellor to the prince, had been Sir John Savile's chaplain at Thornhill, where he had himself, during the 1490s, set up a great *Tree of Jesse* in the east window, close to the Savile *Resurrection of the Just*.[40] Sir John had powerful friends at court, and in March 1503, when he made his will, was able to name as his feoffees Thomas earl of Surrey, later second duke of

---

[35] n.III: Wayment, *Fairford*, pp. 26 and 95.

[36] The v is shown by the accentuation of the bowed and pointed cross-piece of the A. It was the late Prof. Francis Wormald who first read this inscription correctly. The second inscription, on the border of his brigandine, reads IVGESANSBESOI (judge out of a job), and seems to refer to his forfeiture of the stewardship of Wakefield, about the end of the year 1500, while remaining for the time a justice of the peace: Wayment, *Fairford*, pp. 95–6.

[37] Richard III had, on 11 Feb. 1484, appointed him captain of the Isle of Wight: *Calendar of Patent Rolls Ed. IV, Ed. V and Ric. III* (London, 1901), 410.

[38] 'Dodsworth's Yorkshire notes', *Yorkshire Archaeological Journal*, 8 (1883–4), 488. The work of rebuilding the choir 'att the oversight of the said Sir John' was finished in 1493; the window containing the inscription survives in a much damaged condition. Cf. Burlison and Gryll's tracing (*c*. 1870), Victoria and Albert Museum, Department of Prints and Drawings E. 1951–1952.

[39] Wayment, *Fairford*, pp. 1, 96 and n. 97.

[40] The window survives, though much restored. See 'Dodsworth's Yorkshire notes', p. 489.

Norfolk, and Sir Reynold Bray, the king's receiver-general for the Warwick lands. By this time the nine eastern windows (I, n.II–V and s.II–V) and the great west window with the *Last Judgement* had probably been finished, as well as the four in the north clerestory. The most natural explanation of the Prince of Wales' feathers in four of the south side windows of the nave (s. VI–VIII and s. X) is that the whole operation was financed by the council of Wales.

Sir John Savile died in March 1505, and although some work seems to have been carried out during the next few years, including the lower register of the *Judgement of Solomon*, the glazing must still have been incomplete at the death of Henry VII: the twelve Prophets in the north nave aisle (n. VIII, VII and VI), stylistically speaking the most advanced work in the church, had still to be done. We must suppose that about 1512 Wolsey undertook to 'oversee' the completion of the glazing, with the same function that Sir John Savile appears to have had at the beginning of the century: a function that Wolsey himself was to assume in a draft indenture of 1518 when he was to direct the work of Pietro Torrigiano in producing a tomb intended for Henry and Catherine.[41] The Fairford glass was no doubt painted at Westminster,[42] and the probability is that Wolsey, in supervising its completion, asked the king's glazier to include his own image in the guise of a minor character: surely the most convincing portrait of him that has survived.

---

[41] See below, pp. 262–3.   [42] Wayment, *Fairford*, p. 95.

CHAPTER 5

Cardinal Wolsey and the goldsmiths

PHILIPPA GLANVILLE

A gold bowl ... within the cover the cardinal's arms enamelled ... 103 oz. A holywater stock ... with a sprinkyll ... graven with a griffon, a lion and a Cornish chough, cross keys and cardinals hats 145½ oz.

The King's Jewels 1532

Cardinal Wolsey is notorious for his love of splendour and in particular his lavish use of goldsmiths' work, so vividly recalled by George Cavendish and criticized by Polydore Vergil and Hall. Although there is no full inventory of Wolsey's possessions, his goldsmiths' bills and the descriptions of the plate seized by the crown enable a partial reconstruction of how and why he accumulated so much, who his goldsmiths were and how he manipulated his massive holdings to flesh out his role as prince of the church and statesman. Wolsey's attitude to conspicuous display has to be seen in the context of the expectations of contemporary society, as becomes clear when the state occasions he organized are compared with those of an earlier era, or those of the French or Flemish courts. All this splendour depended on the goldsmiths of London and their control both of the alien craftsmen and of the imported plate which the English so admired.

I

Cardinal Wolsey shared, if he did not exceed, his master's understanding of the psychological significance of conspicuous display. His stage management of Cardinal Campeggio's arrival in London as papal legate in November 1518 is typical, although on this occasion his tactics failed. The twelve mules he sent to supplement Campeggio's eight had dummy coffers covered with red cloth 'as though they had been full of Treasures', but due to an accident the actual contents were exposed as being merely 'olde Hosen, broken Shoen and roasted Fleshe ... and muche vile baggage'.[1] In Giustinian's assessment of Wolsey's personality and way of life, he stressed goldsmiths' work as a constant feature of the cardinal's personal setting. 'He always has a sideboard of plate worth 25,000

[1] Hall, pp. 592–3.

ducats, wherever he may be ... In his own chamber there is always a cupboard with vessels to the amount of 30,000 ducats.'[2] The Italian commented that this lavish show was characteristic of the English nobility, an observation borne out by contemporary plate inventories. In 1509 John de Vere, earl of Oxford, mentioned in his will almost 15,000 Troy ounces of silver plate and 240 ounces of gold, and the duke of Buckingham left well over 6,000 ounces at his fall. In 1533 Bishop Nicholas West left over 6,000 ounces and Lord Dacre and Sir Christopher Dacre had more than 6,500 ounces of plate valued a year later.[3]

George Cavendish vividly evoked the theatricality with which Wolsey both displayed and relinquished his wealth in plate to the king's agents on 19 October 1529, setting it out on tables in a series of rooms at York Place, with baskets underneath full of broken plate. Although the indentures to which Cavendish refers have not survived, we do have the incomplete series of accounts for plate and jewels supplied by Wolsey's goldsmith Robert Amadas between 1517 and 1529, and a statement of the plate remaining at Cawood in November 1530.[4] Given that during his retreat to Esher following his fall, Wolsey lacked even the basics of tableware, it is evidence of his partial return to favour that the Cawood plate a year later weighed over 6,500 ounces. In weight of metal this is far in excess of the 1,300 ounces of Serjeant Keble in 1500, the 2,700 left by Viscount Lisle, the 4,000 or so at The Vyne in 1541 (which exclude chapel plate) or the duke of Suffolk's holdings in Southwark in 1535, more than 5,500 ounces. The stock of plate ready for sale in the counting-house of Robert Amadas in 1532 was half as much.[5] However, when the content of the Cawood plate is analysed and compared with the cardinal's earlier orders from Amadas, it emerges as a relatively modest and makeshift provision, dominated by everyday tableware and drinking vessels. Few of the objects bore Wolsey's arms or elaborate decoration, and none was noticeably large or heavy. Apart from a cross, there were no mounted hardstones nor exotica such as ostrich eggs, and none of the spectacular buffet pieces, which are characteristic of the inventories of men of rank and frequently appear in the possession of the wealthier livery companies. In other words, the Cawood inventory is a further reminder of how much status Wolsey had lost in 1529.

Wolsey's use of plate as the principal element of display in his chapel and

[2] R. Brown (ed.), *Four Years at the Court of Henry VIII* (London, 1854), II, p. 314 and I, p. 79.
[3] Oxford Inv., W. H. St J. Hope (ed.), 'The last testament and inventory of John de Veer, thirteenth earl of Oxford', *Archaeologia*, 66 (1914), 329–38; Buckingham Inv., Staffordshire Record Office, D 641/1/3/10; West Inv., PRO, PROB2/488; Dacre Statement, *LP*, Addenda (i) 933; P. Glanville, *Silver in Tudor and Early Stuart England* (London, 1990), chapter 1.
[4] Cavendish, p. 99; *LP*, IV (iii), 6184, 6748: PRO, SP1/56, fols. 223–31, PRO, E36/171.
[5] Keble Inv., E. W. Ives, *The Common Lawyers of Pre-Reformation England. Thomas Kebell: a Case Study* (Cambridge, 1983) or Wiltshire Record Office 88/5/179; Lisle Inv., M.St Claire Byrne (ed.), *The Lisle Letters*, 6 vols. (London, 1981) VI, pp. 189–91; Sandys Inv., E. W. Chute, *History of The Vyne* (Basingstoke, 1888), pp. 52–5; Suffolk Inv., Lincoln Record Office, Ancaster MSS X/A/14; Amadas Inv., PRO, PROB2/486.

dining chamber was characteristic of his time. So was the diversity of sources from which his plate came; some was commissioned in London, Bruges or Paris, other pieces were bought new or secondhand, and had his arms, badge or motto added in enamel or engraving; others again came as diplomatic gifts or, a smaller category, his dues at New Year. Because his heraldry is so distinctive – the chough and griffin, the cardinal's hat and pillar, the motto 'Dominus mihi adjutor' and lions – his large display of plate can be recognized in the royal Jewel House lists of 1532, 1547 and 1574.

Historians of Tudor England have tended to ignore the part played in courtly society by goldsmiths and their work. This is perhaps understandable, since little plate survives from the first half of the sixteenth century. The rarity of Tudor plate today may be gauged from the fact that the entire volume of English silver now surviving from the late medieval and early Tudor period is less than the stock of plate held in his counting-house by Robert Amadas, court goldsmith to Henry VIII, at his death in 1532. Many of the pieces which do survive, such as the Howard Grace Cup, in the Victoria and Albert Museum (plate 55), the earliest known piece of Renaissance plate, or Lady Margaret Beaufort's Cup at Christ's College, Cambridge, are relatively light and have lost the jewels which originally enhanced them. Other pieces, such as the standing mazer at All Souls College, Oxford, have been heavily restored and others again, such as the late fifteenth-century Anathema Cup (Pembroke College, Cambridge) have lost their covers. The gilding on some has worn away to a pale lemony colour and others have been so thickly regilded in the nineteenth century as now to appear almost brassy. This treatment has been meted out to the silver given by Bishop Richard Fox to Corpus Christi College, Oxford. This is a fascinating group of early Tudor silver, much of it dating from the last phase of Gothic in England, just before the 'antique' style swept through the workshops of northern Europe, in the decade between 1510 and 1520.[6]

Although there is a paucity of objects and of illustrations, there is, however, an immense wealth of documentation which reveals both the form and function of early Tudor plate. Goldsmiths' work is unique among the decorative arts in that the raw materials, gold, silver and precious stones, retain their value, and can be re-fashioned repeatedly as circumstances require. Because of this inherent value and because there was always a lively second-hand market for worked silver, inventories and bills are usually precise, quoting not only the description but also the rate per ounce and the weight of each piece. When assaying the Dacre plate prior to melting it, valuers could identify six different standards of alloy besides sterling, the finest being plate imported from Paris and the worst being 'untouched' (without hallmarks), still with its low-grade solder. The different

---

[6] For Fox's plate, see T. Wilson, 'Bishop Fox's Crozier', *The Pelican* (1980–1), 8–27; M. Campbell, 'Bishop Fox's Salt', *The Pelican* (1983–4), 39; P. Glanville, 'Bishop Fox's Ablution Basins', *The Pelican* (1983–4), 77. For Tudor silver generally, see Glanville, *Silver*.

values by weight put on plate have a real meaning, conditioned primarily by their precious metal content, and by a further allowance for the quality of the fashion or workmanship. Hence objects can sometimes be tracked through successive changes in ownership down to the virtually inevitable final re-fashioning. This process, from the goldsmith's shop to the melting pot, might take only a few years. The 1521 inventory of the Jewel House of Henry VIII contains some 900 entries. Only seventy-four of these pieces can still be identified in the Jewel House of Queen Elizabeth in 1574.[7] The 1520s, of course, saw an abrupt and dramatic change in the style of English silver, with the arrival of Renaissance motifs such as 'antique boys', moresques, grotesques, dolphins and mermen: so, given this flood of new motifs, the Jewel House inventory taken after the death of Robert Amadas in 1532 might be considered a more revealing benchmark of the survival of plate, with these recent pieces perhaps being retained after the less fashionable older ones had been melted down. However, exactly the same policy of discarding old plate was followed: of the 977 sets listed in 1532, only ninety can be identified as still in the Jewel House in 1574. Many of these, the most highly fashioned and the gold vessels, came from the plate of Cardinal Wolsey, given up in 1529. When plate was perceived as 'battered, bruised and unfit for service' it was unsentimentally consigned to the melting pot, whether to be refashioned into some more appropriate form, to pay the goldsmith's bill or merely to realize its cash value.

Because plate was the essential indicator of status, it was crucial in the ritual of gift-exchange which was the visible cement holding the hierarchy together; it also played an essential role in every ceremonial occasion. This was acknowledged in the emphasis which chroniclers such as Hall and ambassadors such as Niccolo Sanuto gave to display, in an instinctive understanding of the pomp and theatre which underlay medieval and Renaissance kingship. When Sanuto was entertained at Richmond in May 1515, the Italians sat down to dinner only after 'witnessing a display of gold plate of most immense value'. Hall commented on the feast of the two kings in 1520, 'the riches of vessel, plate and Iuelles surmounteth the witte of man to expresse', and of the chapel plate at Ardres, he 'suppose(d) neuer suche like were seen'.[8] Goldsmiths' work provided the backdrop to every one of the ceremonial set-pieces of the state and the church, whether it was the English royal chapel at the Field of Cloth of Gold, in which three altars were completely equipped with gold plate, one for Wolsey, one for the king and one for the queen, or the famous banquet laid on by Wolsey for the French ambassadors at Hampton Court in 1527. Cavendish's account of his

---

[7] A. J. Collins (ed.), *Jewels and Plate of Queen Elizabeth, the Inventory of 1574* (London, 1955); E. Trollope (ed.), 'King Henry VIII's jewel book', *Reports and Papers of the Associated Architectural Societies*, 17 (1884), 155–229.

[8] Hall, pp. 606, 618. In 1518, Giustinian compared Wolsey's York Place banqueting hall to the tower of Chosroes the Sassanian because of its decoration of massive vases (vassi) of silver gilt (*Four Years*, II, p. 225).

ostentation on the last occasion has been quoted many times, but the point to note was that the elaborate gold plate laid out on Wolsey's sideboards remained on display, none of it actually being taken off for use. This served as a telling illustration of the wealth of the cardinal and it was by no means a unique demonstration.[9]

Whether in a secular or religious context, the aim of such public exhibition of goldsmiths' work was to create a spectacular display of treasure to dazzle visitors, as Erasmus stressed in his admittedly ironic account of visits to Walsingham and Canterbury: 'you would say that Midas and Croesus were beggars if you saw that vast assemblage'. The shrine of Thomas Becket was the richest in England, embellished with precious metals and massive stones: 'gold was the meanest thing to be seen there'. Some jewels, it was claimed, were larger than the egg of a goose. The prior demonstrated the finer points, touching each exhibit with a white wand, and telling the name in French, the value and the name of the donor.[10]

The same theme occurs in the descriptions of court displays under Henry VII. When he received Catherine of Aragon into England for her betrothal to his son Arthur, the feast following the joust between the duke of Buckingham and the marquis of Dorset was held in Westminster Hall, which was hung with gold thread tapestries: 'in its upper part a royal cupboard was made and erected . . . in length all the breadth of the Channcery, and in itt was set seven shelves or haunches of goodly Height, furnished and filled with goodly and rich Treasure of Plate as could be seene, great part whereof was Gold'. Later that evening, after the disguising, a solemn procession of two hundred lords, knights and esquires entered Westminster Hall, each one bearing either a spice plate or a cup of precious metal, to refresh the guests, 'yet more to be wondered, for that the Cupboard was nothing touched but stood compleat garnished and filled, seemingly not one diminished'. Two days later, on Sunday, another banquet was held in the Parliament Chamber, again with a lavish and theatrical display of plate, most of it gold.[11]

Comments by writers both English and foreign, stressing the number of shelves and quality of the plate displayed, are an index of the contemporary significance attached to such an exhibition. This was not necessarily achieved from the host's own resources; it was common practice to borrow or hire in order to achieve the rich effect, as happened in the livery companies. When one of their members was to serve his turn as sheriff or mayor, then the company gathered its

[9] Cavendish, pp. 69–70.

[10] J. G. Nichols (ed.), *Pilgrimages to Saint Mary of Walsingham and Saint Thomas of Canterbury by Erasmus* (Westminster, 1849), pp. 55–6.

[11] T. Hearne (ed.), *Johannis Lelandi de Rebus Britannicis Collectanea*, 6 vols. (Oxford, 1774), v, pp. 357–73. Similar terms were used for the reception of Philip and Joanna of Austria at Windsor in 1506: 'a great and rich cupboard which continually stood in the Great Hall with all gilt plate' (J. Gairdner (ed.), *Memorials of King Henry VII*, Rolls Series 10 (London, 1858), p. 300).

resources, both collective and personal, to ensure that a decent show was made during their colleague's year of office. In 1515, when the Drapers' Company held a well-documented election feast, five members of the company were responsible for lending between them some 160 pieces of plate, many drinking cups, but also eight large ewers and basins. On this occasion, the number of diners and their guests was far beyond the normal resources of the company. Two lists of plate belonging to the Goldsmiths' Company, both of the 1520s, may relate to a loan (proposed or already arranged) of their silver to assist in an official entertainment. Alternatively, these lists of the company resources may have been prepared at the time of one of the extraordinary demands for loans made by the king and cardinal in 1522 which fell so heavily on the livery companies.[12]

These institutional inventories, which have survived among the papers of Cardinal Wolsey in the British Library, demonstrate the normal Tudor ownership pattern for both livery companies and private owners, in that most objects carried the badge or arms of the owner, and they are dominated by plate for drinking and plate for ritual handwashing. These two were the dominant sections in all domestic plate lists, followed closely by elaborate salts and dining plate. Other categories comprised lighting equipment such as sconces, candelabra and lanterns, and miscellaneous categories including standishes (inkstands), toilet silver, boxes and silver for hawks or dogs. Plate for the chapel was another heavy drain, which for members of the nobility might run to several thousand ounces, since it included not only the vessels for celebrating the Mass, such as chalice, paten and cruets, but also ablution basins and devotional objects. Wolsey's plate was massive and elaborate. The holywater sprinkle described at the opening of this paper was heavier than any other single piece in the Jewel House in 1532. A generous provision for chapel and devotional plate was customary among the nobility and princes of the church. Lady Margaret Beaufort bequeathed 1,800 ounces of chapel plate to Christ's College, Cambridge.[13] In 1533 Catherine of Aragon retained in her closet more than 600 ounces of silver-gilt for her daily worship, despite her diminished status as princess dowager.[14] Henry VIII's bastard son, the duke of Richmond, had rather more plate for his chapel, including a massive 101-ounce cross, with figures of Mary and John, enamelled and 'pounced with roses'.[15] In 1532, Robert Amadas had in stock in his counting-house six devotional images (of Saints Agnes, Paul, Peter, Edmund,

[12] A. H. Johnson, *The History of the Worshipful Company of the Drapers of London*, 5 vols. (Oxford, 1914–22), II, pp. 6–7; P. Glanville, 'The Company's Plate in the 1520s', *Goldsmiths' Company Review* (1984–5), 19–22; BL, MS Additional 24,359, fols. 43–4 and MS Additional 34,367, fol. 1.

[13] R. F. Scott (ed.), 'On a list preserved in St John's College of the plate and vestments bequeathed by the Lady Margaret to Christ's College', *Communications of the Cambridge Antiquarian Society*, 9 (1899), 349–67.

[14] Catherine of Aragon Inv., PRO, SP1/75, fols. 150–2 (*LP*, VI, 340)

[15] Richmond Inv., J. G. Nichols (ed.), 'Inventories of the Wardrobe, Plate, Chapel Stuff etc. of Henry Fitzroy, Duke of Richmond and of the Wardrobe Stuff at Baynard's Castle of Katherine, princess Dowager', *Camden Miscellany*, III (1855), p. 6.

Anthony and Nicholas) weighing between 55 and 72 ounces.[16] All these statues and most of the elaborate sets of altarplate vanished either during the Reformation or in the difficult years of Elizabeth's reign, when she could be criticized for the use of altar candlesticks in her private chapel and when All Souls, for example, found it expedient to transfer its pair of liturgical ablution basins from the chapel to the domestic plate lists.

The necessary task of impressing foreign visitors and guests with a prince's splendour could be achieved in a number of ways. Henry VIII advertised the magnificence of his reception for the French ambassadors at Greenwich in 1527 by opening up the temporary Banqueting House to the public: 'these two houses with Cupbordes, hangynges, and all other thinges the kyng commaunded should stand still, for thre or foure daies, that al honest persones might see and beholde the houses and riches, and thether came a great nombre of people'. Henry's display at Greenwich rivalled that arranged for Wolsey at Hampton Court as part of the same visit. The Greenwich display, as Hall describes it, had as its centrepiece a cupboard with seven shelves, all dressed with fine gold. A second cupboard was all of 'massy plate of siluer and gilte, so high and so brode that it was maruaile to beholde'.[17] In addition, the ewery boards (the places from which the silver for washing was distributed) were laden with massive ewers and basins 'so great that euery Lorde grudged to beare theim'. That this is not mere hyperbole can be seen from the immense weight and size of the gold basins given to Wolsey by Francis I (333 ounces) or of the basins left in the Jewel House at the time of the sale of Charles I's possessions in 1649/50. One souvenir of the Jewel House of Henry VIII weighed over 500 ounces; when it is realized that the normal weight for a silver basin (when empty) was between forty and eighty ounces and that it would be heavier by a ewerful of rosewater once the diners had washed their hands, it can be seen that the bearers of basins might be in real difficulties.

The task of manipulating these massive pieces of silver, whether the traditional medieval pair of ablution basins or the basin and accompanying ewer, was on occasions of state an obligation undertaken by members of the nobility. When Cardinal Wolsey celebrated a Mass at St Paul's in September 1518, in the presence of the king and the French ambassadors, the basins for washing were brought by three earls, followed by two dukes and a marquis. Again, when Wolsey sang Mass at Greenwich in February 1521, the earl of Essex brought the basin, the duke of Suffolk took the assay (sample) of the water and the duke of Norfolk, the towel.[18] However offensive to these high-born men their service to the 'butcher's son' might seem, this ceremonial involving dukes and earls was not peculiar to the English court.

Welcoming and housing foreign visitors was a considerable strain on the Jewel House. Henry VIII expected Wolsey to set out at least as lavish a display of plate at York Place or Hampton Court as the king himself did; indeed, the shortage of an

[16] Amadas Inv., PRO, PROB2/486. [17] Hall, pp. 722 and 724. [18] Hall, pp. 594 and 629.

adequate London palace except Bridewell between 1512, when Westminster was damaged by fire, and 1530 when Henry took over and extended Wolsey's York Place (renaming it Whitehall) meant that the cardinal was relied upon to make a show on behalf of the king. When in 1527 the French embassy arrived in England to arrange the Treaty of Perpetual Peace, on Wolsey's instructions Robert Amadas delivered to the five most distinguished of the party a carefully graded issue of plate (probably from his personal stock rather than from the Jewel House). Each man had, as a minimum, a pair of pots and a basin and ewer, plus a set of three drinking bowls with one cover; in addition, the French bishop who led the party had a pair of flagons 'chased with water flowers'. To enable the courtier Sir Anthony Browne to lay their table, Amadas issued the following day two pairs of gilt salts, the larger 'low square with a cover', weighing fifty-eight ounces, plus candlesticks, slip-end spoons, trenchers, chargers, platters, dishes and saucers, the normal content of a garnish of serving plate. Nothing like this survives today, with the exception of an unmarked waterpot at Magdalen College, Oxford, and a pair of French pots at All Souls.[19]

Not only was magnificence considered necessary in the displays on ceremonial occasions, munificence was also a necessary princely obligation. Ambassadors expected to be presented with a 'cupboard' or set of plate on their return home. The precise content of the cupboard varied, but the gifts made to the Scottish ambassadors at the time of the marriage of Margaret, daughter of Henry VII to James of Scotland in January 1503 are typical. The senior figure always received some gold plate, while the other members had sets in silver gilt. The archbishop of Glasgow, the leader of the embassy, received a cup of gold, six great standing pots, silver 'pounst' (i.e. chased), twenty-four silver drinking bowls with their covers, a ewer and basin and a chafing dish. Henry VIII's gifts to the departing admiral of France in 1518–19 were substantially more lavish: a gold cup 'garnished with great perle', a garnish of tableware, a pair of basins, a set of drinking bowls and four pairs of great pots for the buffet, 'which liberalitie the straungiers much praised'. The full extent of Wolsey's gifts from Francis I cannot be clearly stated, but the gold plate alone identifiable in the 1532 Jewel House inventory as being from that source weighed more than 1,500 ounces.[20]

Such a gift might not be of matching plate; indeed it was considered worthy of note when the plate was 'all of one sute', since this substantially added to the estimation in which the gift was held both by the donor and the recipient. When Henry VIII was being advised about the possibility of buying a splendid set of cupboard plate in Bruges, which had become available from the estate of Erard de la Marck in 1538, his agent urged him to buy the pieces because of their great

[19] For the plate issued to the French ambassadors in May 1527, see BL, MS Egerton 2603, fols. 14–15. For the Magdalen silver, see J. Hayward, 'Tudor Plate of Magdalen College, Oxford', *Burlington Magazine*, 125 (1983), 260–5.

[20] *Lelandi Collectanea*, IV, pp. 258–64; Hall, pp. 595–6.

beauty and because they were all matching. Henry was in competition with Francis I for the plate and he does not seem to have proceeded with this acquisition.[21]

Not only were ambassadors rewarded with plate, but their employers also expected an exchange of gifts. When Henry VIII met Margaret of Austria, regent of the Low Countries, at Tournai in 1513, the exchange of gifts included gold plate. The pieces presented on the English side were all lavished with badges of the Tudors, enamelled roses and imperial crowns or portcullises. A similar obsession with quasi-national symbols emerges in Wolsey's gifts to Francis I at the Field of Cloth of Gold, when the French king received (among other plate) a great gold salt crowned with the English patron saint, St George with the dragon. In return, Wolsey received sets of gold ewers and basins with Francis's initials and with his badge of friars' girdles.[22]

Fashionable antique ornament, which was so prominent both in the gifts to and the purchases of Wolsey, and even apparent in his final remnant of plate at Cawood, seems to have been less significant to his master, the king. The inventory clerks compiling the Jewel House check list on the death of Amadas in 1532, when commenting on 'antique work', were frequently identifying objects which had come from Wolsey, either as gifts or as part of the involuntary transfer of all his plate made by the cardinal when he left York Place in 1529. This may indicate a lack of enthusiasm for antique work on Henry's part in the 1520s or an unwillingness to spend on display plate when he could acquire it by other means; in 1533–4, Henry's bastard son, the duke of Richmond, received gilt pots which were 'graven above the swage of the foote with antique work' but these were probably part of Wolsey's plate originally.[23]

The New Year's gift exchange was the most significant of the ceremonies involving plate and one for which both goldsmiths and donors prepared carefully, as is clear from the instructions which the duke of Buckingham wrote in November 1520 shortly before his fall. The gifts for Henry, Catherine and Wolsey were to be 'of the best and newest faccone'.[24] The king took a close and critical interest in the gifts presented to him by the court at New Year. From 1538 a vivid pen-picture exists of Henry 'leaning against the cupboard, receiving all things' and watching his treasurer of the chamber, Sir Brian Tuke, listing and valuing his presents: this was written by John Husee for Arthur Plantagenet, Lord Lisle, bastard son of Edward IV and lord deputy of Calais.[25] Both the anxiety and the relief as to his present's reception expressed by Lisle's London agent must have been typical emotions for those dependent on the king's favour. Henry's love of

[21] *LP*, XIII (ii) 47.
[22] J. Finot, *Inventaire Sommaire des Archives Départementales du Nord* (Lille, 1895), p. 178. Plate broken in April 1533 included much of Wolsey's: *LP*, VI, 338.
[23] *LP*, V, 1799. Richmond Inv., Nichols (ed.), *Camden Miscellany*, III (1855), p. 12.
[24] *LP*, III (i) 1070.
[25] *Lisle Letters*, V, no. 1086.

plate and jewels was second only to the cardinal's and it was important to keep to certain conventions which governed the New Year's gift exchange. Those from leading noblemen were expected to be of considerable value, either in coin, or, more often, the equivalent in plate. In the 1520s Wolsey regularly gave the king a gold cup weighing sixty ounces or more and supplied by Robert Amadas, at a cost of well over £100 (£117 in 1523–4). In return he received in 1528, at least, a cup of forty ounces, more than any of the nobility. Amadas's own offerings were more modest: in 1531–2, his last year at court, he gave the king six sovereigns in a white paper.[26]

Amadas was one of between four and seven principal goldsmiths normally supplying the king's New Year gifts, to be issued by the Jewel House in return. Canny suitors would take his advice about the appropriate sort of offerings to make to the king. He had the lion's share of this trade, as in 1521 when he provided seventy-three items out of the 250 or so ordered from seven Londoners. Although these orders were a steady source of income, running annually at between £800 and £1,500 during Amadas's working life, they comprised largely standard items – salts, cups, bowls, spoons and so on – of no great elaboration, on which the charge for 'fashion' was effectively fixed. These were contract prices, which rose slowly over time. In the 1480s Nicholas Warley was being paid 5s an ounce, but in 1513, the goldsmith William Holland complained when ordered to make a New Year's gift of two great pots for the queen that he 'cannot live to make such curious work at the price therein written'.[27]

Working towards this tight annual deadline caused difficulties for court suppliers. Amadas, Twistelton, Holland and the other goldsmiths fulfilling Jewel House orders for plate to be issued to the donors of gifts, arranged staged payments on account in April, May or June each year. The pressure intensified up to December, since not only the king, but all noblemen and officers of state expected to receive gifts of plate or money on New Year's Day. The Goldsmiths' Company reprimanded John Gardiner (Amadas's former apprentice) in December 1538 for failing to bring a gilt crown, intended for the cover of a posset pot, for assay and 'touch' (hallmarking). His defence was that Morgan Wolff, the king's goldsmith was harrying him to have it ready for the king, hence his omission.[28]

II

The name of Robert Amadas, Wolsey's principal goldsmith, has frequently been mentioned in the first part of this paper, and in the second part the well-documented career of the richest goldsmith of early Tudor England will be examined in a little more detail. Amadas was the son and nephew of London

[26] *LP*, IV (ii) 3748, V, 686. New Year's gifts rolls are listed in *Jewels and Plate of Queen Elizabeth*, p. 248.
[27] *LP*, I (i) 1549, III (ii), p. 1544.   [28] Goldsmiths' Company, Minute Book H, fol. 74.

goldsmiths and followed the traditional path to trade success for an energetic citizen with an inherited craft but no personal wealth. He married the grand-daughter and heiress of Sir Hugh Bryce, who until his death in 1496 had been the leading goldsmith at the Mint. The Amadas family association with Bryce was of long standing: he had been apprenticed to Robert's uncle John in 1453. Amadas also followed in Bryce's footsteps by linking himself with the crown, first through the Mint, then as a direct supplier of goldsmiths' wares to the court. The forced loan which Henry VIII demanded from the City in 1522 is a useful indication of comparative wealth; Amadas gave £400, far more than any other member of his company. The next largest contribution, of £150, was from Sir Thomas Exmew, knight and alderman, and the rest of the seventy-two goldsmiths named each gave well under £100.[29]

The traditional picture of Henry VII as a man with no appreciation of goldsmiths' work and its role in the monarch's environment is dramatically contradicted by hard financial facts: between 1491 and 1509, he spent some £200,000 or even £300,000 on plate and jewels.[30] Yet his son's accession brought a marked shift in royal expenditure on conspicuous display, and as the amounts of the treasurer of the chamber and the more detailed Revels Accounts show, one favourable to Amadas's career.[31] The young king dressed for his jousts and revels in gold-embroidered garments or costumes sewn with gold letters and devices, and he clothed his courtiers and even his guard in similar style. Fancywork in gold and silver, 'gold stuff for the disguisings', jackets for the guard made of green satin embroidered with gold and silver spangles, and even horse harnesses of goldsmiths' work predominated in Amadas's early court orders, far exceeding in value the annual contracts for New Year's plate. In September 1510 he was paid £266 for 'letters, wreaths, hearts and roses of fine gold', all to be worn by the king and queen at their revels. Some were lost, others 'given by the King to lords and ladies of his jacket', or 'for pleasure suffered to be taken'. Of the 439½ ounces of gold, comprising hearts, 259 initial HS and 219 initial KS which Henry and Sir Thomas Knyvett wore in the revels held at Westminster Palace on 13 February 1511, Amadas received back less than half. An example of these little gold trifles, made to be sewn on to the royal garments, is a miniature whistle shaped like a pistol, which by family tradition was the king's first love-gift to the young Anne Boleyn.

In one exceptional year, 1513, Henry spent over £2,400 with Amadas and with Mortemer the court embroiderer, on gold-embroidered jackets for his guard alone, for his meeting with the Emperor Maximilian. But even that looks modest

---

[29] I am grateful to Gordon Glanville for sharing his meticulous work on Amadas and to the wardens of the Goldsmiths' Company for allowing me access to their records. Much of what follows draws on P. Glanville, 'Robert Amadas, Court Goldsmith to Henry VIII', *Proceedings of the Silver Society*, III/5 (1986), 106–14. T. F. Reddaway and L. Walker, *The Early History of the Goldsmiths' Company, 1327–1509* (London, 1975), pp. 276–7, 285–6.

[30] S. B. Chrimes, *Henry VII* (London, 1972), p. 217.   [31] *LP*, II (ii), pp. 1444–73, 1490–1517.

beside the £2,000 spent in July 1513 for horse harness and 'trappers' of goldsmiths work, and Amadas's expenditure of £462 'for garnishing a headpiece with crown gold, garnishing a salet and mending a shapewe (helmet)'. The king's sister Mary's betrothal to Louis XII of France stimulated further massive orders for jewels, plate and gold-embroidered textiles for her. At the same time, state business also brought orders to Amadas; in March 1514 he was paid £1,576 for making a new great seal and for jewels. Issues and gifts of plate for foreign ambassadors formed a large part of Amadas's orders in the 1520s, particularly between 1527 and 1530, when important embassies from France, from the emperor and from the pope arrived in London: in October and November 1529, for instance, Sir Brian Tuke paid Amadas on two occasions for plate delivered to Cardinal Campeggio.[32]

Another of the regular Jewel House orders to Amadas was for gold collars and chains, traditional marks of royal favour. Gold livery collars of ss, interspersed with enamelled Tudor roses, knots and portcullises, can be seen in several of Holbein's portraits, and one survives among the London mayoral regalia. Although unmarked, the collar, originally presented to Sir John Alen, may be taken as typical of one facet of Amadas's work: the 'Jewells of Golde and Stonys' in his counting house included a 'George with a Garter' valued at 42s 6d, a silver cramp-ring, a pomander of base gold set with pearl and stone, bracelets 'for a Mannys nek' and for an arm, and caskets set with pearls. By far the most valuable items were two gold chains, one with a cross weighing only 23½ ounces, appraised at over £50. If not for the king, these were doubtless intended for one of the noblemen and courtiers so prominent among Amadas's customers: the nine 'Sperat' (hopeful) debtors listed in his inventory as owing a total of £2,052 included Suffolk, Huntingdon, Northumberland, Wiltshire, Dorset and Sussex, as well as his Mint colleague Lord Mountjoy.[33]

Amadas's success as a court supplier can be assessed partly by the offices he later achieved. From the earliest entries in Henry VIII's chamber accounts, the size of the orders he received stands out. He was usually paid by the customary method of a warrant but sometimes, as in 1515, special orders slipped through the system. On 7 April he was paid £102 12s 4d 'upon a book syned for making of divers things for the French Queen bought of him'. Control of expenditure in the royal household was always a problem; when Wolsey proposed a thoroughgoing reform in 1519, Amadas was to be responsible for auditing, an indication of the acumen with which he was credited by the cardinal, and of the trust Wolsey reposed in him. Amadas was acting as master of the jewels from 1524, replacing Sir Henry Wyatt, and was the first trained goldsmith to achieve this office at the heart of the court, although letters patent granting him the title and salary of £50 a year were not sealed until 20 April 1526. He was receiving exchequer payments

[32] *LP*, v, pp. 315–16.
[33] PRO, PROB2/486. Another version of this list, with different names and total is in *LP*, VI, 924.

as treasurer of the jewels in the last year of his life, and as direct evidence of the royal favour, he was granted a profitable wardship in 1518. The ward, Richard Scrope, heir to a Wiltshire family, was later to marry his daughter, so reinforcing the family's wealth and standing.[34]

While Amadas's parallel career as Mint official is too complex to be discussed in detail here, it was undoubtedly the mainspring of his prosperity. Although his father and uncle apparently had no direct Mint connection, Amadas's marriage to Elizabeth Bryce probably gave him his opening, and he subsequently had a long career as Mint deputy. With his son James, Bryce had had a joint appointment as porter and clerk at the Mint from 1472, which had continued under Henry VII; these apparently minor titles conceal a major financial influence. Although the date of Amadas's marriage to Elizabeth is not known (it certainly antedates 1503), he was a close family friend before 1498, when he witnessed the will of Sir Hugh's widow. The first recorded event in Amadas's association with Mint affairs came the following year, when he was appointed joint keeper of the exchange at the newly established Leadenhall exchange, with the duty of taking in old, worn clipped and foreign coin, a constant problem to the financial stability of the Tudor coinage. When Henry VIII came to the throne, Amadas was sufficiently experienced and trusted to be chosen by the new master of the Mint, William Blount, Lord Mountjoy, as master-worker jointly with Edward Jourden.[35]

Amadas's working life saw several attempts to grapple with the problems of the English coinage, culminating in Wolsey's currency reforms of 1526, which introduced the George noble and crown in gold and a lighter silver coinage. Throughout the decade 1510 to 1520, when his activities both as Mint officer and as court supplier of jewels, plate and silver-gilt devices for 'disguises' are well documented, he and Jourden were almost every month taking delivery for melting of hundreds of pounds in coin, from refuse groats to refuse gold. Amadas's expertise was clearly acknowledged by the crown when Henry VIII (unsuccessfully) attempted to persuade the regent of the Netherlands to revise exchange rates for English coin in 1514. Amadas was one of the two Mint representatives who met the Flemish mint masters at Goldsmiths' Hall. A decade later, in 1526, when Archbishop Warham needed advice on the new issue of the Canterbury mint, it was Amadas to whom he turned.[36] The names of two Italian bankers who operated in London, Niccolo Duodo of the Pisani and Antonio Cavallari of the Frescobaldi, among his debtors, are another hint of the ramifications of his financial dealings.

The opportunities for those goldsmiths associated with the Mint were con-

---

[34] *LP*, II (ii) 4263; G. R. Elton, *The Tudor Revolution in Government. Administrative Changes in the Reign of Henry VIII* (Cambridge, 1953), pp. 38–9.

[35] C. E. Challis, *The Tudor Coinage* (Manchester, 1978), pp. 45–6, 63–4 and his forthcoming history of the Goldsmiths' Company in the sixteenth and seventeenth centuries.

[36] Challis, *Coinage*, pp. 67, 71–2.

siderable; in the generation before and after Amadas, Sir Hugh Bryce and Sir Martin Bowes were, as he was, among the wealthiest men in the city. Their prosperity came not from their official fees, but from the 'wastage' occurring in the refining and recoining process. Amadas himself reported collecting some £700 worth in September 1525. Some was probably good enough to sell on again, although only credited at its melt price. Amadas was twice accused by Lord Mountjoy of drawing improper profits from the Tower Mint. By delaying repayments Amadas could employ the king's bullion in his own large-scale money lending activities, and by keeping for himself the filings or scrapings of precious metal which could be sifted out from the sweepings of the Mint floor he could add to his own stocks of gold and silver. When called to account for such malpractice, Amadas resorted to disingenuousness, deliberately misunderstanding the point about sweeping. 'We know not what it means to find any manner of profit in sweeps of a house', he claimed, 'except a man have lost a thing afore and to sweep the house and to search if he can find the same thing again', an extraordinarily brazen defence from a man with forty years' experience of his craft and its practices.[37] The three years between 1527 and 1530 saw an enormous increase in Mint output: the total face value of new silver coinage introduced was over £213,000, whereas in the three years following, it was £90,000 only. The opportunities offered by this enormous volume of bullion to an energetic, knowledgeable and unscrupulous Mint official were considerable. It may be significant that when elected alderman of Bread Street Ward in October 1529, Amadas did not, as he had in 1523, attempt to escape it by pleading pressure of his official duties, but asked that he be excused personal attendance at ward meetings only 'if he shall continue in the King's service'. The fall of his patron, Cardinal Wolsey, may well have shaken Amadas's confidence in his ability to survive at the Mint after Lord Mountjoy's accusations. It is also possible, however, that this by now elderly goldsmith may have felt unwilling any longer to face the struggle of refuting such charges, for he had, earlier in 1529, applied via Wolsey, to the Mercers' Company, requiring them to elect him to the office of mayor of the staple at Westminster 'being desirous of some quiet room or office'.[38] None the less, he remained in office both at the Mint and at the Jewel House until his death, supplying the usual large share of the 1531–2 New Year's plate issues, and dying some time before May 1532.

In Amadas's will (made 3 July 1531), he left the customary bequests to the city's prisons, seven lazar houses, Barking Abbey and his parish church of St Mary Woolnoth, but none was markedly generous, with the exception of £10 for a silver-gilt image of Our Lord for the High Altar of St Mary's. A truer reminder of the whole focus of his professional life is his request that his executors buy the

[37] Ibid., p. 80.
[38] Ibid., pp. 78–80; J. D. Alsop, 'The Mint Dispute of 1530–32', *British Numismatic Chronicle*, 51 (1981), 197–200; *LP*, IV (iii), App. 243.

king a gold cup worth £100 'to be gracious to my wife and children in their suits and causes'. His company was left £20, plus individual payments to all in the livery; but it provided for none of his executors and the overseers were all major figures at court – Sir Thomas More, the duke of Norfolk and Richard Rich. Sir John Daunce, Amadas's long-standing colleague in Mint and Jewel House affairs was left a substantial bequest, £10 'to pray for my soul'.[39] The reason for this bequest may not be unconnected with the fact that Sir John was one of the commissioners who audited the Jewel House after Amadas's death; the commissioners found that Amadas's estate owed the king 'for plate lacking' over £1,760. His widow had other problems too, being vehemently and vociferously loyal to Queen Catherine, and prophesying disaster for the king, called in her book of prophecies the 'Mould warp' (mole), because of his association with Anne Boleyn. Thomas Cromwell, recognizing the crucial role of the treasurer of the jewels, ensured his success at court by taking over Amadas's office immediately it was vacant.

Amadas's civic career was that of a man almost totally absorbed in his Jewel House and Mint duties and anxious to avoid civic office if at all possible. Elected alderman of Farringdon Ward Without in March 1523, he was 'removed and rejected for divers great and urgent considerations'; in other words, Wolsey sent to the mayor, asking that he be discharged because he was the 'king's servant'. His name barely occurs again in the civic records, although he was elected and sworn in as alderman of Bread Street in November 1529. Almost from his first appearance in the Goldsmiths' Company Minute Book in 1492 as a *lowys* (young freeman), Amadas's relations with his craft had a hint of irregularity and of influence manipulated to his benefit. Three years after the death of his father, William, in 1491, with whom he had presumably trained (although there is no record of his apprenticeship), Amadas paid 13s 4d as belated acknowledgement of his unpaid dues for apprenticeship. By 1503, he was sufficiently well established to pay his fine and be admitted to the category of 'young men' of the company. Although he deferred his first term of company office, as renter warden, the following year, paying a fine of 40s, he was by 1505 clearly active both in the craft and in his specialized business of the exchange of money. In that year, he was one of forty-seven goldsmiths granted pardons for unspecified trade offences and was also fined by the company for selling wares below sterling, which had not been brought to the Hall for assay and touch at Bristol Fair.[40]

Amadas moved steadily up through the livery hierarchy, becoming prime warden in 1524, while building up his heavy commitments as supplier of luxury goods, as court officer and as master-worker at the Mint. Clashes of interest inevitably arose from the pressures of dealing with a demanding, competitive

[39] PRO, PROB11/25/7.

[40] A. B. Beaven, *The Aldermen of the City of London* (London, 1908), I, p. 73 and II, p. 169. Goldsmiths' Company Minute Book A, fol. 416, 'Fynes for myswerking and for dysobedience'.

and display-conscious young monarch: in 1511, when Amadas was fourth or punch warden, responsible for hallmarking, he committed the cardinal offence of removing the puncheons from the hall, unprecedented behaviour aggravated by his allowing the company beadle, Edward Frodsham, to 'touch plate because he might not tarry but must go to dinner'. The wardens rapidly called a special private assemble of all the past wardens to discuss these offences. Edward Frodsham was expelled from his post and his lodging while Amadas was to pay a very heavy fine of £5 or to give a gilt cup weighing 22 ounces.[41] Even when prime warden, Amadas paid the minimum attention to company affairs commensurate with his office: his presence is recorded at only six assemblies and obits between April 1524 and July 1525.

At his death, Amadas's workshop in his large house in Aldersgate Street was fully equipped, and the presence of three standing beds in the adjacent men's chamber offers a clue to the number of workmen he employed. The valuable stock of materials in his counting-house included uncut gems, seedpearls, gilt beads, spangles, gold wire and components such as the silver 'amells' or bosses for arms, to be set into basins, ewers and cups: all this indicates that his workshop was still active. The 'Jewels, Gold and Stonnys' were valued at £239 14s 8d, the stock of plate at £629 3s 3½d. However, Amadas took only a handful of apprentices, unlike Sir Hugh Bryce, who took at least twenty and this indicates that in Amadas's long career as court supplier, he must have relied heavily on outworkers and journeymen.[42] Several names of subcontractors occur in association with his, notably Robert Cowpar and John Harlam. Although their names are rarely recorded, occasional references demonstrate the dependence, at court level, on alien craftsmen-specialists in jewellery, stone-cutting or engraving. Amadas worked in partnership with several men such as Cornelius Hayes or Henry Holtswejler of Düsseldorf, who was active in London from at least 1514. Many alien craftsmen skilled in the precious metals and allied trades were employed directly by the king, and Amadas supplied jewels alongside Jacques Marin and Jacques Langelois of Paris, John van Ulrike and Alexander of Bruchsal, who was also engraver to the king.[43] Workmen named as debtors in Amadas's inventory include John Baptist, the king's Italian goldsmith, and Grumbold, presumably also a craftsman, but probably of Flemish origin.[44] Barely glimpsed in royal records, these alien craftsmen appear most prominently in the Minute Books of the Goldsmiths' Company, either in lists of those granted licence to work or when an English master goldsmith was in dispute over some matter

---

[41] Goldsmiths' Company Minute Book b/c, fols. 77–8, 83, 137.

[42] Amadas had a shop from at least 1510, when his servant Jenkin was accused of enticing away another goldsmith's customer: Goldsmiths' Minute Book b/c, fol. 37.

[43] P. Glanville, *Silver*, chapter IV; Challis, *Coinage*, pp. 61–2; J. F. Hayward, *Virtuoso Goldsmiths and the Triumph of Mannerism, 1540–1620* (London, 1976), pp. 109, 282.

[44] Goldsmiths' Company Minute Book I, fols. 271–2. Grumbold may, however, be an anglicization of Grimaldi.

concerning them or their work. When Edward Seymour, earl of Hertford, was disputing his unpaid bill with Nicholas Trappes in 1544, for instance, the goldsmith eventually brought as witnesses the German workmen responsible, to attest that he had not inflated but merely passed on their charges.[45]

Although the social standing of Amadas's family is hard to assess, his career evidently brought him considerable wealth. At his death the total value of his goods, hopeful or 'Sperat' debts and ready money was £3,844 19s 9¼d, and he had two country houses in addition to his main London property in Aldersgate Street, which also incorporated his workshop and two counting houses. He had a taste for paintings unusual even among the great men of his time; apart from painted hangings depicting the royal arms and portraits of Henry VIII and Edward IV, which were hanging in the hall of his London house, he had eleven sets of pictorial and carved panels.[46] The private chapel was fully equipped, not only with two sets of vestments and a printed Mass Book but also with a pair of ablution basins, a pair of cruets and two paxes all wholly gilt, plus parcel gilt holy water stocks and sprinkle, and a sacring bell, an assemblage characteristic of aristocratic or episcopal chapels. His dining table and buffet were equally lavishly set with plate, although its variety was relatively limited. Of the eighty-eight items in his plate cupboards, over a third (thirty-four) were drinking vessels of various kinds, cruses, goblets and standing cups with covers, a 'pece' without a cover, a nut and 'a pot with a haunce[47] with gilt knob'. The other silver was all, except for a pair of candlesticks, directly associated with eating and serving food or drink. Such ewers and basins, flagons, pots and other drinking vessels were the sort of plate thought suitable for ambassadors and for involuntary royal guests such as the duke of Buckingham, imprisoned in the Tower in 1521.[48]

Amadas was the goldsmith used by many of the court, but Wolsey was by far his largest client, from 1517 at least. Wolsey's orders were not only immensely lavish but also very varied, including commissions for imported plate such as massive candlesticks from Bruges, chased with the cardinal's badges, or Paris plate. At Amadas's death, the cardinal, and another of Henry's victims, the duke

---

[45] Goldsmiths Company Minute Book H, fol. 67; M. Blatcher (ed.), *Report on the Manuscripts of the Most Honourable The Marquess of Bath preserved at Longleat, Volume IV, Seymour Papers 1532–1686*, Historical Manuscripts Commission 58 (London, 1968), pp. 99, 100–2; Longleat House, MSS, Vol. IV fols. 53, 66.

[46] Compare S. Foister, 'Paintings and other works of art in sixteenth century English inventories', *Burlington Magazine*, 123 (1981), 173–180.

[47] The meaning of the word *haunce*, hance or hans, found in Tudor plate lists, was formerly uncertain. From this reference and from the list of rates for goldsmiths' work drawn up by a committee of the company in 1516, it is clear that the word is a direct transfer from the French term *anse* (Latin *ansa*), meaning handle. The fashion for drinking beer or ale from a squat pot with a handle, a drinking vessel made in stoneware, delft and glass as well as in silver-gilt, was sufficiently new in the sixteenth century for this type of vessel to have to be qualified with the additional detail in Amadas's otherwise frustratingly brief inventory. See P. Glanville, 'Tudor Drinking Vessels', *Burlington Magazine Special Supplement*, September 1985, 19–22.

[48] 'King Henry VIII's jewel book', pp. 215–16.

of Buckingham, were the leading names in his list of 'Desperat Debts'. Amadas had supplied the duke with the plate necessary to exercise his notoriously expensive hospitality at Thornbury Castle, but the cardinal ran up the larger bill, a staggering £1,600, when equipping his new colleges with jewels and plate during the 1520s.[49]

Although Amadas's stock of plate at his death included a few gilt pieces with antique work valued at 4s 4d the ounce, or 4d more than the standard rate for gilt, his inventory gives little indication of the style of his personal plate, with the exception of his spoons, which were slip-topped or had lion finials. By the time he died, designs for silver in the Renaissance manner had been circulating among northern goldsmiths for well over a decade, although England was a little behind France and Flanders, and indeed at this time derived its new ornament largely through the medium of Flemish craftsmen and French painted ornament. It is in Cardinal Wolsey's patronage that we find perhaps the clearest evidence for the penetration of such forms into court silver. His purchases stood out not only in their scale but also in their consciousness of continental fashion. Indeed, the unique interest of Robert Amadas's career lies in his position at the centre of court patronage at a time when his craft, together with others such as sculpture and manuscript illumination, was first affected by the Italian Renaissance. In gold-smiths' work, as in other fields, the enormous scale and intense concentration of Cardinal Wolsey's patronage, a patronage which was vital to Amadas during the central years of his career, made an important contribution to the dissemination of continental styles at the court of Henry VIII; a king who, in this respect at least, could only follow in his minister's footsteps.

[49] *LP*, iv (iii) 6748(15); B. J. Harris, *Edward Stafford Third Duke of Buckingham, 1478–1521* (Stanford, 1986), pp. 76–9, 92, 132–3.

CHAPTER 6

Wolsey's foreign policy and the domestic crisis of 1527–8

S. J. GUNN

Of all the portfolios that cluttered the desk of Thomas Wolsey, chancellor, legate and chief minister, that for foreign policy was always one of the most important, and was often the most important of all. It was important to Henry VIII, whose reputation and dominance among the rulers and pundits of Europe was a vital element in the image and self-image of magnificent kingship. It was personally important to Wolsey, a man gratified to acknowledge applause from the European audience, and well aware of his own international significance as a prince of the church. This much historians recognize, as no one can fail to do in considering the time and energy devoted by the cardinal to the trivial minutiae of diplomatic bartering, or the formulation of impossibly sweeping schemes for the political salvation of Christendom. Yet there is a temptation to dismiss the diplomatic wrangling as a pointless waste of time, and the international statesmanship as a hopeless waste of hot air. Wolsey, we feel, should have spent his effort neutralizing political rivals at court, or overhauling medieval government, not chasing diplomatic chimeras. But we fail to understand the priority which cardinal and king accorded to foreign affairs, because we divorce international politics from domestic politics and problems of government, as Wolsey was never free to do.

The last four years of Wolsey's ministry demonstrate with especial force how his management of the king's business was a seamless web, in which the conduct of foreign affairs depended on, and in turn determined, developments in many other areas of the minister's responsibility. This made the successful conduct of an active and adventurous foreign policy – the sort the king wanted – a task of formidable intellectual and political complexity. Wolsey had to take account of the changing objectives and capacities of the rulers of all the significant European states, and the relations between them; of the internal politics of England's leading neighbours, France, Spain, Scotland and the Netherlands, and the possibility of exploiting these to England's advantage; of the effects of foreign policy on England's economic and social stability; and of the importance of visibly successful management of foreign affairs in the maintenance of the king's trust in him, and of his dominance among the king's advisers, many of whom had strong views about foreign policy and were active as ambassadors, negotiators and generals. Finally, from 1527, Henry's determination to secure from the pope an annulment of his marriage added another degree of difficulty to Wolsey's handling of European affairs, one which in the end tested his skill beyond its limits.

Before 1525, Wolsey had succeeded in offering Henry the satisfaction of a high profile in European power-politics without high risks. War with France appealed to the king for many reasons, and Wolsey first demonstrated his formidable administrative skills in the organization of military and naval supplies for the campaigns of 1512 and 1513.[1] But war cost money, and demanded reliable allies who were hard to find. Wolsey made his debut as an international statesman in 1514 by negotiating not merely a peace with France, but one under which Henry's sister married King Louis XII, Henry kept the conquered city of Tournai, and the king and his courtiers received large French pensions.[2] This was not, as it might have been, the signal for English withdrawal from continental politics. First there were plots with Louis XII against Ferdinand of Spain; then, after Louis's death and the accession of the bellicose Francis I, plots with the Swiss and the Emperor Maximilian against French domination in northern Italy. When the European powers came together despite English machinations to keep them apart, Wolsey hijacked a papal initiative for a general truce and a crusading alliance to produce the Treaty of London of October 1518: this brought all Christendom together at peace under English leadership, and ended the unprofitable confrontation with France by a new marriage settlement and the sale of Tournai.

In 1519, Henry was kept in the limelight by a brief but respectable run in the election for the imperial crown. Next year, his reconciliation with Francis was celebrated in the glittering showmanship of the Field of Cloth of Gold. By then, Wolsey was already weighing up the possibilities open to England in the impending clash between the new emperor, Charles V, king of Spain and lord of the Netherlands, and his natural rival Francis. Both France and Charles's conglomerate empire were far richer and better-armed than England, but Henry could still command centre-stage by one of two means. Either the king and his cardinal could arbitrate a peaceful settlement, or they could exploit the conflict to renew English conquests in France. Characteristically, Wolsey prepared to do both. At Calais and Bruges in 1521 he unsuccessfully played honest broker between the continental giants, while at the same time extracting the best

---

[1] S. J. Gunn, 'The French wars of Henry VIII', in J. Black (ed.), *The Origins of War in Early Modern Europe* (Edinburgh, 1987), pp. 28–47; Pollard, pp. 18–20. I am grateful to C. S. L. Davies and Dr E. K. Cameron for their helpful comments on this chapter, and to the Warden and Fellows of Merton College, Oxford, and the University of Newcastle upon Tyne for research fellowships which enabled me to write it.

[2] For what follows, see J. J. Scarisbrick, *Henry VIII* (London, 1968), pp. 51–107, 125–40; R. B. Wernham, *Before the Armada: the Growth of English Foreign Policy, 1485–1588* (London, 1966), pp. 85–110.

possible terms from Charles for an offensive alliance, to be concluded should his arbitration fail.[3] The years of war which followed were not without successes, and deep though temporary incursions were made into French territory. But Wolsey's attempts to fund the final push into France, following the capture of Francis I at the battle of Pavia, were defeated by widespread resistance to unparliamentary taxation, and Charles capped his failures to provide full support for earlier English campaigns with evident unenthusiasm for large-scale annexations by Henry during the captivity of the French king.[4]

So, in August 1525, Wolsey began the last phase of his foreign policy by making peace with France, and demanding that Francis be freed. Charles released Francis in January 1526, under the crippling terms of the Treaty of Madrid; these terms Francis soon repudiated, leaving his sons as hostages in Spain. The threat of complete imperial dominance in Italy enabled Francis to assemble a league of Italian states, including the papacy, to fight Charles by the Treaty of Cognac in May 1526.[5] English diplomacy had encouraged the formation of the league, and provision was made for Henry to enter it as 'protector', but he had no good reason to pour large subsidies into the drain of Italian warfare, and Wolsey spent the summer of 1526 expostulating Henry's goodwill towards the league, but insisting on his inability to participate. To the Italians, as to France, Wolsey offered England's mediation between the emperor and his enemies, to unify Christendom against the twin threats of Lutheran subversion and Turkish conquest, threats brought home in the summer of 1526 by the diet of Speyer and the Hungarian defeat at Mohács. A universal peace made by English negotiation, like that of 1518, remained the aim of Wolsey and the king for the next three years, but the understandable lack of trust between Charles, with his well-developed sense of imperial dignity, and Francis, with his talent for tearing up treaties, made this an unattainable objective. Wolsey had both to press Charles to concede a peace, and to guard against an independent Franco-imperial settlement, sealed with royal marriages, which might leave England diplomatically and dynastically isolated.

To stand any chance of success, Wolsey had to move ever deeper into alliance with the French. In August 1526 England and France contracted not to treat separately with the emperor. In April 1527 perpetual peace was declared between the two countries, a French marriage was settled for Princess Mary, Henry's only

---

[3] J. G. Russell, 'The search for universal peace: the conferences at Calais and Bruges in 1521', *Bulletin of the Institute of Historical Research*, 44 (1971), 162–93; P. J. Gwyn, 'Wolsey's foreign policy: the conferences at Calais and Bruges reconsidered', *Historical Journal*, 23 (1980), 755–72.

[4] G. W. Bernard, *War, Taxation and Rebellion in Early Tudor England: Henry VIII, Wolsey, and the Amicable Grant of 1525* (Brighton, 1986).

[5] For general narratives of European, and especially Italian, politics between the treaties of Cognac and Cambrai, see K. M. Setton, *The Papacy and the Levant, 1204–1571*, 4 vols. (Philadelphia, 1976–84), IV, pp. 238–327; J. Hook, *The Sack of Rome, 1527* (London, 1972); for French policy, R. J. Knecht, *Francis I* (Cambridge, 1982), pp. 208–20; for English policy, Wernham, *Before the Armada*, pp. 113–21; Scarisbrick, *Henry VIII*, pp. 142–233.

legitimate child, and it was agreed to make war on Charles if he refused final offers for peace. That summer, Francis was elected to the Order of the Garter, Henry to that of St Michael. In August, Wolsey himself crossed to France, but nothing came of the peace conference he hoped to conduct there. He met no more success with the plan he conceived to exploit the captivity of Pope Clement VII, who had been at the mercy of Charles V's mutinous troops since the sack of Rome in May. Those cardinals who remained at liberty were summoned to meet Wolsey at Avignon and establish under his leadership a caretaker government for the entire church, able to arbitrate peace in Europe (and settle Henry's divorce). But only four cardinals appeared, and the pope refused absolutely to delegate his powers to the cardinal of England.

The one important thing Wolsey did do in France was to explain to Francis I the marital manoeuvres of his good brother and perpetual ally King Henry, who had resolved by spring 1527 on his need to divorce and re-marry.[6] Henry's affection for universal peace, Italian liberty and the friendship of France was not entirely due to a small favour he needed from the pope, but England's diplomatic freedom was seriously cramped by the fact that nothing but diehard opposition to any plan for Henry's divorce from Catherine of Aragon could be expected from her nephew Charles V, or indeed from a pope under his influence. If Francis and Charles could not for the moment be reconciled, then England could choose only the French side in the continuing struggle, and this had to be done as resolutely as possible in order to win grateful French assistance in the persuasion of the pope. Thus Henry found himself in January 1528 at war against Charles V, a war declared in Spain by reluctant English ambassadors acting in concert with the French, on Charles's refusal of the latest peace terms. English efforts to restart negotiations for a general settlement, and to neutralize the conflict by a truce with the Low Countries, began almost as soon as this phoneyest of phoney wars had started, but only the truce took hold. Francis and Charles occupied 1528 with the exchange of increasingly insulting challenges to personal combat, while they watched the French army under Marshal Lautrec brush aside imperial opposition to march the length of Italy, only to dissolve outside Naples from the effects of dysentery, typhus and malaria.

This failure, and others which followed, disposed the French to look for peace, and Charles's concern over Germany and desire to visit Italy for his imperial coronation, had the same effect on him. But the English truce with the Low Countries, which also covered the latter's border with France, had opened contact between Margaret of Austria, regent of the Netherlands, and Louise of Savoy, mother of Francis I. In autumn 1528 it was they, not Henry and Wolsey, who began the moves that would lead to the 'Ladies' Peace of Cambrai' in August 1529. Even in summer 1529, Wolsey still hoped that he might preside over the making of peace in Europe, but his increasingly desperate efforts to secure the

---

[6] E. W. Ives, *Anne Boleyn* (Oxford, 1986), pp. 102–9.

king's divorce made him no longer credible as an honest broker, and Francis I and his ministers comprehensively outmanoeuvred the cardinal to keep him from exerting any influence over the final settlement.[7] Despite French assurances of continuing goodwill, Cambrai left England isolated, Henry firmly married to Catherine, and Wolsey in dire straits. Thomas Wolsey, the minister who rose to power largely through his handling of foreign affairs in the war and peace of 1512–14, fell largely through his failure to solve the king's problems by diplomatic means. It is hard to judge what chance he ever stood of success. No amount of pressure on the pope would necessarily have made him give way to Henry on an issue which questioned papal authority at a very inopportune time. No amount of pressure on Charles V would necessarily have made him abandon Catherine's cause. Wolsey was merely the chief minister in one of Europe's peripheral monarchies, and one whose direct influence on the great powers could be exerted only where they clashed along the borders of France and the Netherlands, not in Italy where their struggles more immediately affected papal policy. As we shall see, this drove him to desperate measures. But diplomacy offered him more hope of obtaining the king's desires than any other avenue; and until 1529, the man who had conjured up the unlikely successes of 1514, 1518 and 1521 had good reason to think that he had yet to find the diplomatic problem he could not overcome.

The significance of foreign policy in Wolsey's career, and especially in these final years, was reflected in the demands it placed upon him. Diplomatic duties could elicit from the aging cardinal miracles of physical endurance, like that wonderingly recorded by his gentleman-usher George Cavendish: while in France in 1527, Wolsey sat at his desk writing letters from 4 a.m. until 4 p.m., 'all w[hiche] season my lorde never roose ons to pis, ne yet to eate any meate, but contynually wrott his letters w[ith] his owen handes'.[8] In negotiations too, Wolsey's stamina was tested by sessions of four or more hours' length, and on the day he hammered out the final form of the truce of June 1528 with the ambassadors of France and the Netherlands, discussions lasted from the morning until 2 a.m.[9]

Diplomacy, whether conducted in person or by letter, also called on Wolsey's impressive range of tactical skills. His capacity for the use of deceptive small print struck the French ambassador, Jean du Bellay, who noticed, as the Netherlands' envoys had not, that Wolsey's draft for the truce restored the terms of English trade with the Low Countries not to the *status quo ante bellum*, but to the position

[7] R. Scheurer, 'Les relations franco-anglaises pendant la négociation de la paix des Dames (juillet 1527-août 1529)', in P. M. Smith, I. D. McFarlane (eds.), *Literature and the Arts in the Reign of Francis I. Essays presented to C. A. Mayer*, French Forum Monographs, 56 (Lexington, 1985), pp. 142–62.

[8] Cavendish, p. 61. In all quotations, punctuation and the use of u, v, i and j have been modernized, and other languages usually translated into English.

[9] V.-L. Bourrilly, P. de Vaissière (eds.), *Ambassades en Angleterre de Jean du Bellay* (Archives de l'histoire religieuse de la France, 1905) (hereafter *AAJB*), pp. 195, 269, 291.

one year before the outbreak of war, thus negating all the steps taken by the Netherlands' government in the commercial disputes preceding and during the rupture.[10] Similarly, the cardinal's bland assurance to Charles V that a clause in the treaty of Windsor of 1522, promising Henry an indemnity for English participation in the war against France, was merely a sop to English opinion and would never be implemented, left the emperor bleating like the victim of a peculiarly unscrupulous second-hand car salesman when his failure to pay the indemnity was quoted as an English *casus belli* in 1528.[11] When necessary, Wolsey could delay by negotiating in slow motion, as he did with the representatives of the League of Cognac in autumn 1526.[12] But more often he drove discussions on with a range of histrionic tricks. His language was colourful: he frequently swore by his holy orders, said that he would rather lose an arm or 10,000 crowns than have to break a promise or put unworthy proposals to the king, and in one memorable interview asserted that he would rather be hacked in pieces than give bad advice, would give a finger for two hours' conversation with the king of France, and would bet his head that the emperor would observe the treaty he was proposing.[13]

As a former schoolmaster, Wolsey retained an ability to lose his temper to frightening effect. In France he stormed out of a meeting, and refused to return until Louise of Savoy came and asked him to, 'and by that means', recorded Cavendish, 'he brought ther matters to passe that byfore he cowld not atteyne nor cause the councell to graunt'.[14] He tried similar tactics in the truce negotiations, breaking an impasse with 'an extremity of wrath, the like of which I have never seen in him before', accusing the French and Netherlandish delegates of trying to kill him with frustration, and threatening to conclude a bilateral truce with the Low Countries and then 'give up to the devil practices of peace and war and all the things of this world, and set himself to serving God'.[15] When dealing with one set of ambassadors, like the French in spring 1527, Wolsey would match fits of anger with sessions where he took each envoy aside in turn to recount gently his devotion to their cause. He undermined their negotiating position, by assuring them that their king's views as reported by the English ambassadors in France were more moderate than those they had presented; then he tried to hurry them into a settlement with news of Italian attempts to negotiate a truce unfavourable to France. When they made a substantial concession, he 'esteemed it as much as if we had presented him with a pair of gloves', and pressed for more; when they asked him to give way, he said he would not do so for half the kingdom of France.[16] Yet he knew when to stand firm and when to yield: a

[10] Ibid., p. 283.
[11] Bodleian Library, Oxford, MS Fr c 1, fol. 14v (*LP*, IV (ii) 3884).
[12] *LP*, IV (ii) 2388, 2445.   [13] *AAJB*, pp. 31–2, 196, 238, 266.   [14] Cavendish, p. 58.
[15] *AAJB*, pp. 274–5.
[16] *LP*, IV (ii) pp. 1398, 1401, 1403–4; PRO, PRO31/8/137, fol. 297v (*LP*, IV (ii) 2974).

memorandum of thirty-five points raised in the final drafting of the Anglo-French treaty marked only six as those on which Wolsey would concede nothing, and the remainder as agreed either on the French suggestion, or on a compromise.[17] Wolsey applied similar techniques to the difficult task of reconciling two sets of foreign envoys in the truce negotiations, warning the imperialists that French success in Italy might cause them to withdraw from the talks, then telling the French that Margaret of Austria's council disapproved of the truce and might soon persuade her to recall her representatives.[18] In the last five days of the three months of talks, he pressed each delegation in turn to match concessions just extracted from the other side, until he reached an agreed draft treaty.[19] No one who negotiated with Wolsey doubted his ability. Ambassadors excused their failures to outmanoeuvre him with exasperated epithets about 'a man as difficult as any in the world', or 'the most rascally beggar in the world, and the most devoted to the interests of his master'.[20]

Yet even Wolsey had his limitations. Though other councillors helped him in negotiations, and some important discussions took place at the French or Spanish courts where Wolsey had to trust English ambassadors to carry out his instructions with skill, in diplomacy as in other spheres of ministerial activity he probably delegated too little of his work to his subordinates. His involvement in every detail ensured that everything was done to his exacting standards, and his astounding work-rate certainly impressed the king. But these long hours of diplomacy distracted him from other areas of government, and 1527 and 1528 saw no initiatives in domestic policy to compare with those begun in the post-war lull of 1525–6, which had covered not only the cardinal's old favourites, justice and enclosure, but also Wales, the North, the royal household, the council and the coinage.[21] In 1527, the growing problem of Lutheranism combined with the continual press of business in chancery and star chamber during the legal term to make Wolsey glad to have a breathing-space when forced to postpone his trip to France: in the time before his departure, as he told the king, 'I may do moche good, aswel in keping of your terme, as in the ordering of thise sedicious prechers, and other thinges tending to the weale and quiete of your people.'[22] Wolsey must at times have been frustrated by his inability to deal with so many different problems at once. The extent to which foreign affairs had to take

[17] PRO, PRO31/8/137, fols. 46–8 (*LP*, IV (ii) 3010).   [18] *LP*, IV (iii) App. 168, 179.

[19] *AAJB*, p. 300.

[20] Bibliothèque Nationale, Paris (hereafter BN), MS Fr 20994, fol. 206r (*LP*, IV (iii) App. 106).

[21] J. A. Guy, *The Cardinal's Court: The Impact of Thomas Wolsey in Star Chamber* (Hassocks, 1977), pp. 45–50, 120, 123; P. L. Hughes, J. F. Larkin (eds.), *Tudor Royal Proclamations*, 3 vols. (New Haven and London, 1964–9), I, pp. 110–13; J. J. Scarisbrick, 'Cardinal Wolsey and the common weal', in E. W. Ives, R. J. Knecht, J. J. Scarisbrick (eds.), *Wealth and Power in Tudor England. Essays presented to S. T. Bindoff* (London, 1978), pp. 45–67; C. E. Challis, *The Tudor Coinage* (Manchester, 1978), pp. 68–72; see above, pp. 17–19.

[22] *StP*, I, p. 193.

precedence, because they involved a response to uncontrollable external events, can have been little comfort to him.

On the other hand, the trials of diplomacy had their personal compensations. There was the elation produced by a difficult job well done: Cavendish noted that Wolsey entertained the French ambassadors at Hampton Court in November 1527 at the peak of the Anglo-French alliance, 'lawghyng & beyng as mery as ever I saw hyme in all my life'.[23] There was the chance to advance the cause of his colleges, and of his son Thomas Wynter, with bulls from the pope, building stone from France, and a Parisian education for the boy.[24] There were substantial pensions from France, Spain and Milan, and lavish gifts of plate.[25] Wolsey may not have been open to bribery by continental powers, but it did his finances no harm that kings and their ambassadors believed he was.[26] And whether he enjoyed the exaggerated reverence with which he found himself treated or not, a wide range of contemporaries believed that his diplomatic pomp pandered to a proud heart.

Magnificence was a political weapon, and one Wolsey was ready to use. He briefed his household before they left Calais in 1527 that while in France they were to treat him with the respect due to the king, since he was the king's appointed lieutenant there.[27] When he was waited on at dinner with more servile ritual than Francis I, then, perhaps he was making a statement about Henry's superiority.[28] But our suspicions might be aroused by the fact that the French ambassadors to England were taken aback by Wolsey's equality with his own king in the display of his coat of arms and other symbolic actions.[29] Self-importance was not just a matter of ritual. So visible was Wolsey's supremacy in the management of Henry's foreign relations, that it became easy to think that it was the cardinal and not the king who really mattered. Wolsey's anxiety to protest to Henry in 1527, that he wished to take over the administration of the church during the pope's captivity, not 'for any auctorite, ambicion, commodite, private proufite, or lucre, but only for the avauncement of Your Grace's secrete affaire', suggests what the cardinal thought the king might be thinking.[30] It would have taken a strong man indeed to resist entirely the urge to megalomania cultivated by the pageants with which Wolsey's advent in France was greeted, with their messianic portrayal of the 'cardinalis pacificus', saviour of Christendom.[31] We cannot judge the exact state of Wolsey's ego, but his

[23] Cavendish, p. 70.
[24] LP, IV (ii) 2868–9, 2879, 3562, 3955, 4259, 4294, 4307, 4365, 4374, 4645, (iii) 5212.
[25] LP, IV (ii) 2682, 2830, 2865, 2944, 2987, 3026, 3041, 3153, 3619, 3690, (iii) App. 86; CSPM, 798.
[26] CSPS, III (ii) 16, 32, 37, 210, 252; LP, IV (ii) 3839.
[27] Cavendish, p. 61.   [28] CSPV, IV 151.
[29] V.-L. Bourrilly, F. Vindry (eds.), Mémoires de Martin et Guillaume Du Bellay, II, Société de l'Histoire de France (Paris, 1910), p. 36.
[30] StP, I, p. 278.
[31] S. Anglo, Spectacle, Pageantry and Early Tudor Policy (Oxford, 1969), pp. 225–30.

diplomatic behaviour did little to give the lie to the accusations of his enemies that greed and pride were his besetting sins, for greed and pride were the occupational diseases of international statesmen. Apparently self-aggrandizing and unsuccessful diplomacy was a ready target for those who wished to criticize Wolsey at home, as Skelton's *Speke, Parott* showed.[32] Whether overstated grandeur diminished his diplomatic effectiveness is another question, one the papal nuncio in France answered in the negative in his pen-portrait of Wolsey at Amiens: 'although in all his outward acts he shows excessive pomp and great ostentation, nevertheless, in speaking, in behaviour and in negotiation, he reveals an intellect capable of every greatness, proper to any undertaking or affair, because he is a dexterous and gracious man, full of glorious and noble intentions'.[33]

The foremost of those intentions does seem to have been to satisfy Henry VIII. The king took a more consistent and informed interest in foreign policy than in most other areas of government, and this both eased and complicated Wolsey's task. King and cardinal could work as a very effective double-act, using audiences with the king, 'simple and candid by nature', to encourage ambassadors frustrated by the cardinal's obstructiveness.[34] Wolsey could use the king's disapproval as an excuse for refusing to contemplate concessions, or win goodwill from an ambassador by stressing the trouble he had had in persuading Henry to accept a proposal.[35] Henry enjoyed lecturing envoys on such themes as the benefits of universal peace, but was equally happy to leave the grind of detailed negotiation to his minister.[36] They regularly discussed important issues together, enabling Wolsey to conduct matters by his 'wisedom, discretion and fidelite', having 'had mutual conference with the kinges highnes . . . knowing the intencion and mynde of his grace therein, by mowthe'.[37] When they were apart, Wolsey took care to send on news from abroad as it reached him, keeping Henry in touch with the latest developments.[38] At all times the most significant decisions, above all those of war and peace, rested with the king, and Wolsey never questioned the fact; indeed, he found it politic to refer to all the best ideas on policy, whatever their origin, as Henry's own.[39]

Of course there were hitches in this working relationship. The king's greed for information, especially about the diplomatic showmanship of his fellow-monarchs, left Wolsey apologizing that his account of the pageants at his entry into Boulogne in 1527 was insufficiently circumstantial. He begged the king 'not to impute it to my necligence, but oonly to th'obstinacy of my mule, whiche by

[32] G. Walker, *John Skelton and the Politics of the 1520s* (Cambridge, 1988), pp. 69–94.

[33] A. Desjardins (ed.), *Négociations diplomatiques de la France avec la Toscane*, II, Collections des Documents inédits sur l'Histoire de France (Paris, 1861), pp. 981–2.

[34] *CSPM*, 733.   [35] *CSPS*, III (ii) 39; *LP*, IV (ii) 2974, p. 1398, (iii) App. 148.

[36] *CSPM*, 733, 734; *CSPS*, III (ii) 37, 189.

[37] *LP*, IV (ii) 4080, 4217; *StP*, I, pp. 192–3.   [38] *LP*, IV (ii) 3147, 3178, 3243, 3851, 4409.

[39] *StP*, I, pp. 197, 265.

the [terri]ble noyse of the goneshot was driven to suche a malyncoly that I had inogh to do to kepe my self opon her back; whereby I had no commodite to [hear]e or beholde advisedly anything that was [done]'.[40] More seriously, Henry had a dangerous taste for the red herrings that clogged Wolsey's diplomatic in-tray. He was enthusiastic about the unlikely plan for a marriage between his bastard son Henry, duke of Richmond, and a Portuguese princess, under which the couple would be endowed with the duchy of Milan: Wolsey had to assure him twice that this was only an imperialist ruse to separate England and France.[41] Fortunately, Henry never took hold of the wish expressed by unspecified 'great men' in Germany that he should be elected king of the Romans in preference to the emperor's brother Ferdinand.[42]

Most frustrating for Wolsey must have been the king's occasional obstinate insistence on politically unrealistic points of detail. Towards the end of the lengthy truce negotiations, Henry suddenly became obsessed with the idea that Margaret of Austria should be bound to compensate Englishmen robbed on the high seas by Spaniards, out of the goods of Spaniards resident in the Low Countries. Wolsey commented wearily: 'I do mervayle that the kynges grace doth no better ponder the effecte of the saide truxe, and with whome the same is treated, and to what places and limites the same dothe extende.'[43] Brian Tuke, who had been involved in the negotiations, explained at length to the king the benefits of the truce as arranged, and the impossibility of Margaret's compliance with such extravagant demands. Though Tuke was in agony with kidney stones, he seems to have managed not to convey Wolsey's impatience, even though Henry reopened the subject the morning after Tuke thought he had answered all the king's objections. Finally Henry was satisfied, and turned to suggesting remedies for Tuke's condition; having understood how Wolsey, by his 'high and special policie', had obtained the best possible terms from Margaret's ambassadors, the king commented approvingly, 'Ye, by God, they delt with no fole.'[44]

Henry could be still harder to satisfy on matters closer to his heart, and it was the entanglement of foreign policy with the king's divorce that wrung from Wolsey his most slavish assurances of devotion to his master's cause.[45] However great Wolsey's dedication and industry, though, he could not readily please the king, because to place political pressure on the pope in direct competition with Charles V required an independent influence on Italian politics which England could not exercise.[46] In this the divorce presented in an acute form the problem confronting all Wolsey's attempts at significant intervention in the European politics of the later 1520s, which centred on the struggle for Italy. Henry could not

---

[40] LP, IV (ii) 3289.   [41] LP, IV (ii) 3028, 3051, 3287, 3317, 3362, 3381, 3400.   [42] LP, IV (ii) 2961.
[43] StP, I, p. 190.   [44] LP, IV (iii) 4332–3, 4404; StP, I, pp. 295, 297–8.   [45] StP, I, pp. 194–5.
[46] Wernham, Before the Armada, p. 119; G. de C. Parmiter, The King's Great Matter: A Study of Anglo-Papal Relations 1527–1534 (London, 1967), pp. 11–66; Scarisbrick, Henry VIII, pp. 198–233; H. A. Kelly, The Matrimonial Trials of Henry VIII (Stanford, 1976), pp. 21–59; LP, IV (ii) 3312, 3715, 3750–1, 3913.

win honour or territory by fighting in Italy, and the campaigns of 1522–5 suggested he could not even do so by reconquering areas of France. The alternative was to make peace, 'an acht of as good, hey and perpetual memoyry as any acht that thas ben doen in the tyme of our remembrance', as John Hackett, Henry's representative in the Netherlands, put it.[47] That would give Henry, in the words of the Italian ambassadors at his court, the 'glory, to unite all the other princes for the weal of Christendom'; in the words of Charles V, the 'honour that there [in England] so good a work as peace should be achieved'; in the words of Wolsey, 'the glory and honour thereof, and of al the good successes', which 'shal principaly be ascribed unto Your Highnes'.[48] A policy of arbitration enabled Henry to take the moral high ground on an impressive range of issues, from the defence of Christendom against the Turk, through the protection of Rome against 'the moste detestable, cruell and mauldict tirannye of the emperialles', to the 'good of Italy, which consisted in its freedom from servitude and tyranny'.[49] But contemporaries knew that Henry wanted more than a good reputation and a warm glow inside.

English arbitration was a matter of power, probably – though it is a dangerous phrase to use – a matter of the balance of power. Wolsey offered Henry through peace what he had offered him in 1521 through war, that 'by your wysdome and counsel . . . the gretest parte of Crystendome shalbe rulyd and governyd'.[50] This could not be achieved by mere isolationism. As Wolsey explained to Sir Thomas More, Englishmen hoping to play a significant role in Europe without involvement in alliance politics and even warfare were like men in a fable, who hid in caves to avoid a rainstorm which drove insane those it wetted: they would emerge to find that they could not control the wet fools outside.[51] Instead, England's weight must be used to correct the emperor's dominance in Europe, because, as acute observers in the Netherlands noted, from England's point of view '[yt] were not convenyent for the welt of Cristyn[dom]' that Charles V 'schowld hawe all hi[s] wyll and mynd of the kyng of France and els where, lyke as he dessyrys to hawe, for he showld wyx too grett a lord'.[52] And, in theory at least, the harder it was to bring Charles to reason, the more England could extract from France. As Wolsey told Henry, 'the more difficulte the said Frenche king dothe nowe fynde with th'emperor, the gladder and more easy shal Your Grace have hym to treate and conclude with the same, in all thinges according to Your Graces desire'.[53]

[47] E. F. Rogers (ed.), *The Letters of Sir John Hackett 1526–1534* (Morgantown, 1971), p. 137.
[48] *CSPM*, 734; Haus-, Hof-, und Staatsarchiv, Vienna (hereafter HHSA), Belgien PA17, fol. 305r; *StP*, I, p. 180.
[49] W. Bauer, R. Lacroix (eds.), *Die Korrespondenz Ferdinands I*, II (i), Veröffentlichungen der Kommission für neuere Geschichte Österreichs, 30 (Vienna, 1937), p. 31; *CSPS*, III (i) 588; *StP*, I, p. 190; *LP*, IV (i) 2227, 2233, 2243, (ii) 2604, 3197; *CSPV*, IV, 74.
[50] Gwyn, 'Wolsey's foreign policy', p. 772.
[51] J. A. Guy, *The Public Career of Sir Thomas More* (Brighton, 1980), p. 23.
[52] *Hackett Letters*, p. 98.   [53] *StP*, I, p. 226.

This approach, however, posed two major problems. The first was the danger that Francis, Charles or the Italian states might settle their differences without reference to England, a threat evoked again and again by reports of secret Franco-Spanish negotiations or of rival initiatives for an arbitrated peace, notably those sponsored by the pope.[54] Once England herself had entered the war, Henry and Wolsey had to look more kindly on papal offers of arbitration, though they tried to claim the credit for any settlement made after their rupture with Charles, on the grounds that they had 'brought the enemy of peace to reason by force'.[55] But they would always have preferred a peace negotiated in England like that of 1518, or one made by Wolsey elsewhere like that projected in 1521, or even one made in Spain by English and French ambassadors acting under Wolsey's instructions. The longer negotiations lasted, though, the more the other powers suspected English motives, especially once the divorce became public. As Margaret of Austria warned Charles V in January 1529, Henry and Wolsey would not design a settlement 'without regard to their private profit, and to take advantage of the king of France and perhaps also of the emperor'.[56]

Somehow Wolsey had to bring Francis and Charles to his negotiating table before they found one of their own. But to do so, he had to intervene in the Italian power-struggle, and here lay the second problem. All sorts of schemes were mooted for English occupation of disputed territories during peace talks, and even for the provision of a papal bodyguard at English expense, but none of them was very practical, and no attempt was made to implement them.[57] Second best was to send English money to Italy, with an English representative capable of exploiting the impact of such expenditure on the Italian powers, and this was tried with Sir John Russell's mission to Rome in early 1527. Russell sent back assurances that Henry 'never spent monney, that shall sounde more to your honour, than this', for the pope 'estiemyth hym self as greately bounde to Your Highnes, as ever pope was to anny prince'. But the practical results of Russell's trip were negligible.[58] Meanwhile it became ever clearer that the League of Cognac was a broken reed, because its members did not trust one another sufficiently to act in concert.[59] The only way England could manipulate events in Italy was through the French; so Henry and Wolsey nagged Francis and his council into prompting Marshal Lautrec to advance faster in order to increase pressure on Charles and the pope.[60] It was a lamentably indirect procedure, and it left king and cardinal waiting anxiously for news from Italy, whence letters arrived during Lautrec's campaign at an average rate of one every six days. Worse

---

[54] *LP*, IV (ii) 2679, 2705, 2707, 3002–3, 3028, 3047, 3271–2, 3319, 3321, 3411, 4034, 4063, 4244.
[55] *LP*, IV (ii) 4002, 4897; *AAJB*, pp. 133–4.
[56] HHSA, Belgien PA18/3, fol. 30r.
[57] *LP*, IV (ii) 2556, 2638, 2891, 2948, 3047, (iii) App. 160; *Négociations diplomatiques*, pp. 851–5.
[58] D. Willen, *John Russell, First Earl of Bedford* (London, 1981), pp. 17–21; *StP*, VI, p. 563.
[59] Setton, *The Papacy and the Levant*, III, p. 259.
[60] *LP*, IV (ii) 3350, 3485, 3661, 3713, 3717, (iii) App. 147.

still, Henry and Wolsey could not really be sure whether they wanted Lautrec to succeed or not, for Charles V insisted throughout 1528 that he would not hand back Francis's sons and make peace while a French army remained in Italy, while Francis held out for good terms as long as it still seemed likely that he might conquer Naples.[61] Given Charles's determination, and the large resources of his empire, a single French victory might not be enough to compel him to a peace on England's terms. A French defeat might well lead to peace, as indeed it eventually did, but it would leave the pope to the mercy of the emperor and impede Henry's divorce. Italy alone would not necessarily provide the answer to all Henry's problems, even if he and Wolsey could find the means to seek it there.

Wolsey's task was further complicated by other factors. The maintenance of Henry's neutrality and the need to assert his territorial sovereignty led to awkward diplomatic incidents when French, Flemish and Spanish ships took to attacking each other just outside Calais, Southampton and Sandwich, in Rye harbour, and even, in one spectacular incident, in a running battle up the Thames from Margate to the Tower wharf.[62] Henry demanded action over such affrays, declaring that the French 'may aswell . . . take a Flemyng upon the lande, in any parte of his reame, as oute of any of his said havons'.[63] Wolsey had the difficult task of complaining strenuously without upsetting the French.

The cardinal was also severely limited in the concessions he could offer the French to secure a close alliance. He may have had some real enthusiasm for the idea of terminating the long and wearing conflict between England and France – it would have fitted well with his more general efforts to pick up the threads of Henry VII's policies – and he explained to Henry in glowing terms how the achievement of peace would be to the king's 'eternall honour, glory, and renowne, and to the repose, enriching, and tranquilite of your realme and subjectes for ever'.[64] But to achieve perpetual peace, the English right to the French crown had to be signed away, and some significant compensation was necessary. After initial attempts to get Boulogne, or the county of Guines, Wolsey settled on a pension, payable in salt, from the kings of France to the kings of England for ever. He also had to be very careful over the exact terms of Princess Mary's French marriage, lest the unthinkable happen and Henry die while his sole heiress was an unmarried minor in French hands, or lest Mary's son – the future king of England – turn out more French than English.[65]

In diplomacy with the French there were at least plenty of such issues to haggle over, but in formulating English grievances against Charles V, Wolsey had the opposite problem. From late 1525 English ambassadors had been instructed to badger the emperor about his debts to Henry under the treaty of Windsor of 1522, but whenever the question was raised, Charles expressed his entire willingness

[61] *LP*, IV (ii) 3826.
[62] *AAJB*, pp. 162, 167–8, 174–5; Hall, p. 748; *LP*, IV (ii) 3556, 3621, 3782, 3887, 3956, 3976.
[63] *StP*, I, p. 283.   [64] *StP*, I, p. 250.   [65] *LP*, IV (ii) 2675, 2728, 2771, 2773, 2974, 3105.

to pay, but his temporary inability to do so.[66] This did not make very convincing material for a mortal quarrel between the king and the emperor, and Henry could hardly say he was going to war to stop Charles meddling in the English royal divorce. The English declaration of war in early 1528 had to consist largely of complaints about the emperor's failure to make peace at England's request, a charge readily answered by the fact that it was not Charles but Francis who had broken the Treaty of London to start the war, and then broken the Treaty of Madrid to restart it.[67] The thinness of English claims against Charles would have made it alarmingly hard to justify serious Anglo-imperial conflict without compromising Henry's honour, and this reinforced more practical reasons for Henry's and Wolsey's reluctance to fight the emperor.

Yet Henry and Wolsey could not take such decisions without reference to others. The French were their allies, indeed after April 1527 their perpetual allies, and they had to be sufficiently satisfied with the English alliance to oblige Henry in his dealings with the pope. The English declaration of war itself was made to allay French suspicions that the English ambassadors in Spain had secret instructions not to declare war on Charles even if he did refuse the joint French and English peace ultimatum.[68] In fact the English negotiators did have secret instructions, telling them that 'the king[es] special and grettest desire is to conduce ev[er]ything, if it possibly may be doon . . . by wey of peaxe & frendely man[er], w[ith]oute com[m]yng unto any hostilitie w[ith] th'empero[ur], if by any politique p[er]suasions or good exhortations he can be contented to com[m]e unto reason'; but Henry could not admit this, and had to promise the French that he would punish his envoys for their unwillingness to intimate war.[69] The declaration of hostilities was just one episode in a continuing struggle between French determination to commit England's resources to the war against Charles, and English reluctance.

Even before the treaty of April 1527 bound Henry to fight to compel Charles to make peace, Francis was complaining that the slow progress of Wolsey's peace initiatives would waste that summer's campaigning season.[70] In May 1527, when there was no prospect of joint Anglo-French military action for at least a year, there was much talk of the duke of Suffolk and his army of 10,000 Englishmen who would join a large French army to invade Flanders, as there was of the enlarged Calais garrison which would raid the borders of the Low Countries.[71] But by March 1528, when Henry and Charles had been at war for two months, though preparations had begun to set an army on foot, Wolsey and other councillors told the French ambassadors that it would not be ready before late June.[72]

---

[66] *LP*, IV (i) 1628, 1655, 1799, 1928, 2023, 2040, 2095.   [67] *LP*, IV (ii) 3884.

[68] *LP*, IV (ii) 3826, 3831–2, 3871, 3873, 4564.

[69] CUL, MS EE 4.27.11, fol. 4r (*LP*, IV (ii) 3144); *AAJB*, p. 130.   [70] *LP*, IV (ii) 3042.

[71] *LP*, IV (ii) 3088, 3138; *CSPM*, 799, 800, 809; *CSPV*, IV 97, 99; *CSPS*, III (ii) 69.

[72] *LP*, IV (iii) App. 153–4, 156, 158.

By April the English were talking of a landing in July; then in May, to encourage the French, the date came back to mid-June, and Wolsey and Suffolk began detailed strategic planning.[73] Troops were mustered in London, but by 20 May the captains were told to disband them.[74] By this stage Wolsey's truce nego-tiations were near enough to completion to close the option of an invasion of Flanders, but he had to maintain support to France in other ways, for Francis's impatience was such that he had begun to threaten the termination of the salt pension should Henry fail to do his duty against Charles.[75]

That duty became in the end a matter of money. Between August and November 1527, Henry contributed £47,499 15s to the maintenance of Lautrec's army in Italy.[76] In February 1528, Wolsey held out hope of further help for Lautrec, and nearly three months later some was paid, but only by the remission of an instalment of Henry's French pension rather than in cash from the English royal coffers.[77] By then the French were requesting support for Lautrec equiv-alent to the sums Henry would have spent on the invasion of Flanders, and this prompted further promises, quibbles and delays until a treaty was signed in July, regulating such contributions until the end of November.[78] In October the haggling over the contribution to the French army in Italy began all over again.[79] Making war by subsidy was never a very reliable business – it had fallen flat in 1516, when Wolsey tried it against the French – but in 1527–8 it was the only option that offered any hope of keeping the French alliance in good repair and winning concessions from Charles and the pope. At least, by the late spring of 1528 it was the only such option, for by then Wolsey's great gamble to solve the problem of England's powerlessness in a Europe obsessed with Italy had failed beyond repair.

The gamble was to follow through his *renversement des alliances* by joining France to threaten and, if necessary, attack England's old ally, the Netherlands. It was a strategy frequently recommended to Henry and Wolsey by Italian rulers, who wished to distract the emperor by a body-blow to the land of his birth, for what Charles himself called 'the natural love which we bear towards [the Low Countries] above all others' was well known.[80] It was also advocated by the French, who saw the opportunity to continue Louis XI's expansion of France's northern borders, and who argued that Charles's greatest fear was of damage to the Netherlands, 'esteeming not at all, in comparison with those countries, anything he might lose in Italy'.[81] It was tempting too because the Netherlands seemed weak, liable to prove an easier prey for Henry the conqueror than France

---

[73] *LP*, IV (iii) App. 160, 165, 173.   [74] Hall, p. 749; *AAJB*, p. 259.   [75] *AAJB*, p. 253.
[76] *LP*, IV (iii) 5515.
[77] *AAJB*, pp. 148, 151.
[78] *AAJB*, pp. 244, 257, 261–2, 267, 271, 308–9, 312–14; *LP*, IV (ii) 4516, 4523–4, 4542, 4617, 4642, (iii) App. 180–1, 186.
[79] *LP*, IV (ii) 4879.   [80] *Korrespondenz Ferdinands I*, p. 178.
[81] *LP*, IV (i) 2260, 2369, 2829; *AAJB*, p. 132.

had done. The English defection in 1525 had prompted Margaret of Austria to make truce with the French, beset as she was by mutineers, heretics, urban rioters, tax-refusers, and provincial estates trying to negotiate separate truces with the enemy.[82] In 1526 unrest and insolvency continued, and she warned Charles that the Low Countries were incapable of warfare; early in 1527 she was known to have asked him for permission to seek another truce should war break out.[83] Merely the threat of war might have proved enough to make the Netherlands collapse into the sort of confusion that had dogged the reign of Charles's grandfather Maximilian, and this in turn might have forced Charles into English-sponsored peace talks, whatever the Italian situation. In July 1528, Margaret of Austria herself described to the emperor the probable effects on the Low Countries of simultaneous war with England to the west, France to the south, and the pro-French duke of Guelders to the east:

> It would not have been possible to keep and defend this country, having few troops and those disobedient, no money, and subjects unwilling to help; while war on all sides, with the French, English, and those of Guelders, would have completely taken away the passage of trade, and the practice of fishing, which would have impoverished the people so much that it would have been impossible for them (even had they been willing) to help and contribute to the expenditure necessary to sustain war and defend the country on so many sides. And it is likely that the invasion of this country and the small resistance to it which would have been possible, the deprivation of trade and interruption to fishing, would have caused commotions and rebellions, which in the absence of Your Majesty would have been difficult to remedy.[84]

The Anglo-French invasion, as we have seen, did not materialize, but that is not to say that it could not have done. Earlier in the decade, English armies had been raised and shipped to France within nine or ten weeks, and this was the timetable proposed in the Anglo-French discussions.[85] The idea of raiding the Low Countries from Calais came much nearer to fruition, as both Charles and Margaret thought it would: on 1 February 1528, he wrote to her to fortify Gravelines, Bourbourg and Dunkirk, the towns most readily attacked from Calais, while as early as September 1527 she had expressed concern that the English would try to 'surprise two or three towns to increase their territory of Calais and encroach on this side of the sea'.[86] The English plan was to send 1,000 men to Calais under William, Lord Sandys, one of Henry's most able commanders. But Calais was in no state to receive them. In July 1527, when Wolsey passed through, the town was in great need of repairs, food supplies, and wages for the garrison, 'al which fautes, errours and lakkes', Wolsey assured the king with characteristic comprehensiveness, 'I trust to redubbe, afore my retourne

82 A. Henne, *Histoire du Règne de Charles-Quint en Belgique*, 10 vols. (Brussels, 1858–60), IV, pp. 49–81.
83 Ibid., pp. 105–66; *LP*, IV (ii) 3185.   84 HHSA, Belgien PA18/2, fol. 185r.
85 S. J. Gunn, 'The duke of Suffolk's march on Paris in 1523', *English Historical Review*, 101 (1986), 598–600.
86 HHSA, Belgien PA18/1, fol. 3; PA17, fol. 163r.

unto Your Highnes'.[87] Yet by November the garrison had not been paid for nine months, and the town was running seriously short of grain.[88] By January 1528, soldiers were selling their beds to buy food, mutiny seemed imminent, and the commanders were at their wits' end.[89] Sandys fell ill, delaying his crossing from February into March, and by that stage poverty and discontent were also rife in the frontier fortress of Guines which was to be his base of operations.[90] Serious preparations for his expedition continued through March and April, as Sandys sent his armour to Guines, raised a company of cavalry, and sent out letters to raise footsoldiers throughout southern England.[91] But Wolsey must have been glad when Margaret's readiness to negotiate a truce relieved the need to risk the Calais expedition: both Calais and Guines remained restless, under-supplied and insecure throughout 1528 and into early 1529.[92]

The threat from Calais was not the first step in Wolsey's campaign against the Netherlands. That had been taken in May 1527, once the Anglo-French alliance was secure but long before the English declaration of war against Charles. Wolsey forbade the English cloth fleet to sail to the great international fairs of Antwerp and Bergen-op-Zoom, where the majority of England's cloth, her main manufactured export, was usually marketed.[93] The cardinal later claimed that this had been done at the request of the English merchants, and there were troubles over the monetary policies of the English and Netherlandish governments which might be used to justify a rupture, but this was mere window-dressing.[94] Wolsey's real motive was to harm the economy of the Netherlands, which had grown since the start of the century to become the greatest entrepôt in Europe, and thus to put political pressure on the regent and the emperor.[95] As a by-product, he hoped to revitalize Calais, which in July 1527 was nominated as the mart town for all English cloth exports.[96] But English exporters were reluctant to use Calais. As a garrison town with a small harbour, they argued, it was unsuitable for large-scale trade, and, despite Wolsey's negotiation of privileges for English merchants in France equivalent to those they had enjoyed in the Low Countries, it was difficult to distribute their cloth except through the accustomed networks.[97] The result was that English cloth travelled overland from Calais to

[87] *StP*, I, p. 213; *HKW*, III (i), pp. 344–5. [88] *LP*, IV (ii) 3569, 3611.

[89] *LP*, IV (ii) 3651, 3655, 3865, 3894, 3938.

[90] *LP*, IV (ii) 4026, 4122, (iii) App. 156.

[91] *LP*, IV (ii) 4043, 4127, 4191, 4199; *AAJB*, p. 192. It is not always easy to separate the preparations for Sandys's expedition from those for Suffolk's invasion, for which it was to be the prelude.

[92] *LP*, IV (ii) 4330, 4393, 4395, 4494, 4936, 5051, (iii) 5466, 5504. [93] *CSPM*, 806; *CSPS*, III (ii) 66, 69.

[94] *CSPS*, III (ii) 113; R. Macquereau, *Traicté et recueil de la maison de Bourgogne* (Louvain, 1765), p. 330; *Hackett Letters*, pp. 109–10; G. Schanz, *Englische Handelspolitik gegen Ende des Mittelalters*, 2 vols. (Leipzig, 1881), I, pp. 62–5.

[95] H. Van der Wee, *The Growth of the Antwerp Market and the European Economy*, 3 vols. (Louvain, 1963), II, pp. 121–38.

[96] *Tudor Royal Proclamations*, I, p. 115.

[97] *CSPS*, III (ii) 75; Hall, p. 729; *StP*, I, pp. 218–20, VII, pp. 4–5.

Antwerp, decreasing its competitiveness in the market and stimulating the native cloth industry to expansion, based on growing imports of Spanish wool.[98] Wolsey's action did have some ill-effects on the Netherlands' economy – one Antwerp merchant specializing in the English trade had to sell off his houses and annuities to avoid bankruptcy in 1528, while interest rates in Antwerp rose from twelve or thirteen per cent to over twenty-one per cent between 1526 and mid-1528 – but these troubles were insufficient to force Charles's hand.[99]

Indeed, the vigour and success with which Charles and Margaret responded to the Anglo-French threat decided the trial of strength initiated by Wolsey in favour of the Netherlands. At sea the Spanish and Flemish fleets and privateers had the better of the English and French, so much so that even during the truce negotiations, when a show of strength might have reinforced Wolsey's position, the English fleet was under orders to protect Flemish ships plying to England, and to try to prevent Franco-Spanish conflict, at least during the two months of unmolested trade following any rupture which England and the Netherlands had guaranteed one another under the *Intercursus Magnus* of 1496.[100] Charles's determination to resist what he saw as the entirely unjustified aggression of his enemies prompted him to despatch letters in September 1527 to all his subordinates, Margaret included, ordering them to defend his possessions at all costs, and to sell or mortgage his demesnes to do so.[101] Margaret was not shy of drastic financial expedients. She implemented an almost complete stop on the payment of government pensions between February and May 1528, and took hurried loans from her leading councillors and officials, and from Antwerp merchants, to fund her defensive preparations.[102] These included not only repairs to fortifications, and the strengthening of garrisons along the border with France, but also the installation of artillery at Gravelines, the maintenance of several thousand troops in Holland and Zeeland, and the fortification of ports and dikes, to resist an English landing.[103] In October and November 1527, she had sent spies from Antwerp and Arnemuiden to tour the harbours of Normandy and England and investigate invasion preparations.[104] They cannot have found much, but the invasion-scare took hold in the Netherlands anyway, enabling Margaret to obtain large-scale taxation for defence against the English

---

[98] *CSPV*, IV 235; *StP*, VII, pp. 4–5; Van der Wee, *Antwerp Market*, I, p. 530.

[99] Van der Wee, *Antwerp Market*, II, pp. 146, 149–50.

[100] R. Macquereau, *Ce est la maison de Bourgogne* (Paris, 1841), pp. 74, 77–8; *CSPS*, III (ii) 371, 541; Hall, p. 749; *LP*, IV (ii) 4066, 4193, 4670, 4677; *AAJB*, pp. 177–8; *Hackett Letters*, pp. 140–1; HHSA, Belgien PA18/1, fol. 60.

[101] *Korrespondenz Ferdinands I*, pp. 121–2; HHSA, Belgien PA17, fols. 307–10.

[102] Archives Départementales du Nord, Lille (hereafter ADN), B2345, *passim*.

[103] ADN, B2345, *passim* and fols. 54r, 180r, 186r, 187r; B2351, fol. 379r; HHSA, Belgien PA18/1, fol. 150r; Macquereau, *Ce est la maison*, p. 89.

[104] ADN, B2350/82565.

threat as well as the French.[105] Meanwhile Charles took counter-measures against England on the European scale.[106] He tried to marry his recently-widowed sister, Mary of Hungary, to James V of Scotland, and made more general moves to set the Scots against the English. He instructed Margaret to negotiate with the Hanseatic towns to cut off supplies of Baltic grain to England. Most alarming, he planned a rendezvous at the mouth of the Thames, or in the Channel near Calais, between a Spanish fleet carrying 2,000 troops, and a large Flemish fleet carrying 6,000 German mercenaries. In the Netherlands it was believed to be fear of this potential assault, which may have aimed to put Charles's brother-in-law the exiled king of Denmark on the English throne, that caused Henry and Wolsey to seek the truce.[107]

In fact a far more potent determinant of English action was Margaret's sudden arrest of all English merchants in the Netherlands on 21 February 1528. This was a breach of the *Intercursus*, under which free trade should have continued well into March. But Margaret justified it by Henry's detention of the Spanish ambassador – his response to Charles's detention of the French and English envoys in Spain, as a guarantee of the safety of the Spanish ambassador in France – and by a temporary stop on all shipping, made in England when news of the declaration of war first broke.[108] Then as now, such diplomatic technicalities served as a cover for political manoeuvres. Margaret's action gave her English hostages, of whom she would have been deprived by Henry's instructions, sent to his merchants in mid-February, to withdraw from the Netherlands.[109] It also forced the English government to make the first move towards negotiating a truce, for the immediate requests for the merchants' release enabled her to protest her desire for amity with England, and send ambassadors to pursue a settlement there, while maintaining pressure on Henry and Wolsey by a total cessation of trade.[110] And as the truce negotiations progressed, Margaret repeatedly made capital out of her dealings with the arrested merchants. In March, she cited her willingness to release them as an earnest of her enthusiasm for a truce; in April, she cited their release (effected by 16 March) and the restoration of free trade as a demonstration of her desire to 'kepe good lowe and amyte' with Henry; and in June she used her readiness to help them recover their merchandise from Flemish pirates to foster

---

[105] Macquereau, *Ce est la maison*, p. 51; HHSA, Belgien PA17, fol. 387r; *Korrespondenz Ferdinands I*, p. 240; J. D. Tracy, *A Financial Revolution in the Habsburg Netherlands. Renten and Renteniers in the County of Holland, 1515–1565* (Berkeley, 1985), pp. 61–2.

[106] *Korrespondenz Ferdinands I*, pp. 179–80, 250–3; HHSA, Belgien PA17, fol. 390r.

[107] Henne, *Charles-Quint*, IV, p. 173; Macquereau, *Ce est la maison*, p. 75; C. Weiss (ed.), *Papiers d'état du Cardinal de Granvelle*, I, Documents inédits sur l'histoire de France (Paris, 1841), pp. 347–8; ADN, B2345, fol. 175r; W. Tyndale, 'The practice of prelates', in H. Walter (ed.), *Expositions and Notes on Sundry Portions of the Holy Scriptures, together with the Practice of Prelates*, Parker Society (Cambridge, 1849), p. 334.

[108] *LP*, IV (ii) 3946, 3958–9, 4008, 4018; ADN, B2345, fol. 169v; *Hackett Letters*, pp. 115–18.

[109] Bodl. MS Ashmole 1116, fol. 121r (*LP*, IV (iii), App. 151); *Hackett Letters*, pp. 126–7.

[110] *Hackett Letters*, pp. 123–5.

further goodwill.[111] On the other hand, she maintained economic pressure on England with a new tax on English wool imports in March.[112] English merchants in Spain similarly tried to withdraw in December 1527, were arrested on the outbreak of war, and were released by June 1528.[113] But it was the relationship with the Netherlands around which English policy revolved, and through which English policy failed.

It was not the case that Henry and Wolsey had set their hearts on a vigorous war against the Netherlands and found it impossible. The official position was that Henry was most unwilling to make war, and for once the official position was the truth.[114] In March 1528 Henry even told the French ambassador that he had shown more enthusiasm for the war before it was declared than he did afterwards, because he thought that such a show of boldness would force Charles to make peace.[115] In private discussions with Wolsey and More, he tried to judge the exact amount of sabre-rattling required to satisfy the French, but not to provoke Margaret into detaining the merchants and their goods any longer.[116] Yet Wolsey always tried to keep several options open in his management of Henry's foreign relations, and the success of such initiatives as the French peace of 1514, the imperial alliance of 1521, and the French peace of 1525 rested on his ability to do so. War with the Netherlands was such an option, and its usefulness as a tool of Wolsey's policy towards Charles relied on its credibility. Once war had been declared, that credibility had to be maintained, or the French would grow restless and Charles would see no reason to listen to Wolsey's talk of peace. As Henry resolved on 1 March, 'seeyng he must algates to the warre, he wold do it substancyally, and as it shold be don'.[117] But a war fought from a chaotic Calais against an enemy already gaining the upper hand in the economic struggle, bristling with garrisons, refreshed with new grants of taxation, and contemplating seaborne attacks on England was not the push-over that had been envisaged in 1527. Margaret had called Wolsey's bluff. As the truce negotiations drew near to a settlement in mid May, it was Margaret who felt able to reject various French proposals, and by the time the truce was concluded in June, it was Wolsey who was worried lest Margaret, conscious of her growing strength, should 'utterly desiste from the treatyng of the said truxe'.[118]

England's failure to make more of a show of fighting the Netherlands was of immediate significance in the international struggle. Margaret rejoiced that the

---

[111] *CSPS*, III (ii) 373; *Hackett Letters*, pp. 131–3, 145–8; H. J. Smit (ed.), *Bronnen tot de geschiedenis van den handel met Engeland, Schotland en Ierland*, II (i), Rijks Geschiedkundige Publicatiën, 86 (The Hague, 1942), pp. 367–8.

[112] Schanz, *Englische Handelspolitik*, II, p. 68.

[113] *CSPS*, III (ii) 463; *StP*, VII, p. 85; *LP*, IV (ii) 3648; G. Connell-Smith, *Forerunners of Drake: A Study of English Trade with Spain in the Early Tudor Period* (London, 1954), p. 78.

[114] *StP*, I, pp. 284–6.   [115] *LP*, IV (iii) App. 158.   [116] *StP*, I, pp. 285–6.

[117] *StP*, I, p. 281.

[118] *AAJB*, pp. 272–4; *StP*, I, p. 292; *LP*, IV (iii) 4285, 4340.

French, 'who have begun war against us, in the confidence that the English would do the same, are perplexed and astonished'.[119] She thought it strengthened Charles's position, and it demonstrably strengthened her own. She was able to turn the troops and money intended for defence against England to the war on her eastern border against the duke of Guelders and his allies, the rebel subjects of the bishop of Utrecht.[120] The duke, who had invaded Holland in March 1528 with encouragement from France and, allegedly, England, lost control of Utrecht and Overijssel and was forced to make peace with the emperor in October.[121] The French lost their second front against Charles, and all eyes returned to Italy.

Wolsey's policy did not merely fail to coerce the Netherlands. It destabilized England to the extent that the truce became not just a useful preliminary to the elusive general peace, but a necessity to prevent the sort of collapse in England that had been expected in the Low Countries. First, it caused political turmoil among councillors and people alike. The very idea of an intimate alliance with France, the traditional enemy, had aroused considerable opposition. In April 1527 handbills circulated in London, criticizing the cardinal for advising Henry to marry his daughter to a Frenchman, and Wolsey betrayed a certain oversensitivity by sending an all-night watch armed with light artillery onto the streets, and ordering the summary imprisonment for six weeks of a family whose apprentices had – accidentally, they claimed – thrown dirt from a gutter at the French ambassador's servant.[122] Similar measures were taken in July against 'sedicious untrewe and sclaunderous rumours' in the capital, and in November the presence of another French embassy prompted further rumblings, leading Wolsey to order the mayor to forbid discussion of the king's affairs.[123] It was incidents like these that gave both French and Spanish envoys grounds for talking of a violently anti-French public opinion, though the experience of Mary's later Spanish marriage might suggest that the popular fear was more one of foreign domination in general. Wolsey must have felt that he could not please the London populace whatever he did, for his efforts to fund war against France earlier in the 1520s had roused them to even greater hostility than did his reconciliation with the old enemy in 1527.[124]

There was equally firm evidence of dissension on the council. Wolsey had faced difficulties in domestic politics over his foreign policy before: his fencing with France in 1515–18 upset the francophile duke of Suffolk, the cautious earl of

[119] HHSA, Belgien pa18/1, fol. 155r.

[120] Henne, *Charles-Quint*, iv, pp. 177–96; ADN, b2351, fol. 379r.

[121] P. J. Meij et al., *Geschiedenis van Gelderland, II, 1492–1795* (Zutphen, 1975), pp. 54–9; Macquereau, *Ce est la maison*, p. 61.

[122] Hall, pp. 720–1; CSPS, iii (ii) 66, 69.

[123] L. Lyell, F. D. Watney (eds.), *Acts of Court of the Mercers' Company, 1453–1527* (Cambridge, 1936), pp. 749–50; Hall, p. 733.

[124] Walker, *John Skelton*, pp. 103–15.

Shrewsbury, and other councillors, and the lavish expenditure and false bonho-
mie of the Field of Cloth of Gold were an important step in the alienation of the
duke of Buckingham.[125] But from 1527 such opposition was more sustained and
more significant. Exeter, a nobleman closely linked to the queen (who was known
to abhor the French alliance for obvious reasons), comforted the Spanish
ambassador in February 1527, after Wolsey had lectured the unfortunate envoy
before a group of English councillors on how his own and his master's obstinacy
were the only obstacles to peace.[126] The chronicler Edward Hall heard in early
1528 that there were debates about foreign affairs in the council every day:
Wolsey took the French side, but others disagreed.[127] As long as such disagree-
ment did not get out of hand, it could be useful to Wolsey, who regularly told
French ambassadors of the great opposition he faced, in order to win their
sympathy and moderate their demands.[128] Many different councillors were
involved in diplomatic discussions and negotiations between 1526 and 1529, and
they toed the line when Henry seemed committed to the French alliance, as the
duke of Norfolk did in stressing the strength of the amity with France to the
vicomte de Turenne in April 1527.[129] So Wolsey's more extravagant claims that
he was the only man in England prepared to countenance alliance with France
must be taken with a pinch of salt, as ambassador Du Bellay's rather sardonic
accounts of his conversations with the cardinal suggest he knew. Indeed,
England's adherence to France survived Wolsey's fall, since it was the only
solution to the problem of Charles V's control over the pope.[130]

On the other hand, Wolsey may have been right to think that he had become
identified with the present, and potentially disastrous, pro-French policy to a
dangerous extent. For the politician around whom opposition to the cardinal
naturally coalesced was a known favourer of the emperor. Thomas Howard,
duke of Norfolk, was the most active lay peer in attending the council, and, as
lord treasurer, held one of the kingdom's greatest offices. From family tradition,
economic self-interest, a genuine concern for public order and, Wolsey suspected, a bloody-minded determination to say the opposite to the cardinal, he
counted himself a good imperialist.[131] His views emerged in various ways: a row
with Wolsey in the king's presence in April 1527 which made the cardinal feel ill
for several days; an ability to ask for good news about peace negotiations with the

---

[125] S. J. Gunn, *Charles Brandon, Duke of Suffolk c. 1484–1545* (Oxford, 1988), pp. 54–62; G. W. Bernard,
   The Power of the Early Tudor Nobility: a Study of the Fourth and Fifth Earls of Shrewsbury (Brighton,
   1985), pp. 16–26; B. J. Harris, *Edward Stafford, Third Duke of Buckingham, 1478–1521* (Stanford,
   1986), pp. 171–2.
[126] *CSPS*, III (ii) 37.   [127] Hall, p. 748.
[128] *LP*, IV (ii) pp. 1398, 1403–4, 1411; *AAJB*, pp. 162, 195–6, 359–65.
[129] *LP*, IV (ii) pp. 1399–1407, (iii) App. 106; *CSPS*, III (i) 341, (ii) 8, 37, 189; *AAJB*, pp. 191–2, 244.
[130] Wernham, *Before the Armada*, pp. 123–32.
[131] H. Miller, *Henry VIII and the English Nobility* (Oxford, 1986), p. 103; *CSPS*, III (ii) 81, Further
   Supplement, p. 438; A. G. Dickens (ed.), *Clifford Letters of the Sixteenth Century*, Surtees Society,
   172 (Durham and London, 1962), p. 106; *AAJB*, p. 365; cf. *LP*, IV (iii) App. 125–6.

emperor in a way which made it clear what outcome he favoured; and, most seriously, a leading role in a conspiracy to criticize the minister during his absence in France.[132] So long as he retained the king's confidence, Wolsey might happily have ignored Norfolk's dissent, forcing the duke to cooperate with the cardinal, as he had done in the past, or risk the king's disapproval. But as Henry's impatience over the divorce mounted, the cardinal needed ever more urgently to demonstrate his competence and success in European politics, lest the king, perhaps encouraged by Norfolk and others, begin to think his minister dispensable.

Success abroad to reinforce Wolsey's position at home was all the harder to achieve, because the war against the Netherlands broke the common tenets of English political wisdom. England's 'ancient amity' with the Low Countries and their rulers, the dukes of Burgundy, was held dear not only by the Dutch noblemen who wrote emotional letters to Henry in March 1528 begging him to eschew war, but also by many Englishmen.[133] Edward Lee, the English ambassador in Spain, wrote to Wolsey in June 1527, arguing that '[th]is amitee between [th]e hows[es] of Englond, B[our]goigne and Castill is awncient and hid[er]too inviolate, fownded opon long lyne in old blodd, in wiche beeing evermor[e] to [th]is daye devoyed of all quarell[es] and demaund[es], for none of th[em] hathe against [th]e oodr anye titles, can not bee mater of breache and dissention, speciallie to mortall warr.'[134] Such views had to be changed, and Wolsey set about a propaganda campaign. In autumn 1527, and again in February 1528, he orated in star chamber to the judges, lords and JPs on the benefits of the French alliance for peace, trade and tourism, and on the iniquities of Charles V, conjuring up images of the streets of Rome after the sack littered with the anatomical debris of bishops and cardinals.[135] Du Bellay noted that news of French successes in Italy was spread about by the government, in the hope of inflaming the people against the Spaniards and Flemings, and Margaret of Austria complained about anti-imperial libels and sermons promoted by Wolsey.[136] Proclamations about the sack of Rome were read in the churches of London, ordering church plate to be sold off to pay for the war to save the pope from Charles.[137] At court, plays and pageants celebrated English peacemaking and efforts to rescue the church.[138]

Yet Wolsey did not have the field to himself. Margaret had instructions from Charles to spread in England the justifications of his behaviour towards Francis and Henry commissioned by Wolsey's imperial counterpart Gattinara, to con-

---

[132] *LP*, IV (ii) p. 1411; PRO, SP1/45, fol. 193 (*LP*, IV (ii) 3663); *CSPS*, III (ii) 224; Cavendish, p. 44.
[133] *LP*, IV (ii) 4036–7, 4071–2.
[134] BL, MS Cotton Vespasian C IV, fol. 140 (*LP*, IV (ii) 3152).
[135] Cavendish, pp. 64–5; Hall, pp. 742–4.
[136] *AAJB*, pp. 35–6; *Hackett Letters*, p. 114; HHSA, Belgien PA18/1, fol. 120r.
[137] *CSPS*, III (ii) 189.
[138] Anglo, *Spectacle*, pp. 211–37.

vince 'those who are good Englishmen' that peace with Charles was best, 'although their king may not be happy with it'.[139] The pamphlets were printed in a number of editions in spring 1528, though whether any were sent to England is unclear.[140] In March Charles told her to play dirtier still, and stir up the people of England against the king's divorce; a copy of this letter was intercepted by the French, and must have caused considerable consternation at the English court.[141] Meanwhile books denouncing Wolsey as the author of the divorce, and as an obsessive candidate for the papacy who wished to punish Charles V for failing to arrange his election, were printed in Spanish and Dutch and duly circulated in the Netherlands.[142] They may well have been versions of the *Diálogo de Mercurio y Carón*, written by Charles's humanist secretary Alfonso de Valdés to justify his master and vilify his enemies, among them the ambitious, greedy, tyrannous and deceitful cardinal of England.[143]

By March 1528, Margaret of Austria's efforts to stir up the people of England were unnecessary, for the effects of Wolsey's economic warfare had done so already. In that month Margaret paid a reward to one Vincent Pepin, who brought her news of the 'mutacions qui estoient en Angleterre', risings of the common people in various places in favour of peace and alliance with Charles and his Low Countries.[144] The wave of unrest in early March was a response to lay-offs in the cloth industry, prompted by rumours of Margaret's arrest of English merchants. In Essex a letter was intercepted, reporting the saying in London that no cloths would be bought for export 'w[ith]out that we can cause the comyne to aryse, for to complayne to the kyng and shew hyme how they be not halff set a wourke'.[145] In Suffolk, the duke of Norfolk forestalled a movement to petition him for the continuation of clothworking, by taking steps 'to quenche the brewte of stoppyng and arrestyng of o[ur] marchantes in Flandres', and persuading forty master-clothiers to put their workmen back to work.[146] In Gloucestershire and Wiltshire no one acted so fast, and large bodies of clothworkers gathered at Westbury and Devizes. Local notables had to disperse these assemblies with fair words, and convey urgently to king and cardinal the need to restore cloth exports or face further trouble.[147]

---

[139] *Korrespondenz Ferdinands I*, p. 179; J. W. Headley, *The Emperor and his Chancellor: a study of the imperial Chancellery under Gattinara* (Cambridge, 1983), pp. 86–113.

[140] ADN, B2345, fol. 191r; I. A. Nijhoff, M. E. Kronenberg, *Nederlandsche Bibliographie van 1500 tot 1540*, 3 vols. in 6 (The Hague, 1923–61), I, nos. 700, 1483, 1624–5, II, nos. 3495–6.

[141] HHSA, PA Belgien 18/1, fol. 114v; *LP*, IV (ii) 4112.   [142] Tyndale, 'Practice of prelates', p. 322.

[143] A. de Valdés, *Diálogo de Mercurio y Carón*, ed. J. F. Montesinos, Clasicos Castellanos, 96 (Madrid, 1929), pp. 96–102, 139–41, 165–73. I am grateful to Dr S. L. Adams for this reference.

[144] ADN, B2345, fol. 328r; HHSA, Belgien PA18/1, fol. 120.

[145] PRO, SP1/47, fol. 165 (*LP*, IV (ii) 4129); *LP*, IV (ii) 4145.

[146] PRO, SP1/47, fol. 89 (*LP*, IV (ii) 4044); Hall, p. 745; D. N. J. MacCulloch, *Suffolk and the Tudors: Politics and Religion in an English County, 1500–1600* (Oxford, 1986), p. 298.

[147] *LP*, IV (ii) 4043, 4085, 4191. It is possible that the reports of trouble in Gloucestershire rested on confusion between Westbury (Wilts) and Westbury-on-Trym (Glos).

The government's response was to order all clothiers to keep their men supplied with work, but this arrangement could not last long unless the merchants bought the cloth from the clothiers.[148] Wolsey, who had reportedly threatened various London merchants with the Tower in February unless they continued to buy cloth, confronted them again in March, and, using the threat that the king would break the privileges of London's wholesale cloth mart at Blackwell Hall, extracted a promise that their purchasing would continue.[149] At least Henry did not, as it was rumoured in Mons, have the offending merchants beheaded.[150] Yet however much Wolsey bullied the merchants, the industry could not return to normal until the truce was signed. Olive-oil imports from Spain were needed to soften the wool before it could be combed, and if the truce were not completed before mid-June, English traders would miss the great Sinksen mart at Antwerp and the depression would deepen.[151] Unrest in clothmaking areas continued after mid-March, in Somerset at the end of the month, in Kent in April, where petitioners asked Archbishop Warham for repayment of the forced loans they had given the crown in 1522, and in Kent again in May, when there was talk of assembling a 'company to get corne of the riche men', conspiring with Londoners, killing gentlemen, and murdering the cardinal.[152] No wonder Wolsey was anxious to conclude the truce.

It was on events like these that William Cecil would base his famous adage, that 'the people that depend uppon makyng of cloth ar of worss condition to be quyetly governed than the husband men'.[153] In an attempt to preserve social stability in future trade depressions, English governments would make a habit of doing what Wolsey had found it necessary to do, ordering clothiers to keep on their outworkers at the accustomed wages even when they could not sell their cloth for export.[154] No future English government would deliberately cut off trade with the Low Countries as Wolsey had done, and in 1563 it was Margaret of Parma, regent of the Netherlands, who cited the events of 1527–8 to argue the effectiveness of economic warfare against England.[155] Yet Wolsey's policy did not seem stupid in 1527. It was based on careful research – Sir Thomas More was sent down to Blackwell Hall in May 1527 to study the trade between clothiers and

[148] *LP*, IV (ii) 4058.   [149] *AAJB*, pp. 158–60, 180; Hall, pp. 745–6.

[150] A. Louant (ed.), *Le Journal d'un bourgeois de Mons, 1505–1536*, Commission Royale d'Histoire (Brussels, 1969), p. 288.

[151] *StP*, I, p. 294, VII, p. 73; *Hackett Letters*, p. 144; *AAJB*, p. 272; W. R. Childs, *Anglo-Castilian Trade in the Later Middle Ages* (Manchester, 1978), pp. 109–11; E. Kerridge, *Textile Manufactures in Early Modern England* (Manchester, 1985), pp. 157–8; *LP*, IV (ii) 4432, 4638.

[152] Kerridge, *Textile Manufactures*, pp. 14–23; J. C. K. Cornwall, *Wealth and Society in Early Sixteenth Century England* (London, 1988), pp. 71–8; *LP*, IV (ii) 4141, 4173, 4188–90, 4192, 4226, 4236, 4243, 4276, 4287, 4296, 4299–300, 4310, 4331; PRO, SP1/48, fol. 84 (*LP*, IV (ii) 4310 (ii)); P. Clark, *English Provincial Society from the Reformation to the Revolution: Religion, Politics and Society in Kent 1500–1640* (Hassocks, 1977), pp. 22–3.

[153] R. H. Tawney, E. Power (eds.), *Tudor Economic Documents*, 3 vols. (London, 1924), II, p. 45.

[154] Kerridge, *Textile Manufactures*, pp. 208–9.

[155] G. D. Ramsay, *The Queen's Merchants and the Revolt of the Netherlands* (Manchester, 1986), p. 13.

London merchants – and sound precedent.[156] Admittedly, Edward IV had rejected the chance to ally with France against the Low Countries in 1478, finding the state of English opinion, the dangers of economic disruption and the weakness of his claims against the house of Burgundy as convincing disincentives as they were in Wolsey's day.[157] But Henry VII had diverted English cloth exports from the Netherlands to Calais three times, and each time this blow to the Low Countries had helped to extract political or commercial concessions from Maximilian or Philip the Fair.[158] On the third occasion, Wolsey had almost certainly seen the policy in operation, as chaplain to Sir Richard Nanfan, deputy of Calais.[159] Henry VII's schemes worked, as Wolsey doubtless intended his to work, because the exchange trade and cloth-finishing industry of Antwerp and Brabant were so damaged by the English withdrawal that the Antwerpers begged their rulers to accede to Henry's wishes.[160] Henry imposed his boycotts with characteristic thoroughness, and though there were economic ill-effects on England, notably those prompting the attack on the London Steelyard in 1493, his policy – as in many other matters – must have seemed to Wolsey a good model to follow.[161]

Unfortunately there were at least five differences between the situation of Henry VII's reign and that of 1527–8, which combined to scuttle Wolsey's policy. Antwerp's decades of boom had made the Netherlands' economy stronger and less susceptible to English coercion. Concurrently the English cloth trade seems to have become more firmly locked into the London–Antwerp route, increasing disruption and opposition to the move to Calais.[162] English exports of raw wool, which had increased during Henry VII's suspensions of the cloth trade, and compensated for the fall in cloth customs, had by 1528 reached the low point of a long decline.[163] England's population had begun a substantial rise, increasing the importance of the cloth industry as an employment and as a by-employment for up to half the cottage-farmers in some areas; total cloth production had risen by more than ten per cent since the last of Henry VII's stoppages.[164] All these developments would have impeded Wolsey's imitation of Henry VII. What made it impossible was the failure of the harvest of 1527, the third worst harvest of the

[156] Guy, *Public Career of Sir Thomas More*, p. 13.

[157] C. L. Scofield, *The Life and Reign of Edward IV*, 2 vols. (London, 1923), II, pp. 222–31.

[158] Wernham, *Before the Armada*, pp. 68–95.   [159] Pollard, p. 13.

[160] O. de Smedt, *De Engelse Natie te Antwerpen*, 2 vols. (Antwerp, 1950–4), I, pp. 115–19.

[161] PRO, E101/414/6, fol. 121v; A. A. Thomas, I. D. Thornley (eds.), *The Great Chronicle of London* (London, 1938), p. 249.

[162] J. D. Gould, *The Great Debasement: Currency and the Economy in mid-Tudor England* (Oxford, 1970), p. 120.

[163] Ibid.; E. E. Rich (ed.), *The Ordnance Book of the Merchants of the Staple* (Cambridge, 1937), pp. 9–18; T. H. Lloyd, *The English Wool Trade in the Middle Ages* (Cambridge, 1977), p. 283; E. M. Carus-Wilson, O. Coleman, *England's Export Trade, 1275–1547* (Oxford, 1963), p. 72.

[164] J. Thirsk (ed.), *The Agrarian History of England and Wales volume IV, 1500–1640* (Cambridge, 1967), p. 425; Carus-Wilson and Coleman, *England's Export Trade*, p. 139.

entire sixteenth century. Wheat prices were on average more than double what they had been in 1526–7, and the surveys of grain stocks organized by Wolsey in November and December 1527 showed that most villages' supplies would run out in March 1528.[165] In contrast, food had been in good supply when Henry VII diverted the cloth trade. The average price of wheat during Henry VII's embargos rarely passed above 6s a quarter; in 1527–8 it was more than 13s 4d.[166] Hungry people bought food in preference to clothing, so domestic cloth sales must have fallen almost as severely as exports, exacerbating the problems of unemployment and poverty already caused by the break in trade.[167] And hungry people were restive. From the late summer of 1527 onwards, noblemen and courtiers had been sitting more frequently than usual at quarter sessions, working on the grain commissions, punishing vagabonds and arresting rioters.[168] The spring of 1528, the worst point of the grain crisis, would have been unsettled enough without mass unemployment in the cloth industry. As it was, many of Henry's leading subjects spent a tense spring and summer trying to contain unrest in the area of their 'rule', and doubtless pondering – as Henry himself may have done – the wisdom or otherwise of Wolsey's confrontation with the Netherlands.[169]

The cardinal did his best to make his foreign policy solve these domestic problems. He badgered the French to let him import their corn into England, and urged Margaret to free Baltic grain destined for England which she had arrested in her ports.[170] But the very fact that these rulers could, at the right diplomatic price, allow grain to pass to England, mocked Wolsey's impotence. The price of wheat in England had been below that on the continent throughout the 1520s; in 1527–8 the English price was higher by a greater margin than it had been for sixty years.[171] In the Low Countries, indeed, 1527 was not an especially bad harvest in a hungry decade.[172] Margaret had to take measures to control the movement of grain and to discipline vagabonds; seven children were crushed to death at a dole of bread in Mons, but public order and the national war effort survived, thanks in part to the sophisticated systems of poor relief recently instituted in several of the Netherlands' largest towns.[173] Wolsey's threat to the Netherlands did not

[165] R. W. Heinze, *The Proclamations of the Tudor Kings* (Cambridge, 1976), pp. 99–102; D. Dymond, 'The famine of 1527 in Essex', *Local Population Studies*, 26 (1981), 29–40; W. G. Hoskins, 'Harvest fluctuations and English economic history, 1480–1619', *Agricultural History Review*, 12 (1964), 34–5; *LP*, IV (ii) 3587.

[166] Hoskins, 'Harvest fluctuations', pp. 44–5.   [167] *Agrarian History*, pp. 625–6.

[168] PRO, KB9/504/27, 29, 39, 144; KB9/510/31; *LP*, IV (ii) 3552, 3625, 3664, 3691, 3712, 3811, 3822, 3883, 4012; *AAJB*, p. 44.

[169] *LP*, IV (ii) 4414, 4455, 4501, 4627, (iii) App. 163.

[170] *LP*, IV (ii) 4065, 4662; L. Lalanne (ed.), *Journal d'un bourgeois de Paris sous le règne de François Premier (1515–1536)*, Société de l'histoire de France (Paris, 1854), p. 323; *CSPV*, IV, 188, 205, 208, 210, 212, 235; *AAJB*, pp. 31–2, 184–5; *Hackett Letters*, p. 135.

[171] *Agrarian History*, pp. 851–2.

[172] Van der Wee, *Antwerp Market*, I, pp. 177, 186, 192, II, pp. 150–2.

[173] C. Laurent, J. Lameere, H. Simont (eds.), *Recueil des ordonnances des Pays-Bas, deuxième série, 1506–1700*, 6 vols. (Brussels, 1893–1922), II, pp. 481–2, 487; *Bourgeois de Mons*, p. 283; P.

survive, and in the long run neither did he. In 1525 he had failed to fund a war for Henry and stirred up rebellion in the process; in 1528 he failed to impose a peace for Henry and stirred up more rebellion in the process. It was humiliating for a king to have his foreign policy dictated by the clothworkers of Westbury and Devizes, but that was what European opinion plainly thought had happened in 1528. It confirmed the continental image of an England governed by its unruly and chauvinistic lower classes, and suggested unflattering parallels with the last English king to face rioting clothworkers in a year of trade stoppage and high grain prices, the weak-minded Henry VI.[174] Wolsey complained stiffly to the French ambassador that French councillors had reportedly been making patronizing excuses for English irresolution in the struggle against Charles, saying that they 'understand well that over here they cannot properly be masters of their people'.[175]

For Wolsey the comparison with 1450 was more chilling still, casting him in the role of William de la Pole, duke of Suffolk, the chief minister toppled by popular disorder and noble disaffection on the failure of an unpopular and pro-French foreign policy. The parallel may have struck him with a frisson when he read the depositions of the Kentish conspirators of May 1528, men who talked of the deeds of Jack Straw and Robin of Redesdale: they planned to send the cardinal to his death in a boat, a memory, perhaps, of the boat in which Suffolk had been beheaded off Dover on his way into exile.[176] All Wolsey's brilliant diplomatic wrangling, all his careful plans to bring kings, emperors and uncooperative popes to Henry's feet, had foundered on the opposition of starving weavers, when the demands of internal stability forced him to curtail his bold foreign policy. Worse than that, the threat to internal stability had been greatly exacerbated by the effects of Wolsey's already controversial diplomatic manoeuvres, and his apparent responsibility for the domestic crisis heightened the lack of confidence in his policies created by his unconventional attachment to France. No doubt he might have weathered the storm, especially had he devised some new means to secure the king's divorce. But in 1529 he could offer only the old diplomatic routes, and on the experience of 1527–8 his foreign policy looked not just threadbare but positively unsafe.

That impression had been created not by Wolsey's incompetence, but by the dangerous and multifaceted interaction between international power-politics

Bonenfant, 'Les origines et le caractère de la réforme de la bienfaisance publique aux Pays-Bas sous le règne de Charles-Quint', *Revue Belge de Philologie et d'Histoire*, 5–6 (1926–7), 887–904.

[174] P. Rickard, *Britain in Medieval French Literature, 1100–1500* (Cambridge, 1956), pp. 181–2; M-R. Thielemans, *Bourgogne et Angleterre: relations politiques et économiques entre les Pays-Bas bourguignons et l'Angleterre, 1435–1467* (Brussels, 1966), pp. 208–9; J. N. Hare, 'The Wiltshire risings of 1450: political and economic discontent in mid-fifteenth-century England', *Southern History*, 4 (1982), 15–26; R. A. Griffiths, *The Reign of King Henry VI: the Exercise of Royal Authority, 1422–1461* (Berkeley, 1981), pp. 610–49.

[175] *AAJB*, p. 266.   [176] *LP*, IV (ii) 4310; Griffiths, *Henry VI*, pp. 676–84.

and England's political, economic and social condition. Wolsey was not stymied by abler statesmen, richer monarchs or braver generals. His policy was always unlikely to succeed to perfection in the difficult circumstances he faced, but it was at least a vigorous and intelligent attempt to solve his problems. It was fundamentally sabotaged by the rainstorms of April and May 1527 which ruined the English harvest.[177] This treacherous weather may have dented the cardinal's great faith in the diplomatic effectiveness of the stars (one chronicler recounts that he timed his departure for France to fit the best positions of Jupiter and Venus).[178] But Wolsey's real confidence rested rather in his own skill. It is a tribute to the agility of his mind that by 1530 the lesson of 1527–8 had impressed itself indelibly upon him. In his desperate machinations for an international conspiracy against England, which would destroy the king's confidence in those who had supplanted him and force his restoration to power, open war between England and the Netherlands played a central part. When trade was interrupted, intended Wolsey, 'th'englishmen sholde make insurreccion', causing Henry's councillors to totter and fall.[179] When Wolsey projected this from internal exile in Yorkshire, it was rightly accounted high treason. When he had unintentionally effected it as the king's chief minister, it was the boldest gamble of an imaginative but never unfettered diplomatic career.

[177] Dymond, 'Famine of 1527', p. 29.
[178] *Report on Manuscripts in the Welsh Language, I,* Historical Manuscripts Commission, 48 (London, 1898), pp. v–vi.
[179] L. R. Gardiner, 'Further news of Cardinal Wolsey's end, November-December 1530', *Bulletin of the Institute of Historical Research,* 57 (1984), 103–4.

CHAPTER 7

The cultivation and promotion of music in the household and orbit of Thomas Wolsey

ROGER BOWERS

Of Wolsey's personal interest or tastes in music, no direct testimony survives. In view especially of Cavendish's silence on the matter, it is conceivable that he had little or none beyond the conventional contemporary pleasure in background sound for entertainment purposes, having been always too preoccupied with affairs of state ever to develop or indulge any particular sympathies in this direction. Yet even if this were so, it would be of little significance for any evaluation of the role of Wolsey as an employer of musicians and promoter of music. For from the moment that he was first elevated to the episcopate, as bishop of Lincoln early in 1514, he belonged to and moved in strata of society in which it was an uncontested convention for the patron's household to incorporate, commensurate with his status, various groups of musicians, including, especially, a personal chapel of the household, copiously equipped and fully staffed. In this respect indeed, no great churchman or secular grandee of the early sixteenth century could decently avoid being an agent for the promotion of music and the patronage of musicians; and few failed to appreciate the extent to which the maintenance of an elaborate musical establishment could contribute to its employer's political and social ends, by promoting an image and aura of splendour and wealth, of diplomatic potency and political weight.

The objective informing the maintenance of an elaborate chapel of the household was far more than merely the ordering by competent staff of the daily devotions of a great man. It was a means of advertising publicly the patron's devotion to Holy Mother Church, and also, at a time of incipient schism, the integrity of his religious orthodoxy. It was no less a channel for a conspicuous display of his wealth and magnificence, so establishing his status in the eyes of those with whom he dealt in business both diplomatic and political; and in its execution of the religious ritual, it manifested the resources in creative and executive talent that its employer held at his personal command. The chapel was a vehicle for pageantry and spectacle no less than any other principal department of a Tudor court, which was manifested in the splendour of the appointments of the buildings in which it performed its duties, in the magnificence of the ornaments, relics, Mass vessels, and other equipment with which it encrusted its enactment of ceremony and ritual, and in the expertise and virtuosity brought to bear upon its projection of the music of the liturgy by the men and boys by whom the chapel was staffed. Lastly, the chapel's services might symbolize and actively promote the unity and mutual charity of all the lord's household staff.[1]

Wolsey's household chapel was not a building, but a body of personnel and its equipment. These attended permanently upon their employer, and performed the liturgy for the good estate of his soul in the chapel of whichever palace, mansion or castle he happened at any given time to be occupying. The ritual text, ceremonial action and plainsong monody of the early-sixteenth-century Latin liturgy were prescribed by the thousand-year tradition of the church itself. However, of the ten authorized services a day, a body so largely peripatetic would not attempt to sing more than just those of greatest significance. These were High Mass of the day and the daily Lady Mass (the votive Mass of the Virgin Mary), plus the principal Hours – Matins and Lauds (perhaps just on festivals), Prime, and Vespers with Compline followed by the evening intercessory votive antiphon.

Like all the non-monastic liturgical Uses, the Use of Salisbury – the standard secular Use of lowland England from Somerset to Cheshire and the Wash – required for its execution three ranks of clergy. These consisted of a body of men in the orders of priest to be 'clerks of the upper form'; of other adult men, in lesser orders or lay, as 'clerks of the second form'; and of boys with unbroken voices, to be the 'clerks of the lowest form'. The constitution of the personnel of Wolsey's chapel necessarily reflected this basic liturgical requirement – in just the same way as the obligatory physical arrangement of the choirstalls in the several chapel buildings reflected, on each side of the choir, the need for the three hierarchical levels. Cavendish enumerated the personnel of Wolsey's chapel in a degree of detail that reflects the pride that was taken in it. He listed the dean of the chapel, always 'a great clarke and a devyn',[2] and the sub-dean, who between them bore responsibility for the efficient management of the chapel and its personnel. There followed, as the clerks of the upper form, twelve singing priests under a 'Repetor of the Quyer', probably an experienced and senior musician in priest's orders, an expert liturgist who rehearsed the singers in the plainsong items proper to each successive service. With these were associated a gospeller and an epistoler principally to intone the gospel and epistle at celebrations of Mass, who in strict usage should have been in the orders of, respectively, deacon and subdeacon, but who at this period were often older men fully ordained to the priesthood. In addition to the master of the choristers there were sixteen further lay singing-

---

[1] K. Mertes, *The English Noble Household, 1250–1600* (Oxford, 1988), p. 148.

[2] For Dr Robert Shorton, dean in 1526 (*LP*, IV (ii) 3086), see A. B. Emden, *A Biographical Register of the University of Cambridge to 1500* (Cambridge, 1963), pp. 525–6; and for his successor, Dr Richard Duke (or Duck), dean in 1527 (*LP*, IV (ii) 3216), see Emden, *A Biographical Register of the University of Oxford to 1500*, I vol. in 3 (Oxford, 1957–9), p. 602.

men to be the clerks of the second form, and to complete the personnel, twelve singing-boys as choristers.[3] Excluding the ancillary staff and the two senior priest-administrators, the working singing complement of Wolsey's chapel totalled thirty-two men and twelve boys – more than one-tenth of his entire salaried household.[4]

Cavendish's enumeration was of the chapel at probably the greatest dimensions that its employer ever saw fit to raise it, no doubt during the latter part of his career as the king's chief minister. Its personnel had not always been so extensive, but probably it was never a modest organization; in 1521, for instance, it had numbered a dean and sub-dean, ten chaplains, ten gentlemen lay clerks (including the master of the choristers) and ten choristers.[5] Even at these numbers, totalling thirty singers, the chapel had been grand enough, and Cavendish's latest enumeration probably represented not only its apogee, but in fact the greatest number that Wolsey actually thought it prudent to employ. That in numbers it matched the greatest cathedral choirs in the land (London St Paul's, Salisbury and York) probably mattered little, since it far outmatched them in quality. What did matter was that had it grown any larger, it would totally have eclipsed Henry VIII's Chapel Royal itself. For virtually all of his reign, at least from 1511 until the 1540s, this stood established at the dean, thirty gentlemen (normally the sub-dean and nine other chaplains, plus twenty lay clerks), and ten choristers.[6] Wolsey, that is, did not shrink from exceeding in numbers of staff even his master's own Chapel Royal; however, he does appear to have considered it prudent to keep the margin of excess decently restrained.

[3] The ancillary staff included a yeoman and two grooms of the vestry, and a servant of the master of the choristers to assist him in looking after the boys. Cavendish, pp. 19–20.

[4] Cavendish, pp. 200–1. Cavendish also recorded (pp. 20, 22–3) that 'Of doctors [i.e., of divinity or law] & chapplens attendyng in his Closett to sey dayly masse before hym he had xvj[en] persons'. These clearly are personal chaplains, advisers and confidants, entirely distinct from the liturgical and musical chapel body.

[5] This was the chapel body which, with three ancillary staff, was included in the household which accompanied Wolsey on his embassy to France in 1521: BL, MS Harley 620, fols. 27v, 44v–45r, and *passim*. When Sir John Hawkins wrote his *A General History of the Science and Practice of Music* (London, 1776; repr. New York, 1963), p. 384, he had available to him some version of Cavendish that enumerated Wolsey's chapel as follows: dean, sub-dean, 'repeater of the choir', ten chaplains, gospeller, epistoler, master of the choristers, twelve lay clerks and ten choristers. These proportions, lying between the 1521 figures and those in the version of Cavendish printed by R. S. Sylvester, do represent a wholly plausible stage in the evolution of the constitution of the personnel of Wolsey's chapel; they may also suggest that at some stages in its history, Cavendish's narrative has existed in more than one recension.

[6] The chapel Henry VIII inherited from his father had stood at a dean, twenty-six gentlemen (the sub-dean plus six or eight chaplains, with nineteen or seventeen clerks) and twelve boys (PRO, LC2/1, fol. 4r (1500), fol. 68v (1503), fols. 131r, 141v (1509); LC9/50, fols. 208v, 209r (1509)). This had been modified as above by 1511 (LC2/1 fol. 170r), and in terms of the adults retained these proportions through 1520 (SP1/19, fol. 267v), 1524 (E179/69/23), c.1535 (SP1/37, fols. 98r–100r) and 1547 (LC2/2, fol. 33r). The number of choristers remained at its reduced figure of ten at least until 1543 (E101/423/10, fol. 89r), but had been restored to twelve by 1545 (C66/785, m. 44), at which number it still stood in 1547 (LC2/2, fol. 15v).

Moreover, Wolsey's role as an employer and patron of musicians by no means ceased with his dismissal from the king's service as lord chancellor in 1529. As cardinal archbishop of York he was still an ecclesiastic enjoying both substantial status and the income to support it, and his need of an archiepiscopal household and personal chapel and choir was in no way diminished by his fall from political power. Indeed, within the household attending him on his journey north towards York in the spring of 1530 were still 'such syngyng men as he than had remaynyng with hyme',[7] doubtless to form the nucleus of his prospective archiepiscopal household chapel.

Wolsey's chapel was peripatetic, and normally sang wherever he was resident. Naturally, it accompanied him on his major public diplomatic adventures abroad, for instance to France in 1521 and 1527,[8] and doubtless to the Field of Cloth of Gold in 1520, even though no explicit reference to its presence there has yet been found.[9] It would have been natural for the chapel to be in attendance upon its master whenever, in his capacity as priest as well as chief minister, he celebrated Mass on some great occasion of state. In 1521 the Venetian ambassador observed that for Wolsey, celebrating Mass on public occasions was unusual, 'he not having done so for many years, save at Guines [i.e., the Field of Cloth of Gold, 1520]'.[10] Nevertheless, Wolsey did take the opportunity to mark, in this most conspicuous of ways, his particular diplomatic triumphs when opportunity arose – in St Paul's Cathedral in 1518, for instance, and twice in 1526, in spectacles of thanksgiving for the successful conclusions of peace treaties;[11] at the Mass following the betrothal ceremony in 1518 of Princess Mary and the Dauphin François,[12] and at the High Mass concluding the interview of the kings at the Field of Cloth of Gold in 1520.[13]

Otherwise, much of the chapel's observance of the liturgy took place not in great churches but in what were probably the relatively small chapels of Wolsey's principal residences – York Place, The More and Durham House; larger, probably, and not a little grander, was the chapel of Hampton Court palace. Only rarely, indeed, would the chapel not have been in attendance upon its employer. Exceptionally, however, for a space of seven and a half weeks in August and

---

[7] Cavendish, p. 133.

[8] BL, MS Harley 620, *passim*; MS Harley 542, fol. 73r; J. G. Nichols (ed.), *The Chronicle of Calais in the reigns of Henry VII and Henry VIII*, Camden Society 35 (1846), p. 40.

[9] His retinue of 300 persons on this occasion certainly included twelve chaplains and fifty servants of gentleman status: J. G. Russell, *The Field of Cloth of Gold* (London, 1969), p. 191.

[10] *CSPV, 1520–6*, 151.   [11] *CSPV, 1509–19*, 1085, 1088; *LP*, IV (ii) 4481; *CSPV, 1520–6*, 1223, 1262.

[12] *CSPV, 1509–19*, 1085, 1088.

[13] *CSPV, 1520–6*, pp. 29, 55, 74–5; Russell, *Field of Cloth of Gold*, pp. 172–6. However, when Wolsey celebrated Mass in St Paul's Cathedral to mark the conclusion of peace between England and France in November 1527 (*CSPV, 1527–33*, 201), Cavendish noted that Mass was sung not by Wolsey's chapel but by the choirs of St Paul's and the Chapel Royal (Cavendish, p. 67). Hall noted a number of instances in which Wolsey celebrated Mass on occasions of supreme diplomatic importance: see Hall, pp. 594, 618, 629, 640, 711, 734.

September 1526, the dean, sub-dean, chaplains, clerks and boys of Wolsey's chapel all found themselves lodged at St Albans Abbey – evidently while Wolsey was pre-occupied elsewhere, though it has proved difficult to ascertain where, and with what.[14]

Although no complete list of the names of the singers in Wolsey's chapel choir is known for any period, yet some idea of its personnel can be gained from stray references. The names of all the chaplains and clerks (but not of the choristers) who accompanied him to France in 1521 can be recovered from the petty cash accounts of the embassy;[15] other names can be recovered haphazardly from the lay subsidy rolls of 1524 and 1525,[16] and four further names from the account in 'The Chronicle of Calais' of Wolsey's visit there in 1527.[17]

Within the household the thirty-two priest-chaplains and clerks of Wolsey's chapel counted as gentlemen, the highest rank of household staff, and all were expected to be professional singers and masters of not one but of a range of repertoires and techniques. The boys were expected to be as expert as the men, and it was the job of the master of the choristers to see that they were so. The staple fare of all was the immense annual cycle of the plainsong of the liturgy. This incorporated both solo and choral performance, and to solo episodes it would be expected that, when suitable, individuals would also possess the skills of elaborating the plainsong by improvising counterpoint to it according to the standard prescriptions for descant, counter and faburden.

Of an importance probably greater than either of these, however, was the capacity of the chapel singers as a body to realize and give voice to one of the greatest glories of the late medieval English church – the spectacular, expansive

---

14 PRO, E315/272, fols. 63v, 64r. The circumstances under which Wolsey detached the chapel from his household on this occasion are not clear. The chapel can hardly have needed so much sabbatical leave to learn the music for the ceremonial opening of Cardinal College, Oxford, on 19 October. In fact, until 12 August 1526 Wolsey had been at Hampton Court (LP, IV (ii) 2372, 2388, 2392). Thereafter, although correspondence flowed in to him unabated, very little left his hand until early October; apart from the despatch of three letters from The More, two on 4 September (LP, IV (ii) 2454, 2455) and one on 29 September (LP, IV (ii) 2493), where he was and what he was doing is not at all evident. (It may be noted that LP, IV (ii) 2424, 2445 and 2535 are undated; 2457 belongs not to 1526 but to 1525.)

15 BL, MS Harley 620, passim.

16 PRO, E179/69/9, 69/10. These are merely lists of names with their assessments; the offices held are not specified. Since these documents are lay subsidy rolls, the ordained clergy of Wolsey's chapel would necessarily be excluded; the lay clerks are included, but not all can be identified. Presumably, some of the older choristers also appear; the occurrence of the names John Sheppard (on 69/9 only) and Thomas Causton among those with minimum assessments of 4d is certainly thought-provoking, but is just as likely to be the product of coincidence.

17 Chronicle of Calais, p. 40; however, recourse to the original (BL, MS Harley 542, fol. 73r) is necessary to make clear that the bracket identifying the 'gentlemen of the chapell' encloses only the four names Phelippe, Avery, Berepe and Burban, and not the next six as well. As a source, this late-sixteenth-century transcript of a lost original is less than ideal; unfortunately a corresponding list contemporary with Wolsey and bearing his signature (BL, Cotton MS Caligula D x, fols. 103–4) stops short before reaching the names of the members of the chapel.

and virtuosic repertory of liturgical and para-liturgical choral polyphony. Music of this kind had first been developed and exploited by the English in about the 1460s. Composed in five or six or more parts for the full chorus of boys and men, it served particularly to lend special distinction to the chapel's performances on its most public occasions, and no less to distinguish the daily celebrations of High Mass, Lady Mass and the evening votive antiphon, plus – by the 1520s – the hymns and Great Responsories of the Office on festivals. It was for the rendering of music of this kind that there had been chosen factors so fundamental as the particular balance of boys' voices to men's in choirs of this type, and there need be little doubt that its ability to make a spectacular and impressive show on suitable occasions with choral polyphony was the principal criterion by which an employer judged how good and effectual a service his chapel was doing him.

It is most regrettable that not a single book of the plainsong service, or of the polyphony, of Wolsey's chapel is known to survive. Nor has any comprehensive inventory of its books or other musical paraphernalia yet come to light.[18] The absence of such sources prevents the realization of any more than the vaguest conception of the nature and extent of what has been lost. Nevertheless, it seems certain that Wolsey's collection of working chapel volumes was a notable one. Certainly, he was avaricious to lay his hands on any quality collection of chapel books that appeared to become available for acquisition. For instance, on the death in 1527 of Henry Percy, fifth earl of Northumberland, Wolsey made clear to his son and heir that it was his pleasure to have for his own possession the books that had formerly belonged to the chapel of the deceased. The new earl reluctantly complied; Wolsey's haul was four antiphoners, 'such as I thynk wher nat seen a gret wyll', five graduals, an ordinal, a manual and eight processioners.[19]

However, among the grander buildings in which Wolsey's chapel conducted the liturgy was the chapel of Hampton Court, of some of the more valuable possessions of which there yet survives an inventory of May 1523.[20] The appurtenances of worship there included an organ described as 'a grete paire of

[18] The chapel items were unfortunately not included in the principal working inventory of Wolsey's household goods, that was drawn up early in 1522 and progressively updated through to 1529: BL, MS Harley 599, fols. 1–112. This item was calendared under the date 1530 (*LP*, IV (iii) 6184) as if it were a confiscation inventory. However, it is clearly the product of several hands, over several years; the appearance of one item in the original layer and hand recording goods already procured on 22 December 1521 (fol. 34v) and of an addition to the first layer dated 12 May 1522 (fol. 48v) shows that the original layer was compiled early in 1522.

[19] T. Percy (ed.), *The Regulations and Establishment of the Houshold* [sic] *of Henry Algernon Percy, the fifth Earl of Northumberland* (London, 1770), pp. 429–30. The young lord Percy had been brought up in Wolsey's household, and the cardinal was rather apt to treat him as merely an erring boy (Cavendish, pp. 29–30, 150, 155); he did at least contrive to retain the remaining books of his father's chapel, claiming that 'they [are] not worth the sending nor ever was occupied in my Lords Chapel'. For the late earl's chapel, and some idea of the nature of Wolsey's haul in books, see R. Bowers, 'The vocal scoring, choral balance and performing pitch of Latin church polyphony in England, c.1500–58', *Journal of the Royal Musical Association*, 112 (1987), pp. 57–64.

[20] BL, MS Harley 599, fols. 113–21.

Organs' and possibly sufficiently large to have been a permanent fixture, plus two 'smaller paire of Organs', which were compact instruments probably of only small compass. The latter could be set up on a mere trestle-table of wainscot, and one case for the bellows and another for the keyboard, action and pipes was all that was needed to make either of them fully portable.[21] Repertory manuscripts of the period show that the organ could be used to play voluntaries at suitable points in the Mass or Office, and to alternate with voices during the performance of plainsong items – but not yet to accompany the voices.

The books whose value was enough to make them worth listing included a printed missal and another 'grete booke of paper in printe' of unknown content. Of greatest interest, however, is the occurrence of 'A priksongbooke in printe'.[22] No printed book of polyphony for church use had yet been produced in England, nor indeed anywhere outside northern Italy and Rome. It is intriguing to imagine the singers of Wolsey's chapel having available to them the contents of one of the early prints of masses or motets from the presses of either Ottaviano Petrucci or Andrea Antico (the only two music printers of any substance to have appeared by 1523). Indeed, if this really was a single volume of choirbook dimensions, rather than a set of part-books, then its identity appears to be limited to only three possible publications: Petrucci's *Motetti A* (1502) and *Motetti de Passione ... B* (1503), and – perhaps the most probable of the three – Antico's *Liber Quindecim Missarum* (1516).[23] The fact that this volume was kept permanently at Hampton Court and not included among the books that formed part of the chapel's peripatetic equipment indicates, perhaps, that principally it was thought of as an item of interest to the curious rather than of practical repertorial performance. Nevertheless, some possible consequences of an admission to English compositional procedures of examples of continental practice by such a route may conceivably be seen in some of the works of the composers in Wolsey's chapel, and are noted below.

Although no comprehensive idea of the scope and character of Wolsey's chapel's repertory of polyphony can really be grasped, yet some small insight into the nature of the music it was expected to handle can be derived from consideration of the compositions that survive under the names of men known to have been among its members – even though it is possible in only a few cases to be certain that such music was written actually during their employment by Wolsey.

As composers, the most distinguished of Wolsey's chapel musicians were Richard Pygott, Avery Burnett and John Mason. Richard Pygott was probably the first, and equally probably the only occupant of the office of master of the choristers of Wolsey's chapel. As Richard Pygott of Westminster, servant of the

---

[21] Ibid., fols. 116v, 119r.   [22] Ibid., fol. 118r.

[23] This volume comprehended four Masses by Brumel, three each by Antoine de Févin, Josquin des Près and la Rue, two by Mouton, and one each by Pipelare and Roselli.

cardinal of York, he occurs as early as January 1517,[24] and certainly was in office as master of the choristers by December that year.[25] Thereafter his name and office occur frequently[26] until 1527,[27] and in all likelihood he served Wolsey until his fall.

Of Pygott's five works with sacred texts, only one survives complete. This, 'Quid petis, o fili?', is for devotional rather than ecclesiastical use, and is discussed later.[28] His remaining works are all liturgical or para-liturgical. Two are for five voices: a setting of the votive antiphon *Salve regina, mater misericordie*, and a four-movement Mass *Veni sancte spiritus*. Both pieces survive in isolated part-books originating little if at all later than *c.*1530,[29] and seem very likely to have been written for Wolsey's chapel. Both compositions survive also in a set of part-books of *c.*1539–40, from which one book is unfortunately missing;[30] however, it has proved possible for the music to be completed.[31] At a total of some 1150 semibreves, the setting of *Salve regina* is immensely extended; it is indeed one of the most elaborate and expansive pieces of its period, extremely florid in style and making great technical demands of its singers. In a similar vein, the Mass *Veni sancte spiritus* is among the most ornate that survive from its time.[32] A further Mass by Pygott, for six voices, was listed on an inventory of the contents of the volumes of polyphony used in the chapel of King's College, Cambridge, in 1529,[33] but is not known to have survived.

Of the remaining two compositions attributed to Pygott, one is a fragmentary setting for four voices of *Domine, secundum actum meum*, the sixth responsory at Matins in the Office of the Dead;[34] the other is a setting of a votive antiphon to St Thomas of Canterbury, *Gaude pastore christi gregis*, probably originally in five parts

[24] *LP*, II (ii) 2838. [25] BL, MS Harley 599, fol. 44r (*LP*, IV (iii) p. 2766).

[26] 1518: PRO, SP1/16, fol. 206v (*LP*, II (ii) 4055); 1521: BL, MS Harley 620, fols 13v, 26v, 27v, 28r, 44v; 1524: PRO, E179/69/9; 1524–5: BL, MS Egerton 2886, fol. 263r.

[27] PRO, C82/588, no. 4: Signet Bill in favour of 'Richard Pigot, Maister of the Children of the Chapell with the moost Reverend fader in god your moost trusty Counsaillour the lord legate de latere'. In the calendar of this item (*LP*, IV (ii) 3142) Pygott is incorrectly described as master of the children of the Chapel Royal. Pygott's name appears on a list of the gentlemen of the Chapel Royal calendared (*LP*, IV (i) 1939 no. 10) under the date 1526. In fact, the original document (PRO, SP1/37, fols 98–100) is undated, and there seems to be no good reason to follow the compilers of *LP* in associating it with the promulgation of new household statutes in 1526; the names on the list unequivocally date it rather later, to *c.*1535.

[28] See below, pp. 194–5. [29] BL, MS Harley 1709, fol. 26r and BL, Add. MS 34191, fol. 4v, respectively.

[30] The 'Peterhouse part-books', now CUL, MSS Peterhouse 471–4; see N. Sandon, 'The Henrician part-books at Peterhouse, Cambridge', *Proceedings of the Royal Musical Association*, 103 (1976/7), 106 and R. Bowers, entry relating to Peterhouse MSS 471–4 in I. A. Fenlon (ed.), *Cambridge Musical Manuscripts 900–1600* (Cambridge, 1982), p. 132.

[31] N. Sandon, 'The Henrician Part-Books belonging to Peterhouse, Cambridge', 2 vols, PhD dissertation, unpublished (University of Exeter, 1983), II, pp. 62–95 and 455–522 respectively.

[32] Ibid., I, pp. 215, 263–4, 301.

[33] F. L. Harrison, *Music in Medieval Britain*, 2nd edn (London, 1963), p. 433.

[34] Winchester College, muniment 12845; see A. Rannie, *The Story of Music at Winchester College* (Winchester, [n.d.: *c.*1970]), pp. 2–3 (with facsimile).

but of which only the highly melismatic bass part now survives, in a volume copied not later than *c.*1530.[35] Among the large corpus of surviving polyphonic votive antiphons, surprisingly few are on texts addressing St Thomas; being votive to the name-saint of Thomas Wolsey, it is not improbable that this piece was composed by Pygott in particular satisfaction of his perceived obligations to his employer at the time of its composition.

Pygott's music is of high quality, commending comparison even with John Taverner for his ability to combine cogency of detail with large-scale logic. Particular note has been taken of his precocious fondness for imitative writing,[36] and it is tempting to speculate that there can be detected here some influence arising from the availability among the books at Hampton Court of printed continental polyphony of the first fifteen years of the sixteenth century.

Among the gentlemen of Wolsey's chapel who accompanied him in his household on his embassy to France in 1527 was a Master Avery,[37] and he can certainly be identified with the 'Master Averie' by whom two compositions still survive. One is an *alternatim* organ setting of *Te deum laudamus*,[38] the hymn or canticle concluding Matins on festivals; the other is a four-movement Mass 'Ut re mi fa sol la'. This latter survives uniquely in the Forrest-Heyther set of part-books datable to *c.*1528–30,[39] and thus can with some certainty be dated to the period of its composer's employment with Wolsey. To the attribution 'Master Averie' in one of the part-book sources of the Mass, a later hand has added the surname 'Burton'.[40] The annotator was almost correct; 'Master Averie' seems quite certain to be identifiable with the Avery Burnett who, after Wolsey's fall, occurs as a gentleman of the Chapel Royal in *c.* 1535 and up until 1541.[41]

The keyboard setting in a polyphonic guise of the alternate plainsong verses of *Te deum laudamus* is an extended essay in two- and three-part writing, but cannot claim to be particularly inventive or interesting. The Mass, however, is rather

[35] BL, Add. MS 34191, fol. 23r.

[36] N. Sandon, 'Pygott, Richard', in S. Sadie (ed.), *The New Grove Dictionary of Music and Musicians*, 20 vols. (London, 1980), xv, p. 483. The biographical detail in this article requires slight revision in the light of note 27 above; and see Sandon, 'The Henrician Part-books belonging to Peterhouse, Cambridge', I, pp. 181–90.

[37] *Chronicle of Calais*, p. 40.

[38] J. Caldwell (ed.), *Early Tudor Organ Music*, Early English Church Music, VI (1968), p. 1. It survives only in BL, Add. MS 29996, a source of the later 1540s.

[39] J. Bergsagel, 'The date and provenance of the Forrest-Heyther collection of Tudor masses', *Music and Letters*, 44 (1963), 240.

[40] J. Bergsagel, 'Avery', in Sadie (ed.), *The New Grove Dictionary*, I, p. 745.

[41] PRO, SP1/37, fol. 99r (calendared in *LP*, IV (i) 1939 no. 10, under the erroneous date 1526); *LP*, XIII (ii), p. 283; *LP*, XVI, p. 726. Avery Burnett must be distinguished from David Burton (with whom he has frequently been confused); Burton occurs exclusively as a gentleman of the Chapel Royal, from 1511 (PRO, LC2/1, fol. 170v) until 1529/31 (*LP*, V, pp. 310, 325) – an occurrence of his name in 1542 (*LP*, XVII, 1012 no. 54) is retrospective to 1526. A few other instances are known in which a composer (e.g. Lionel Power) was blessed by a forename so unusual that it alone sufficed to identify his works.

more remarkable.[42] It is of enormous length; the four movements performed end-to-end last for some forty minutes. Such duration, and its dense and expansive six-part scoring for treble, alto, two tenors (one full-range, one low-range) and two basses, shows the choir for which it was written to have been capable of meeting immense demands made on its stamina and technical skill. The Mass includes, in particular, a variety of resourceful examples of the contrasts of fully scored writing for chorus with passages for a kaleidoscopically inventive array of solo ensembles, such as are the hallmark of the most ambitious enterprises of this most fecund period in English musical history.

It has to be admitted that the Mass is not great music. Its sheer length appears to have caused the composer to outrun his powers of melodic inventiveness, and even the extent of his technical facility at times. His huge edifice is built on almost the simplest material conceivable: the six adjacent pitches of the hexachord, which give the Mass its title and occur in the tenor part as a *cantus firmus*. No other example of this particular technique is known in English music of the period, though it had been briefly in vogue on the continent a little earlier. It is tempting to see again in this instance a possible influence and stimulus provided by the availability to Burnett of the printed volume of continental polyphony at Hampton Court.

John Mason first occurs as a lay clerk in the choir of the collegiate church of St Mary, Eton, from June 1501 until Christmas 1506.[43] Evidently he proceeded to take priest's orders soon after, and he turned his musical accomplishments to good account by spending a year in Oxford frequenting the schools of the university and, as John Mason, priest, taking the degree of Mus.B. in February 1509.[44] Immediately he became a chaplain in the choir of the college of St Mary Magdalen (of which Wolsey was a former fellow), and served also as master of the choristers, until June 1510.[45] Thereafter, no reference to him has been found until his occurrence as one of the chaplains in Wolsey's household chapel choir in 1521.[46] By this time, he clearly had friends in influential places, and he was soon adding to his benefices canonries (not necessarily residentiary) and prebends of Salisbury (1523) and Hereford (1525), and one of the royal preferments to a

---

[42] J. Smart (ed.), *Avery Burton* [sic]: *Mass 'Ut, re, mi, fa, sol, la'*, (Mapa Mundi, London, 1982). Smart has supplied the second bass part missing from the source. See also P. Phillips, 'A commentary on Avery Burton's [sic] *Mass on the Hexachord*', *Early Music*, 6 (1979), 218, and (but only in the light of Phillips's article) L. Brothers, 'Avery Burton [sic] and his Hexachord Mass', *Musica Disciplina*, 28 (1974), 153.

[43] Eton College, Audit Rolls 31–4; Audit Book 1, pp. 14, 28, sub tit. *Stipendia Capellanorum et Clericorum*.

[44] Oxford, Bodleian Library, Archives of the University, Register of Congregation G (1505–16), fols. 68v (supplicat, 30 January 1509), 70r (admission, 12 February 1509).

[45] Magdalen College, Oxford, Liber Computi 1490–1510, fol. 230r; Liber Computi 1510–30, unfoliated (first fascicle), sub tit. *Stipendia Capellanorum et Clericorum*.

[46] BL, MS Harley 620, fols. 14v, 27v, 44r.

Mortimer chantry in Chichester cathedral (1523).[47] Considering that two or three of the priests of Wolsey's chapel were transferred to the chapel choir of Cardinal College, Oxford, in or after 1526,[48] it is perfectly conceivable that the *dom* Mason who was a chaplain of Cardinal College in 1529/30, and served briefly as acting master of the choristers following the departure of John Taverner in March 1530, may be identified with the present John Mason.[49]

Of Mason's four surviving compositions, all appear to be for five voices. Three are votive antiphons, two on texts votive to St Mary – *Ave Maria. Ave fuit prima salus* and *Quales sumus, o miseri properantes* – while one, *Vae nobis miseris*, is a Jesus antiphon. The fourth, *O rex gloriose*, is a setting of the (ritual) antiphon during Lent to *Nunc dimittis*, the canticle at Compline. Since all survive uniquely in the Peterhouse part-books of *c.*1539–40, none can be shown for certain to date from the time of Mason's employment in Wolsey's orbit, and none is complete; nevertheless, all four have proved to be restorable.[50] Mason emerges as a respectable second-division composer of fair talent; the sheer length of the prose texts he chose to set provoked a style more syllabic and less melismatic and expansive than that of many of his contemporaries.

Apart from the three composers, little has been discovered about such remaining members of Wolsey's chapel whose names are known. Robert Phillips had been a chorister of the Chapel Royal in 1514,[51] and occurs as a lay clerk of Wolsey's chapel in 1521 and 1527.[52] After Wolsey's fall, he returned to the king's service as a clerk of the Chapel Royal,[53] evidently as one of its star singers.[54] Richard Bower had become a lay clerk of Wolsey's chapel by 1524;[55] like Phillips, he subsequently transferred to the Chapel Royal, probably on Wolsey's fall. There he continues to occur until 1559,[56] having succeeded William Crane as master of the choristers in 1545.[57]

The liturgical music – and especially the choral polyphony – of the first third of

[47] J. M. Horne (comp.), *Fasti Ecclesiae Anglicanae 1300–1541*, II (Hereford diocese), p. 48; III (Salisbury diocese), pp. 88, 78; A. B. Emden, *A Biographical Register of the University of Oxford, A.D. 1501 to 1540* (Oxford, 1974), pp. 386, 657; B. Rose, 'John Mason: a clarification', *Musical Times*, 113 (1972), 1231; Sandon, 'The Henrician Part-books belonging to Peterhouse, Cambridge', I, pp. 171–7.

[48] See below, pp. 197–8.   [49] PRO, E36/104, pp. 18, 19.

[50] Sandon, 'The Henrician Part-books belonging to Peterhouse, Cambridge', II, pp. 19–30, 166–94, 280–98, 299–316. In an independent restoration by Dr Bernard Rose, *Quales sumus* and *Vae nobis* have been recorded by the choir of Magdalen College on Argo ZRG 846.

[51] BL, Add. MS 21481, fol. 151v (*LP*, II (ii), p. 1464).

[52] BL, MS Harley 620, fols. 27v, 44v et alibi; MS Harley 542, fol. 73r (as 'master phelippe'); *Chronicle of Calais*, p. 40.

[53] Recorded from *c.* 1535 (PRO, SP1/37, fol. 99r) until 1552 (BL, MS Stowe 571, fol. 36v). He appears to have served a period as precentor of King Henry VIII's College – the successor institution to Wolsey's Cardinal College Oxford – around 1541: *LP*, XVI, 580 no. 32.

[54] J. Pratt (ed.), *The Acts and Monuments of John Foxe*, 8 vols, 4th edn (London, 1887), V, pp. 465–70. This is Foxe's narrative of the life and martyrdom of Robert Testwood, for whom see further below, pp. 198–9, 205.

[55] PRO, E179/69/9, 69/10.   [56] BL, MS Lansdowne 3, fol. 200r.   [57] PRO, C66/785, m. 44.

the sixteenth century made considerable demands on the technique and training of those to whom its performance was committed; indeed, in the eyes of their employer, the music might well have failed in one of its principal purposes had it not done so. The rapid articulation of the coloratura vocal style of the late fifteenth century had been supplemented, rather than supplanted, by the greater rhythmic restraint of its successor style; meanwhile, the demands made on ensemble, breathing, intonation and sheer physical stamina as well as vocal virtuosity remained undiluted. The quality of the choirs maintained to execute this music in the great aristocratic households and the major churches duly became a source of immense pride to their employers; and consequently there emerged eager competition among them to secure the services of the ablest singers.

Since at least the reign of Richard III, the crown had regularly replenished the ranks of the Chapel Royal through application of the royal prerogative rights of impressment and purveyance, whereby the persons and services of skilled artificers and executants could be requisitioned for the king's service. A royal commission was issued to some appropriate member of the chapel establishment, empowering him to scour the country, visiting cathedral, collegiate and other churches taking the ablest singing men and boys for service in the Chapel Royal. The most potent way in which any of the most prestigious of the remaining choral institutions – especially those of royal foundation or connection – could secure the recruitment of competent singers ready trained was therefore to purchase from the king a comparable commission, commonly called 'the Plakard', endowing it likewise with a royally delegated right to impress into its own service men and boys from other institutions. Cathedrals and churches among the likely victims could then seek to preserve themselves from the potentially devastating effects of such predation by purchasing from the king his letters of immunity. Thus could be created an elaborate edifice of privilege and counter-privilege, from which probably the king's treasury ultimately benefited as much as anyone else.

Wolsey knew well how this system could be played. It is possible that he had himself had some brief experience of managing a major household chapel choir, since it appears that he may have served, in an acting capacity, as dean of Henry VIII's Chapel Royal for some period during 1510.[58] It is not surprising, therefore,

---

[58] On 3 October 1510, eighteen months after Wolsey's appointment as dean of Lincoln, the sub-dean and chapter addressed to their 'Ryght wyrschipffull and our speciall goode Maister' a letter endorsed to 'Mr dean of the kinges chappel and dean of lincoln' (Lincolnshire Archives Office: Archives of the dean and chapter of Lincoln, Register A. 3. 4, fol. 15v). This is puzzling, since both before and after this date William Atwater is known to have occupied the office of dean of the Chapel Royal. Nevertheless, it seems unlikely that the chapter of Lincoln would be in error in their address to their own dean, and the probability is that Wolsey had been appointed to be acting dean during some temporary incapacity of Atwater. (There is, however, another explanation, of some remote degree of possibility. Wolsey's predecessor, Geoffrey Simeon, had been both dean of Lincoln and dean of the Chapel Royal. It is conceivable that the letter of October 1510 was

that it was during his brief tenure of the bishopric of Lincoln that, on 9 June 1514, his dean and chapter secured under the signet from the king letters of immunity granting their cathedral choir freedom from predation by all and any persons 'auctorised by our lettres of commission or otherwise to take and Reteyn any singing men or children' – impressment for service in the Chapel Royal alone excepted.[59] And it was by the use of such rights of impressment, obtained from a grateful king, that Wolsey maintained the standards of his own chapel choir, once he had himself become the employer of a household chapel comparable to the king's. No actual document is known to exist, but certainly by 1523/4 Wolsey had obtained such rights – which his servants might exercise for purposes rather exceeding those ostensibly intended. In that year, the choir (of cathedral character and standard) maintained in the parish church of St Botolph, Boston (Lincolnshire), by the gild of St Mary there, twice received predatory visits from Wolsey's servants. On the first occasion, a servant of the lord cardinal and another singer arrived. It cost the gild 20s to buy them off, and on the later occasion, when the predator was Richard Pygott himself, the master of the choristers of Wolsey's chapel, the gild invested 26s 8d 'to have his good will in regard to the singing boys' – i.e., for Pygott *not* to take any away with him.[60] In 1527, Wolsey's chapel was one of four institutions which enjoyed these royal rights of impressment and were expressly exempted from the effect of the grant of immunity issued to the Master and Fellows of the collegiate church of the Holy Trinity, Pleshey (Essex), on behalf of their six singing-boys.[61]

Wolsey, moreover, had no intention of allowing his own chapel to be impoverished by the impressment of his singers, and, as lord chancellor, he was in a position to see that the texts of signet bills delivered to him to be issued as letters under the great seal reflected this. Thus in 1528 the Provost and Fellows of King's College, Cambridge, obtained from the king two complementary sets of rights, firstly of immunity from further vexatious impressment of their own singers, and secondly of themselves impressing singers from other choirs for their own service – but the same four choirs, including Wolsey's chapel, were granted specific immunity from such depredation by the agents of the Cambridge college.[62] On top of these rights of impressment, moreover, Cavendish observed that Wolsey's chapel enjoyed the benefit of occasional augmentation by 'dyvers Reteynours of connyng syngyng men that came at dyvers sondrie pryncypall

addressed by some thoughtless clerk using an obsolete formula once appropriate for Simeon, but not for Wolsey. Nevertheless, such a hypothesis hardly seems very likely.)

[59] Ibid., Register A.3.3, fol. 65v.

[60] *Regarda diversis personis* ... servienti domini Cardinalis et alii Cantatori veniencibus usque boston pro Choristis habendis xxs ... Magistro pygot Cantatori servienti domini Cardinalis pro benevolencia sua pro pueris xxvjs viijd: BL, MS Egerton 2886, fol. 263r.

[61] PRO, DL12/44/2; the three other choirs whose commissions to impress remained effective at Pleshey were the Chapel Royal, St Stephen, Westminster, and St George, Windsor.

[62] PRO, c82/609, no. 189. This immunity from depredation by King's was extended also to its sister college, St Mary, Eton.

feastes'.[63] The feelings of their employers, as their ablest singers set off for Wolsey's chapel at the onset of the major feasts of the Church's year, just when they were needed most sorely by their regular churches, can well be imagined, but the cardinal's will, no doubt, was not one to be thwarted.

Indeed, there may have been many instances in which, to secure the permanent transfer of a coveted singer, Wolsey merely needed to make his pleasure known, without resort to his sub-regalian privileges. At some time in perhaps the late 1510s, William Warham, archbishop of Canterbury, wrote to Wolsey confirming that through Dr Bennet, Wolsey's chaplain, he understood that 'your grace is desirose to have one Clement of my chapel which syngeth a basse parte' – whom Warham, with at least an outward show of dutiful meekness, duly sent to Wolsey by return.[64] This 'Clement' may well have been Clement Wymer, who is recorded as one of the chaplains of Wolsey's choir in 1521.[65] If even Warham felt it impolitic to resist such an expression of the lord legate's pleasure, it is hard to imagine any other of even the upper ecclesiastical aristocracy of the period responding otherwise.

Of the high competence of Wolsey's chapel choir there can be little doubt. In 1515, Niccolo Sagudino, himself an amateur keyboard player and a reputable judge, had observed of the members of Henry VIII's Chapel Royal that their voices were 'more divine than human, not so much singing as carolling (*non cantavano ma jubilavano*)'; the basses, in particular, he thought to be unequalled anywhere in Europe.[66] Nevertheless, barely three years later it was reckoned that Wolsey's chapel was superior to the Chapel Royal – and it was the king who was doing the reckoning, and the king was not amused. It appears that it may have been during the celebration of the Twelve Days following Christmas 1517 that Henry began to suspect that Wolsey's chapel might be more skilful than his own, and he proceeded to devise a test. The two chapels were summoned,[67] and a piece of music unknown to both was given to them to sing at sight. This proved to be 'bettre and more suerly handlydde' by Wolsey's chapel than by the king's, a fact which William Cornysh, master of the Chapel Royal choristers, was not able to deny.[68]

---

[63] Cavendish, p. 20.

[64] PRO, sp1/40, no. 60: H. E. Ellis, *Original Letters Illustrative of English History*, 9 vols. in 3 series (London, 1824–46), 3rd series vol. 2, p. 54. The letter is undated; it is calendared under 1526 (*LP*, IV (ii) 2696), but may well be a few years earlier.

[65] BL, MS Harley 620, fols. 27v (dom Clemens), 45r (ser Clement Wymer).

[66] 'Ditta messa fu cantata per la capella de questa Maestà [Henry VIII], qual veramente è più presto divina che humana; non cantavano ma jubilavano, et *maxime* de contrabassi, che non credo al mondo sieno li pari'; F. Stefani, G. Berchet, N. Barozzi (eds.), *I Diarii di Marino Sanuto* (Venice, 1879–1903), xx, col. 266; calendared in *CSPV, 1509–19*, 624.

[67] On 3 January 1518, 6s 8d was paid by the king to one of his servants 'Riding with a lettre to mr Pigot', which may refer to these proceedings: BL, Add. MS 21481, fol. 280r.

[68] PRO, sp1/16, fol. 174: 'for hys grace [the king] haith playnely schewydde unto cornysche that your graces chiapell is better than hys, and providde the same bi thys reason, that yff ony maner off newe songe schulde be broght unto boith the sayde chiapellis for to be sunge ex improviso then the sayde

What followed shows very clearly the high priority accorded by the great of the land to the competence of the public face of their religious devotions. Henry evinced a particular admiration for the singing of one of Wolsey's choirboys – so much, and perhaps so conspicuously, that Wolsey thought it prudent to offer the boy to Henry for transfer to the Chapel Royal. The offer was made through Richard Pace, the king's secretary, who presently wrote back to Wolsey conveying the king's thanks for the offer, and an imperious request that the boy, though not in good health ('notwythstondynge hys dissease'), be sent to court immediately, 'schewynge that he haith grete neade off him: as itt is true'.[69] It was 24 March; perhaps the services for the Vigil of the Annunciation had shown up more deficiencies among the Chapel Royal choristers. Holy Week and Easter were imminent, and the king was ill-inclined to wait. To discourage Wolsey from prevaricating, Pace wrote again the next day, reminding him that 'yff itt were not for the personall love that the kyngis highnesse doith bere unto your grace, suerly he wolde have owte off your chiapell not chyldren oonly, but also men';[70] and he wrote again the day following, reporting that the king wanted the boy immediately, and would prefer to obtain him without resorting to an official requisition by Cornysh or any other.[71] Pace wrote yet again on 29 March, reporting that Henry was asking daily after the boy.[72]

In fact, Wolsey had already complied, writing to Pace on about 27 March that he had lately despatched to the court (which was then at Abingdon) 'Robyn my boy'.[73] Robin must have arrived later on the 29th; Pace wrote again that day acknowledging receipt, conveying the king's gratitude, and assuring Wolsey that Henry would never have coveted the boy had he not been 'compellydde bi pure necessitie and lakke off chyldren'. Pace also assured Wolsey that he had spoken to Cornysh, to urge him to treat the boy well, 'otherwyse than he doith his owne' – which Cornysh had promised to do.[74] At Abingdon, satisfaction appears to have been universal. Musically the boy was evidently highly gifted, and well trained as a singer of both composed polyphony and of descant improvised to plainsong; even the master of the Chapel Royal choristers accepted the indignity with a good grace. As Pace assured Wolsey on 1 April, 'Cornysche doith gretly laude and prayse the chylde off your chiapell sende hydre, not oonly for hys suer and clenly syngynge, but also for hys goodde and crafty descant; and doith in lyke maner extolle Mr Pygote for the techynge off hym'.[75] What Wolsey, Pygott and young Robin himself thought of the proceedings is not recorded; but few episodes show

---

songe schulde be bettre and more suerly handlydde bi your chiapell than bi hys graces. Cornysche istud plane verum, nullo modo concoquere [sic] potuit.' *LP*, ɪɪ (ii) 4024; Ellis, *Original Letters*, 3rd series vol. 2, p. 49.

[69] Ibid., fol. 173 (*LP*, ɪɪ (ii) 4023).   [70] Ibid., fol. 174 (*LP*, ɪɪ (ii) 4024).
[71] Ibid., fol. 176r (*LP*, ɪɪ (ii) 4025).
[72] Ibid., fol. 198 (*LP*, ɪɪ (ii) 4043).   [73] Ibid., fol. 204 (*LP*, ɪɪ (ii) 4053).
[74] Ibid., fols. 199, 200 (*LP*, ɪɪ (ii) 4044); Ellis, *Original Letters*, 3rd series vol. 2, pp. 51–4.
[75] Ibid., fol. 206v (*LP*, ɪɪ (ii) 4055).

more clearly than this the high priority accorded by the great of the land to their capacity to deploy in the musical establishments of their household chapels the finest performers they could find.

It may be noted, also, that Henry could be magnanimous as well as covetous, and that such traffic was not necessarily all one way. For instance, one of the most outstanding members of the Chapel Royal at this time was its principal composer, Robert Fayrfax; him, it appears, Henry was content to second to Wolsey for several weeks of the year 1520/1[76] – the last year, in fact, of the composer's life.

Of music-making of a secular nature within the household under Wolsey's patronage, very much less is known. Cavendish's enumeration of the membership of the household indicates that Wolsey forebore to retain in his employment such distinguishing marks of secular lordship as trumpeters and simple heralds; however, he did note, among a group of miscellaneous functionaries towards the end of his list, Wolsey's employment of an ensemble of four 'Mynstrelles'.[77] Minstrels, most commonly in teams as small as three or four, were a standard feature of great households of all kinds; it appears that principally their function was to provide background sound at meals, and music for dancing. Socially, their status was much lower than that of the learned chapel musicians; musically, they did not need to be literate, and indeed, their repertories appear to have been wholly unwritten, and the transmission of their craft entirely oral. For these reasons, very little is now known about the character and the scope of their provision of music.[78] The household minstrels of Henry VIII who played for the ball celebrating the proxy marriage of Henry's sister Mary to Louis XII of France at Greenwich in 1514 consisted of an ensemble of four players, on shawm (*piva*), rebec (*violetta*), small pipe (*certo pifaretto*) and lute (or possibly, gittern: *cithara*), 'si accordavano molto bene',[79] and Wolsey's ensemble may well have been constituted very similarly.

Some indication of the character of the functions expected of Wolsey's ensemble is given by Cavendish's account of the kinds of entertainment provided for his hosts by the cardinal on his embassy to France of 1527. At Amiens on 19 August he gave a banquet for the queen mother of France (Louise of Savoy) and other great ladies, which was attended also (ostensibly unexpectedly) by the

---

[76] An allocation *super compotum* on the view of expenses of the king's household, 12–13 Henry VIII (BL, MS Royal 7 F xiv, fol. 148r): pro Vadiis Roberti Fairfax de Capella regia existentis in servicio domini Ducis Eboracensis lxix s. iiij d. At first sight, this entry appears puzzling, since there was no duke of York in 1520/1; almost certainly an error for the *cardinal* of York may be assumed.

[77] Cavendish, p. 20. In default of trumpeters of his own, Wolsey was permitted to take with him on an embassy to France in 1528 two of the king's trumpeters: *LP*, IV (iii) App. 150.

[78] For an illuminating survey of such evidence as does survive of minstrels and their music and duties in a courtly setting, see J. Stevens, *Music and Poetry at the Early Tudor Court*, 2nd edn (Cambridge, 1979), pp. 244–51, 298–309.

[79] *CSPV*, 1509–19, 505; for identification of the instruments, see Stevens, *Music and Poetry at the Early Tudor Court*, pp. 245, 262. See also Hall's descriptions of Wolsey's ceremonial banquets and 'disguisings', e.g. Hall, p. 595.

king, Francis I. In Cavendish's eyes, the feature of this feast was the great 'myrthe and solace' provided for the diners not only in conversation but also 'in instrumentes of musyke setforthe with my lordes mynstrelles'; probably the music was supplied not really to be listened to, but to be appreciated as part of the ceremony and 'honour' of the service of the meal. Following their performance during the banquet, the minstrels played music for the ladies to dance to. So 'Connyngly & dulce' did they play, indeed, that Francis was much impressed, and Wolsey agreed to lend the players to him for the following night. They accompanied the king to a nobleman's house, and duly played on while the company danced the night away. For one of the minstrels it was all too much. Cavendish was not sure whether (as some said) he was actually poisoned, through jealousy that King Francis should so clearly take greater pleasure in Wolsey's minstrels than in his own, or whether he merely injured himself 'with extreme labor of blowyng'; but within a day or two the shawm-player, 'an excellent man in that art', had expired.[80]

Secular music-making in Wolsey's household, however, could also include opportunities for performances of a repertory more learned in nature than minstrel music. The masques with which Wolsey entertained Henry VIII on his visits to the cardinal's household were enhanced and ornamented with composed music of various kinds for performance by voices; indeed, with 'all kynd of musyke and armonye setforthe with excellent voyces bothe of men and Childerne' – evidently the men and boys of the household chapel, wearing (probably quite literally) different hats.[81]

There was scope also for purely recreational music-making, of a more or less informal kind, by the learned musicians of the chapel. Among the contents of a printed volume of *XX Songes*, collected and published in 1530 as a set of four part-books, is a setting by Richard Pygott of a vernacular text, 'By by lullaby; In a drem late as I lay'; unfortunately, only the bass part survives. The text is a simple lullaby, not overtly religious in nature, but apparently intended to be understood as a song of Mary to the infant Jesus.[82] Possibly falling into a similar category, as edificatory music composed for the pleasure and recreation of his singers round their fireside, or for moments of a more reflective nature among the public formalities of Wolsey's court, is Pygott's single work that does survive complete. This is an extended devotional song in carol form for four voices, 'Quid petis, o

[80] Cavendish, pp. 59–60; *LP*, IV (ii) 3365.
[81] Cavendish, p. 25. A description of a masque mounted in Wolsey's household in 1527 (*CSPV*, 1527–33, p. 4) unfortunately makes no mention of the music of the performance. For several instances in which the boys and men of the Chapel Royal performed and sang in a secular capacity at comparable royal masques, banquets and 'disguisings', see Stevens, *Music and Poetry at the Early Tudor Court*, pp. 238–52 *passim*, which also endeavours to identify, among surviving secular songs, items possibly usable on such occasions; S. Anglo, *Spectacle, Pageantry and Early Tudor Policy* (Oxford, 1969), pp. 101–2, 119–21.
[82] E. Flügel, 'Liedersammlungen des xvi Jahrhunderts besonders aus der Zeit Heinrichs VIII', *Anglia*, 12 (1889), 590.

fili?'[83] It is a Nativity song; the three stanzas, in old-fashioned alliterative English written probably many years before, reflect on Mary's delight in her infant son, while the burden, in dog-Latin, invents a dialogue between them. The music is, perhaps, a young man's experimental composition. The burden and first stanza explore an embryonic but genuinely imitative style, in which the music is fully scored à4; each verbal phrase is given its own distinctive musical point in a style melodically and rhythmically restrained, introduced by each voice in turn and discussed with textual repetition where necessary. The composer, however, chose not to continue in this style; for stanzas two and three he reverted to the more traditional style of composition, setting stanza two for duet and three for trio, with little more than polite gestures towards the principle of imitation prior to relaxation into expansive and more rhapsodic polyphony much based on the imperfect consonances of the third and the sixth, very much after the fashion of much of the writing for reduced voices found in the Eton Choirbook polyphony of the 1480s and 1490s.

Surviving in a manuscript of *c.*1520,[84] as – in patches – one of its most advanced compositions, this carol seems quite probably to have been composed while Pygott was working for Wolsey. The text of 'Quid petis, o fili?' is literary, not liturgical; the differentials of pitch between its constituent voices display not the standard lay-out of the ecclesiastical choir, but the 'terraced' scoring eventually to become characteristic of the much later domestic madrigal. Evidently therefore, it was composed not for use in chapel, but for devotional edification and entertainment in a domestic context.

Also to be heard in Wolsey's household on occasions was keyboard music of various kinds. When Dionisio Memo, then organist of the doge's chapel of St Mark, Venice, arrived in England in 1516 (bringing with him his own instrument), he was presented first to Wolsey. Wolsey is reported to have desired to hear him play, and to have taken pleasure in the performance; however, it is not necessary to impute to this a motive entirely aesthetic in nature. Given Henry VIII's well-attested and genuine pleasure in music, Wolsey may well have been principally concerned with estimating Memo's capacity for earning him some credit as a patron who could then introduce Memo on to the king. Henry was indeed very appreciative, and Memo remained at the English royal court for over a year.[85]

Nevertheless, it is just possible that Wolsey was known, or at least believed, to take some genuine pleasure, however oblique, in keyboard music. In any event, Richard Pace, writing to him in 1520 about other matters, thought it might

[83] J. Stevens (ed.), *Music at the Court of Henry VIII*, Musica Britannica 18, 2nd edn (London, 1969), p. 82.

[84] BL, Add. MS 31922; see Stevens, *Music and Poetry in the Early Tudor Court*, pp. 107, 421–2.

[85] *CSPV, 1509–19*, 780, 783; R. Brown, *Four Years at the Court of Henry VIII: a Selection of Despatches written by the Venetian Ambassador*, 2 vols. (London, 1854), I, p. 296; II, p. 97.

interest Wolsey to know in addition that at court 'a newe player uppon the Clavicordes' had been introduced, whose playing the king was enjoying.[86] Further, among the effects listed at Hampton Court on an inventory of January 1523 was 'An Instrument of Musyke in my lordes deynyng Chaumbre'.[87] It seems that such a description could be only of one of the larger keyboard instruments; had it been a positive organ it would presumably have been described as such, so the greatest probability is that it was a virginal or harpsichord, on hand to contribute to the provision, when suitable, of *Tafelmusik*. Such an occasion could well have been provided by the banquet laid on by Wolsey at Hampton Court for the French ambassadors in November 1527, when the service of the meal was accompanied 'with suche a pleasaunt noyce of dyvers Instrumentes of musyke' that the visitors '(as it semyd) ware rapte in to an hevenly paradice'.[88]

In respect of his promotion of the music of the church, Wolsey's patronage extended beyond his own household chapel to the chapels of his two collegiate foundations at Oxford (foundation charter 1525) and Ipswich (1528). At neither college was the observance of the Opus Dei to be in any way subordinate or subservient to its academic purpose; Wolsey himself would probably not have dissented much from the opinion of William Capon, dean of Cardinal College, Ipswich, that 'in our quere standith the honnor of your graces collage'.[89] In neither case did Wolsey leave the worship of the college chapel to be conducted as a secondary priority by the academic members; rather, for each he supplied a fully-staffed professional chapel choir. For Cardinal College, Oxford, the statutory complement of the choir totalled forty-two persons: – a precentor and twelve chaplains, the master of the choristers and twelve lay clerks, and sixteen chorister-boys.[90] The choir of Ipswich College was somewhat less inflated with personnel; at a dean and twelve chaplains, eight lay clerks (including the master of the choristers) and eight choristers,[91] it was placed at around the top of the mainstream of collegiate churches of the second rank.

The importance of high quality in the performance of the music of the Ipswich and Oxford chapels was demonstrated by the efforts taken to secure the services of skilled men to fill the chapel positions. Wolsey had obtained from the king the appropriate commission empowering him to impress singing men and boys for the Oxford choir;[92] thereafter, however, he was content to delegate the application of the commission to a trusted agent, John Longland, bishop of Lincoln. Longland duly applied himself to the finding of 'prestes, singing men and

---

[86] *LP*, III (i) 1010; Ellis, *Original Letters*, 3rd series vol. I, p. 199.   [87] BL, MS Harley 599, fol. 115v.

[88] Cavendish, p. 70.   [89] PRO, SP1/53, fol. 197r (*LP*, IV (iii) 5458).

[90] Her Majesty's Commissioners, *Statutes of the Colleges of Oxford*, 3 vols. (London and Oxford, 1853), II section 11, pp. 13, 49–51; PRO, E36/102, fols. 3v–4r.

[91] PRO, C66/652, m. 32 (royal licence of foundation); J. C. Cox, 'The Cardinal's College, Ipswich', in W. Page (ed.), *The Victoria County History of Suffolk*, 2 vols. (London, 1902–7), II, pp. 142–3; A. F. Leach, 'Ipswich School', ibid., pp. 328–32.

[92] PRO, SP1/39, fol. 239r (*LP*, IV (ii) 2564).

queresters' for Cardinal College, and in September 1525 Wolsey wrote to him acknowledging his success so far in obtaining personnel and retaining them to enter the college for its formal opening a year hence, on the feast of St Frideswide (19 October) 1526.[93] Wolsey had also, it appears, come to some arrangement with the king and William Crane, who had succeeded William Cornysh in 1523 as master of the choristers of the Chapel Royal,[94] apparently for the release or secondment of some singers from the king's Chapel Royal. With his own recruits, plus the provision of some personnel from Wolsey's own household chapel, Longland felt confident that he could 'truste and doubte nott but you shall have an honorable gud quere ther of singinge men and Children as well in brests as in cunnynge'.[95]

Of particular moment was the appointment to the principal musical post in each college, that of master of the choristers, whom at Cardinal College the statutes themselves required to be *musices peritissimus* – 'very highly skilled in music'. Men of such competence, however, could command high salaries, and clearly considered themselves to be in a seller's market. Longland's initial choice as master of the choristers for Cardinal College, Oxford, Hugh Aston – then master of the choristers at the collegiate church of St Mary, Leicester[96] – evidently opted ('considering his greate wages which he allegith in perpetuite there') to haggle over the matter.[97] Wolsey seemed not too concerned, and was content to leave the resolution of the appointment to Longland's discretion.[98] Longland did not persevere with Aston, but made a second choice, John Taverner, lay clerk and probably master of the choristers at the collegiate church of the Holy Trinity, Tattershall (Lincolnshire).[99] Taverner likewise prevaricated, alleging 'thassurans and profite of his lyvinge att tatessall: and that he is in way of a gud mariage, whiche he shuld loose if he dydd reamove frome thens'.[100] Nevertheless, his reluctance proved to be soluble, and before Whitsuntide 1526 he had accepted the appointment, and with the royal commission was busy, in Boston among other places, impressing singers in time for the formal opening of Cardinal College in October that year.[101] Among the chaplains and clerks of the Cardi-

---

[93] PRO, sp1/39, fol. 118r (*LP*, iv (ii) 2457, there misdated to 1526). Wolsey was writing to advise Longland that the opening was being delayed from the date previously determined, 25 March [1526].

[94] Although formally appointed only in 1526 (PRO, c82/574, no. 28), Crane had in fact been in office since Cornysh's death in 1523: see e.g. BL, MS Egerton 2886, fol. 299v.

[95] PRO, sp1/39, fol. 239r (*LP*, iv (ii) 2564, there misdated to 1526).

[96] A. H. Thompson (ed.), *Visitations in the Diocese of Lincoln, 1517–1531*, 3 vols, Lincoln Record Society 33, 35, 37 (Lincoln, 1940–47), iii, p. 222.

[97] Only a year before, Aston had shown at least an interest in moving from Leicester to become master of the choristers of the choir maintained in the parish church of St Botolph, Boston (Lincolnshire): BL, MS Egerton 2886, fol. 263r.

[98] PRO, sp1/39, fol. 118r (*LP*, iv (ii) 2457).

[99] Thompson, *Visitations in the Diocese of Lincoln, 1517–1531*, iii, p. 112; BL, MS Egerton 2886, fol. 296r.

[100] PRO, sp1/39, fol. 239r (*LP*, iv (ii) 2564).

[101] *Regarda data diversis personis* … magistro Taverner in adventu suo cum Commissione pro Cantatoribus vjs viijd … Roberto Lyne Capellano in adventu suo usque boston cum Commissione

nal College choir in September 1529, John Kyttley, Clement [Wymer] and Nicholas Lentall had served previously in Wolsey's household chapel, and likewise possibly Masters Reynold and Mason. Others, however, were from Taverner's own 'country'; John Radley and Thomas Lawney he had brought from Boston, and John Lyster from Tattershall.[102]

Finding the right man to train the choir of Cardinal College, Ipswich, apparently proved to be an enterprise little less taxing. On the day that the college opened, 8 September 1528, the office of master of the choristers was being discharged by one Mr Lentall, evidently Nicholas Lentall, on secondment from Wolsey's household chapel where he had been listed as a lay clerk in 1524 and 1525.[103] Lentall was competent, 'sober and discrete, and bringeth up your Choresters very wele'; to Wolsey, however, his own chapel was of greater importance than the newest of his colleges, and shortly before Christmas he recalled Lentall to his own household, much to the dismay of the dean of Ipswich, William Capon, who lamented Lentall as 'the kay [keystone] of our quere' who had 'set every thyng in so good ordre and made us very good Childern'.[104] However, the replacement found for Lentall, Robert Testwood, was a specialist choirtrainer of professional standard and experience. For seven years early in the sixteenth century he had been a chorister of Henry VII's Chapel Royal;[105] thereafter, he had gained considerable experience in the duties of a master of the choristers, initially at the collegiate church of St Mary, Warwick,[106] before taking up at Whitsun 1524 the appointment from which he was subsequently recruited to Ipswich, that of master of the choristers of the choir of St Botolph, Boston.[107]

However, it is probable that the Ipswich choir was operational for little more than eighteen months or so, and may never have really settled into that level of stability and expertise for which its founder hoped. On the day of its inauguration, the choral staff was almost complete; the dean could report to Wolsey the

Taverner vjs viijd: Boston (Lincolnshire), Borough Archives, MS 4/c/1/1, fol. 25r. For further references to Taverner not hitherto noted, see ibid., fols. 25r, 25v.

102 Ibid., fol. 24r; BL, Harley 620, fol. 27v.; PRO, E36/104, p. 19; BL, MS Egerton 2886, fol. 296v; Thompson, *Visitations in the Diocese of Lincoln, 1517–1531*, III, p. 112. Nicholas Lentall occurs among the lay clerks of Wolsey's chapel in 1524 and 1525: PRO, E179/69/9, 69/10. In 1528, Taverner, Lawney and Radley were all implicated with others in association with Thomas Garrett, a protestant bookseller and evangelizer who serviced a small heretical cell in Oxford; however, Taverner's and Radley's flirtation was evidently only trifling. Neither was in orders or had any pretensions to theological expertise, and Wolsey, on being apprised of their involvement, dismissed them as 'unlearned' and so saved them from committal to custody: PRO, SP1/47, fol. 111 (*LP*, IV (ii) 4074). Thomas Lawney may well be identifiable with the man of the same name who later served Charles Brandon, duke of Suffolk, as a chaplain: S. J. Gunn, *Charles Brandon, Duke of Suffolk c.1484–1545* (Oxford, 1988), p. 162.

103 PRO, E179/69/9, 69/10.

104 BL, Cotton MS Titus B 1, fol. 282r (see Ellis, *Original Letters*, 1st series vol. 1, pp. 186–9, (*LP*, IV (ii) 4778)); PRO, SP1/51, fol. 124v (*LP*, IV (ii) 5052).

105 PRO, SP1/73, no. 141 (*LP*, V, 1764).

106 PRO, SC6/Henry VIII/3730 (1523/4), sub tit. *Pensiones vicariorum Clericorum et Chorustarum*.

107 BL, MS Egerton 2886, fol. 295r.

presence of a sub-dean, precentor and six chaplains (a shortfall or four), eight lay clerks and nine choristers. The singing-men had been well chosen, 'very well brested with sufficient Cunnyng for theyr Rowmes and som of theym very excellent'; however, they were very disgruntled with their pay, 'alleging for theyr selffes how they had moche better wages there from whense they came fro', and they were little better satisfied with the food.[108] By April 1529 the men of the choir were somewhat depleted; one, mourned as 'a very good descanter', had died 'of an Inposteme', and another, Mr Mowlder, although 'a good quereman' had had to be dismissed 'For he wolde not come to the quere but at his owen pleasure'.[109] Mowlder may very well be identifiable with William Moulder who had been master of the Lady Chapel choir at the abbey of St Augustine, Bristol, in 1503, and occurs as a gentleman of the Chapel Royal in 1511 and 1520.[110] If such petulance represented his method of registering displeasure at an unsolicited and unwelcome secondment from the Chapel Royal to Ipswich, then it suggests the possible drawbacks inherent in any scheme of recruitment by impressment. Nevertheless, the dean of Ipswich, William Capon, could record that as master of the choristers, Robert Testwood was 'a very synguler cunnynge man', who was giving such excellent service in training the boys that 'I thynke verely there be no better children within the Reame of England';[111] despite the vicissitudes of the time, therefore, the music of the chapel of the Ipswich college may have succeeded in contributing something to the reflected glory of its founder and patron.

The choir of Cardinal College, Oxford, however, distinguished by greater numbers, higher prominence, and time enough to achieve poise and stability, seems much more likely to have met in full its founder's expectations.[112] It has been shown that among its repertory, the choir included the contents of the most important set of part-books still surviving from the first third of the sixteenth century.[113] The original layer of this set of six books consists of eleven festal Masses in five and six parts, many on the grandest scale. The collection begins with John Taverner's own Mass *Gloria tibi, Trinitas*, and proceeds with four by

[108] BL, Cotton MS Titus B 1, fol. 281v (Ellis, *Original Letters*, 1st series vol. 1, pp. 186–9 (*LP*, IV (ii) 4778)). The value of a chaplainship was £8 5s 4d p.a., and of a clerkship £6 10s 4d p.a. (PRO, SP1/47, fols. 281r–2v); the complaints were not unjustified.

[109] PRO, SP1/53, fol. 197v (*LP*, IV (iii) 5458).

[110] Gloucestershire Record Office, MS D674a z3, sub tit. *Officium Elemosinarii*; PRO, LC2/1, fol. 170r; SP1/19, fol. 267v.

[111] PRO, SP1/53, fol. 197v (*LP*, IV (iii) 5458).

[112] Even so, not even Cardinal College was immune from a casual obstreperousness among the choirmen that could express itself in wildcat, or even (in three or four cases) persistent, absenteeism: PRO, SP1/47, fol. 9v (*LP*, IV (ii) 3961); and cf. Ellis, *Original Letters*, 3rd series vol. 2, p. 139.

[113] Oxford, Bodleian Library, MSS Arch. F e.19–24 (*olim* Mus. Sch. e.376–81); see J. Bergsagel, 'The date and provenance of the Forrest–Heyther collection of Tudor masses', *Music and Letters*, 44 (1963), 240–58. A detailed inventory of the contents appears in A. Hughes, *Medieval Polyphony in the Bodleian Library* (Oxford, 1951), pp. 43–4.

Robert Fayrfax (Chapel Royal, but of prominent South Lincolnshire family), and one each by Avery [Burnett] (Wolsey's household chapel), John Marbeck (Beverley Minster), William Rasar (St George, Windsor and King's College, Cambridge), Hugh Aston (St Mary, Leicester), Thomas Ashwell (St George, Windsor, Holy Trinity, Tattershall, and Lincoln and Durham cathedrals) and John Norman (Eton College and St David's cathedral). The eleven Masses that had been copied into the books before the premature abandonment of the project in 1530 appear to show a certain predilection for pieces by Taverner's East Midlands countrymen. Equally illuminating, however, is consideration of their liturgical destination, since the collection is conspicuous by the predominance of items on broadly applicable *cantus firmi* that render them usable on many occasions in the church's liturgical year. One is proper to Trinity Sunday, one to the feast of the Resurrection and one to St Alban; but each of the rest is appropriate to whole seasons (the Nativity, Lent) or to feasts in general of St Mary or Jesus, or incorporates a completely non-committal *cantus firmus* such as Burnett's Mass *Ut re mi fa sol la*. As such, their principal character is as one large institution's working collection of large-scale pieces for High Mass, illuminating at once the taste of the choirmaster by whom it was compiled and the expansive luxuriance of the manner in which High Mass was celebrated in Wolsey's principal permanent foundation.

A few traces survive of the extent to which – when he could advert to it – Wolsey's personal interest did influence the music of the chapels of his foundation. A letter of 28 July 1528 indicates that he was concerned for the quality of the boys' choir soon to be inaugurated at Ipswich, and wished it to be strengthened by the transfer there of two of the choristers from Oxford. It was arranged that Taverner himself should take four of his ablest boys to Hampton Court so that Wolsey could hear them sing; he himself would then choose 'such ij as shall stand with his graces pleasure' for translation to Ipswich.[114]

Further, there are among the statutes of Cardinal College, Oxford, certain directions for the conduct of chapel worship that appear to display particular features which represent personal predilections of Wolsey himself. These include the singing in polyphonic settings, following Vespers and Compline each evening, of three specific votive antiphons; one to the Trinity, one to the Virgin Mary, and one to St William of York. This latter saint, otherwise of little more than purely local veneration, had been adopted as a patron by Wolsey, as one of

---

[114] PRO, SP1/235, fol. 290 (*LP*, Addenda (i) 599). The writer, Nicholas Townley (clerk of the works at Cardinal College, Oxford), went on to advise his addressee, Thomas Alford (one of Wolsey's most highly-regarded servants), that Taverner would bring with him to Wolsey 'all those bookes of Songe' that [Nicholas] Lentall had left in Oxford 'with Mr Gouff' (presumably Mr Goffe, one of the chaplains in the choir of Cardinal College, Oxford: PRO, E36/104, p. 19). It is unfortunate not to be able to deduce more about the nature or purpose of this transaction.

Example 1   Commemoration of Thomas Wolsey as founder of Cardinal College Oxford in
setting by John Taverner of 'O Wilhelme, pastor bone'.

his predecessors (died 1154) as archbishop of York; indeed, the Cardinal College
statutes elevated his feast from comparative obscurity to the status of a Greater
Double.[115] There survives among John Taverner's output a setting of a votive
antiphon addressed to Jesus, of which the opening words, in its earliest source
of *c.*1539–40, are: 'O Christe Jesu, pastor bone, / Cleri fautor et patrone'. It has
been shown, however, that this is but a modified version of a versified prayer
which occurs in several contemporary Primers with the opening words 'O
Wilhelme, pastor bone', and is votive to St William of York. There is every
probability that Taverner composed the music to this original text, for performance as the votive antiphon to St William specified by the Cardinal College
statute. In its earliest surviving source, the concluding portion of text includes a
prayer for Henry VIII as *fundator*: 'fundatorem specialem / serva regem nunc
Henricum'. In its failure to rhyme, this couplet stands out from the rest of the
text as probably spurious. It seems clear that the whole textual modification
was undertaken after 1532 at King Henry VIII's College, Oxford, the successor
institution to Cardinal College, and it has very plausibly been surmised that the
original (rhyming) text was: 'fundatorem specialem / serva Thomam cardinalem' (see example 1). This votive antiphon provided Taverner with musical
material from which he derived a five-voice Mass which in its single source
survives under the highly improbable title 'Small Devotion'. It has been
suggested that this title was derived from a carelessly written rubric 'S. Will.
Devocio' (Sancti Willelmi devocio), and that the Mass was written by Taverner

115 Her Majesty's Commissioners, *Statutes of the Colleges of Oxford*, vol. II, section 11, pp. 56–8.

at Cardinal College for performance on the feast of St William – perhaps on 21 March 1527, the tercentenary of his canonization.[116]

Two more of Taverner's compositions seem certain to have derived from his three and a half years at Oxford, having been written to satisfy express requirements of Wolsey's statutes. Each evening at 7.00 p.m. three votive antiphons were to be sung in chapel by the choir: the two Mary antiphons *Salve regina, mater misericordie* and *Ave Maria*, and a Jesus antiphon, *Sancte deus, sancte fortis*. It was specifically required that *Ave Maria* be divided into three sections separated by pauses while the bells were rung.[117] Taverner's setting responds to these requirements exactly, by bringing the music to a full close after *Ave* and after *Ave Maria*. In its sole surviving source, Taverner's *Ave Maria* is followed by his setting of *Sancte deus, sancte fortis*, almost certainly composed as a companion piece, as the Cardinal College statutes required.[118] Taverner was the outstanding English composer of the period between Dunstable and Byrd; although there is every likelihood that considerably more of his finest music was written in response to the opportunities presented by his recruitment to manage the choir of Wolsey's Cardinal College, no more has yet been identified among his output for certain.

The role of music in the great households of the early Tudor period – whether of king, magnate or ecclesiastic – was as a functional craft rather than an aesthetic statement, and in this respect Wolsey's household neither was, nor could have been, very much different from any other. Indeed, it is easier to discern, in the many aspects of the promotion of music in Wolsey's household and his academic colleges, the special magnificence of a final flowering of the traditions and values of the Middle Ages, rather than any experimentation with, or foreshadowing of, the novel qualities and aspirations of the High Renaissance. Indeed, in so far as Wolsey's chapel operated, through its prominence, as an arbiter of taste in England during the late 1510s and 1520s, it may even have delayed the reception into England of the changing approaches to composition then evolving on the other side of the English Channel. Certainly, if any tentative conclusion at all can be drawn from consideration of those few surviving items of polyphony that do seem likely to have been composed for Wolsey's household chapel, by Pygott and Burnett for instance, it would be that one abiding criterion of composition for the cardinal was sheer expansive luxuriance and grandeur, with all the impersonality of presentation that was inseparable from such extended and melismatic articulation of the verbal text. Such largeness of scale promoted an ostentatious and

---

[116] Harrison, *Music in Medieval Britain*, p. 341; D. Stevens, *Tudor Church Music* (London, 1961), pp. 16, 33; Harrison, letter in *Music and Letters*, 46 (1965), 382; H. Benham, *Latin Church Music in England, 1460–1575* (London, 1977), pp. 151–2, 229. The Mass *Small Devotion* is discussed in D. Josephson, *John Taverner, Tudor Composer* (Ann Arbor, 1975), pp. 142–4.

[117] Her Majesty's Commissioners, *Statutes of the Colleges of Oxford*, II, section 11, p. 165.

[118] H. Benham (ed.), *John Taverner: Complete Works*, vol. 2, Early English Church Music XXV (1981), pp. x–xi, 92, 131.

highly successful monumentality, but militated against adoption of the principles of musical concision and responsiveness to the natural rhythm (and even the meaning) of the text which were being articulated and explored in the contemporary music of northern France and the Low Countries.

Indeed, what characterized Wolsey's own arrangements throughout was the thorough incorporation of traditions long-established and, in some instances, possibly already moribund. Immediately noticeable, for instance, in the constitution of every one of the choirs of his foundation is the particular disposition of its sacerdotal (and, sometimes, clerkly also) element. In the two Colleges Cardinal of Oxford and Ipswich and in his own chapel alike, the chosen priestly staff consisted of a head (precentor, dean and 'Repetor' respectively) plus twelve others; at Cardinal College, Oxford, the clerks of the second form consisted likewise of the master of the choristers and twelve lay clerks.[119] Such a constitution was responding not to any demands inherent in the liturgy or its plainsong, or, apparently, in the polyphonic repertory of the choir; rather, its recommendation lay in its religious symbolism, the head plus twelve subordinates serving as an edifying memento and reflection of Jesus plus the disciples. In actual fact, it may not have been at all practicable to divide the number of adult singers into priestly and lay according to such proportions. Men in priest's orders who were also fine singers were difficult to find, far more so than laymen;[120] more forward-looking patrons – not least the king, in respect of the Chapel Royal – had now abandoned unthinking and impractical respect for such arcane symbolism.[121] Rather, in the chosen constitutions of their choirs, they opted for proportions between the constituent sections that minimized the numbers of priests, maximized the lay clerks, and placed high on their priorities the establishment of a satisfactory balance between the voices of men and those of boys.[122] Elsewhere than in Wolsey's foundations, that is, modern practical and musical considerations were taking precedence over medieval symbolic religious representation.

Equally noticeable is the absence of response by Wolsey to a major continental innovation to which he was, perhaps, exposed as much as any other English grandee. It seems clear that traditionally throughout Western Christendom, the plainsong and polyphony of the medieval church services had always been performed by voices alone, unaccompanied by instruments. At some time around the beginning of the sixteenth century, however, an innovation (eventually to be of the highest significance) was introduced to the performance of

---

[119] See above, pp. 179–80, 196. In addition, Wolsey originally intended that the bedesmen at Cardinal College, Ipswich, should number thirteen: PRO, c66/652, m. 32r.

[120] As witness the vacancies at Cardinal College, Ipswich, in 1528: see pp. 198–9 above. Observations on these lines were becoming commonplace by the time of the royal visitations of the cathedrals, 1547–9.

[121] For the constitution of the Chapel Royal during the first half of the sixteenth century, see p. 180 and n. 6 above.

[122] Bowers, 'Vocal scoring, choral balance and performing pitch', pp. 67–8.

polyphony by – among others – the chapel of Philip the Fair, archduke of the Netherlands, and the French Chapel Royal. This was the enhancement of the singing, when desirable, by the addition of an extra layer of splendour and display through the instrumental doubling of the constituent voices in the polyphonic music, most commonly by cornetts and sackbuts. Wolsey encountered the performance of polyphonic Masses thus performed by the French Chapel Royal on at least a couple of occasions: in 1520 at the Mass which he himself celebrated at the conclusion of the interview of the kings at the Field of Cloth of Gold,[123] and in 1527 in Amiens Cathedral during his embassy to France – where the attendance of 'Cornettes and Sakbuttes' among the singers of the French Chapel Royal struck Cavendish as so great a novelty that he made special mention of it in his reminiscences written nearly thirty years later.[124] From France and the Low Countries the practice soon spread, if patchily, to Spain, to parts of Italy and to southern Germany – but not at all to England, Wolsey's exposure to it notwithstanding; there is no evidence to suggest that he sought to emulate this, or indeed any other, contemporary innovation in his arrangements for music.[125]

Indeed, it is not easy to discern any respect in which the dispositions made by Wolsey in his household and colleges for the provision of music proved to be of any particular significance for the future, or of lasting influence, example or effect. Certainly, the amplitude of his munificence gave opportunities to composers of talent – especially Taverner and Pygott – to develop their craft under his patronage. Beyond that, however, the patronage of the great cardinal represented the summation of a departing age rather than the harbinger of a new one. Illuminatingly, for instance, the compilers of the constitution and statutes of King Henry VIII's College, the successor to Cardinal College, Oxford, drew scarcely at all on Wolsey's statutes for their inspiration, but rather on exemplars of other origin, most particularly, those of St George's Chapel, Windsor. In turn, the

---

[123] D. Fallows, 'The performing ensembles in Josquin's sacred music', *Tijdschrift van de Vereniging voor Nederlandse Muziekgeschiedenis*, 35 (1985), 34 and n. 23; and see references to original sources (though not their interpretations) in S. Anglo, 'Le Camp du Drap d'Or et les entrevues d'Henri VIII et de Charles Quint', in J. Jacquot (ed.), *Les Fêtes de la Renaissance*, 3 vols. (Paris, 1956–75), II, pp. 125–6, and P. Kast, 'Remarques sur la musique et les musiciens de la chapelle de François I au Camp du Drap d'Or', ibid., II, pp. 135–6.

[124] Cavendish, p. 54.

[125] It may be noted that although the *presence* in church of players of instruments on occasions of state importance – especially marriages – was by no means unknown on the continent even prior to *c*.1500 (see e.g. footnotes 7–12 of Fallows, 'Performing ensembles in Josquin's sacred music', pp. 55–7), yet it seems certain that their service was not to accompany or participate in either the polyphony or the chant, but rather to perform in the church their normal courtly duties of performing fanfares, sounding arrivals and departures and so on – as expressly executed, from the roodloft of the cathedral, by the state trumpeters on the occasion in 1527 at Amiens noted above: Cavendish, p. 54; *CSPV, 1527–33*, 156. It was likewise in the chapel of Henry VIII's palace of Greenwich in February 1522, at a High Mass celebrated by Wolsey to mark the reception of the papal bull conferring on the king the title of *Fidei Defensor*. After Mass was concluded the bull was read out, and it was at that point, not during the mass, that the 'trumpettes blew, the shalmes and saggebuttes plaied in honor of the kynges newe style': Hall, p. 629.

statutes compiled in the early 1540s for the New Foundation cathedrals took as their model those of King Henry VIII's College; and these in turn supplied models for the reduction and reformation of the Old Foundation cathedral choirs during the reign of Edward VI. The examples presented by Wolsey's own foundations were of no account in the developments immediately to come; ironically, those of the royal successor college in Oxford were seminal.

Wolsey's own household, of course, soon began to evaporate in the aftermath of his dismissal from his office of lord chancellor and the withdrawal of the king's favour in the autumn of 1529. Some of his singing-men remained with him,[126] apparently to become the nucleus of his household chapel as archbishop of York, but essentially his chapel was dispersed. Several of the ablest men – Pygott, Bower, Burnett and Phillips – were promptly absorbed into the Chapel Royal.[127] In the uncertainty surrounding the future of Cardinal College, Oxford, it seems that the ablest among the musicians there were leaving for alternative employment by early in 1530. Mason became precentor and canon residentiary of Hereford;[128] William Whitbroke is subsequently encountered as a senior minor canon at London St Paul's, and Thomas Lawney as vicar choral of the collegiate church of St Stephen, Westminster.[129] By the end of 1530 Cardinal College, Ipswich, had been fully dissolved, and its choir disbanded and dispersed; and for not all the musicians, perhaps, was the landing a soft one. For instance, if Robert Testwood, master of the choristers at Ipswich, hoped to return to the position of master that he had left at St Botolph, Boston, he was due to be disappointed, since it appears that when a vacancy occurred there early in 1530 it was in fact his opposite number in Oxford, John Taverner, who had gone to fill it.[130] Indeed, prior service with the cardinal may not necessarily have been the most desirable of recommendations; despite his evident ability, even Testwood spent an uncertain time in London in only insecure employment before eventually obtaining a position as singing-man (and probably, given his experience, as master of the choristers) at St George's Chapel, Windsor.[131] The dispersal of Wolsey's musicians was evidently thorough; before many months had passed

---

[126] Cavendish, p. 133.
[127] Pygott occurs as a gentleman of the Chapel Royal until April 1547 (PRO, E179/69/50); for the others, see above, pp. 186, 188. On the chapel list of *c*.1535 (PRO, SP1/37, fol. 98r) the names of Phillips, Burnett, Bower and Pygott, with Hugh Rhodes and Thomas Byrd, occur together as a group, and it is tempting to speculate that all six had joined simultaneously in a single draft from Wolsey's chapel.
[128] For references, see above, n. 47.
[129] Josephson, *John Taverner*, pp. 79–83; Harrison, *Music in Medieval Britain*, p. 288; PRO, E301/88.
[130] In 1538/9 the Gild of St Mary in Boston collected 13s 4d as rent of a house in the churchyard of St Botolph's church that formerly had been let to Taverner 'pro camera sua', and which, from its prior record of occupancy, can be shown to have been reserved for singing-men of the choir maintained in the parish church by the Gild: Boston, Borough Archives, MS 4/c/1/2, fol. 1v (for further references to Taverner at this period see fols. 7v, 11r.).
[131] PRO, SP1/73, no. 141 (*LP*, v, 1764); Pratt, *Acts and Monuments of John Foxe*, v, pp. 465–70.

after September 1529, it must have seemed to many who made their living by practice of the musical crafts as if the great cardinal had never been.

Nevertheless, it appears that somewhere in Wolsey's diocese of York, someone was moved by the news of his death in 1530 to reflect in verse upon his passing, and to give to the text a setting in music. The three-voice 'Ballad of the death of the Cardinal' survives on fly-leaves incorporated into the binding of an incunabulum from the library of Ripon Minster;[132] perhaps it was the work of one of the vicars choral there. The words are little better than doggerel; fortunately, the music succeeds in rising above the text in quality. It uses a plain and restrained style to express the tormented self-pity of Wolsey's ghost, and even when hovering on the brink of cliché, contrives nevertheless to retain poignancy and dignity, not least in the refrain with which (or with a version of which) each of the four stanzas closes. As a rare survival of extended secular composition from the second quarter of the sixteenth century, it is printed in full as Appendix A below.

[132] BL, Add. MS 50856. This source has recently undergone conservation, and the music fly-leaves are now bound in as fols. 19–21. For a brief description, see Stevens, *Music and Poetry in the Early Tudor Court*, pp. 435 (song 61), 467 (source 76).

Ballad of the death of the Cardinal

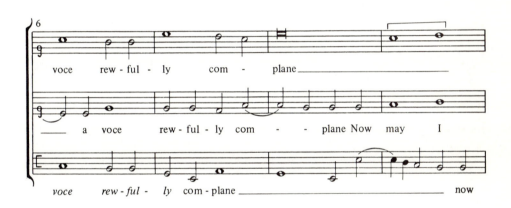

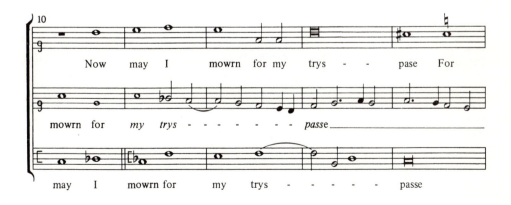

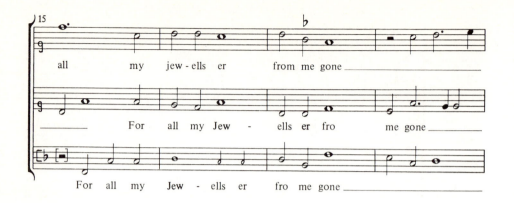

-te _____ *and drede o - - ver all,* _____ for my   gret

and drede   o - ver all, _____ for

drede   o - ver   all _____ for   my _____ gret pryde _____

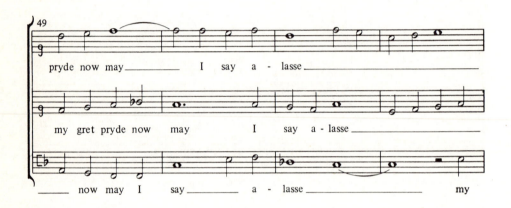

pryde now may _____ I say a - lasse _____

my   gret pryde now   may   I   say   a - lasse _____

_____ now may I   say _____ a - lasse _____ my

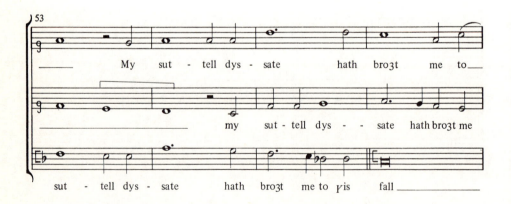

_____ My   sut - tell dys - sate   hath   broȝt   me   to _____

_____ my   sut - tell dys - - sate   hath broȝt me

sut - tell dys - sate   hath   broȝt   me to ƿis   fall _____

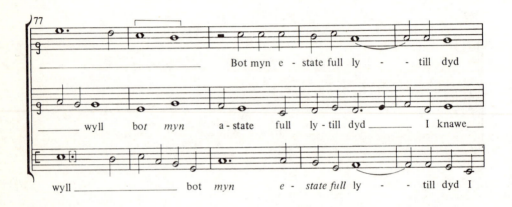

-us   Mi - se - re - re   me - i   de - - - - - - - us.

- - se - re - - re   me - i   de - - - - - - us.

-us   mi - se - re - - re   me - i   de - - - - - us.

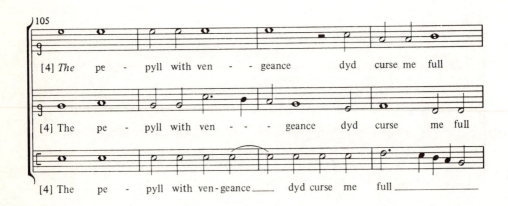

[4] *The*   pe - pyll   with   ven - - - geance   dyd   curse me   full

[4] The   pe - pyll   with   ven - - - geance   dyd   curse   me   full

[4] The   pe - pyll   with   ven - geance____   dyd curse   me   full_____

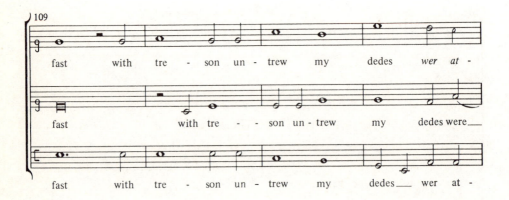

fast   with   tre - son   un - trew   my   dedes   *wer   at* -

fast   with   tre - - son un - trew   my   dedes were____

fast   with   tre - son   un - trew   my   dedes____   wer   at -

NOTES

Source: London, British Library, Add. MS 50856, fols. 19v–21r.
Medium: Manuscript, on paper.
Notation: Black void, standard early-sixteenth-century mensural.
Lay-out: *Cantus Collateralis.*
Title: A ballet of þe deth of þe Cardynall
Attributions: [None]

Editorial apparatus

□ = ligature
All ties and single bar-lines are editorial; double bar-lines at section-closes represent final bars (single or double) in original.
All notes printed small, all material [in square brackets], and all verbal text in *italics* are editorial (supplying omissions or *lacunae* in original).

Accidentals:

Original source mutations are represented by modern accidental, printed large, in staff, at interval first affected.
Original source mutations to *recta* hexachords having continuing effect into succeeding (modern) bars are represented by modern accidental, printed small, in staff, as appropriate.
Original source mutation to *ficta* hexachord (14.1.1) is considered to last for one interval only.
Editorial realizations of *recta* and *ficta* usage are represented by modern accidental, printed above note affected.

Clefs and Signatures:

i: clef G, line 2, throughout. 1.1.0 for duration of one staff, 18.1.0 for duration of two staves: clef G, line 2, supplemented by clef f, line 5, to promote solmization of f'' as fa in c-hexachord.
ii: clef c-fa, line 2, throughout.
iii: clef c-fa, line 4, throughout; except at 11.iii.0 for duration of two staves and 48.iii.1x2 for duration of one staff: clef c-sol, line 4.

Overlay of music to text:

On manuscript, text entered first in script unspaced except for small gaps to accommodate line-end melismas (such melismas on final syllables seem to be characteristic of English vernacular song in the early sixteenth century). Source overlay of music to text is clear where setting is syllabic, and this is retained in edition. At brief melismas in refrain, overlay only casual; in edition some (unobtrusive) editorial imposition of consistency.
Ligatures not broken; musically imitative beginnings of phrases exploited.

Commentary:

The manuscript source is of poor legibility and in places seriously damaged, with loss of music and text through staining, tearing and rubbing. However, this transcription was originally made in 1971, when several passages were still faintly legible (under u/v light) that now have been utterly obscured by the necessary processes of conservation. In the refrain, and occasionally in the stanzas (particularly between stanzas 1 and 4), several corrupt or damaged passages have been restored by comparison with repetitions preserved undamaged elsewhere in the composition; these are not noted in the Commentary below.

13.I.0   a-hexachord mutation (c-mi), written *altera manu*

22.II.3   semibreve in MS

23.II.1   semibreve in MS

38.III.4   minim rest in MS

40.III.2×3   f-hexachord mutation (b-fa)

42.I.3   spyryalte; in II and III spūalte (= spiritualty?)

46.II.1 – 48.II.1   not in MS; some editorial supply of music essential here

50.III.1×2   f-hexachord mutation (b-fa)

57.I.2 – 60.I.4   in MS:

58.II.0   f-hexachord mutation (b-fa)

90.II.4   semibreve in MS

93.I.4   semibreve in MS

111.I.1   minim, pitch *b'*, in MS

120.II.1   text: Therfore my body lyeth now pale & faynt

121.III.1   semibreve in MS

Performance:

Three solo voices, or very small chorus. *Either* male voices (boy treble, alto, tenor) sounding at written 'apparent' pitch; *or* adult male voices (alto, tenor, bass), sounding a fourth or fifth lower than written 'apparent' pitch (i.e. around *F* or *G* to *c''* or *d''*).

CHAPTER 8

Wolsey and ecclesiastical order: the case of the Franciscan Observants

KEITH BROWN

On 16 January 1525 Dr John Allen, Cardinal Wolsey's commissary-general and Dr Henry Standish, bishop of St Asaph, arrived at the convent of the Franciscan Observants adjacent to the royal palace at Greenwich to conduct a visitation of the house in the cardinal's name.[1] But as Edward Hall and the author of the 'Grey friar's chronicle' relate, they found on their arrival that nineteen of the friars had absconded rather than face their visitors. In the circumstances there was nothing for it but to abandon the visitation and return on another day.[2]

By their action the absconders had laid themselves open to a charge of apostasy. As apostates, according to the statutes of their order they had automatically rendered themselves excommunicate;[3] and on the following Sunday another member of their community, Father John Forest, publicly proclaimed their excommunication at St Paul's Cross. By the time the visitors re-appeared some days later, some of the offenders had returned. These, remarkably, were consigned not to one of the Observants' own prisons, but to the porter's ward at York Place: and one particularly recalcitrant individual, Brother John Raynscroft, was sent to prison at the London Greyfriars before submitting to the cardinal and being allowed to return to Greenwich. Some at least of the remainder apparently fled the country and headed for Rome to lodge a protest in the Curia, pursued by a demand from Wolsey that they should be arrested and punished for the sake of his honour and that of the Holy See. But they could not be found and their ultimate fate remains a mystery.[4]

Many of Wolsey's contemporaries took a rather jaundiced view of his dealings

---

[1] This paper is substantially based upon sections of my unpublished D.Phil. thesis 'The Franciscan Observants in England, 1482–1559' (University of Oxford, 1986: hereafter cited as 'Observants'), which has been provisionally accepted for publication in the Oxford Historical Monographs series. I should like to thank all those who have commented on the paper, but all responsibility for its contents remains my own.

[2] Accounts of this incident and its aftermath are given in 'Chronicon . . . ex registro fratrum minorum Londiniae', ed R. Howlett in *Monumenta Franciscana*, vol. II (Rolls series vol. V, 1882), p. 190 and in Hall, p. 691.

[3] 'Abbreviatio statutorum tam papalium quam generalium edita apud Barcinonam . . . [1451]', ed. M. Bihl in *Archivum Franciscanum Historicum*, vol. XXXVIII (1945), VI, 37–8, 41.

[4] *LP*, IV (i) 1750.

with the English church. Those who formulated charges against him in 1529 laid a number of specific allegations. He had, it was said, hijacked the rights of patronage to benefices of both laymen and clerics. He had introduced delays and punitive exactions through his assertion of his legatine jurisdiction over probate of wills (in particular through the joint commission by means of which he had effectively usurped Archbishop Warham's Canterbury prerogative jurisdiction). He had confiscated the goods of deceased bishops. He had milked the clergy through his effective control of preferments and elections of heads of houses and the procurations exacted by his agents when conducting his legatine visitations – all of which, it was alleged, gravely prejudiced the maintenance of monastic hospitality and led to an increase in the number of robbers and vagabonds wandering abroad. He had suppressed religious houses, justifying his actions by spurious and scandalous accusations of depravity and carrying on in wilful disregard of the rights of founders other than the king. Finally – and perhaps worst of all – through his interference with episcopal jurisdictions he had acted as the 'impeacher and disturber of due and direct correction of heresies'.[5]

What underlay these accusations, of course, was the collective indignation of vested interests; angered by the intrusion of a foreign jurisdiction into the area of their legal and patronal rights and by the upsetting of the established order which this entailed, and determined that if they were to have any say in the matter this kind of thing was never going to be allowed to happen again. Given the vehemence of their reaction, it is hardly surprising that it is a picture of Wolsey's role as a subverter of ecclesiastical order which has tended to carry the day. But to give Wolsey his due, this was hardly intentional. After all, his 'high honour' derived first and foremost from his position as a prelate of the church. Broadly speaking, his policy can be said to have been two-fold: to establish and consolidate his control over the church's institutions and to reform the mores of the clergy. A fundamental area of his concern lay with the religious, and in particular with the exempt religious. In this respect, if it can certainly not be claimed to be in any way typical, the story of his attempts to visit and correct the Greenwich Observants nevertheless supplies some illuminating glimpses into the manner and effects of his dealings in this area.

It is a commonplace that Wolsey succeeded in erecting a system of ad hoc, individual ambassadorial powers, expressly delegated by an individual pope to an individual legate for a strictly limited period into a perpetual plenipotentiary authority which effectively transcended the lifetime of an individual pope. That he did so was not simply a matter of pure self-aggrandizement. Good servant of the church of Rome that he was, Wolsey was as much the faithful servant of the king of England. If his reforming intentions were unprecedented in their scale, he

---

[5] In general, Edward Lord Herbert of Cherbury, *The Life and Reign of King Henry the Eighth* (London, 1672), pp. 294–302 (baldly summarized in *LP*, IV (iii) 6075); Hall, pp. 655, 765–6; *LP*, IV (iii) 5749. On the matter of probate, Pollard, pp. 193–6 and *LP*, III (ii) 2752.

could look back upon established precedents. The last years of the fifteenth century and the early decades of the sixteenth constituted an age of sweeping ecclesiastical reforms – and of great reforming cardinals – in the major powers of Western Europe. Wolsey could, and doubtless did, look to the examples of Cardinal Cisneros in the Spanish Kingdoms and of Cardinal d'Amboise in France. Equally, he served a dynasty which took very seriously its responsibility towards the upholding of standards of morality in general and due propriety in religious observance in particular.

Basing himself substantially upon his experiences as an exile in the courts of Brittany and France, Henry VII had founded his claim to legitimacy, in part, upon a role which he had established for himself as a moral leader: both as the reformer of Englishmen's political conduct – the bringer of unity to a nation riven by faction – and as the sponsor of improved religious observance. As such, he had from the beginning taken an active interest in religious reform. As early as 1487 he had petitioned Pope Innocent VIII for authority to reform lax Cluniac, Cistercian, Premonstratensian and other houses: which had issued in the bull *Quanta in dei ecclesia* and its successors, empowering Archbishop Morton to visit and reform exempt religious. He had shown an active interest in the re-introduction of the converse into English Cistercian life. And – most important for our purposes – he had taken the struggling community of Franciscan Observants established at Greenwich by Edward IV and, by founding new houses and securing the transfer of houses of Conventual Franciscans, had turned the movement into one of the powerhouses of early sixteenth-century English religious life.[6]

In this respect, as in others, Henry VIII was his father's son, not least because he was married to a veteran of the court of Cardinal Cisneros; and to this extent his characteristic concern with the moral conduct of others, which can on the face of it seem rather hypocritical, makes a good deal of sense. In the early Tudor consciousness, political and moral ascendancy were inextricably linked. Here the king's instinctive preference for delegation and the availability of a ready supply of talent in the form of Thomas Wolsey met with the inherited ambition of a still-young dynasty to match the achievements of its European rivals. There may be a significant parallel here in that Wolsey was pressurizing the pope for powers to visit the exempt and non-exempt religious as early as 1515; and that apparently the issue was seen as separate from that of the legacy as such.[7]

Where Wolsey was concerned, however, it is undeniable that this mixture of motives meant that his reforming objectives were fatally flawed. 'Nothing', growls the admittedly partial Edward Hall, 'was reformed but came to more

---

[6] On Henry's religious outlook in general, A. Goodman, 'Henry VII and Christian renewal' in K. Robbins (ed.), *Religion and Humanism* (Studies in Church History vol. 17, Oxford, 1981), pp. 115ff. On his role in the introduction of the Observants into England, 'Observants', pp. 29ff.

[7] *LP*, II (i) 780.

mischief'.[8] It was not just that reform was undermined by rapacity; although Wolsey was undoubtedly operating what might in another age have been described as an ecclesiastical protection racket. John Palsgrave, in his detailed list of charges against Wolsey couched in the form of an imaginary set of 'remembrances', describes his measures for reforming the secular clergy as 'for the most [part] prohibitions of such things as we had faculties to dispense with';[9] and Wolsey himself was compelled to confess to the king that he had received payments from exempt religious houses to permit them 'to have their old visitors'.[10] In a grasping age, however, he can hardly be blamed for out-grasping the rest. In an age when personal power and authority depended upon the maintenance of one's 'state' he can hardly be blamed for seeing the church as a convenient milch-cow.

Nor did the weakness lie altogether in the ostentatious and comprehensive exercise of the legatine jurisdiction by Wolsey's servants; although Hall's picture of Dr Allen riding 'in a gown of velvet, with a great train', being 'received into every religion with procession, as though the legate had been there' no doubt goes some way towards explaining his more general accusation that Wolsey encouraged the clergy to 'wax proud'.[11] And it is true that the sheer comprehensiveness of the visitation programme transcended any popular conception of the extent of the need for reform. Admittedly little detail survives – very few visitation articles and injunctions for example[12] – but in his long complaint against Wolsey drafted in 1529 Lord Darcy refers in this context to 'religious houses, abbeys, charterhouses, nunneries close [and] open, friars of all orders and others that were exempt under bulls'. Most interesting here is Darcy's reference to the Carthusians, taken with another, tantalizing complaint about the 'orgueillous visitation and search' made 'rigorously and suddenly' at the Bridgettine house at Syon. For together with the Observants these were the orders which were conventionally lumped together by contemporaries as demonstrating outstanding qualities in their religious life.[13]

This last point, however, does give us a clue to the fundamental reason why Wolsey the reformer was bound to fail. Reform among the religious is at root a matter of reforming the individual spirit; and legislation, while invaluable in establishing norms, must be applied with care and with a real feeling for the spiritual dimension. This Wolsey conspicuously lacked. His reforming legislation – in so far as it can be recovered – is apparently based upon the constitutions laid

---

[8] Hall, p. 593.   [9] *LP*, IV (iii) 575 (p. 2577).

[10] Herbert, *Life and Reign of King Henry the Eighth*, p. 164 (*LP*, IV (ii) 4509).

[11] Hall, p. 593.

[12] For these, Dom David Knowles, *The Religious Orders in England*, vol. III (Cambridge, 1958), pp. 82–3.

[13] *LP*, IV (iii) 5749 (pp. 2550–1). The identification of the three orders was made by, among others, the English Black Monks, in protesting against the severity of the reforming statutes which Wolsey attempted to impose upon them in 1522 (cited by Knowles, *Religious Orders*, III, 159).

down by a previous grand reformer, Pope Benedict XII.[14] But here the resemblance ceased. Benedict – a Cistercian – had at least some feel for the nature of the religious life. Still less was Wolsey a Cisneros; himself, as a Franciscan Observant, representative of the modern religious reform movements.

In this connection it is particularly ironic that Wolsey should have chosen, of all the English religious, to visit and correct the Observants. The Greenwich convent had been the first house in England of this country's only representative of the fifteenth-century reform movements among the religious. The Observance had emerged in Northern Europe at the end of the fourteenth century as a conscientious response to a prevailing laxity of observance within the Franciscan Order as a whole.[15] It had come late to an England where the unreformed friars' excesses had never been quite so marked as they had been on the Continent. And although the Greenwich house had originally been established by Edward IV in 1482,[16] the English Observance was overwhelmingly an early Tudor creation. In particular, it can be argued that Henry VII's action in securing the transfer to the Observants of the three former Conventual houses at Canterbury, Newcastle and Southampton in 1499, and above all his foundation and endowment of the new convent adjacent to the reconstructed royal palace of Richmond shortly after the turn of the century, represented the king's attempt to imitate in a small way the Cisnerian reform movement of contemporary Spain, as a tribute to that first, ill-fated Aragon marriage which was intended to mark the Tudors' arrival among the great ruling dynasties of Europe.[17] Both Polydore Vergil and Henry VII himself, in his will, testify to the first Tudor's peculiar devotion to the friars:[18] a devotion perpetuated by his second son and Catherine of Aragon and reflected in the devotional preferences of the court.

In a very real sense, then, the Observants stood in England as symbolic of late-medieval catholic propriety. And they enjoyed a reputation to match: a reputation which transcended their mere numerical presence, for in England their numbers probably never much exceeded the total of something over 150 friars who can be traced at the time of their forcible suppression in 1534.[19] There are good reasons for supposing that their reputation was deserved. For one thing the English community had been established by importing friars from the province of Cologne; and although by this time it was predominantly English in

[14] Knowles, *Religious Orders*, III, 159.
[15] An admirable account of the origins of the Regular Observance in Northern Europe is given by D. Nimmo, *Reform and Division in the Medieval Franciscan Order* (Bibliotheca Seraphico-Capuccina 33, Rome, 1987), part III.
[16] A. G. Little, 'Introduction of the Observant friars into England', *Proceedings of the British Academy*, 10 (1921–3), 455–71.
[17] 'Observants', pp. 32–40; A. G. Little, 'Introduction of the Observant friars into England: a bull of Alexander VI', *Proceedings of the British Academy*, 27 (1941), 155–66; HKW, III, pp. 195–6.
[18] Polydore Vergil, *Anglica Historia* (ed. D. Hay, Camden Society 3rd series 74, 1950), p. 146; T. Astle (ed.), *The Will of King Henry VII* (London, 1775), pp. 29–33.
[19] This total is derived from biographical data in 'Observants', appendix 1.

composition it always retained something of its international character. As a result, in contrast with the comparative insularity of many contemporary English religious it remained very much an arm of an international movement, maintaining its links with the general chapters of the order and subject to periodic visitation by foreign superiors.[20] For another, given the circumstances of its establishment in England it owed a particular duty to the king, as founder, to preserve its standards intact: a duty bolstered by the inevitable comparison with a body of Conventual friars who themselves maintained rather higher standards of observance than did most of their continental counterparts.[21] And finally there is the litmus test of the 1530s, when as a result of their principled stand against Henry VIII's divorce from Catherine of Aragon and his demand that they subscribe his oaths in favour of the royal supremacy and the Boleyn succession they were to suffer the forcible suppression of their community in August 1534.[22]

So their moral character, on the face of it, makes the fact of Wolsey's visitation remarkable. Even more remarkable, not least to the chroniclers, was their reaction. The roots of this reaction must be sought in the early history of the reform. The Northern European Observant movement had been established – as has already been remarked – essentially as a reaction against a prevalent and frequently scandalous laxity within the Franciscan Order as a whole. And it had grown up in an atmosphere of incessant conflict with the superiors of the unreformed, Conventual majority. The root of the trouble had lain in the standards which the reformers had sought to adopt. They stood in general for a decent, moderate level of poverty and for the maintenance of the common life; and in particular against abuses such as the handling of money and the widespread practice of securing perpetual incomes from rents. But this was all. These were not the eremitic extremes of the earlier, outlawed Spiritual movement. They were in fact nothing more nor less than the moderate observance, in an essentially urban context, laid down by the order's 'second founder' St Bonaventure and which were supposedly binding on all the friars.

As a result the reformers had shown up the Conventuals in front of their lay patrons, they had abstracted alms from them and so, not surprisingly, they had found themselves being persecuted. They had, however enjoyed considerable lay support and with this behind them had found their salvation first in the person of the Avignonese pope Benedict XIII and then in the Council of

---

[20] Ibid., pp. 49–50.

[21] In particular, they had not succumbed to the continental vice of deriving perpetual incomes from rents: see G. Abate (ed.), 'Lettera del P. Tommaso Cudvero [i.e. Cudnor] vicario della provincia minoritica d'Inghilterra al rev.mo padro ministro dell'ordine', *Miscellanea Francescana*, 29 (1929), 113–14.

[22] 'Observants', chapter 4. Knowles, *Religious Orders*, III, 206–11. Knowles's brief account of the Observants, while inaccurate in some details, succeeds very well in encapsulating the essential flavour of the community.

Constance. In 1415 the Council (largely following Benedict) had authorized the Observants in the provinces of northern France to conduct their own affairs under superiors who were nominally to act as vicars of the provincial and general ministers but who in practice were virtually independent of them. This principle – extended to other provinces and made universal by Pope Eugenius IV in the bull *Ut sacra* in 1446 – was to last until 1517. But the Conventual friars could not accept what appeared to them as schism and the century after Constance was marked by continual internecine strife. While the Conventuals, stressing the primacy of the vow of obedience, demanded that the Observants should renounce the vicars, the Observants fruitlessly demanded as a quid pro quo that the Conventuals should accept a measure of reform. By the turn of the sixteenth century, in most provinces Observant friars at least equalled Conventuals in numbers (England was a notable exception here): and the conflict was finally resolved in 1517 by Pope Leo X who, in effect, declared the Observants to represent the true Order of Friars Minor, transferred the ministry into the hands of the Observants' vicars and partitioned off the Conventuals into a separate order.[23]

This chequered history had embedded one lesson very deeply into the Observants' collective psyche. This was that it was imperative to the maintenance of the standards which they had professed that they must be able to govern their own destiny: in practice, that they must preserve their absolute jurisdictional independence of any power short of Rome. Their particular form of piety had made them highly popular both among influential laymen and in the Roman Curia; their inter-provincial links remained strong and they had acquired highly developed lobbying skills. This instinct – as the events of the early 1530s were to show – surpassed even the English friars' loyalty to the king as their founder. So it is understandable not only that they should have resisted Wolsey's unwanted interference in their affairs, but that they should have done so with a conspicuous degree of success.

Wolsey had first been granted powers to visit and reform the exempt and non-exempt religious in June 1518; jointly with his fellow-legate Campeggio – in England to promote a crusade against the Turk – and in the same form as an authority granted to another of Leo X's legates, the cardinal of Luxembourg, in France. On Campeggio's departure from England these powers had devolved upon Wolsey alone. With other powers granted subsequently these had been periodically renewed and ultimately, in January 1524, conferred by Clement VII for life.[24] Employing these powers, by August 1524 he had evidently already made one attempt to visit the Observants and had been successfully rebuffed. He

---

[23] For the period to 1446 the best account is Nimmo, *Reform and Division*, part III; thereafter H. Holzapfel, *Handbuch der Geschichte des Franziskanerordens* (Freiburg im Breisgau, 1909), pp. 126ff. and J. R. H. Moorman, *A History of the Franciscan Order from its Origins to the Year 1517* (Oxford, 1968), pp. 479ff.

[24] Pollard, pp. 179–82 and refs. there cited.

responded by sending to Rome for an additional bull to enable him to override their claim to exemption from his jurisdiction.

This bull was granted on 21 August. A. F. Pollard noted of it that 'it apparently removes all the impediments to Wolsey's plenitude of power which might arise out of previous ecclesiastical constitutions from Otto and Ottobon downwards'. But neither he nor, more surprisingly, Dom David Knowles apparently noticed that the terms in which it is couched clearly refer specifically to the Observants. In spite, it states, of the fact that powers already granted to Wolsey were intended to be sufficient to override all exemptions, some exempt religious had attempted to prevent his visitation by obtaining a prohibition in the Curia or elsewhere: firstly on the ground that they were not required to submit to such a visitation from any legate whose powers were not specifically mentioned in their rule or privileges; and secondly because they interpreted their obligation to their minister-general to mean that without his consent they might not offer obedience to, or in any way submit to the jurisdiction of anyone else without offending against the rule of St Francis. The bull therefore specifically removes all such impediments to Wolsey's plenitude of power.[25]

The bull had not been won without a struggle. The Observants were extremely influential in Rome and counted among their number two cardinals, Ara Coeli (Christopher of Forli, who had been the first Observant minister-general after Leo X had split the order in 1517) and Sancte Crucis (Francis Quinones, the current minister-general). Before it had been granted both Ara Coeli and the pope had written to Wolsey begging him to desist from the visitation: not, they assured him, because the friars had any objection to Wolsey himself as visitor, but because they feared the establishment of a precedent for other provinces and for England under a successor.[26] Clement VII was clearly being harried from all sides. He had accompanied the bull with a timid little letter in which he assures Wolsey that the friars are quite ready to receive his visitation, but again urges him to tread carefully for the greater good of Christendom.[27] But at the same time, in private audience with John Clerk, bishop of Bath and Wells, he had persuaded Clerk to write home in an altogether different and more urgent vein, exhorting Wolsey 'for God's sake to use mercy with those friars, saying that they be as desperate beasts past shame, that can lose nothing by clamours'.[28] In return Wolsey, thanking the pope for the bull on 21 October, assured him that he would

---

[25] T. Rymer, *Foederae, Conventiones, Literae, etc.* (London, 1704–15), XIV, 18–20; Pollard, p. 182 n. 4; Knowles, *Religious Orders*, III, 159.

[26] *LP*, IV (i) 477–8.

[27] 'Jacobi Sadoleti Epistolae Pontificum Romanorum Nomine Scriptae' no. 37, in P. Lazeri (ed.), *Miscellaneorum ex MSS. Libri Bibliothequae Colegii Romani Societatis Jesu*, I (Rome, 1754), pp. 439–40. *LP*, IV (i) 569 curiously misplaces this letter in 1519 and attributes it to Leo X.

[28] *LP*, IV (i) 610.

use his legatine jurisdiction with such moderation and discretion that no complaint could arise.[29]

However, the matter had not ended with the issue of the bull. By the time it had appeared from the papal chancery the friars had already obtained a two years' exemption from its effects which they had managed to slip through under the nose of Girolamo Ghinucci, auditor of the apostolic chamber and absentee bishop of Worcester. Ghinucci, understandably embarrassed, attempted to excuse himself to Wolsey by saying that he could not possibly keep an eye on everything that went on in his office, and both he and Wolsey tried to have the exemption cancelled; which in fact they did not succeed in doing until November of the following year.[30] But by now the cardinal's patience was exhausted; and notwithstanding the exemption he put in train preparations for the visitation of Greenwich, with the results outlined at the start of this paper.

We do not in fact know whether Wolsey attempted to visit any of the other houses of Observants at this time. Perhaps not. But at any rate the issue was still simmering at Rome in the summer of 1525, by now abetted by the fortuitous presence of an Observant chapter. By this time Pope Clement was receiving protests about Wolsey's activities from the Dominicans as well. Clerk reported at the end of July that the Black friars had in the end been content to submit to the cardinal's jurisdiction. But the Observants were an altogether different matter. Clerk related the details of an interview in which a harassed Clement had again begged him to exhort Wolsey in his name 'to deal moderately and to meddle with them as little as may be. For they be clamorous people, importunate, bold and past shame; and because they have nothing to lose and have great assistance here in the court and credit everywhere else among the lay people.'[31] The pope had managed to put the matter off pending the arrival of the minister-general and would perhaps write to Wolsey once more urging moderation: but he did not want this to be interpreted as prejudicial to the legacy. Clerk had tried to play down the seriousness of the situation, claiming 'that there was no lucre, no glory, no envy that could move your Grace to do anything against them; for they were poor, evil and few, and of little estimation in comparison of other religious in England'. And in order to calm the pope down he had told him that Wolsey was letting the matter rest for the moment. The matter may in fact have been allowed to drop. At any rate the lifting of the friars' exemption in November is the last we hear of it.

At this point we must retrace our steps in order to take another look at the nineteen Greenwich friars who had absconded in January 1525. To see the matter in something like its true perspective it must be appreciated that – even granted

[29] A. Theiner (ed.), *Vetera Monumenta Hibernorum et Scotorum Historiam Illustrantia* (Rome, 1864), pp. 544–5. *LP*, IV (i) 759 is an extremely cursory summary.

[30] *LP*, IV (i) 587, 1750.   [31] Ibid., 1521.

that Greenwich was the mother-house of the English community – in a community of only 150 or so friars this figure would represent certainly a substantial proportion, and very possibly even a majority of the complement of the house. Besides which, the abandonment of the vow of obedience which their flight involved was a step which would not have been taken lightly.

Admittedly the Franciscan vow of obedience is to a degree ambiguous. On one hand St Francis himself had desired that his followers should give their elected superiors absolute obedience; but on the other the superior does not wield power so much as exercise stewardship – hence the terminology of ministry and guardianship – and the rule specifically allows for dissent on conscientious grounds. However, what it does not do is permit open revolt. The dissenter is enjoined instead meekly to endure punishment and persecution.[32] The whole edifice depends essentially upon the exercise of charity by both sides. Nevertheless we should not make the mistake of thinking the regime a liberal one. Informing on one another's faults was a way of life, and bodily compulsion readily resorted to. A variety of punishments was practised ranging from a bread-and-water diet to an imprisonment so rigorous that deaths in prison were by no means unknown.[33]

In this light two possible explanations suggest themselves as to why the absconders should have acted as they did. There are of course several reasons why the friars should have been affronted by the prospect of the visitation and by the manner in which it was likely to be carried out. For one thing Wolsey was technically acting illegally in prosecuting his visitation while the two years' prohibition remained in force. And the irony of a visitation of an order which to contemporaries represented the acme of religious virtue by a figure popularly represented as a picture of clerical ostentation was calculated to bring out all the friars' traditional anticlerical instincts. There were two further, more specifically Observant factors at work. One concerns the personnel involved in conducting the visitation. It was not so much John Allen who would have concerned them, in spite of his notoriety as a perjuror.[34] Wolsey's most monumental act of tactlessness was to appoint Standish as his assistant. He may have been, like Allen, a regular doer of the cardinal's business; but he was also the man who in his time perhaps more than any other represented the epitome of the Conventual friar, and so the tradition against whose excesses the Observance itself represented a reaction and whose inferiority in matters of observance had been proclaimed to the world as recently as 1517.[35] There must also be a suspicion that, notwithstanding the friars' genuine poverty, Wolsey's agents would have insisted on

[32] On the nature of Franciscan obedience, Nimmo, *Reform and Division*, pp. 34–47.

[33] 'Abbreviatio Statutorum', c.6. cf. Jerome Barlow and William Roy's 'Burying of the Mass' (ed. E. Arber as *Rede me and be nott wrothe, For I say no thinge but trothe* (London, 1871)), p. 90, where the community is depicted as a nest of backbiters. On deaths in prison, *LP*, VI, 115, 116, 118.

[34] Arber (ed.), *Rede me*, p. 57; Pollard, p. 193 n. 4.

[35] On Standish, Knowles, *Religious Orders*, III, 53–5.

receiving a substantial fee for conducting the visitation. This would certainly have touched an exposed nerve: and not only because one of the distinguishing marks of the Observants (and one which marked them apart from the Conventuals) was their return to the early Franciscan practice of refusing to handle money.[36] The specific issue of malicious demands for money procurations by Conventual visitors had been one of those which had propelled the early friars along the road to jurisdictional independence in the early years of the fifteenth century.[37]

This, however, does not of itself serve to explain the breakdown of discipline within the friary when the superiors finally caved in and submitted to Wolsey's visitors. The matter goes deeper. To some extent the explanation probably lies in the manner in which the visitation brought out into the open the latent conflict of loyalties inherent in the friars' situation. Up to a point this was a simple conflict between their allegiance to their order and to its jurisdictional independence short of Rome, and to the king who was their founder, patron and protector and whose chancellor and chief minister Wolsey was. But at the same time the situation must have been complicated by the intricacies of the friars' patronal relationships. Although it is impossible to prove, it does seem very likely that many individual friars were personally related to members of the court and royal household.[38] What is more demonstrable is that – like those other austere orders with which contemporaries habitually connected them, the Carthusians and the Bridgettines – the Observants attracted to their ranks a good number of late vocations. Frequently these were men with impressive academic backgrounds; and frequently – like John Ryckes, formerly of Corpus Christi College, Cambridge and best known as the author of the *Image of Love*, or like William Peto, with a distinguished career behind him in both universities, men of a distinctly humanist stamp. The Observants had always mistrusted the traditional university schools and their paraphernalia of formal degrees as profoundly injurious to good observance. The English friars maintained no connection with the Franciscan Schools at Oxford or Cambridge and there are good grounds for thinking that the intellectual atmosphere of the Observant friaries was rather more akin to the fashion of the English court than to traditional friary scholarship.[39]

This, combined with their asceticism and the standard of their life, gave them a ready entrée as confessors and spiritual advisers into the counsels of court

---

[36] Arber (ed.), *Rede me*, p. 76. On the contrast between the two on this point see 'God speed the plough', an early sixteenth-century lament on behalf of the honest husbandman whose author pointedly distinguishes between the Observants, who beg 'corn or meat' and the Conventuals, who demand money (printed in W. W. Skeat (ed.), *Pierce the Ploughman's Crede* (Early English Text Society original series 30, 1867), p. 71).

[37] Nimmo, *Reform and Division*, pp. 524–5.   [38] 'Observants', pp. 72–4.

[39] Ibid., pp. 89–91, 96–101. On Ryckes, E. Ruth Harvey, 'The image of love', in *A Dialogue Concerning Heresies*, ed. T. Lawler et al. (The Yale edition of the complete works of St Thomas More, VI, New Haven, 1981), pp. 727ff.

figures, and particularly of court ladies, of whom the most important was the queen herself. The range of Father Hugh Rich's acquaintance, uncovered after he had become implicated with the 'Nun of Kent's' treasonous prophecies in 1533, bears this out.[40] Of course this kind of relationship brought benefits both ways. Among the English Conventuals, as among the other orders of friars, the failure of mendicancy alone to supply a decent standard of living had for long resulted in an unhealthy dependence of individual friars upon individual benefactors. The Observants maintained the common life and succeeded to a remarkable degree in remaining poor in the midst of riches: the essentially traditional satirical condemnation which they attracted was in their case not at all fair.[41] However material corruption is one thing; personal loyalty is another. And the Observants' loyalties were in part to a milieu in which Wolsey was habitually despised for his low birth, worldly churchmanship and limited intellectual attainments.

For these reasons the friars found themselves caught in something of a dilemma. Ultimately the leadership came to the conclusion that they must submit to the cardinal's jurisdiction. Friar Forest may well have helped to swing the balance here, as he was to do during the events of the early 1530s. Forest's origins are maddeningly obscure (and the search is not much helped by the smokescreen thrown up by later generations of Catholic martyrologists in the light of his ultimate execution in 1538). The favour in which he clearly stood with the king may in part reflect a relationship with Edward and Miles Forest of the king's chamber, although this is based upon no more than the coincidence of names. He was however academically distinguished: he was a Doctor of Divinity and was one of the order's leading preachers during these years, a regular performer both at court and at St Paul's Cross. And, although it is impossible to attach any specific office to him, it is clear that he was highly influential in the friars' counsels.[42]

So there is a strong case for explaining away the mass apostasy of January 1525 as essentially a conscientious reaction – complicated by outside loyalties – against the subjection of their community to an outside jurisdiction whose values were irreconcilable with the friars' own, and against their leaders' ultimate failure to

[40] *LP*, VI, 1468 (1–3), VII, 72 (1).   [41] Arber (ed.), *Rede me*, pp. 79, 82ff.

[42] Forest was probably aged somewhere over fifty at this point (cf. M. A. S. Hume (ed. and trs.), *A Chronicle of King Henry VIII, in Spanish* (London, 1889), p. 78). He had joined the order by 1512 (PRO, PROB.11/17 fol. 66v) and was a Doctor of Divinity by 1526 (Guildhall Library, London, MS 9531/10 fol.157v; PRO, PROB11/23 fol. 66v). But he had certainly acquired this distinction before taking the habit: Anthony à Wood's surmise that he had studied with the Oxford Conventuals is clearly based upon a failure to distinguish clearly between the two branches of the order (*Athenae Oxonienses* (ed. P. Bliss, London, 1813–20), I, 107). There is no very good reason to accept the oft-repeated assertion that he was Catherine of Aragon's confessor: this appears to be based upon the highly unreliable testimony of the Franciscan martyrologist Thomas Bourchier (*Historia Ecclesiastica de Martyrio Fratrum Ordinis Divi Francisci, etc.* (Ingolstadt, 1583), p. 25v; 'Observants', pp. 195–201). On his preaching and court roles, William Tyndale, *The Practice of Prelates* (ed. H. Walter, Parker Society, 1849), p. 302 and Sir H. Ellis (ed.), *Original Letters Illustrative of English History* (London, 1824–46), 3rd series, II, 249ff., 253ff., 257ff. (*LP*, V, 1525, VI, 116, 168).

resist its encroachment. There is however a further complicating factor. For this we need to return to the letter with which Clement VII accompanied his bull of 21 August 1524. In it he refers to the pretext upon which Wolsey had based his request for the faculty as being to correct an outbreak of dangerous theological radicalism with Lutheran overtones.[43]

Wolsey has hardly enjoyed a reputation as an effective heresy-hunter. Aside from his symbolic book-burnings his actions rather give the impression that he did not really care about heresy very much except in so far as it carried seditious overtones. In spite of strong and repeated hints from Rome he never sent a heretic to the stake. He was accused in 1529 of having prevented a pair of bishops from carrying out an enquiry into heresy at Cambridge: and, however unwittingly, he succeeded in importing heresy into Oxford through his appointments to fellowships of Cardinal College.[44] And yet he made this, on the face of it, remarkable charge against a community which in the early 1530s was to take a principled stand in support of Catholic orthodoxy and whose members knew well the strength of the bonds which tied them to the papacy. Was there any truth in it? If so it would provide an excellent reason for friars to wish to make their escape. Or was this just another of the 'untrue surmises' such as those with which Wolsey was to be accused of blackening the name of the religious whom he wished to suppress;[45] a lever which he could bring to bear against one of the pope's principal anxieties in the attempt to get what he wanted?

At first sight there is evidence to suggest that there might have been some truth in the charge. Certainly, in the course of time two Greenwich friars did surface in a new, protestant, guise on the continent – one of whom, William Roy, matriculated at Wittenberg in June 1525 and so may conceivably have been one of the apostates of the preceding January.[46] And in October 1528 another member of the community, John West, made the remarkable throwaway assertion that not only were more of the friars guilty of Lutheranism but that the fathers of the house 'be willing to maintain these rebellious heretics (Roy and his partner-in-crime Jerome Barlow) in their mischief, and they pray to God that they must never be taken'.[47]

As we shall see, West had his own reasons for seeking to blacken his superiors' names at this point. However, there are certain prima facie reasons for supposing that Lutheran tendencies might have found a home at Greenwich. I have already referred to the friars' continental origins. Even at this stage the English community contained many friars of Low-Countries and Rhineland origins and for this

---

43 'Jacobi Sadoleti Epistolae', no. xxxvii.
44 Herbert, *Life and Reign of King Henry the Eighth*, p. 301 (*LP*, IV (iii) 6075). On the lack of burnings, Pollard, 208–15.
45 *LP*, IV (iii) 5749 (p. 2550).
46 P. Smith, 'Englishmen at Wittenberg in the sixteenth century', *English Historical Review*, 37 (1921), 422.
47 *Hackett Letters*, no. 94; *LP*, IV (ii) 5043.

reason it is highly likely that they maintained close contacts with the foreign mercantile community in London through which they might have imbibed Lutheran ideas. I have also referred to the intellectual climate of the friaries: and it is a truism of the age that – up to a point – comparatively little separated Erasmus and Luther. Something of what the friars' heretical tendencies might in fact have amounted to can possibly be gleaned from the output of the two continental refugees, Roy and Barlow.

Roy was most probably of French Jewish background. He was a member of a Calais family which certainly had close connections with the English court.[48] His chief notoriety has lain in his role as William Tyndale's helper in the production of his English New Testament; and in this connection a number of writers have been misled by J. Rendel Harris's uninformed guesswork in his work on *The Origin of the Leicester Codex of the New Testament*[49] into attributing to him a degree of intellectual brilliance which he did not possess. Probably the most that can be said for him is that he did possess a certain flair for languages – primarily spoken languages, it must be noted.[50] A more obvious characteristic was that garrulous boastfulness which was Tyndale's despair;[51] and if Sir Thomas More is to be believed he was in fact something of a religious dilettante.[52] As far as his working association with Tyndale is concerned he was clearly never more than an amanuensis; and if one looks at his own published works one finds little in the way of theological precision.

Jerome Barlow was a somewhat later apostate than Roy – he encountered Tyndale at Worms in about May 1527 on his way to meet Roy at Strassburg – and his background is quite obscure. But he was an altogether different kind of character and, as Tyndale pictures him, an altogether more sympathetic figure than Roy.[53] However he shows no evidence of precise theological thinking either. With the exception of his best-known work the *Burying of the Mass*, which shows clear signs of Roy's involvement, his published work appears to have consisted entirely of rehashes of old Lollard tracts of an essentially anticlerical nature.[54]

[48] See the preface to his 'Brief dialogue', ed. A. Wolf as *William Roye's Dialogue Between a Christian Father and His Stubborn Son* (Vienna, 1874). On the family's court connections, *LP*, ɪ (ii) 3567.

[49] J. Rendel Harris, *The Origin of the Leicester Codex of the New Testament* (London, 1887), pp. 47–9. Harris's conjecture rested upon a single inscription recording that the earliest known owner of his codex was a 'frater Froy'.

[50] *LP*, ɪV (iii) 5667.

[51] Tyndale, *The Parable of the Wycked Mammon*, ([Antwerp], 1528) (A. W. Pollard and G. R. Redgrave (eds.), *A Short-Title Catalogue of Books Printed in England, Scotland and Ireland, and of English Books Printed Abroad, 1475–1640* (London, 1926), no. 24454; A. Hume (ed.), 'English books printed abroad, 1525–35: an annotated bibliography' in *The Confutation of Tyndale's Answer*, ed. L. A. Schuster et al. (The Yale edition of the complete works of St Thomas More, VIII, New Haven, 1973), appendix ʙ, no. 6), prologue, sigs. A.ii.r–v. Tyndale's comments on Roy and Barlow are printed in A. F. Pollard (ed.), *Records of the English Bible* (London, 1911), pp. 119–21.

[52] *Confutation of Tyndale's Answer*, p. 8.   [53] *Mammon*, sig. A.ii.v.

[54] For a list of Barlow's works (not all of which survive) see his confession in T. Wright (ed.), *Three Chapters of Letters Relating to the Suppression of the Monasteries* (Camden Society original series,

One characteristic which links all of their works is that they are not actually very Lutheran. The nearest either of them comes to theological discrimination is in Roy's *Brief Dialogue Between a Christian Father and his Stubborn Son*, which suggests a doctrinal movement away from Luther and towards Zwingli.[55] But this was a loose translation rather than an original work; and if More was right in attributing to Roy the anonymous translations of Luther's exposition of the seventh chapter of 1 Corinthians and Erasmus' *Paraclesis* which appeared at Antwerp, bound together in 1529, then he can rather be accused of eclecticism.[56] The *Burying of the Mass* may have been inspired by the reputation of, if not by actual acquaintance with a contemporary German work.[57] It outdoes all the rest in the vehemence of its criticism of Wolsey and the English clergy generally (and the Observants in particular). But it, and Barlow's other known works, are not much more than knocking-copy aimed against real or imagined clerical excesses, and have no real theological axe to grind beyond a preference for Scripture over ceremony.

So perhaps we must seek Roy's and Barlow's primary motivation elsewhere. The answer may lie in the type of character which the Observants would tend to attract into their midst. Theirs was no easy vocation, yet it was one which held an attraction alike for the sons of the wealthy and for some of the best minds of its day. It was essentially a focus for religious idealism, a means of expressing rejection of the spiritual complacency and worldliness which afflicted much of the mainstream church: characteristics put into stark relief by Wolsey's conduct. The Observance would not be the only hard vocation which attracted a few who would ultimately come to regret their choice. There is something of this in both Roy and Barlow.[58] Perhaps in this connection Wolsey himself can be accused of touching-off an outburst of more-or-less vulgar Lutheranism by his own actions. It may also be significant here that while Roy evidently ended up by being burned as a heretic in Portugal,[59] Barlow eventually submitted to the king. In doing so he praised the king's 'so excellent learning and singular judgement of the truth, which endeavoured not only to chase away and extirp all heresies, but also to see

---

26, 1843), pp. 6–7 (and see note 60, below). The original sections of Barlow's 'Proper dialogue between a gentleman and a husbandman' of 1530 (also printed by Arber) are made of much tamer stuff than the 'Burying of the Mass'.

55 A. Hume, 'William Roye's "Brefe Dialoge" (1527): an English version of a Strassburg catechism', *Harvard Theological Review*, 60 (1967), pp. 307ff; L. A. Schuster, 'Thomas More's polemical career, 1523–1533', in *The Confutation of Tyndale's Answer*, pp. 1171–3.

56 *Short-Title Catalogue*, no. 10493; Hume, 'English Books', no. 10; More, *Confutation of Tyndale's Answer*, p. 8. More is supported on this by W. A. Clebsch, 'The earliest translations of Luther into English', *Harvard Theological Review*, 56 (1963), pp. 77ff.

57 This was Niclaus Manuel's *Krankheit der Messe*, published at the start of 1528 (C. H. Herford, *Studies in the Literary Relations of England and Germany in the Sixteenth Century* (Cambridge, 1886), pp. 33ff.).

58 See in particular Tyndale's comments on Barlow, *Mammon*, sig. A.ii.v. cf. the case of the Carthusian Andrew Borde (E. M. Thompson, *The English Carthusians* (London, 1930), pp. 412–14).

59 More, *Confutation of Tyndale's Answer*, p. 8; John Foxe, *Acts and Monuments* (ed. J. Pratt, London, [1887]), IV, 696, 753.

a reformation of slanderous living, for the restraint of vice in all estates, to the furtherance of virtue and advancement of God's Word': not just a grovelling apology but, apparently, a reflection of the atmosphere of anti-Wolsey propaganda which pervaded the court in the months which followed the cardinal's fall.[60]

If this is so, however, what are we to make of Friar West's remark? Once again we need to draw out the context in which the remark was uttered. His case represents quite another angle of the story of Wolsey's interference in the friars' affairs. John West was a stepson of the London goldsmith Sir Thomas Exmew and by now a fairly senior friar within the Greenwich convent, since at least by late 1528 he held the offices of preacher and confessor. It is also clear that for some time before this he had been active in Wolsey's service.[61] Friars had traditionally played an active role in their patrons' affairs (one needs only think of the example of Friar Brackley in the *Paston Letters*[62]). And the Observants were not altogether exceptional in this respect. As they had retained something of the full vigour of their international links they could make themselves particularly useful on the international front. In the earliest years of Henry VIII's reign their provincial vicar, Bonaventure Langley, had been employed on diplomatic missions to the king's sisters, Margaret in Scotland and Mary in France.[63] But here again there were obvious risks to the maintenance of proper observance: and in West's case it is clear that his client relationship with Wolsey was leading him to act as an independent operator in the Brackley mould, comparatively free of the discipline of his order. Moreover, it apparently enabled him to breach with impunity his vow of poverty. In a revealing letter to Wolsey early in 1529 he pleads for the cardinal's aid in a dispute over his stepfather's will.[64] In the process he reveals himself to have inherited lands at Hackney from his mother, Lady Elizabeth Exmew, which he had proceeded to sell to his sister and her husband, and as the inheritor and possessor on his own account of various items in gold and amounts in cash. In short, by his own admission West stands accused as a *proprietarius*, the

---

[60] Wright, *Letters*, pp. 6–7. A good deal of ink has been expended on the question of whether Friar Jerome can be identified with Bishop William Barlow (see esp. E. G. Rupp, *Studies in the Making of the English Protestant Tradition* (Cambridge, 1949), pp. 62ff. and most recently A. M. McLean (ed.), *The Work of William Barlowe* (The Courtenay Library of Reformation Classics no. 15, Sutton Courtenay, 1981), pp. 169–70, 178–81. Much of the confusion stems from the fact that the surviving ms of Friar Jerome's confession (BL, MS Cotton Cleopatra E.iv fol. 146) is evidently written in the same hand as a letter of William Barlow to Thomas Cromwell (BL, MS Cotton Caligula B.iii fol. 195) and is signed 'William Barlo'. However many of the works listed in the confession are certainly those of Friar Jerome and in my view the muddle can most sensibly be sorted out by hypothesizing that both documents are in fact later transcripts made by one who himself confused the two individuals.

[61] E. Arber (ed.), *The First Printed English New Testament* (London, 1871), p. 33; *LP*, IV (ii) 4810, 5043; IV (iii) 5275.

[62] For Brackley see J. Gairdner (ed.), *The Paston Letters, 1422–1509* (Edinburgh, 1910), vols. II–IV, *passim*.

[63] *LP*, I (ii) 2394, 2423, 2440; II (i) 80, 138.   [64] *LP*, IV (iii) 5275.

holder of individual property outside the friary vilified in successive versions of the statutes of the order.[65]

West had left England for Antwerp at the beginning of August 1527 charged with a special mission by the cardinal.[66] The appearance from the presses of Tyndale's English New Testament – in the original Cologne quarto fragment and the Worms octavo edition of March 1526[67] – had marked a sea-change in the battle against Lutheranism in England. What had been by and large an essentially intellectual debate – albeit one overshadowed by the dire penalties which accompanied theological dissent taken to extremes – conducted chiefly within the bounds of Oxford and Cambridge, was now in danger of being transformed by the appearance of a printed vernacular protestant literature into a matter for popular debate with obvious subversive potential.

But it had been the appearance of Roy's *Brief Dialogue* and the *Burying of the Mass* which had really stirred the cardinal. In his prologue to the former Roy had let the cat out of the bag by identifying Tyndale as the translator of the New Testament, and himself as his helper. Now the English authorities knew who they were looking for; and besides, the vicious lampooning in the *Burying of the Mass* supplied Wolsey with a very personal imperative for doing something.

Initially Wolsey's main targets were Tyndale and Roy as perpetrators of the English New Testament (at this point the authorship of the *Burying of the Mass* seems to have been unknown in England): but the commission which West was given under the great seal was to involve him more generally in seeking out and securing the apprehension of various other English fugitives; notably an English merchant at Antwerp, Richard Harman, who had been identified as a key link in the chain along which Tyndale's scriptures were conveyed to England.

We shall not be concerned here in any great detail with West's campaign, carried on with the willing but thankless co-operation of the king's ambassador at the court of Malines, Sir John Hackett.[68] It is enough to say that West had a frustrating time of it. In Antwerp he ran across Francis Birckmann, a Cologne stationer who was probably well known to his countrymen among the English friars through his outlet in London:[69] and from him he learned (not altogether

[65] 'Abbreviatio statutorum', III, 13–15, vi.24.
[66] He carried letters dated 5 August: *LP*, IV (ii) 4810.
[67] *Short-Title Catalogue*, nos. 2823–4; Hume, 'English books', nos. 1–2.
[68] The campaign against Harman can be traced in *Hackett Letters*, 67ff. and in the pages of *LP*, IV. But Miss Rogers was mistaken in thinking (p. 155 n. 7) that the three individuals named in Wolsey's commission to Hackett were Harman, his wife and a fugitive English priest, Richard Akerston. Hackett makes clear (*Hackett Letters*, 68; *LP*, IV (ii) 4511) that the latter two were arrested on the initiative of the margrave of Antwerp; and in the light of West's later activities it is much more likely that Wolsey was after Tyndale and Roy, by now known in England as collaborators on the New Testament edition.
[69] *Hackett Letters*, no. 78; *LP*, IV (iii) 4693. On Birckmann, E. G. Duff, *The Printers, Stationers and Bookbinders of Westminster and London* (Cambridge, 1906), pp. 195ff.

correctly) that the *Burying of the Mass* had been produced by Roy, Barlow and Tyndale. A plot was hatched to arrest them at Cologne; but when West arrived there he found that all the available copies of both this and Roy's dialogue had been removed from the market by the prompt action of the ever-helpful Sir Herman Rinck, an imperial knight who had long been a faithful servant of Henry VIII and his father.[70]

In fact West never did catch up with either Tyndale, Roy or Barlow. Back in Antwerp, his best efforts and those of the governor of the Merchant Adventurers, Sir John Style, failed to turn up any evidence to incriminate Harman; and the cardinal's subsequent prevarication on the issue revealed the English case against him to be a man of straw. Although Harman was arrested and held, the fact that he held burgess rights at Antwerp meant that the emperor's council was reluctant to allow his extradition and demanded that concrete evidence should be produced first. This neither Wolsey nor West was able to do. Four times Hackett succeeded in preventing Harman's acquittal for lack of evidence; but ultimately he could not prevent first his release on surety and ultimately, at the end of February 1528, his complete acquittal. Whereupon for his trouble he found himself faced with defending himself against a damages suit.

During the course of his activities on the cardinal's behalf West had on a number of occasions received money from Hackett and Style; and on more than one occasion application had been made through Hackett for a dispensation from the cardinal which would allow him to relinquish his habit.[71] It is hardly surprising that his superiors should have taken exception to all this. Matters came to a head after his return from the continent in October 1527. He had returned, partly to try by means of personal representation to get some action out of Wolsey in the Harman affair, and partly to continue his own investigations in London, in particular into Roy's recent daring return to London to visit his mother at Westminster. Once in England he found his superiors taking an unhealthily keen interest in all that he was doing: furthermore the provincial minister and the guardian of Greenwich went to Wolsey to demand the revocation of his commission. At one point he is found appealing to Sir Brian Tuke, the treasurer of the king's chamber, in a tone of desperation, for his assistance in obtaining from Wolsey either a dispensation from his vows or else 'a letter of obedience under my Lord's broad seal': failing which, he feared, the horrors of the Greenwich prison beckoned.[72]

On this at least the cardinal evidently did not let him down. West both survived the crisis and for the time being retained his habit. He is last heard of in the summer of 1529 chasing Roy and Barlow across East Anglia, accompanied by another Greenwich friar, John Lawrence.[73] He was apparently no longer among

---

[70] *Hackett Letters*, nos. 79, 81, 87 (*LP*, IV (ii) 4694, 4725, 4826).

[71] *LP*, IV (ii) 4810; Arber (ed.), *First Printed English New Testament*, pp. 32–6.

[72] *Hackett Letters*, no. 94; *LP*, IV (iii) 5043.   [73] *LP*, IV (iii) 5667.

the friars some three years later,[74] and it is unlikely to be pure coincidence that his disappearance at least roughly parallels the cardinal's fall.

It was in his appeal to Tuke that West made his remarkable claim that the fathers of the house were harbouring and protecting Lutherans. He offers it as an explanation of his superiors' hostility; and he combines it with accusations of their opposition, and hence disloyalty to the king and Wolsey. They have, he complains, 'taken great indignation at me because I have sped so well . . . they cannot speak among them a good word of my Lord's Grace and the King's. And because I do reprove them of their ill sayings they go about all that they can to put me to trouble and vexations and desolations.' It is all a rather obvious gambit by a desperate man, designed to ensure action on his behalf by interpreting his persecutors' motives in the blackest possible light, by allying heresy with disloyalty. To this extent it succeeded. But that is not to say that the specific accusation that the fathers supported Roy and Barlow, and prayed that they might not be apprehended, might not have had a grain of truth in it. It simply reflects one of the characteristics of the Observant regime. In claiming, in effect, that the friars' opposition to Wolsey overrode even their concern for doctrinal orthodoxy, West is actually underlining the extent of their desire to maintain their jurisdictional independence. The Greenwich superiors were not in any way expressing their approval of heresy. Rather, they were saying that the disciplining of Roy and Barlow, as professed friars, belonged first and foremost to them.

This, surely is the nub of the matter. Throughout this business it was the Greenwich fathers, not Wolsey, who had the better grasp of the realities of the situation; in appreciating that in the long run the question of jurisdiction, rather than of doctrinal orthodoxy per se, was the more important; in appreciating that a cure imposed from outside was likely in the long run to have consequences which were worse than the disease. In the end, Wolsey's interference in the friars' affairs had achieved nothing positive. If there had been 'Lutheranism' abroad in the Greenwich convent it was nothing which the friars could not handle themselves by means of their own internal mechanisms. If anything, Wolsey had made matters worse, in so far as his interference had tended to drive nascent dissidence over the walls and out of control.

This, however, was by no means the whole story. The passage of time and a broadening of perspectives have done much to mellow the Pollardian orthodoxy that Wolsey in effect taught Henry VIII how to be head of the church. His activities left their mark on different areas of the church in different ways and to differing degrees. And one might have thought that a movement which had unquestionably maintained a good deal of the vigour of its founders would have been quite able to shake off the effects of the cardinal's interference. Yet even here echoes of his overbearing presence continued to reverberate after his fall.

---

[74] In particular his name does not appear in a list of senior members of the community compiled for Thomas Cromwell's benefit in September 1532 (*LP*, v, 1312 (ii)); 'Observants', appendix 3.

For Wolsey had succeeded, as the friars had feared from the start, in establishing some dangerous precedents whose usefulness was not to be lost on his pupil Thomas Cromwell when, a few years later, he came to contend with their opposition to the king's divorce and its consequences. On one level there was Wolsey's use of the Observant–Conventual divide as a useful means of imposing discipline upon the Observants from outside. His use of a Conventual prison in 1525 as a means of dealing with a recalcitrant friar was to be used to greater effect by Cromwell seven years later. And the cardinal's employment of the Conventual Standish was to be developed into the wholesale subjection of the Observants to the more compliant Conventuals in the autumn of 1534, as a final vindictive solution to the problem of their intransigent opposition to the royal supremacy.[75]

But at a deeper level, there lay the insidious after-effects of Wolsey's patronage, which in the different circumstances of the early 1530s would help to open new divisions within the community. There is a link between the events of the late 1520s and the early 1530s in the figure of West's 1529 companion John Lawrence. His name recurs in Cromwell's correspondence in 1532–3 as an informer against the fathers of the community. And Lawrence was not alone. There was by this time a distinct dissident party among the friars, which was ultimately to place its loyalties to the king, Cromwell and the Boleyns above its loyalty to the community and the community's general alignment with the Aragon interest. The party was a small one, and not all of its members had been part of the Observant community of the 1520s: but in part it does seem to have been linked together by a common client-loyalty to Wolsey. And in feeding information to Cromwell and the king it succeeded in severely compromising the community's attempts to retain its integrity in an increasingly hostile atmosphere.[76] To this extent, at least, Wolsey made a significant contribution to bringing about the community's ultimate downfall.

[75] 'Observants', pp. 141–3, 198–201.   [76] Ibid., pp. 147ff.

CHAPTER 9

Cardinal Wolsey and the satirists: the case of Godly Queen Hester re-opened

GREG WALKER

Thomas Wolsey is perhaps unique among Tudor statesmen in his capacity to provoke normally reserved historians to flights of rhetorical condemnation. It is not simply that scholars have examined his administrative record and found it wanting. With Wolsey there has always been a temptation to moralize the criticism, indeed to make a suspect moral judgement the basis of the political analysis. Most readers will, no doubt, be familiar with accounts of the cardinal's career which see his own moral failings as central to his methods of government and to his eventual fall from power. His megalomaniacal ego, his greed, his colossal pride (as expressed through his buildings), his acquisitive policies and his love of pomp and ceremony are the central motifs of many a study. The net result is usually not so much a political biography as an exemplar in the *Fall of Princes* tradition of improving literature. Perhaps the most extreme example of this tendency is Garret Mattingly's remarkable description of an entirely carnal cardinal,[1]

> [the] unwieldy hulk of corrupted flesh bearing perilously the supple, powerful, brain, a demoniac incandescence of ambition and pride driving and lighting from within the bloated, rotting, body.

It is difficult to imagine any other individual attracting such evident loathing. Even perennial schoolroom villains such as Empson and Dudley have fared better. But, unlike Wolsey, they were not churchmen, and history reserves its most damning judgements for those villains who were also princes of the church. Thus we are presented with Wolsey painted in a number of unattractive guises: as the autocrat who prevented the humanist reform of the church which would have forestalled the Reformation, as the epitome of the moral and spiritual failings of the late medieval church, but most often as the hypocritical sinner, the man whose flagrant abuse of every Christian principle made him an object of loathing to all who encountered him. Wolsey, we are told, was personally deeply unpopular, and it was the man, rather than the offices he held, which provoked

[1] G. Mattingly, *Catherine of Aragon* (London, 1942), p. 174. I am very grateful to the President and Fellows of the British Academy for the generous award of a Postdoctoral Fellowship which enabled me to complete this paper.

that unpopularity. It will be the object of this essay to question that assumption and to suggest rather that in fact the reverse was the case.

Any attempt to revise our view of Wolsey's contemporary reputation (and particularly his reputation as a leader of the church), however, faces a seemingly insurmountable barrier in the mass of material critical of him which survives from the early sixteenth century. Even in his own lifetime Wolsey attracted an almost unrivalled degree of attention from the authors of satires, complaints and invectives. From the 1520s alone there survive as many as eight literary works which were written either wholly or partly in dispraise of the cardinal. From John Skelton's poetic satires, through the anonymous invectives *Of the Cardinal Wulse* and the *Impeachment of Wolsey*, to John Palsgrave's ironic 'Articles' and Jerome Barlowe's *Burial of the Mass*, a wide range of material exists which seemingly supports the view that Wolsey's bad historiographical press is only a pale reflection of a contemporary reputation of staggering unpopularity.[2]

Yet such critical accounts as these, and those others which appeared following his death, should not be accepted as straightforward representations of Wolsey's personal reputation, still less as accurate descriptions of the man himself. For they were designed to pursue ends other than simply the castigation of the cardinal, and were shaped by motives beyond the moralizing subject matter which they initially present. In each case, as I have suggested elsewhere, what appears to be an analysis of Wolsey's character or motivation, proves on closer examination to be more a product of calculated special pleading to political ends.[3]

As A. F. Pollard, Peter Gwyn and J. J. Scarisbrick have demonstrated, Wolsey's posthumous reputation was more a product of his position and of the political and religious circumstances of the 1530s than of his own character or actions.[4] He was perhaps the first victim of English Reformation propaganda. And he was a victim who enjoyed little sympathy. As the most obvious representative of Roman authority in England he inevitably became the focus of protestant attacks upon what they saw as a corrupt and vainglorious catholic church. And it is in this light that protestant accounts of his supposed vanity and greed should be read, as indictments of an allegedly worldly and material church, not as specific accounts of Wolsey's own personality. Moreover, whilst catholic controversialists were eager to write in defence of their church, they were less prepared to defend Wolsey's maligned reputation. For them an alternative, but equally damning, logic applied. Wolsey was seen as the man who at best collaborated in, and at worst instigated, the 'King's Great Matter', the 'divorce' from Catherine of Aragon which led to the break with Rome. Thus, ironically,

---

[2] For the view that such accounts must 'represent accurately the condition of public feeling', see P. L. Wiley, 'Wolsey's career in Renaissance English literature', unpublished Stanford University PhD dissertation, 1943, p. 3.

[3] G. Walker, *John Skelton and the Politics of the 1520s* (Cambridge, 1988), chapters 3–5.

[4] Pollard, pp. 4–5; P. J. Gwyn and J. J. Scarisbrick, *Cardinal Wolsey* (Sussex Tapes, 1981).

Wolsey secured a reputation amongst catholics as the betrayer of their church at the same time as he appeared to protestants as the very embodiment of it. Historical accident and subsequent events thus contrived to produce a situation in which he was castigated by everyone and defended by no one (except perhaps by George Cavendish, his gentleman usher, who wielded the two-edged sword of his *Life of Wolsey* in his master's defence). In such circumstances the historical individual was soon buried beneath a huge weight of polemical invention, an uncomfortable position which he has occupied until well into the present century.

The focus of the present paper is not, however, the posthumous vilification of Wolsey, but those literary treatments which circulated during his lifetime and particularly those which relate to his administration of the church. For it was these texts which provided the critical material upon which the later accounts elaborated. And here again, as what follows will demonstrate, there were more factors at work than initially suggest themselves. Here too the attack on Wolsey was not an end in itself, but rather a means towards wider political ends.

I

John Skelton's satirical poems, 'Speke, Parott', 'Collyn Clout' and 'Why come ye nat to courte?', written in 1521 and 1522, provide both the most extensive and the most intensive critical treatments of Wolsey which survive. And in these texts as elsewhere the allegations laid against the cardinal are ostensibly moral in origin. It is his unnatural pride and arrogance which make him an abomination as head of the church:

> So rygorous revelyng, in a prelate specially;
> So bold and so braggyng, and was so baselye borne;
> So lordlye of hys lokes, and so dysdayneslye;
> So fatte a magott, bred of a flesshe-flye . . .
> So myche crossyng and blyssyng and hym all be shrewde;
> Suche pollaxis and pyllers, suche mulys trapte with gold –
> Sens Dewcalyons flodde, in no cronycle ys told.
>
> ('Speke, Parott', ll. 506–9, 516–18)[5]

These vices, coupled with his avarice, create the corrupt, flamboyant monster of popular legend. Supposedly reporting criticisms levelled against the entire higher clergy by their lay opponents, Skelton provides, in 'Collyn Clout', a comprehensive picture of a simoniacal, slothful cardinal, too busy indulging his own vices to attend to the parlous state of the church or the pitiful condition of its lay charges. The bishops,

---

[5] All references are to texts in V. J. Scattergood, ed., *John Skelton: the Complete English Poems* (Harmondsworth, 1982).

>   kepe so harde a rule,
>   To ryde upon a mule
>   With golde all betrapped,
>   In purple and paule belapped;
>   Some hatted and some capped,
>   Rychly bewrapped,
>   God wotte, so theyr great paynes,
>   In rotchettes of fyne raynes,
>   Whyte as mares mylke;
>   Theyr tabertes of fine sylke;
>   Theyr styrops of myxt golde begared,
>   There may no cost be spared:
>   Thyr moyles golde dothe eate,
>   Their neyghbours dye for meate.
>
> ('Collyn Clout', ll. 307–20)

>   Some say ye sytte in trones
>   Lyke *princeps aquilonis*
>   And shryne your rotten bonys
>   With perles and precyous stonys. (ll. 344–7)

Such charges are, however, conventional. As has been argued elsewhere, satirists had made precisely the same points, in much the same language, about bishops and archbishops, cardinals and popes for centuries.[6] And it is far from clear that such accusations represented the immediate concerns of contemporary laymen and women. Criticisms of clerical wealth, pride and ceremonial pomp were endemic to late medieval society, and like many endemic phenomena they seem to have lain largely unnoticed beneath the surface of political and social life, unthought of on a day-to-day basis. Thus it is doubtful that anyone, unless specifically prompted, would have cited Wolsey's ceremonial poleaxes and pillars as a major social or political evil. But such charges, like all stock assumptions and prejudices, were there to be picked up and used by those with other axes to grind, who might add them to a catalogue of other charges to broaden and strengthen their appeal. And this is precisely how Skelton used them.

In 'Speke, Parott' the poet's aim was to attract royal patronage by criticizing Wolsey at a time when he seemed to have aroused Henry's distrust. Thereafter, in 'Collyn Clout' and 'Why come ye nat to courte?', his object was to secure patronage from the wealthier citizens of the city of London. Hence he forged his satires to appeal to their current concerns, most notably their objection to the forced loans of 1522 imposed by Wolsey, who himself acted as chief commissioner for London. Thus we find Skelton deftly manipulating these conventional criticisms of clerical wealth in order to turn them into attacks upon the loans. In the passage quoted above, for example, the reference to prelates on thrones,

---

[6] A. R. Heiserman, *Skelton and Satire* (Chicago, 1961), pp. 190–243; Walker, *John Skelton*, chapter 4.

adorned 'with perles and precyous stonys' leads immediately into a stark contrast with the situation endured by the hard-pressed citizens of London.

> But howe the commons gronys,
> And the people monys,
> For prestes and for lonys,
> Lent and never payde
> But from daye to daye delayde,
> The communewelth decayde. (ll. 348–53)

Again, Wolsey's personal vices and his supposed dominance of Henry VIII are cited, not as grievances in themselves, but as part of the criticism of the loans. The laymen complain, Collyn reports, that the bishops,

> gyve shrewd counsell
> Agaynst the communewell
> By pollynge and pyllage
> In cytes and vyllage
> By taxynge and tollage. (ll. 358–62)

The supposedly moral judgements upon Wolsey must be read in the light of the poet's overall purpose, which was to produce as effective a criticism of the forced loans as possible. Conventional jibes at worldly prelates were added to the satires in order to give them greater substance and to widen their appeal. They should not be mistaken for the object of the attacks, nor for personal criticisms of Wolsey the man. They were, in effect, a given element, a standard ingredient in all anti-clerical satires. Thus simply to identify them in any given text is hardly productive. It is how they were used in each case, and to what ends, which is significant.

II

To illustrate this proposition in more detail what follows will concentrate upon one of the later literary attacks upon Wolsey, the dramatic *Enterlude of Godly Queen Hester*. This text is selected for detailed study both because it rarely enjoys close attention and because it seems to shed new and revealing light upon reactions to Wolsey's administration, particularly to the centre-piece of his administration of the church, the legatine authority. It also seems to display in an exemplary manner traits common to all the literary attacks written in the 1520s; texts to which we shall return at the conclusion of this essay.

The *Enterlude of the Vertuous and Godly Queene Hester* was not printed until 1561, but it is clearly a work of an earlier period. Previous commentators have suggested dates between 1522 and 1527. But, as what follows will demonstrate, it actually forms a part of the attack upon Cardinal Wolsey at his fall in 1529. The play is ostensibly a recapitulation of the Old Testament Book of Esther. The heroine of the title (here named Hester) is chosen as his queen by King Assewerus (Ahasuerus or Artaxerses of Persia). At first she conceals her Jewish origins. But when Aman, the newly appointed chancellor, gains Assewerus' connivance in a plot to massacre the Persian Jews, she reveals her true race at a banquet prepared for the king, and pleads for a royal reprieve for herself and her people. The king, shocked that he has been misled by Aman into so vindictive an act, grants her request, and has Aman executed on the gibbet he had prepared for Hester's foster-father Mordecai.

Elements of the biblical story are omitted from the interlude. Both the callous dismissal of Esther's predecessor, Queen Vashti, which opens the story, and the massacre of the enemies of the Jews which concludes it, are exised, in order to maximize the audience's sympathies for Hester, and for the fate of the Jews. And new elements are added to the story in the form of a satirical conversation between the vices Pride, Ambition and Adulation, and the introduction of a further vice, Hardy Dardy, who seeks employment in Aman's service. But the broad sweep of the original narrative is retained. A closer reading of the detailed treatment of that narrative, however, quickly reveals that the interlude is rather more than a simple rehearsal of the biblical story for moral or theological effect.

Many of the incidental details in the drama are curiously inappropriate. The location of the story should, of course, be Old Testament Persia. But little effort seems to have been expended by the author to create a credible biblical society. On the contrary, the text insists at many points on the contemporary English locus of the action. The reader is presented with a society familiar with friars (l. 502), pursuivants (l. 156) and park keepers (l. 657).[7] When Aman uses a legal weapon to humble a rival, it is not to the Persian law that he looks, but to the very English 'statute of apparell' (l. 378). And when war is mentioned, it is not a biblical foe of the Persians who is feared, but 'eyther ... Scotland or France' (l. 479). These anomalies need not in themselves demonstrate a covert political motive behind the play. Contemporary references of often startling inappropriateness litter the medieval Corpus Christi cycles. But these allusions are not the only idiosyncratic elements in the play. The Jews themselves, whose plight forms the substance of the plot, are also oddly defined. Some of the practices ascribed to them seem appropriate to biblical Jewry, others do not. Like the people of the original story the Jews of *Hester* are 'scattered abroad and dispersed among the people in all ... provinces', practising their own laws.[8] But the duties of these Jewish 'households' (ll. 956–7) are to dispense charity and hospitality to the poor and needy (ll. 943–4) and to pray and conduct ceremonies for the benefit of the wider community (ll. 1096–1102). In addition the author mentions their going on pilgrimage (l. 790) and at one point presents them singing hymns

---

[7] All references are to the text in W. W. Greg, ed., *The New Enterlude of Godly Queene Hester* (Louvain, 1904).

[8] Esther, 3:8 (Authorized Version).

(l. 861). Reference to such practices makes it evident that the play is something more than a simple narrative of the sufferings and triumphs of biblical Jewry. In fact it casts in the role of the persecuted Jews the religious orders of the last years of the 1520s.

What the play provides, as what follows will exemplify, is an attack upon Cardinal Wolsey for his intrusion into the affairs of the religious houses and into the prerogative rights of the secular clergy.[9] In the text there are echoes of a number of the accusations of personal failings laid against Wolsey by Skelton and others. Aman, the Wolsey figure, is said, for example, to be so proud that Pride himself has to travel in poor array in his jurisdiction (ll. 373–90) and so vain that he has retained,

> al [the] flatteres, and al crafty clatterers
> That dwell fourtye myle aboute. (ll. 395–6)

But it soon becomes evident that the author is chiefly interested, not in Wolsey's alleged flaws of character, but in one specific aspect of his ecclesiastical administration.

In 1524 Wolsey began the suppression of a series of small English religious houses, whose incomes he transferred to the Oxford college which he was in the process of founding. Between 1524 and 1529 a combination of papal bulls and royal warrants authorized him to suppress a total of twenty-nine houses, in order to realize a yearly income of 3,000 ducats towards the maintenance of Cardinal College. It is in the light of these suppressions that the defence of the religious contained in Hester's defence of the Jews is to be read.

Precisely why the playwright should have been so interested in these suppressions is not, however, immediately evident. It is certainly the case that Wolsey's commissioners were active over a wide geographical area. But such activity was hardly new. Bishop Alcock of Ely had suppressed the nunnery of St Radegund to found Jesus College, Cambridge, in 1496. Richard Fox, bishop of Winchester, had endowed Corpus Christi College, Oxford, with the revenues of suppressed houses in 1517. And John Fisher, bishop of Rochester, had endowed

---

[9] That Aman is a figure for Wolsey will be made clear by what follows. Note in the present context, however, that both are chancellors of the realm and control the law courts. Aman, like Wolsey, is also head of the church (ll. 424–36). There are also numerous echoes of Skelton's anti-Wolsey satires in the treatment of Aman. He is 'this ravenous wolf' (l. 180) and 'this carnifex' (l. 840). Skelton's jibes at the *vitulus* or 'bull-calf' ('Speke, Parott', ll. 59, 347–52, 377–80; 'Why come ye nat to courte?', Decastichon, ll. 1–10) may also be alluded to in the reference to 'the bull nor the calfe' (l. 550). Compare also the attacks upon Aman's domination of the law courts in lines 399–416, with the criticisms of Wolsey's administration of the court of star chamber in 'Why come ye nat to courte?', ll. 184–204 and 314–45. The numerous allusions to papal symbols of authority and the absence of any references to religious radicalism and heresy would seem to refute the suggestion that the play was a product of the fall of Thomas Cromwell, written around 1541 to praise the duke of Norfolk for his role in that event (see I. Lancashire, *Dramatic Texts and Records*, p. 22). The arguments for and against suppression of the religious houses come at ll. 311–21; 475–8; 737–46; 943–70.

his college, St John's, Cambridge, with the property of two nunneries in 1524. Nor were the houses suppressed by Wolsey in the 1520s particularly large or significant institutions. They were small houses, generally on the margins of independent viability. Only four contained more then eight occupants, and only five enjoyed an income in excess of £100 per annum.[10] Yet Wolsey's suppressions do seem to have aroused an unusual amount of protest and opposition, both at the time and subsequently, at his fall. The townsfolk of Tonbridge, Kent, felt sufficient affection for their local priory to petition Archbishop Warham for its salvation,[11] whilst at Bayham in Sussex local men went as far as forcibly to restore the canons to their abbey, in clandestine defiance of the suppression commissioners.[12] Such acts clearly indicate a degree of local support for the houses concerned. Thus it is possible that the author of *Hester* was prompted to write in order to appeal to such spontaneous local opposition to the suppression of a specific house. But it seems more likely that the play was written somewhat later, after the houses had been dissolved, as part of a more general attack upon the engine of the suppressions, Wolsey's legatine authority. For what is perhaps more interesting is that criticism of the suppressions surfaced again at Westminster, after Wolsey's fall from grace in 1529, as one of the charges levelled at the cardinal in the lords' articles. Among these articles, which share a number of suggestive coincidences of theme and approach with the text of *Hester*, was the assertion that[13]

> the said Cardinal hath not only, by his untrue suggestion to the Pope, shamefully slaundered many good religious houses and good virtuous men dwelling in them, but also suppressed by reason thereof, above thirty [sic] houses of religion.

It would be possible to see the inclusion of such charges in both the lords' articles and the text of *Hester* as simply a reflection of how widespread was popular concern at an obvious iniquity. Might it not be argued that Wolsey was suppressing perfectly good religious institutions in order to finance a college that was little more than a monument to his own vanity, and popular opinion recognized the fact and protested? Similar suggestions have been offered in the past.[14] But a close reading of the texts concerned, and an examination of the political context in which they appeared, suggests that the situation was more complex than this. Indeed, both the lords' articles and *Hester* seem to be the product of specific political motives held by a particular interest group.

The allegations against Wolsey gathered together by the authors of the articles of 1529 are an idiosyncratic collection, combining substantial political charges

[10] D. Knowles, *The Religious Orders in England* (3 vols., Cambridge, 1959), III, p. 161.

[11] *LP*, IV (i) 1470–1, 4920.

[12] J. J. Goring, 'The riot at Bayham Abbey, June 1525', *Sussex Archaeological Collections*, 116 (1978), 1–10.

[13] Lord Herbert of Cherbury, *The Life and Reigne of Henry the Eighth* (London, 1649), Article XIX, p. 269.

[14] See, for example, Pollard, p. 217.

with personal grievances, conventional assertions of wrongdoing and wild accusations of secret malice. These could hardly be the concerted grievances of any one group, nor a reflection of popular opinion, still less a true representation of the views of any one of the signatories. They are too diverse for that. Rather they seem to be a collection gathered at short notice on an *ad hoc* basis. An extended group of councillors was provided with an opportunity to produce formal criticisms of Wolsey by a king anxious to use the cardinal's failure to further his campaign for a divorce. These criticisms, gathered together as a set of articles, were formally compiled on 1 December 1529, possibly as the first step towards an abortive act of attainder. But, as E. W. Ives argues elsewhere in this volume, the first draft of these indictments may have been completed as early as the end of July 1529.[15] What it is important to note, however, is that whenever the original draft was compiled, the initiative in Wolsey's condemnation lay with Henry, not with the lords and clerics concerned. As Edward Hall stated: it was only when 'the nobles and prelates perceived that the kings favor was from the Cardinal sore minished' that 'every man of the Kynges Counsaill, beganne to laye to him suche offences, as they knewe by hym'.[16] Far from acting independently, the lords, here and elsewhere, were actually responding to signals from the king.

The duke of Suffolk's famous declaration at the legatine court at Blackfriars, accompanied by a great clap upon the board with his hand, that 'it was never merry in England whilst we had cardinals among us' was the first of many initiatives stage-managed by Henry and designed to cow church leaders into conceding an annulment, whether in England or in Rome. As both Edward Hall's and George Cavendish's accounts make clear, Suffolk was not working on his own initiative. Henry had already spoken to both Norfolk and Suffolk concerning his frustration with proceedings in the courtroom before the prorogation, and had primed them to encourage the judges to reach a decision. When judgement was not given and the adjournment announced instead, 'with that/ stept forthe the Duke of Suffolk *frome the Kyng And by his commaundement spake*' the fateful words 'with a stought and hault countenaunce'.[17] Having made the speech, Suffolk then hurried out after Henry, the latter having left his gallery as soon as the duke stepped forward, clearly aware of what was about to be said. No more public demonstration of royal dissatisfaction with the judges could be imagined. And with it Wolsey was marked out, again very publicly, as the scapegoat for the failure of the court.[18] This role was expanded by the proceedings taken against him in the autumn of 1529, particularly by Henry's summons of what Lord Herbert describes as 'a council of the Nobles' to sit in star chamber to compile the formalized catalogue of charges against him.[19]

[15] See chapter 11. For the possibility of an act of attainder, see G. R. Elton, *Reform and Reformation* (London, 1977), p. 112. For an alternative view, see Pollard, pp. 256–63.
[16] Hall, pp. 758–9.   [17] Cavendish, p. 90; Hall, p. 758, my italics.   [18] Cavendish, p. 90.
[19] Herbert, *Life and Reigne*, p. 265.

In their haste to comply with Henry's wishes, the attendant lords and commoners seem to have collected suggestions from a number of interested parties, and presented them as their own, with only the minimum of editorial attention. Thus, despite the generally anti-clerical intentions behind the document, and despite the fact that it was eventually signed only by laymen,[20] it is clear that the signatories' parliamentary colleagues, the bishops and the abbots of the greater monasteries, were also influential in its drafting. Otherwise the inclusion of detailed allegations concerning the operation of Wolsey's legatine authority cannot be satisfactorily explained.[21]

Of the forty-four formal charges in the articles, at least eleven concern purely ecclesiastical issues. Five concern the financial exactions imposed upon the regular religious by Wolsey, and the criticisms of monastic practice which he is said to have employed to secure his papal commission to reform them. Neither of these issues is likely to have greatly troubled the majority of the signatories to the indictments. A further three articles relate to legatine interference in the ordinaries' probate jurisdictions, and in promotions to livings in episcopal hands. All of these charges display so detailed a knowledge of the cases concerned that they can only have been compiled with the close co-operation of the interested parties.[22] This need not mean that the lords spiritual were all antagonized by Wolsey's use of his legacy, and consequently acted to voice their collective grievances in the articles. But it does suggest that a group of such clerics, perhaps only small in number, was anxious to see that the type of central interference in their affairs represented by the legatine authority was roundly condemned, certainly by the council, and perhaps even by parliament.

This anxiety was partially the result of a history of friction between Wolsey and elements of the regular clergy which extended well beyond the small-scale suppressions of 1524–8. As early as August 1518 Wolsey, in joint commission with his fellow legate Cardinal Campeggio, received a bull empowering him to visit and reform all religious houses. This need not have caused the religious any

---

[20] The signatories were Lord Chancellor Sir Thomas More, the dukes of Norfolk and Suffolk, the marquises of Dorset and Exeter, the earls of Shrewsbury, Sussex (elevated during this parliamentary session but still subscribing himself 'R. [Viscount] Fitzwa[l]ter' here, although listed among the earls), Oxford and Northumberland, Lords Darcy, Rochford, Mountjoy and Sandys, Sir William Fitzwilliam, Sir Henry Guildford and the judges Sir Anthony Fitzherbert and Sir John Fitzjames. Herbert, p. 274.

[21] Interestingly, Hall's account of the drafting of these articles grants an equal role to the clergy and the lay lords. It is perhaps also significant that he, himself a member of the Reformation Parliament, does not describe the 1 December meeting as a parliamentary committee, but as a meeting of the council. 'When the nobles and prelates perceived that the King's favour was from the cardinal sore minished, every man of the Kynges counsaill beganne to laye to hym such offences as they knewe by hym, and all their accusacions were written in a boke, and all their hands set to it.' Hall, p. 759.

[22] Note the list of deceased clerics whose goods Wolsey is alleged to have seized in article xxx, and the knowledge exhibited in articles xxix, xxvii and xix, of the terms of Wolsey's petitions to Rome, of the acceptance of his legacy by the king, and of the conditional clauses in his bulls permitting the religious suppressions.

serious concern. Such rights of visitation had traditionally rested with the archbishops of Canterbury, whose prerogatives Wolsey's legacy superseded. But neither William Warham (archbishop 1503–32), nor his predecessors Archbishops Dean and Morton, had conducted a general visitation of the southern province. What made Wolsey's authority different was first the fact that it extended to those orders previously exempt from outside interference, and second his declared intention of employing his rights energetically in the interests of reform. The cardinal is known to have ordered visitations of over sixty religious houses, in addition to cathedral chapters, colleges and the mendicant orders.[23] He also took determined steps towards initiating a more general reform of the religious orders. On 19 March 1519 he issued new statutes for the regular Augustinian canons.[24] On 12 November 1521 he summoned the abbots and priors of the Benedictine order to York Place to discuss reform, and at their provincial chapter in February 1522 he formally criticized the order for its avarice and the irregular life of its members, concluding this warning of the need for change by signally descending upon the monks of Westminster for an admonitory visitation.[25] The book of statutes which he subsequently circulated to the Benedictines was sufficiently reformist to arouse a chorus of protest, on the revealing grounds that they asked too much of an order which did not profess to practise the strict discipline of the Observants.

Clearly, despite portraits of Wolsey as an all too erring man of the flesh, ready to wink at even the worst excesses of the late medieval church, the cardinal took the need for reform seriously. And his insistence on the point aroused considerable protest from the religious: not only from those whose laxity he exposed, but also from those less culpable. When he proposed to visit the Franciscan Observants, an order with a reputation for strict adherence to their rule, and for exemplary living, he faced the concerted opposition of a community at Greenwich determined to defend its independence against his interference.[26]

Tension between the more independently minded religious and Wolsey may, then, partially explain the inclusion of religious grievances in the lords' articles of 1529. But this does not fully account for the inclusion of references to the monastic suppressions in these articles. Nor does it indicate why this particular issue, rather than any of the other projects conducted during the period of the

---

23 M. Kelly, 'Canterbury jurisdiction and influence during the episcopate of William Warham, 1503–1532', unpublished Cambridge University PhD dissertation, 1963 [hereafter, Kelly], p. 193. For evidence of Wolsey's earnest in the matter of reform, see the injunctions issued by his agent John Allen at Wenlock Priory in 1523: R. Graham, *English Ecclesiastical Studies* (London, 1929), pp. 132–6.

24 Wilkins, *Concilia*, III, p. 613; P. J. Gwyn, 'Wolsey and church reform', paper read to the Graduate History Seminar at the University of Oxford, 18 February 1985. I am grateful to Peter Gwyn for the chance to discuss and cite his views in this essay, although my interpretation of the evidence differs from his in several important respects.

25 D. Hay (ed.), *The Anglica Historia of Polydore Vergil* (Camden Society, 1950), p. 259; Knowles, p. 159.

26 See chapter 8; Knowles, *Religious Orders*, III, p. 160.

legacy, should have been thought important enough to be taken up in a satirical play.

What made a retrospective defence of the suppressed houses so relevant in 1529 was the possibility that the government was intending to embark upon a second, far more significant, series of suppressions in the last years of the 1520s. For a number of years Wolsey had been considering a scheme for the creation of an unspecified number of new English bishoprics to be financed, like Cardinal College, from the incomes of suppressed religious houses. This time, however, the larger scale of the project required greater financial provision, so it was the greater abbeys which were targeted for conversion into cathedral churches. On 12 November 1528 the cardinal, again in conjunction with Campeggio, who had returned to England to examine the king's matrimonial problems, was granted a bull empowering him to investigate the viability of such a scheme, and to submit proposals for its implementation to Rome.[27] Then on 29 May 1529 a second bull authorized the execution of the plan, allowing the legates to dissolve the relevant monasteries and transform their occupants into secular canons.[28] Moreover, further bulls of 12 November 1528 and 30 April 1529 gave Wolsey still wider powers to dissolve religious houses with fewer than twelve inmates in order to eliminate those institutions unable to fulfil their proper functions. The powers created by these grants threatened a far more widespread attack upon the religious orders than had been undertaken in 1524–8.[29] Only Wolsey's fatal failure to obtain Henry his divorce, and Campeggio's subsequent departure, prevented the implementation of these schemes. The possibility that they might outlive their architect and be revived by the government in the future surely explains the anxiety of the lords spiritual to see the whole notion of suppressions as closely identified with the fallen minister as possible, and thus confined to the political wilderness with him.

It is in this context that the text of *Hester* should be read. The criticisms of Wolsey's authority implicit in the figure of Aman are in fact far more specific than has been suggested by previous commentators. They do not constitute simply an attack upon the cardinal's personal failings, but are a detailed critique of his legatine jurisdiction.

Ambitious clerks, it is claimed, cannot rise quickly to good livings, because Aman controls promotions.

> For yf yt be a good fee, Aman sayeth that longeth to me
> Be yt benefyce or parke,
>   If he espy to [that] . . . promotion, he wyll streyt geve him a portion,
> A lappe of a thowsande markes,
> He shalbe purged cleane (ll. 440–4)

---

[27] Ibid., p. 160.   [28] *LP*, IV (iii) 5667–8.

[29] I am further indebted to Peter Gwyn for the opportunity to read summaries of the chapters on religious reform in his forthcoming study of Wolsey in advance of publication.

This is not simply a generalized allegation of avarice, it is a reference to a specific aspect of Wolsey's legatine jurisdiction. For Wolsey was able, as legate *a latere*, to intervene in the prerogatives of all bishops within their dioceses, and appoint his nominees to the ecclesiastical livings in their hands through the process of prevention. Thus, in the words of the character Ambition,

> my lorde Aman
> Handelles all thynge so,
> That every office and fee, what so ever it bee,
> That maye bee sene and fonnde;
> By his wit he wyl it featche, and or it fal he wil it catche
> That never commeth to the grounde. (ll. 488–93)

Thus Aman's sycophantic nominees gain all the good benefices.

> They solde theyr woll, and purchased a bull,
> Wyth a pluralyte.[30]
>   And lefte predication, and toke adulation,
> And what by mendation, and dyspensation,
> They gat the nomynation, of every good benefyce.
>   So better by flatterynge, then by preachynge,
> To wealthe they dyd aryse. (ll. 430–6)

The same charge is made in the lords' articles, where the giving of benefices by prevention is cited as an example of Wolsey's interventionism,[31] as is the more general issue of exploitation of other's livings raised in the playwright's reference to the 'portion' demanded from each incumbent by Aman.[32]

> Also, the said, Lord Cardinal constrained all Ordinaries in *England*, yearly to compound with him, or else he will usurp halfe or the whole of their Jurisdiction, by prevention, not for the good order of the Diocese, but to extort treasure: for there is never a poore Arch-Deacon in England, but that he paid yearly to him a portion of his living.

There is a similar precision to the lines in which Ambition criticizes Aman's arrogance, and his contempt for learning. For the examples of the chancellor's behaviour which he cites to illustrate his contempt for learned men return us directly to those religious suppressions which are the central issue of the play. In claiming the right to reform the religious orders, those nominally exempt from external authority as well as those open to visitation, and in imposing his own regulations upon them, Wolsey was, the author suggests, vainly exulting his own wisdom above that of the founders of the houses and the creators of their rules.

---

[30] Another of Wolsey's legatine prerogatives was the right to grant dispensations to clerics holding more than one living.

[31] Herbert, *Life and Reigne*, p. 267, article VII.   [32] Ibid., p. 269.

> For all rewlers and lawes, were made by fooles and dawes
> He [Aman] sayeth verely.
>   Ordynances and foundation, without consyderation,
> He sayeth, were devysed.
> Therefore hys Imagination, brings all out of fashion
> And so all is dysguised. (ll. 459–64)

Perhaps the most obvious indication that Wolsey's legatine authority was the true target of the satire is provided by the extended exchange between Pride and the other vices concerning the need to draw up their wills. As a criticism of Wolsey this scene seems curiously oblique, until it is placed in the context of the legatine prerogative. Pride begins the exchange with the observation

> I hearde once a Fryer, as trewe a lyer,
> As anye in the countrey:
> Hee preachhed veramente, that our testamente
> Always readye shoulde bee.
>
> [Adulation:] For at our deathe, we shall lacke breathe,
> And than fare well wee. (ll. 502–7)

After the vices have each symbolically bequeathed their sinful qualities to Aman, they conclude their testaments.

> [Adulation:] . . . by my holydome, I wene it be wysedome,
> For folke often chat, howe men dye in estate [intestate],
> But so shall not wee:
> [Ambition:] No by Sainct An, but yet my Lorde Aman,
> Never the better shalbe:
> [Pride:] No forse so god me save, yf we our wyll myght have
> We woulde he shoulde never thee [thrive].
> Nowe made is our testament. (ll. 568–75)

The allegorical level to all this is quite clear. By bequeathing all their evil characteristics to Aman the vices do indeed ensure that he will never thrive. But there is a clear political meaning to the arguments too. For by ensuring that they do not die intestate, the vices are also ensuring that Wolsey does not benefit materially from their deaths. For under the terms of his legatine commission Wolsey had the right to appoint executors for the estates of those individuals who died intestate, or whose appointed executors would not undertake the task, regardless of the diocese in which the deceased resided. And the cardinal's officers seem vigorously to have pursued this right, particularly after 1523, when a composition between Wolsey and Archbishop Warham led to their exercising a joint jurisdiction throughout the southern province.[33] Thus not only did Wolsey (and Warham) have the right to exact probate fees for the proving of wills worth over 100s in their jurisdictions (a right which brought in the considerable sum of

---

[33] Kelly, 'Canterbury jurisdiction', pp. 60–1.

£530 4s 3d in 1529 alone), they could also take over completely the disposition of estates *ad viam intestati*, and those with unwilling executors. And under the joint administration the suspiciously high proportion of one in ten wills fell into the archbishops' hands through the latter means,[34] prompting allegations of intimidation which were formalized in article XVII of the lords' indictment.[35]

> Also, the Lord Cardinal, by his authority legatine, hath used, if any spirituall man having any riches or substance, deceased, he hath taken their goods as his own, by reason whereof their wills be not performed; And one mean he had, to put them in feare that were made Executors to refuse to meddle.

Again, like the appointments to benefices by prevention which undercut the ordinaries' rights of patronage, and the monastic visitations which intervened in hitherto exempt areas of religious self-regulation, this prerogative was exercised at the expense of others. In this case Wolsey and Warham between them contrived to annex the probate rights of their suffragan bishops who had to compound with their metropolitans in order to retain some of their income.

But if it is possible to identify the issues raised in the play by a comparison with the lords' articles, and with the political situation in late 1529, how are those issues treated, and to what end? Can the charges against Wolsey made directly in the articles, and implied in *Hester*, be accepted as accurate indictments of his administration? The analysis offered thus far might have given the impression of a rapacious legatine jurisdiction which aroused seemingly justified opposition from its victims. But to leave the discussion there would be to simplify the situation to the point of distortion. For there was rather more to the attacks of 1529 than heartfelt opposition to Wolsey himself. It cannot be denied that there were groups and individuals with genuine or imagined grievances against the cardinal who took the opportunity provided by his fall to gain a measure of personal revenge. Among these was Lord Darcy, who provided a series of charges of his own independent of the formal articles presented by his noble colleagues,[36] and who seems to have held Wolsey personally responsible for his own failure to obtain significant royal offices in the North. But beyond such isolated cases of real animosity, most of the apparent opposition to the cardinal was more subtly motivated and more opportunist than it at first appears.

There is little to suggest that the legatine jurisdiction had been exercised illegally. Indeed what evidence there is demonstrates that it was employed only conservatively in many areas. Even Warham, whose correspondence with Wolsey in the early 1520s, full of protests of injustice, is a major source of evidence for the rigorous enforcement of the authority, was permitted to retain many lucrative rights of advocation to his court of audience which Wolsey could have denied him, had he insisted on the full enjoyment of his prerogative.[37] Moreover, the extensive rights of patronage by prevention complained of both in

---

[34] Ibid. [35] Herbert, *Life and Reigne*, p. 269.
[36] *LP*, IV (iii) 5749. [37] Kelly, 'Canterbury jurisdiction', p. 177.

the articles and in the text of *Hester*, were also employed modestly, and then generally in favour of crown nominees rather than Wolsey's own. The legatine jurisdiction was not a corrupt dictatorship in the church conducted for Wolsey's benefit at everyone else's expense. There was certainly a considerable element of venality involved in its implementation which may offend modern perceptions of the religious vocation. But in the context of sixteenth-century episcopal politics this was nothing new. Financial disputes were endemic among the Henrician bishops, as each sought to protect and expand jealously guarded rights and privileges. Thus a degree of opposition to Wolsey's attempt to reconcile the episcopate to the new and overarching authority represented by his legacy was inevitable. All such innovations and attempts to widen prerogatives, however legally valid, aroused opposition. In the period before Wolsey's rise to power Archbishop Warham had undertaken a determined attempt to enforce his archiepiscopal prerogative rights at the expense of his suffragans, which had aroused such heated opposition, led by Bishop Fox of Winchester, that the king had had to intervene before it could be settled, and then with bad grace on both sides.[38] It would be entirely wrong to dismiss the attacks upon Wolsey at his fall as simply well justified grievances aroused by a novel legatine authority exercised by an abnormally rapacious individual. What prompted the opposition to the cardinal was the opportunity provided by his fall to throw off a financial burden and an intrusive jurisdiction, and to establish a claim for future independence.

The clergy were under no illusions about where the real authority behind the jurisdiction lay. It was Henry's influence which had secured Wolsey the legatine commission, and it was Henry's word which could remove it.[39] Hence the appeal to the king inherent in both the lords' articles and *Hester*.[40] But such an appeal had to be carefully worded, for the king who could appoint and dismiss Wolsey could always arrange for another to replace him, and removing Wolsey would be of no benefit to the English clergy if it simply meant his replacement as legate by another royal nominee, particularly if, as was rumoured in 1529, Henry was listening to those who argued for a general despoliation of the church to reduce it to its 'primitive' state.[41] Nor would the lot of the bishops of the southern province be greatly improved if the removal of the legatine jurisdiction led simply to the restoration of Archbishop Warham's own burdensome metropolitan regime. What was needed was so to criticize Wolsey and the legacy that the one was irrevocably linked to the other, and so the political neutralization of the man

[38] Ibid., pp. 45–92.
[39] Hence the tacit acceptance on the part of both Wolsey and the duke of Norfolk, whom the king had sent to him with a message, that Henry had deprived the cardinal of his legacy after his dismissal from office, despite the fact that the legatine commission from Pope Clement in 1524 had been for life: Cavendish, p. 116.
[40] Aman, it must be noted, was both appointed and dismissed by King Assewerus. There is no attempt to portray his authority as a 'foreign' jurisdiction, as the legacy technically was.
[41] *LP*, IV (iii) 5416–17 and 6011.

would leave the unwanted aspects of his legatine prerogative too unpopular to be revived. In the long term, of course, this strategy was to prove fruitless. The royal supremacy in the church, the creation of the vicegerency and the dissolution of the monasteries, more than realized the clergy's worst fears of interventionism, and answered the appeals for personal royal government voiced in *Hester* in decisive and unwelcome manner. But in the short term it may have enjoyed more success. For no attempt was made to appoint a legate in Wolsey's stead, and Warham, albeit he quickly began to reassert the rights of his prerogative courts upon Wolsey's fall,[42] was not to attempt to enforce his rights with the same vigour as he had prior to the legacy.

III

The arguments advanced earlier have stressed the close association between the case against Aman presented in *Hester* and the charges against Wolsey contained in the lords' articles. Both the interlude and the articles, or at least that portion of them which deals with clerical grievances, share a common strategy. Both disguise what are essentially pleas for greater clerical independence with a veneer of concern for royal authority. In order to make their protests politically acceptable to the crown, both documents stress the damage done to the royal prerogative by the exercise of Wolsey's legatine jurisdiction, whilst at the same time presenting complaints which actually concern the infringement of clerical liberties. Always the damage done to the bishops and the regular clergy is portrayed as damage to the crown.

In the first of the articles, which is concerned with the alleged spoliation of the monasteries and bishops' prerogatives, it is the infringement of Henry's own 'prescription' which is stressed. Wolsey had, the lords alleged, obtained the legacy,[43]

> by reason whereof he hath not only hurt your said prescription, but also . . . hath spoiled and taken away from many houses of Religion in this your Realm, much substance of their goods. And also hath usurped upon all your ordinaries within this your Realm much part of their jurisdiction, in derogation of your Prerogative, and to the great hurt of the said Ordinaries, Prelates, and Religious.

Other clerical grievances are similarly presented as defences of the royal dignity. Wolsey's legatine visitations are described as 'to the great extortion of your subjects, and derogation of your laws'. The legacy itself is described as being exercised 'contrary to your gracious Prerogative or Regality', and the execution of the estates of a number of deceased clergymen is termed 'contrary to their wills and your lawes and Justice'.[44]

The author of *Hester* pursues an identical strategy. The play is written as an

[42] Kelly, 'Canterbury jurisdiction', p. 202.   [43] Herbert, *Life and Reigne*, p. 266.
[44] Ibid., pp. 270–1, articles xxv, xxvii and xxx.

appeal to the king, figured in the character of Assewerus, to exert himself and dismiss his legate, ruling personally in his stead. But a closer reading of the text reveals that what the author is actually asking for is a greater degree of self-regulation for the clergy, free from interference of any kind, whether legatine or royal.

The story of Esther drawn from the Old Testament, is framed in the play by a discussion of the responsibilities of a monarch, which finally insists upon the need for the king to dispense with the services of favourites and lieutenants and take up the reins of government himself. Given that in the original story King Ahasuerus had merely removed Haman and replaced him with a new 'lieutenant', Mordecai, this discussion would seem curiously incompatible with the tale it envelopes, were that simply a biblical drama. But in the context of the play's political intentions this 'framing debate' is clearly relevant to the main text.

The opening scene of the play has King Assewerus consulting his council regarding the best means of distributing honours among his subjects. The question arises, where should true honour be bestowed? It is quickly established that virtue should be honoured above all other qualities, and that among the virtues pertaining particularly to a prince, justice is the most admirable. But this moral is taken further by the 'Third Gentleman', who suggests that justice is of no value without the diligence required to implement it. And that diligence must, he argues, be found with the prince himself, 'in his owne person' (l. 64). It is only through strong personal rule that a sovereign brings honour to his realm. For, without such a personal involvement and commitment to good government on the part of the one man who is above temptation, the machinery of justice will appear to be merely an instrument of advancement employed by self-interested courtiers. Even the renowned justice of Solomon, the Gentleman suggests, would have been less effective

> If by hys lieutenante had been done the same,
> Hys honoure shoulde never have spronge so farre . . .
> Nor yet hys subjectes to suche awe and feare,
> He coulde have dryven by no meanes at all
> As he dyd by hys justice personall
> And over thys many a noble man,
> At the prynces Wyll and commaundymente,
> To employe justice, dyd the best they can
> And yet the commons unneth coulde be content
> And why? for in their mynde they thyncke verament
> That either for riches and honour Justis will doe
> And he onely, for the zeale that to Justis he hath to
> Wherefore noble prince, if in youre owne person will ye
> Employe Justis the more youre honour shallbe.

(ll. 71–2, 75–86)

What follows in the play proper is, in effect, the education of Assewerus in the wisdom of this advice. Only after the misfortunes of Aman's ascendancy have been experienced is the lesson brought home to the king. Only then is he able to offer the audience the ostensible moral of the play.

> My Lordes by this fygure ye may well se,
> The multitude hurte by the heades necligence,
> If to his pleasure so geven is he,
> That he will no paine take nor dilligence,
> Who careth not for his cure ofte loseth credence. (ll. 1162–6)

Thus on one level the moral debate complements the satiric theme of the Hester story. The drama whose intention was to criticize Wolsey's legatine authority was contained within a debate which demonstrated that kings ought not to trust such lieutenants as Wolsey with the exercise of authority. But, just as the lords' articles carried the subtext that the best way to preserve the royal prerogative was to restore the traditional liberties of the bishops and the religious orders, so the play insists, despite its call for the king to govern personally, upon the right of the clergy to govern themselves. When Hester gains the removal of Aman, and pleads for the pardon of the Jews, she begs that

> The precepte youre grace sente at Amans desyre,
> Againste me and all the Jewishe nation,
> May be revoked and upon convocation
> A new devised by them that can do best,
> And that sente forthe to set the Jewes at reste. (ll. 1083–7)

The arguments advanced earlier in the play by Hester concerning the divine origins of the religious orders and their immunity from all but divine suppression, are here taken to their logical conclusion in the plea that the churchmen should decide for themselves how they should be governed in future. Significantly Hester requests that 'them that can do best', evidently the clergy themselves, decide their fate, rather than that Assewerus simply contradict his 'precepte' with a new proclamation. In the biblical original the future of the Jews was settled rather more simply and directly. Esther begged Ahasuerus to write new letters to cancel those sent at Haman's request.[45]

> Then the King Ahasuerus said unto Esther the queen and to Mordecai the Jew . . .
> Write ye also for the Jews, as it liketh you, in the King's name, and seal it with the
> King's ring: for the writing which is written in the King's name, and sealed with the
> King's ring, may no man reverse.

At Mordecai's instructions the King's scribes then take down and despatch new directives, permitting the Jews to take revenge upon their enemies.

For all the play's rhetoric concerning the need for a vigorous personal monarchy, the author chooses to omit entirely this declaration of royal authority from his play. Instead of giving Assewerus the chance to reassert his authority over the Jews/church at Aman's fall, he introduces the call for collective, and by definition independent, self-regulation by convocation. This exposes his true

---

[45] Esther, 8:7.

intentions at their most obvious. It may well have been expedient to appeal to the king to act decisively in extinguishing the legatine authority, but it was certainly no part of the author's intention to encourage Henry to take over himself the intrusive regulation of religious affairs which the legacy entailed. To replace one overlord with another was not what was intended. Hence the need, not only for the attack upon the person of the legate, designed to gain the removal of the legacy, but also the stress upon the benefits of a return to the traditional forms of clerical self-regulation. The play has come a long way from a simple denunciation of Wolsey's personality and character.

Hester is, then, an interesting document from an historical viewpoint. It takes us into the midst of the debate surrounding Wolsey's fall and the administration of the church in its aftermath. Thus it is frustrating that so little can be teased from it concerning its author or place of performance. From the material included in the play and the manner in which the text sought to influence royal opinion, it is clear where the author's sympathies lay. It would thus be tempting to attribute authorship, and involvement with the lords' articles to the same source, perhaps a small group of clerics and laymen opposed to both the legatine authority and the more alarming religious reforms beginning to be mooted at court. Given the sympathetic allusions to Catherine of Aragon inherent in the figure of Hester, it would also be tempting to locate this group among those men and women who favoured her side of the 'divorce' debate. And perhaps a performance in or around the court during the Christmas period 1529–30 was intended. But beyond such tentative suggestions little can be said with any confidence.

More can be said about the text in relation to other literary attacks upon Wolsey. *Hester* is a play, not so much about Wolsey, as about the legatine commission. The author includes material critical of Wolsey's character and lifestyle, but he does so primarily to flesh out the portrait of the cardinal as a tyrant in a conventional mould. The play's main political strategy is not to blacken Wolsey's reputation, but to use a reputation already blackened by royal criticism of the cardinal to blacken by analogy the real object of the author's hostility: central interference in the running of the religious houses and diocesan admin-istration. It takes its lead from the royal signal that Wolsey was 'fair game', and uses the consequent atmosphere of anti-Wolsey criticism for its own ends. In this it provides a model for much of the political poetry and drama of the period.

Wolsey's position as head of the church in England and chief minister of the crown made him the inevitable target of complaint. Indeed, as the lightning conductor protecting the king from potentially damaging criticism it was part of his job to do just that.[46] Thus, when one reads what appear to be personal attacks

---

[46] Note in this context his collaboration in the fictional explanation of the failure of the Amicable Grant in 1525. When the demand collapsed in the face of widespread unwillingness (or inability) to pay, Wolsey accepted the blame for the affair, claiming to have initiated the demand without royal knowledge or approval. Thus the cardinal attracted the criticism and the odium of failure, whilst

upon Wolsey the individual it is always necessary to ask whether these are indeed what they seem, or simply another incarnation of the venerable convention of visiting the perceived political sins of the monarch (or any aspect of current policy which fails to find favour) onto his closest advisers.

More specifically, it is hardly surprising that such attacks upon Wolsey increased after July 1529, once the king had clearly signalled his displeasure with the minister and appeared to encourage his denigration. In such circumstances the ability to present criticisms of the newly marginalized minister became a political virtue and a means of obtaining the royal ear. Thus Henry's actions predictably provoked a plethora of responses. And, equally predictably, the authors of a number of such responses saw the opportunity which the exercise provided for the pursuit of their own ends, and laced the material required of them with arguments, suggestions and petitions of their own.

To say that such literature *uses* Wolsey as well as abuses him is not, however, to deny that the cardinal aroused opposition in some quarters. But it is important to identify the specific nature of the criticism to which he was subjected. Where Wolsey does seem to have aroused antipathy – among the citizens of London for example – it was in circumstances in which he, acting as the agent of the crown, made demands, both financial and jurisdictional, which aroused resentment.

As the commissioner who personally presented the city with royal demands for the general proscription and forced loans of 1522, who acted as the intermediary between king and parliament for the subsidy of 1523 and who presented the 'request' for the Amicable Grant of 1525 – all major financial demands which the city found it difficult to meet – Wolsey could hardly avoid provoking the hostility of the citizens. And the same is true of the relationship between the cardinal in his role as papal legate and the sections of the church which he sought to discipline and reform.

The apparent outburst of anti-Wolsey feeling which followed his disgrace in 1529 must, then, be examined with some care. Far from indicating a general popular hatred of the cardinal and widespread satisfaction at his fall, it was comprised of a strictly limited number of discrete elements. Moreover, many of these were the product more of concerns for the future – over how policy would be determined and implemented in the post-Wolsey era – than of genuine interest in Wolsey himself. Hence the renewed concern on the part of the London burgesses concerning clerical exaction and Wolsey's financial demands, which surfaced in the invective *Impeachment of Wolsey* and in the grievances put before the first session of the Reformation Parliament; hence also the revival of protests at the monastic dissolutions and the interventions in the dioceses voiced in the *Impeachment*, in *Hester* and in the lords' articles. Both of these protests were moti-

Henry emerged unscathed from a potentially dangerous political crisis (for an account of the demand see G. W. Bernard, *War, Taxation and Rebellion in Early Tudor England* (Brighton, 1986)).

vated by a desire to see the policies concerned condemned along with their instrument.

Perhaps paradoxically, what a study of *Hester* and the lords' articles also suggests is that criticism of Wolsey, although strictly limited in both extent and motivation, was actually less homogeneous than has sometimes been suggested. It seems that, from the moment of his initial disgrace, not only was there an evangelical attack upon his character and methods of government, voiced by William Tyndale and others, which aimed at the vilification of the Roman church for which Wolsey provided a convenient symbol, but there was also a conservative reaction against him, albeit of a limited extent and of a more subtle nature than might have been expected. This latter capitalized upon Henry's dissatisfaction with Wolsey, using it as the excuse to present arguments against increased central interference in the affairs of the church. For this group, as with the evangelicals, it was not Wolsey himself, but what he could be made to represent, which made him a useful object of abuse.

Such opposition from within the church was not aroused by frustration with Wolsey's alleged opposition to reform, with the poor example which he set of worldly prelacy in action, or with any of the other aspects of his personality which are usually cited as the cause of his unpopularity. Far from reflecting righteous indignation at the venality of the cardinal's financial exactions, or an Erasmian reaction against worldliness, the arguments contained in both *Hester* and the lords' articles articulate a desire that such worldly instruments as probate fees and ecclesiastical court jurisdictions be merely returned to episcopal control. What we see reflected, both here and in much of the other anti-Wolsey literature of the period, is a financial and jurisdictional struggle of the sort which dogged the late medieval church, not a novel moral or factional campaign provoked by unacceptable aspects of Wolsey's personality.

CHAPTER 10

Playing check-mate with royal majesty? Wolsey's patronage of Italian Renaissance sculpture

P. G. LINDLEY

Set up a wretch on hye,
In a trone triumphantlye,
Make him a great astate,
And he wyll play checke mate
With ryall majeste
Counte himselfe as good as he[1]

Only a few fragments survive today of Cardinal Wolsey's patronage of sculpture and this may explain why little effort has been made to assess its importance.[2] The study has, however, a good deal to commend it. Wolsey's most costly sculptural project, his own tomb, can be conjecturally reconstructed on the basis of surviving evidence and its size, ostentation and magnificence reveal much about the cardinal's own self-image and the image he wished to convey to posterity. Its original significance can be gauged by the fact that Henry VIII's own, even grander, monument was clearly inspired by it and that its artist, and even its cannibalized materials, were employed for the royal tomb. Although Wolsey's tomb was undoubtedly his greatest individual sculptural commission, his employment of Italian artists to produce architectural terracottas for the exteriors, and marble fireplaces for the interiors, of his domestic buildings, as well as terracotta figure sculpture for his Oxford college, serves to underline the cardinal's role in consolidating the bridgehead of Italian Renaissance influence in England. This alien style had already reached the country before the death of Henry VII,[3] and had received powerful court endorsement in the commissioning

[1] Skelton, 'Why come ye nat to courte?', ll. 585–90. I am grateful to the Master and Fellows of St Catharine's College, Cambridge, for the Research Fellowship which enabled me to begin work on this essay and to the President and Fellows of the British Academy for the Postdoctoral Research Fellowship which has enabled me to complete it. Richard Morris, Paul Williamson and Simon Thurley have kindly commented on an earlier draft of the paper.

[2] The fundamental study remains that of A. Higgins, 'On the work of Florentine Sculptors in England in the early part of the sixteenth century; with special reference to the tombs of Cardinal Wolsey and King Henry VIII', *Archaeological Journal*, 51 (1894), 129–200.

[3] The often repeated claim that Torrigiano brought the Italian Renaissance to Tudor England (most recently A. P. Darr, 'European sculpture and decorative arts acquired by the Detroit Institute of Arts 1978–87', *Burlington Magazine*, 130 (1988), 495) cannot be sustained. Quite apart from the

of the Florentine sculptor Pietro Torrigiano to produce Margaret Beaufort's tomb in November 1511 and that of Henry VII and Queen Elizabeth of York in October 1512 (plate 56).[4] Scrutiny of Wolsey's patronage demonstrates that by the time of his fall, Renaissance styles were being competently reproduced in England not just by French and Flemish craftsmen but also by native artists. The aims of this paper are therefore four-fold: to reconstruct, on the basis of documentary and other evidence, the form of Wolsey's tomb monument in order to analyse what it can tell us about the cardinal's aims and ideology; to examine briefly its subsequent history; to place it in the context of his other sculptural patronage; and, finally, to examine what significance, if any, this patronage had for Wolsey's contemporaries and for the future.

It is ironic in view of subsequent events that the first evidence for Wolsey's connection with a tomb commission is in the context of the earliest, abortive, project for a monument to Henry VIII and Queen Catherine.[5] In a holograph letter of 1518 now preserved in the British Library, Pietro Torrigiano wrote to Wolsey, expressing his wish to go to Florence, so that he could complete the high altar of Henry VII's Chapel (the contract for which he had received in March 1517) and urging the cardinal to finalize, before he left, arrangements for the works

mid-fifteenth-century penetration of Italian Renaissance forms into England (e.g. the manuscript of Synesius Cyrenensis, *De Laudibus Calvitii* (MS Bodl. 80) translated into Latin from the Greek by John Free for his patron John Tiptoft, illuminated in Padua *c.* 1460–1, and with, on fol. 4v, the title written as if it were on a monument, with classical columns, capitals, pediment and marbled base: see O. Pächt and J. J. G. Alexander, *Illuminated Manuscripts in the Bodleian Library, Oxford, Italian School* (Oxford, 1970), p. 62, pl. LIX, 608a), there are fine examples of Renaissance art in the manuscript illuminations to the poems lauding Henry VII, by the itinerant poet John Michael Nagonius, who visited England in the last decade of the fifteenth century (York Minster Library MS XVI N 2 was unfortunately unknown to F. Wormald, 'An Italian poet at the court of Henry VII', *Journal of the Warburg and Courtauld Institutes*, 14 (1951), 118–19). See also the memorandum on the administration of the Hospital of Santa Maria Nuova in Florence drawn up by Francesco Portinari for Henry VII (Oxford, Bodleian Library MS Bodl. 488) of which fol. 3 is illustrated in F. Saxl and R. Wittkower, *British Art and the Mediterranean* (Oxford, 1948), p. 36.4. Torrigiano was not, almost certainly, even the first Italian Renaissance sculptor to work in England: that honour probably belongs to Guido Mazzoni, who visited England, to design a tomb for King Henry VII, in 1506 (see B. H. Meyer, 'The first tomb of Henry VII of England', *Art Bulletin*, 58 (1976), 358–67; T. Verdon, *The Art of Guido Mazzoni* (New York, 1980), pp. 139–40 and 340–2, with (fig. 91) a reconstruction of Mazzoni's design; see also J. Larson, 'A polychrome terracotta bust of a laughing child at Windsor Castle', *Burlington Magazine*, 131 (1989), 618–24; P. G. Lindley, 'Una grande opera al mio Re: Gilt-bronze effigies in England from the Middle Ages to the Renaissance', *Journal of the British Archaeological Association*, 143 (1990), 112–30). Renaissance works arrived in England as papal gifts and, doubtless, were brought by the Italian mercantile community; the style was also imported, for instance, through the intermediary of French and Flemish manuscripts and books: so that, even if one excludes Raphael's Washington panel of St George (H. S. Ettlinger, 'The question of Raphael's garter', *Burlington Magazine*, 125 (1983), 25–9), often thought to have been brought to England by Castiglione as a gift from Duke Guidobaldo da Montefeltre in 1506, there is a good deal of scattered evidence for the penetration of the Renaissance into England by the death of Henry VII.

[4] *HKW*, III, pp. 218–21; most recently, see Lindley, 'Una grande opera', 113.

[5] Higgins, 'Sculptors', 142.

that Wolsey had promised to obtain for him from Henry VIII;[6] on his return from Florence, Torrigiano would bring back with him the necessary artists and materials. The draft indenture of 5 January 1519 for a monument to King Henry VIII and Queen Catherine which this letter evidently elicited, survives in the Public Record Office.[7] In addition to containing useful information about the (lost) earlier contract for Henry VII's and Queen Elizabeth's monument, it reveals that the new tomb was to cost £2,000, and that it was to be of the same materials as the earlier monument but 'more grettir by the iiijth parte'. Wolsey's role in the commission, as with so much else at the height of his power, was decisive and explicit. The tomb's 'patrone' or 'example' was to be 'after suche manner and forme' as 'shalbe ordered and assigned' by the cardinal.[8] In other words, Torrigiano was to deal directly with Wolsey rather than with the king in designing Henry VIII's and Queen Catherine's tomb. Another clause states that the king was to decide where the tomb was to be set up after its completion, for which four years were allowed. If no place were to be assigned, the sculptor's responsibility to assemble the monument was to be discharged:[9] it is generally assumed that the inclusion of this clause implies that Henry was not very interested in the whole project. The fact that the commission never progressed beyond the stage of a draft indenture must not be allowed, however, to conceal the extraordinary fact that Henry had, in effect, been prepared to delegate control of the form of his monument to Wolsey. Ultimately, of course, the cardinal's position depended on the personal favour and trust of the king, but this draft contract provides tangible evidence of how far Wolsey was enabled by such trust to arrogate decision making to himself. In the same year that the contract was drafted, the Venetian diplomat Sebastian Giustinian stated that 'this Cardinal is the person who rules both the King and the entire kingdom'.[10] This seriously misjudges Wolsey's actual position, but it is easy to see how such an essentially practical view could have been formed.

Although nothing came of this project for a monument for Henry VIII,[11] by 1

---

[6] BL, Titus B vii, fol. 324; E. J. L. Scott, 'A letter of Torregiano', *Athenaeum*, 2743, 22 May 1880, 670–1; Higgins, 'Sculptors', Appendix I.

[7] PRO, SP1/18, pp. 2–5. I am indebted to Margaret Condon for sending me a xerox copy of this document. It is published by W. Illingworth, 'Transcript of a draft of an indenture of covenants for the erecting of a tomb to the memory of King Henry the Eighth, and Queen Katherine his wife', *Archaeologia*, 16 (1812), 84–8.

[8] PRO, SP1/18, p. 3.

[9] It was customary for the sculptor or contractor to set up the monument in a specified place.

[10] R. Brown (ed.), *Four Years at the Court of Henry VIII* (London, 1854), II, p. 314. In May 1516 (ibid., I, p. 227) Giustinian states of Wolsey that 'the will of this most serene King rests in his hands'. Giustinian found by experience that it was necessary to have recourse to the cardinal in all matters, and that, 'should it be requisite to neglect either the King or the Cardinal, it would be better to pass over his Majesty', *CSPV 1509–19*, p. 521. In 1516 he describes him as 'rex et autor omnium' (*Four Years*, I, p. 160).

[11] See also M. Mitchell, 'Works of art from Rome for Henry VIII: a study of anglo-papal relations as reflected in papal gifts to the English king', *Journal of the Warburg and Courtauld Institutes*, 34 (1971), 178–203 and n. 28 below for later projects for Henry VIII's tomb.

June 1524, at the latest, work on Wolsey's own tomb had begun, with another major Florentine sculptor, Benedetto da Rovezzano, in charge of its construction. The evidence for this survives in a letter from Benedetto, dating from 30 June 1529, before Wolsey's fall, but when the latter's position was increasingly uncertain in the light of his increasing difficulties in securing the king's divorce. However, its immediate cause was not Wolsey's sense of impending catastrophe but his instruction, conveyed through Thomas Cromwell, for the sculptor to account for his dealings with Antonio Cavallari, who had just died; Cavallari, purveyor of gold and silver cloths to the king and an important member of the Lucchese mercantile community in London, had acted as Wolsey's funding agent for the tomb.[12] The sculptor explained that his agreement with Cavallari had been a verbal one, that the tomb should not be inferior in workmanship, magnificence or cost to the tomb of Henry VII ('quod non esset minoris operis, decoris et pretii quam sit tumba serenissimi regis Henrici VII').[13] Money was advanced to him as he needed it for the purchase of materials, payment of workmen and expenses, with the understanding that when the tomb was finished it was to be valued by experienced and trustworthy persons, on the basis of the price of Henry VII's monument, regard being had to the superior size of Wolsey's.[14] The cost of the gilding was to be separately assessed as it was not Benedetto's responsibility: we learn from an undated but obviously earlier letter, since it is from Cavallari, that the gilder came from Antwerp and that £380 13s 0d had already been laid out on gilding, only half of which was complete.[15] In total it was going to cost four times the £200 laid out on the gilding of Henry VII's tomb. Between 1 June 1524 and 3 May 1529, 4,250 ducats (£956 5s 0d) had already been spent on the tomb which, according to its maker, was twice as sumptuous, beautiful and skilful as that of Henry VII. Benedetto was anxious to remind Wolsey that he had also been promised both the commission for the high altar of the cardinal's Oxford College

[12] W. Page (ed.), *Letters of Denization and Acts of Naturalization for Aliens in England 1509–1603*, Publications of the Huguenot Society of London, 8 (1893), p. 46. J. Lees-Milne, *Tudor Renaissance* (London, 1951), p. 31, has perpetuated the mistake that Cavallari was one of the workmen. For the Italian merchants, see M. E. Bratchel, 'Italian merchant organisation and business relationships in early Tudor London', *Journal of European Economic History*, 7/1 (1978), pp. 5–32 and G. D. Ramsay, 'The undoing of the Italian mercantile community in sixteenth century London', in N. B. Harte and K. G. Ponting (eds.), *Textile History and Economic History: Essays in Honour of Miss Julia de Lacy Mann* (Manchester, 1973), pp. 22–49.

[13] For an examination of the working procedures for the construction of monuments featuring gilt-bronze effigies in medieval and Renaissance England, see Lindley, 'Una grande opera'.

[14] Jesus College, Oxford, MS 74, fols. 189–90 (pencil foliation), fols. 251–2; Higgins, 'Sculptors', 201–2. Higgins mistakenly described the Masters manuscripts as housed in Cambridge, whereas they are in fact on loan to the Bodleian. Benedetto's letter reveals Wolsey's confidence both in the artist and in Cavallari, and presupposes an agreed model. Effective control of work, subject only to financial constraints imposed through Cavallari, seems to have lain in the hands of the sculptor. Benedetto was himself, it is clear from the letter, also responsible for procuring the materials.

[15] Jesus College, Oxford, MS 74, fol. 191 (a small piece of paper bound into the MS). This is an abstract of Cavallari's letter.

and, more importantly, the commission for Henry VIII's tomb.[16] This attempt to obtain further commissions tends to reinforce other evidence that the sculptor's work on Wolsey's tomb was close to completion.

An inventory drawn up by Benedetto, possibly in October or November 1530, reveals, in fact, precisely how far work had progressed on the monument by Wolsey's fall. The inventory may predate a letter from Wolsey to Cromwell which includes instructions for Cromwell to obtain the sending to York 'of myne image with such part of the tombe as it shall please the King that I shall (have) to the intent that now at my being at my church (of York) I may order and dispose the same for my Buryall which is like, by reason of my heaviness, to be shortly'.[17] The phrase 'with such part of the tomb as it shall please the King that I shall (have)' appears to indicate Wolsey's awareness that Henry VIII intended to make use of its materials. Indeed, the king no more hesitated over plundering Wolsey's tomb than he had earlier delayed in depriving him of York Place, or later paused before redeploying part of the clerestorey of Rewley Abbey Church as a bowling alley at Hampton Court.[18]

Two versions of Benedetto's inventory exist: the shorter one appears to have been drawn up by the artist himself[19] and includes materials unrelated to the tomb project, whilst the other gives slightly more detailed information about the tomb components, including comments on the gilding, which was not the sculptor's responsibility. As far as the tomb is concerned, the only significant difference between them concerns the number of escutcheons with the cardinal's arms and those of the churches to which he had been promoted. The two versions, therefore, can be used in conjunction with one another. The first half of the longer inventory is entitled 'For the King's Highness' and includes those materials which could be re-used in Henry's tomb whilst the second, listing 'Things to be ordered at the King's pleasure' includes the following items, all of which embodied a personal reference to the cardinal and could not simply be redeployed:

1 the image of the cardinal
2 two griffins to go at the feet of the image
3 a cardinal's hat with 12 buttons on strings of copper
4 two escutcheons with the cardinal's arms
5 ten (or fourteen) scutcheons with the arms of the cardinal and the arms of the churches to which he had been promoted

[16] For an intervening (*c.* 1521) project by Baccio Bandinelli for a tomb for Henry VIII, see Mitchell, 'Works of art from Rome', 178–203.

[17] Jesus College, Oxford MS 74, fol. 192 (pen pagination 255); Higgins, 'Sculptors', 163.

[18] *HKW*, IV, pp. 21 and 300–5.

[19] For the inventory (PRO, SP1/52, fols. 22r–24v), see Higgins, 'Sculptors', 203–5 and *LP*, IV (ii) 5113. R. W. Carden, 'The Italian artists in England during the sixteenth century', *Proceedings of the Society of Antiquaries of London*, 24 (1911–12), 171–205, criticizes (195) Higgins' assumption that the shorter draft is the work of Benedetto himself, but the inventory was doubtless translated into English from Benedetto's Italian text.

6 twelve figures of saints each a foot high[20]

7 a crucifix (possibly reflecting the silver high cross 'made after the fashion of that of Cardinal Campeggio' supplied by Robert Amadas[21])

8 two legatine pillars 'keped of the ij angells in their handes'

All of these items were of copper, and each (with the exception of the small coats of arms, which may have been enamelled) is described as fully gilt and burnished. They were all, evidently, ready for assembly. The parts of the tomb which were available for reuse[22] were the following:

1 four nine-foot tall pillars of copper 'curyouslye graven'. Each was constructed of ten sections; only half of one pillar had been gilt and burnished.

2 four kneeling angels to stand at the head and foot of the tomb; each angel was 2 feet 8 inches high. These were gilt and burnished.

3 four 3 feet 4 inches tall angels holding candlesticks, to stand on the great pillars; none had yet been gilded.

4 four 'naked children', 2 feet 9 inches tall, to stand at the head and feet of the tomb to hold the coats of arms. All were gilt and burnished.

5 two large pieces of copper 'garnysshed with sondrye devyses' for the epitaphs, to be fixed to each side of the tomb, each 3 and a half feet long and 2 feet tall, not gilt. Clearly, these had, as yet, no inscriptions.

6 a tomb of touch stone, 7 feet long, 4 feet wide and 2 and a half feet high. It was made in four pieces.

7 four one and a half foot long leaves of copper, for the corners of the tomb; ungilt.

8 the tomb base comprising twelve pieces of black touch and eight pieces of the (more expensive) white marble. It was 8 feet long, 4 feet 4 inches broad and 2 feet high.

9 a step of black touch in eight pieces on which to stand the four great pillars, 9 feet long by 8 feet broad.

10 seven pieces of copper 'lyke cloth of gold' to 'lye uppon' the tomb, all gilt and burnished.

11 four small pillars of copper for the corners of an altar, 4 feet 6 inches high, ungilded.[23]

[20] These doubtless included some of the following: Saints Peter, Paul, Andrew, Margaret, Catherine, Eustace, George, John the Baptist, John the Evangelist, Mary Magdalene, Barbara, Anne, Nicholas, Antony, William of York, James and Philip; these figured in the inventories of York Place and Cawood.

[21] *LP*, IV (iii) 6748 (5).

[22] To my mind, the wording of the inventory need not imply, as Higgins, 'Sculptors', 160 and Mitchell, 'Works of art from Rome', 191, following him, believe, that the 'sarcophagus, base and platform . . . and also the four columns which stood on the platform' were already *in situ* in the Lady Chapel of St George's, Windsor. The fact that there are no fixing marks on the surviving sarcophagus as well as the evidence that most of the columns had still to be gilded, strongly suggests that they all remained in the sculptor's workshop and had yet to be assembled. An indication that the wording cannot be taken unequivocally to prove that items were already in place is provided by the tense change between the first and second versions of the inventory: where the latter has 'A pece lyke clothe of gold in vij peces *standing* upon the tombe', the former has '*to lye* uppon the said tombe' (my emphasis). In general, a tomb would not be set up until all its components had been finished.

[23] These pillars only appear on the longer list. Higgins suggests that it may have been intended to gild all the other ungilded items. This seems very improbable. Clearly, the gilding and burnishing

We never hear again of the eight items in the first group: they must all have been melted down for reuse.[24] The items in the second part of the list could, however, be re-employed as the nucleus of Henry VIII's huge monument – much as Hampton Court and York Place were extended by the king.[25] Henry's tomb, on which Benedetto was now put to work from December 1530 onwards together with Giovanni da Maiano, the other great Italian sculptor employed by Wolsey, was itself never finally completed.[26] Edward VI and Queen Mary seem to have intended to set Henry's tomb up, but never did anything towards this end;[27] Elizabeth funded an expensive model of it in 1574 and also had a survey made of the incomplete monument, but it was never actually erected although it was moved from Westminster to Windsor in 1565.[28] It stood, unfinished but largely intact, in what is now the Prince Consort's Chapel at Windsor until 1645 when the bronze imagery was defaced and sold to pay the Windsor garrison; with the exception of four candlesticks at Ghent, it has now all disappeared.[29] The unda-maged marble sarcophagus and base pillaged from Wolsey's tomb were, however, left in place since their materials were not intrinsically valuable and they were devoid of offensive imagery. They have an extraordinary subsequent history. In 1808, they were moved from Windsor to St Paul's Cathedral: it had been decided that the most fitting use for the redundant remains was to employ them for the tomb of Lord Nelson.[30] To this day, the marble sarcophagus and base can be seen in the crypt of St Paul's (plate 57). The details, dimensions and con-struction of Nelson's sarcophagus as well as considerable documentary evidence for the move from Windsor conclusively prove that it is the one mentioned in

was the last stage of work before shipping and assembly of the tomb and some of this work had still not been completed.

[24] It is unfortunate that the reconstruction of Wolsey's tomb by S. M. Hardie, 'Cardinal Wolsey's patronage of the arts', unpublished M. Litt. thesis, Bristol University 1982, Chapter 2, is based on a mis-identification of Henry VIII's tomb with that of Wolsey. The tomb seen in 1600 by Baron Waldstein (G. W. Groos (transl.), *The Diary of Baron Waldstein* (London, 1981), p. 145) was that of the king.

[25] Higgins, 'Sculptors', 164; *HKW*, IV, pp. 126ff and 300ff; S. Thurley, 'Henry VIII and the building of Hampton Court; a reconstruction of the Tudor palace', *Architectural History*, 31 (1988), 1–57. Cf. also the replacement of Wolsey's arms on the Clock Tower at Hampton Court.

[26] Higgins, 'Sculptors', 164ff for the work of Benedetto da Rovezzano, Giovanni da Maiano and others from 1530–6; Prof. Biddle has shown that work was still in progress in 1543: M. Biddle, 'Nicholas Bellin of Modena: an Italian artificer at the courts of Francis I and Henry VIII', *Journal of the British Archaeological Association*, 29 (1966), 106–121.

[27] Higgins, 'Sculptors', 165.

[28] Ibid., p. 166 and Appendix VII for the reports to the lord treasurer on the work necessary to complete Henry VIII's tomb (BL, MS Lansdowne CXVI. 13 fols. 49–50). See also BL, MS Lansdowne 94 fols. 27–27v for a 'Description of the tombe of K. Hen ye 8th' noted by Mitchell, 'Works of art from Rome', 192, n. 87, and apparently unknown to Higgins. See also E. Auerbach, *Tudor Artists* (London, 1954), p. 143, and *HKW*, III, pp. 320–1.

[29] For which see Higgins, 'Sculptors', 177–81, 186–9 and Appendix VIII, citing *Journals of the House of Commons*, III, 348, IV, 279, 468, 502, 505, and *Journals of the House of Lords*, VIII, 247 and 261.

[30] Higgins, 'Sculptors', 160–3.

Benedetto's 1530 inventory. The base, too, originated in Wolsey's tomb although it seems to have lost five sections of black marble and is now two inches less high and six inches shorter in length than the base listed by Benedetto.[31] These changes probably took place when it was incorporated into Henry VIII's monument.

From this surviving part of the Wolsey tomb, from the details in the inventory and from the evidence of Benedetto's other works, including those he had executed in Florence before he left the city in 1519,[32] it is possible to attempt a reconstruction of Wolsey's tomb. Any reconstruction, however, must be tentative. In the first place, none of the figure and decorative sculpture or bronze embellishments, on which so much depends in the work of a classicizing decorative sculptor such as Benedetto, survives.[33] Secondly, the inventory is not unequivocal and does not reveal, for instance, which, if any, of the bronze figures were in high relief and which were fully three dimensional. Most importantly, though, we know far too little about the sculptor's earlier work in Florence. Benedetto appears to have been exceptionally unfortunate in the fate of his major commissions not just in England but also in Italy.[34] By far his most significant Florentine commission, the shrine of San Giovanni Gualberto, on which he worked between 1505 and 1513, was never set up owing to disputes within the Vallombrosan order who commissioned it,[35] it was severely damaged during the siege of Florence in 1530 and further broken up in 1562. What remains of it is now dispersed between San Salvi, the Badia di Passignano, the Sernigi altar in Santa Trinità in Florence (plate 58) and a private collection.[36] Too little survives of Benedetto's large-scale figure sculpture to enable one to form a clear judgement: his St John, 2.55m high, for the Duomo in Florence and dating from 1512–13, is stigmatized by Sir John Pope-Hennessy as revealing 'in every fold the limitations of a small-scale artist':[37] for Benedetto, finishing Michelangelo's bronze David in 1508 was evidently more important technically than aesthetically. Of the sculptures he must have executed between his leaving Florence in 1519 and his starting work on the Wolsey tomb in 1524 we know next to nothing.[38] And with the loss of

[31] Ibid., p. 162.

[32] The evidence for Benedetto's having left Florence in 1519 is his 1529 letter, in which he mentions that he had not returned to the city to see his wife for ten years (ibid., p. 202).

[33] This loss is only partly supplied by the survival of the four candlesticks originally destined for Henry VIII's monument, sold in the seventeenth century to Bishop Anthony Triest and now in St Bavon at Ghent; ibid., pp. 177–81.

[34] Benedetto is used by Giorgio Vasari, Le Vite, ed G. Milanesi, 4 (1879), pp. 529–36 as an exemplar of the sculptor as the sport of Fate. Bad luck also affected the monograph by E. Luporini, Benedetto da Rovezzano: Scultura e decorazione a Firenze tra il 1490 e il 1520 (Milan, 1964), most of the stocks of which were destroyed in the 1966 Florence flood.

[35] Ibid., pp. 128–31.   [36] Ibid., p. 77 for an analysis of its style.

[37] J. Pope-Hennessy, Italian High Renaissance and Baroque Sculpture (Oxford, 1986), p. 43, fig. 43.

[38] The four bronze pillars supporting the canopy of the high altar of Henry VII's Chapel, which are clearly shown in two early engravings were the work of Benedetto, replacing works by Torrigiano which had failed to bear the weight. They may well have antedated Benedetto's work on Wolsey's tomb.

the components specially made for Henry VIII's tomb, other than the Ghent candlesticks, we are almost entirely in the dark about his work after 1530.

To date, only one work has been attributed to Benedetto's post-1530 period. This is the fountain (plate 59), an impressive work assigned by Pope-Hennessy to that most enigmatic of sculptors, Rustici, which stands in the centre of the gallery in which the Queen's Raphael Cartoons are displayed in the Victoria and Albert Museum.[39] The display presentation for the fountain includes a detailed analysis of its history by Anthony Radcliffe, who instead attributes the fountain to Benedetto. Its recorded history begins at Cowdray, where it is mentioned for the first time by Horace Walpole in 1749. 'I was charmed', he remarks, 'with the front, the court and the fountain.'[40] That Walpole's reference is to the present fountain is confirmed by two Grimm drawings of Cowdray, which show it in the centre of the courtyard. In 1793 Cowdray was burnt down and the fountain, through gift to Lord Robert Spencer, passed to Woolbeding and thence to the museum (on 'permanent loan' from the National Trust).[41] Radcliffe suggests that the fountain was constructed for Cowdray, which was built between about 1520 and 1542, rather than being an early eighteenth-century purchase as Pope-Hennessy contends. It is, after all, quite a coincidence that an unrecorded early sixteenth-century fountain of exactly the right date for Cowdray should have been available in Italy or France for the sixth Viscount Montagu to whom Pope-Hennessy credits its acquisition.[42] Radcliffe argues that the fountain could instead be a work by Benedetto, dating from between 1536 when work on Henry VIII's tomb is sometimes thought to have stopped, and 1543 when the sculptor is found again in Florence.[43] In support of this contention he cites the appearance of Tudor roses on the shaft. One could add that the iconographically anomalous Neptune-like male nude who surmounts the fountain could be a suitable symbol for William Fitzwilliam, lord admiral (from 1536) and builder of Cowdray. Cowdray House, furthermore, features occasional instances of very advanced classical ornament, notably in the coat of arms over the porch, which could reasonably be adduced to suggest the presence of Benedetto's shop in the area.[44] Unfortunately, though, the roses on the fountain's shaft are certainly not Tudor ones and are anyway far from obvious: on the Ghent candlesticks, which undoubtedly emanated from Benedetto's workshop, they are a great deal more prominent. Nor is it by any means clear that Benedetto's work on Henry VIII's tomb actually stopped in 1536. As Professor Biddle has shown, work was

---

[39] J. Pope-Hennessy, 'A fountain by Rustici', *Victoria and Albert Museum Yearbook*, 4 (1974), 20–37.

[40] *Correspondence with George Montagu*, ed. W. S. Lewis, 1 (New Haven, 1941), pp. 98–9.

[41] Pope-Hennessy, 'A fountain by Rustici', 21–2.

[42] Ibid., 23, following W. H. St. J. Hope, *Cowdray and Easebourne Priory* (London, 1919), p. 89.

[43] I am indebted to Anthony Radcliffe for permission to summarize his still unpublished argument.

[44] For Fitzwilliam, see DNB; the coat of arms is conveniently illustrated in M. Howard, *The Early Tudor Country House: Architecture and Politics 1490–1550* (London, 1987), fig. 116.

certainly in progress in 1543,[45] and by the next year it seems to have been under the control of Nicholas Bellin of Modena. In fact, it appears to have been continuing, albeit at a reduced rate, from 1540; it is even possible that it went on, without interruption, from 1536.[46] Anthony Radcliffe's suggestion is, however, a stimulating one and the fountain, which does have northern elements of style, particularly noticeable in the bronze section below the basin, clearly deserves a good deal more attention than it has hitherto received. At the moment, though, it must be considered of doubtful value as an aid in reconstructing Wolsey's tomb.

From Benedetto's inventory, we know that the platform on which the whole monument stood was nine feet long by eight feet broad. The tomb-base of black and white marble on which it rested was eight feet long, four feet four inches wide and two feet high. This means that the four great pillars nine feet high, whose diameter was probably about one foot, must have stood at the side of the sarcophagus and base, where the available space was one foot ten inches on each side. The total height of the pillars, with their three foot four inch tall angels, was a colossal twelve feet four inches. The touchstone sarcophagus is seven feet long, four feet broad and two and a half feet high; the gilt leaves were to fit at the corners, an elaboration of a format which Benedetto had used in the black marble sarcophagus (plate 60) of Piero Soderini in the Carmine at Florence, a work which dates from before 1509.[47] The extraordinary virtuosity of the carving of the Soderini cenotaph, as also in the Altoviti tomb in SS Apostoli, sculpted between 1507 and 1510, where the exquisite white marble sarcophagus is carved with skulls, snakes and harpies (plate 61), indicates the extent of the loss of the 'curyouslye graven' pillars of the Wolsey tomb.[48]

For the kneeling angels (two feet eight inches high) and naked putti (two feet nine inches high) at the head and feet of Wolsey's tomb, we should perhaps look back to Pietro Torrigiano's monument of Henry VII and Queen Elizabeth, where a similar combination is found, although here the angels are elegantly perched on the corners of the tomb.[49] A consideration of Torrigiano's masterpiece highlights

[45] Biddle, 'Nicholas Bellin of Modena', 115. Giovanni Portinari, overseer of work in 1543, was not a sculptor (*pace* Darr, 'European sculpture', 495) but one of the best-known Italian military architectural engineers working in mid-sixteenth-century England (*HKW*, IV, pp. 394, 400, 409, 551, 554, 611, 652–3, 656, 657–60). Since Portinari's role was essentially confined to that of overseer (he also supplied copper for the work), it seems likely that Nicholas Bellin was already in actual charge of work on the tomb by 1543.

[46] Biddle, 'Nicholas Bellin of Modena', 115, n. 3. Stylistically, too, Pope-Hennessy's attribution of the fountain to Rustici is convincing.

[47] Luporini, *Benedetto da Rovezzano*, pp. 134–5.   [48] Ibid., pp. 136–8.

[49] See also the kneeling angels of terracotta which were placed on top of the high altar of Henry VII's chapel. Fragments of these angels, which were destroyed in 1643 (see J. Perkins, *Westminster Abbey: Its Worship and Ornaments*, Alcuin Club Collections 34, 1940, II, pp. 160ff. for the altar: the contract, mistakenly identified as that for Henry VII's tomb, is printed in J. Britton, *The Architectural Antiquities of Great Britain* (London, 1809), II, pp. 23–5 from the contemporary copy of the original contract, Westminster Abbey Muniment 6638') were discovered in 1861 in blocked up windows of the north tower of the Abbey. I am indebted to Mr John Larson, for kindly permitting me to study

one of the problems with Alfred Higgins's reconstruction of Wolsey's monument, a reconstruction which has not been seriously challenged since its publication in 1894.[50] Although the inventory explicitly states that the kneeling angels should be at the head and feet of the tomb, Higgins has placed them at the sides, where they are very uncomfortably related to the epitaphs. Other objections to his reconstruction can also be raised: the figures of saints loosely dotted around the tomb have no precedent in European funerary art and it is unthinkable that they can have been disposed in this manner. The small images of saints were probably intended to be housed in niches cut into the side of the tomb base as in the Orleans tomb, now in St Denis, on which Benedetto worked in 1502.[51] Thirdly, Higgins has given the crucifix to one of the lateral angels whilst another holds a legatine pillar. This, of course, causes a problem, for if one of the angels on the other side is given the second pillar, the remaining angel is left without any attribute. It seems much more likely that a pair of angels, probably at the head of the monument held the crucifix between them, whilst the other pair, at the foot, held the legatine pillars. Finally, the epitaphs are fixed by Higgins to the tomb-base, although the inventory states they were to be fixed to the side of the tomb itself.

Most of these difficulties are resolved in figure 14, although no alternative reconstruction can solve every problem: there are too many uncertainties about the disposition of important elements and about the arrangement of the figure sculpture. The kneeling angels, for instance, could have been deployed on the sarcophagus (fig. 14, a) rather than on its base (fig. 14, b). It is difficult, too, to see how the large bronze panels for the epitaphs, half the length of the sarcophagus and only six inches shorter, could have been satisfactorily related to the curved sarcophagus shape unless they fitted round its contours. Stylistically, the candlestick-bearing angels may have resembled the work of Andrea Sansovino, Benedetto's slightly older contemporary, with whom he had worked and with whose sculpture his own has a great deal in common, but it is difficult to estimate how far, and in what directions, Benedetto's style had evolved since he left Florence.[52]

For our present purposes, however, these doubts about details of the tomb design are less important than the evidence which emerges from *any* reconstruction. Wolsey's documented interest in artistic patronage, it should be stressed, quite apart from his direct supervisory role in drawing up with Torrigiano the design for Henry VIII and Queen Catherine's projected monument, makes it inconceivable that he was not directly involved in the planning of his own

these fragments in the Victoria and Albert Museum Sculpture Conservation studio. Benedetto da Rovezzano reassembled the high altar canopy with new bronze pillars and would therefore have been intimately familiar with it.

[50] But see also n. 24.

[51] Luporini, *Benedetto da Rovezzano*, pp. 114–15. Hardie, 'Wolsey', p. 55 also came to this conclusion.

[52] For Sansovino, see Pope-Hennessy, *High Renaissance Sculpture*, pp. 344–50.

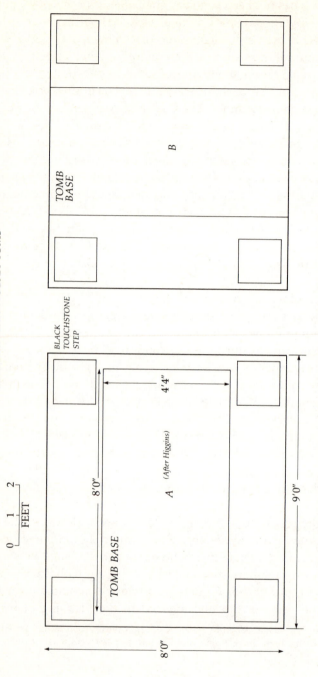

Fig. 14 Conjectural reconstruction of Cardinal Wolsey's tomb, corrected after Higgins. a and b show alternative positions for kneeling angels at Wolsey's head and feet. The angels bearing candlesticks (A, B, C, D) have been posed in a variety of different ways. Ground plan A is to be preferred to B, which leaves insufficient space at the ends.

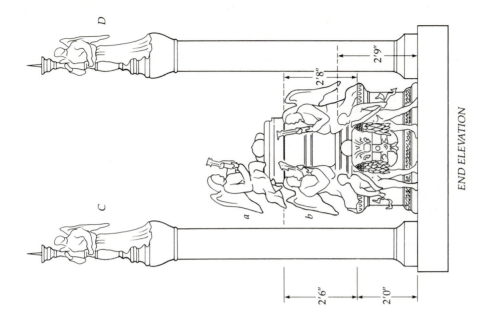

D   C

2'8"

2'9"

a

b

2'6"

2'0"

END ELEVATION

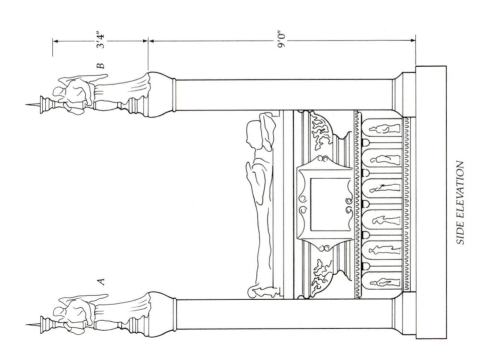

B   A

3'4"

9'0"

SIDE ELEVATION

tomb.[53] There can be no doubt, then, that the basic design directly reflects Wolsey's own ideas. It consequently becomes all the more important to try to establish the context in which Wolsey's tomb should be viewed. Four aspects of the tomb deserve attention here: its scale, the choice of materials, the selection of Benedetto da Rovezzano as the sculptor, and its location.

The early sixteenth century was a period when funerary monuments became increasingly large, memorials in which the power and status of the deceased were trumpeted to posterity. By comparison with Michelangelo's early projects for Pope Julius II's tomb, Wolsey's seems almost insignificant.[54] Compared to that of Louis XII and Anne of Brittany, in St Denis, or the monstrous project apparently contemplated for Henry VIII in the early 1520s, Wolsey's tomb again appears modest.[55] However, Michelangelo's first plan for Julius II's tomb was unrealistically ambitious and by 1532, when only six of the marble statues were anywhere near completion, the initial conception had been dramatically scaled down.[56] In France the monument of Louis XII and Queen Anne was not completed until 1531, and Baccio Bandinelli's grandiose monument for Henry VIII never, apparently, progressed beyond the stage of a model. The period was one of extremely rapid change in tomb design, as in many other areas, and in order to register the real significance of Wolsey's tomb it has to be evaluated by comparison with English tombs completed before 1524 (the latest possible date for the conception of his monument) rather than those conceived or completed after that date. Such comparisons throw a very different light on the project. In England, prominent ecclesiastics had often been commemorated in 'stone-cage' chantry chapels,[57] separate structures within larger buildings, or simply by large tombs. At Winchester Cathedral, there is a remarkable series of stone-cage chapels from the time of Bishop Edington onwards, the most recent of which was that of Richard Fox (d. 1528) (plate 62), completed by 1518, whilst the tradition at Canterbury Cathedral had generally been for less ostentatious monuments: even those of Cardinal Morton (d. 1500) or Archbishop Warham (completed in 1507) hardly bear comparison with the Winchester chapels.[58] But neither the Winchester

[53] For Wolsey's artistic patronage, see Hardie, 'Wolsey'.

[54] J. Wilde, *Michelangelo* (Oxford, 1978), chapter 4.

[55] For the former, see A. Erlande-Brandenburg, *L'église abbatiale de Saint-Denis, II, Les Tombeaux Royaux* (Paris, 1979), and the discussion in B. H. Meyer, 'The first tomb of Henry VII of England', *Art Bulletin*, 58 (1976), 365–6; for the latter see n. 11 above. Cf. also Emperor Maximilian's tomb.

[56] Wilde, *Michelangelo*, pp. 110–13.

[57] The term is that of G. H. Cook, *Mediaeval Chantries and Chantry Chapels* (London, 1968), p. 82.

[58] See, most recently, P. G. Lindley, 'Figure-sculpture at Winchester in the fifteenth century: a new chronology', in D. Williams (ed.), *England in the Fifteenth Century* (Woodbridge, 1987), pp. 153–66. For Canterbury, see R. Willis, *The Architectural History of Canterbury Cathedral* (London, 1845), chapter 7; F. Woodman, *The Architectural History of Canterbury Cathedral* (London, 1981), pp. 255–6. Warham's tomb was originally joined to a small chantry chapel, completed in 1507 (J. Wickham Legg and W. H. St. J. Hope, *Inventories of Christ Church, Canterbury* (Westminster, 1902), pp. 138–47); Morton's monument was constructed after his death (cf. the provisions in his will). I am grateful to Christopher Wilson for information and advice on the Canterbury monuments. The

chapels, nor the grandest erected elsewhere, such as that of Bishop Alcock (founded in 1488) at Ely Cathedral, nor indeed any earlier tomb of an ecclesiastic, could stand comparison with Wolsey's monument.[59] To this generalization, there is only one, very doubtful, exception: the chantry chapel of Cardinal Beaufort at Winchester Cathedral. Beaufort's chapel is interesting because it housed a wooden effigy before the latter's destruction in the Civil War.[60] Such a cheap material is a surprising choice for an enormously wealthy prelate, who made substantial donations to his cathedral church and whose chapel is architecturally of the first rank. It is possible that the wooden effigy was simply the remaining core of a figure like Henry V's in Westminster Abbey, and that it had been covered in gilded plate and stripped at the Dissolution.[61] Apart from this tendentious example, it is impossible to find any real precedent for the scale and ostentation of Wolsey's tomb-monument amongst those of English medieval ecclesiastics.

The choice of extremely costly materials, gilt-bronze and marble, employed for Wolsey's tomb undoubtedly reflects a long tradition in England.[62] But this tradition was almost exclusively confined to royal tombs.[63] Only the mid-fifteenth-century tomb of Richard Beauchamp, earl of Warwick, with a gilt-bronze effigy on a Purbeck marble tomb-chest (plate 63), stands comparison with the regal tombs in Westminster Abbey.[64] Even beside the Beauchamp tomb, though, the sheer size of Wolsey's monument is remarkable. And this must have been the cardinal's intention: Benedetto's 1529 letter indicates that the design explicitly set out to equal or surpass the double tomb of Henry VII and Queen Elizabeth of York, the most recent royal monument, and one which had been completed only a decade earlier. At the lowest possible estimate Wolsey's

site for the tomb of Archbishop Bourchier was granted to him by the prior and chapter on condition that it 'had no superfluous appendages that . . . may sensibly screen the light of the north windows from the altars' (Willis, *Architectural History of Canterbury*, p. 131), and a monument of the Winchester type would not have been permitted in this location.

[59] J. Bentham, *The History and Antiquities of the Conventual and Cathedral Church of Ely* (Cambridge, 1771), p. 183; *VCH, Cambridge and the Isle of Ely*, IV (London, 1967), pp. 72–3.

[60] L. G. Wickham Legg, *A Breife Description of a Journey made into the Westerne Counties*, Camden Miscellany 16 (London, 1936), p 47.

[61] R. N. Quirk, 'The tomb of Cardinal Beaufort', *Winchester Cathedral Record*, 23 (1954), 6–10.

[62] For the medieval tradition see, most recently, L. Stone, *Sculpture in Britain: the Middle Ages* (Harmondsworth, 1972), *passim* (particularly p. 209) and for Torrigiano, see A. P. Darr, 'Pietro Torrigiano and his sculpture for the Henry VII Chapel, Westminster Abbey', unpublished PhD dissertation, New York University, 1980. For a new view of the continuing importance of this tradition in the Renaissance in England, see Lindley, 'Una grande opera'.

[63] For one exception, see below. Thomas Stanley, Earl of Derby (d. 1504), who was also commemorated by a gilt-bronze effigy, married into the future royal family when he took Margaret Beaufort as his second wife in 1482.

[64] R. Gough, *Description of the Beauchamp Chapel, adjoining to the Church of St Mary, at Warwick* (London, 1809); J. G. Nichols, *Description of the Church of St Mary, Warwick, and of the Beauchamp Chapel* (London, 1838); P. B. Chatwin, 'The Effigy of Richard Beauchamp at Warwick', *Antiquaries Journal*, 6 (1926), 448–9; Chatwin, 'Recent Discoveries in the Beauchamp Chapel, Warwick', *Transactions and Proceedings of the Birmingham Archaeological Society*, 53 (1928), 145–57; G. Cope, 'The "Beauchamp Chapel", Warwick: a liturgical-architectural study', *Warwickshire History*, 4 (1978–79), 56–68.

monument cost as much as that tomb – which of course features two gilt-bronze effigies. In size, Wolsey's tomb was certainly superior to Torrigiano's monument. No earlier royal tomb in England could equal it and the great columns with angels bearing candlesticks found no English parallel.[65] Similarly, the gilt bronze pillars supporting the altar could be equalled only by the Henry VII Chapel high altar. The most recently completed French royal tombs, that of Louis XI at Notre-Dame-de-Cléry and Guido Mazzoni's monument to Charles VIII at St Denis (plate 64), with their *priant* figures of the deceased, were splendid and innovative monuments but less grandiose than that of Wolsey.[66]

In late fifteenth-century and early sixteenth-century Italy too, bronze was rarely employed for tombs. Verrocchio's monument for Piero and Giovanni de' Medici in Florence of *c*. 1469 and the tomb of Pope Sixtus IV, commissioned by the future Julius II from Antonio Pollajuolo and finished in 1493, and that of Innocent VIII which Pollajuolo next produced, were the only recent precedents.[67] By contrast, the tombs of Cardinals Ascanio Sforza and Girolamo Basso della Rovere, commissioned from Andrea Sansovino by Pope Julius II to adorn Bramante's rebuilt choir of Sta Maria del Popolo, Rome, were, in spite of their triumphal arch format, essentially only grandiose wall tombs, and were carved entirely of marble.[68] In Rouen Cathedral, the tomb of Cardinal Georges d'Amboise (d. 1510) and of his nephew, then archbishop of Rouen, completed by 1525, was, again, a wall monument with two *priant* figures, and although the sculpture was of extremely high quality, it was of marble and alabaster rather than metal.[69] Wolsey's tomb surpassed all these in grandeur and scale. By any international standards it was exceptional in its size and in the expense of its materials. This was explicitly recognized by Augustino Scarpinello, the Milanese ambassador to England, who, writing in December 1530 of the cardinal's death, states Wolsey

[65] The pillars borne before Wolsey in procession clearly lie behind these four pillars, which may also have been influenced by Charles V's device (for which see E. E. Rosenthal, 'The invention of the columnar device of Emperor Charles V at the court of Burgundy in Flanders in 1516', *Journal of the Warburg and Courtauld Institutes*, 36 (1973), 198–230). They are visually reminiscent of shrines, such as those of St Edward the Confessor at Westminster or that of St Alban in his eponymous abbey church. For the former, see J. G. O'Neilly and L. E. Tanner, 'The shrine of St Edward the Confessor', *Archaeologia*, 100 (1966), 129–154. For the latter, see J. T. Micklethwaite, 'The shrine of St Alban', *Archaeological Journal*, 29 (1872), 201–11; R. Lloyd, *An Architectural and Historical Account of the Shrines of St Alban and Saint Amphibalus in Saint Alban's Abbey* (St Alban's 1873) and *VCH Hertfordshire*, II (London, 1971), p. 494. See also the general survey by N. Coldstream, 'English decorated shrine bases', *Journal of the British Archaeological Association*, 129 (1976), 15–34.

[66] Verdon, *Mazzoni*, pp. 123–34 and pp. 338–40. In contrast to the more intimate and modest tomb of Louis XI, Mazzoni's monument for Charles VIII was the 'most pompous royal tomb effigy imagined up to that date' (Verdon, *Mazzoni*, p. 128). The kneeling figure of the king was of polychromed bronze, the base of black marble and ancillary features gilt-bronze.

[67] J. Pope-Hennessy, *Italian Renaissance Sculpture* (Oxford, 1986), pp. 43–5 and pp. 301–2.

[68] Pope-Hennessy, *High Renaissance Sculpture*, pp. 54–5 and pp. 346–7.

[69] M. Allinne, 'Les Priants du Tombeau des Cardinaux d'Amboise', *Bulletin des Monuments Rouennais* (1909), 79–94. The addition of the *priant* of Georges II d'Amboise was an alteration to the original design of the tomb and the second *priant* was itself modified in 1542 and after 1550.

'had prepared for his remains a more costly mausoleum than any royal or papal monument in the world, so that the King intends it to serve for himself *post multos et felices annos*, having caused the Cardinal's arms to be erased from it'.[70]

Wolsey's choice of Benedetto da Rovezzano as the sculptor of his monument is also significant. The three most recent royal sculptural commissions in bronze and marble had all been awarded to the Florentine sculptor, Pietro Torrigiano. After the latter's departure for Spain in *c*. 1522, Benedetto was his obvious successor. Italian, and specifically Florentine, artists enjoyed a higher status than native craftsmen in much of northern and eastern Europe and large numbers of Italian sculptors made their way to the north at precisely the time when European politics centred on the struggle for Italy. Benedetto, who may already have proved his competence by fashioning new bronze pillars for the high altar canopy of Henry VII's chapel, must have come to England with a high reputation: in the declining Florentine market for monumental tombs before he left the city in 1519, his work was amongst the most important. For Benedetto, the English court must have seemed, as it did to Torrigiano, an arena in which great commissions could be secured, away from the overpowering rivalry and dominating genius of Michelangelo. For the English, the work of Torrigiano or Benedetto – as later of Nicholas Bellin da Modena or Toto del Nunziata for instance – provided the best available examples of a style (or, more correctly, range of styles) which dominated European art as French High Gothic had once done. Wolsey seems to have exerted little personal control over the production of his tomb once the design had been agreed, leaving the detailed supervision to Cavallari. The freedom this gave the sculptor seems to have been important, for Benedetto's tomb would have been the first wholly and unequivocally Renaissance monument in England on a grand scale.[71] Its uncompromising rejection of northern Gothic elements is clear from the form of the surviving sarcophagus and base, which find their closest comparisons in Benedetto's Soderini and Altoviti wall tombs. Wolsey's tomb was, then, a marked stylistic departure from English medieval norms. Its

---

[70] *CSPV*, IV (1527–33), 637; *LP*, IV, Introduction, p. dxcviii. There is no evidence to determine whether Scarpinello ever saw the monument, or whether he had other sources of information.

[71] In the earlier monuments at Westminster Abbey, Torrigiano had been unable to produce wholly Renaissance style monuments owing to the constraints imposed upon him by his patrons. The only earlier tomb which had been entirely Renaissance in style was that of Dr Yonge, for which see C. Galvin and P. Lindley, 'Pietro Torrigiano's tomb for Dr Yonge', *Church Monuments*, 3 (1988), 42–60; this is a much smaller and cheaper wall-tomb, made of terracotta, freestone and marble. I can find no evidence (cf. Pollard, pp. 186–7n) that Wolsey appointed Yonge his suffragan for York in 1514. The words 'Part of' have been accidentally omitted at the beginning of note 3 in the above paper, wrongly implying that the (destroyed, second) tomb of Dean Colet was designed by Torrigiano. In fact, only the niche and bust from the late Perpendicular tomb were the work of the Italian sculptor: see F. Grossmann, 'Holbein, Torrigiano and some portraits of Dean Colet', *Journal of the Warburg and Courtauld Institutes*, 13 (1950), 202–36. The situation was analogous to the chantry chapel of Abbot Islip of Westminster, a late Gothic structure for which Torrigiano supplied the roundel now in the Wallace Collection. Cf. A. P. Darr, 'From Westminster Abbey to the Wallace Collection: Torrigiano's *Head of Christ*', *Apollo*, (1982), 292–8.

Renaissance style as well as its cost and magnificence helped to assert the patron's international status.

In its iconography too, the monument emphasized Wolsey's power, fully justifying Cavendish's remark that Wolsey had 'more respect to the worldly honor of hys person than he had to his sperytuall profession'.[72] No *memento mori* or *transi* balanced the tomb's most distinctive features: the uniquely ostentatious pillars, the escutcheons of his ecclesiastical preferments, and the cardinal's hat which Wolsey received in a splendid ceremony at Westminster Abbey.[73] In an age notably sensitive to display, the response of the observer to Wolsey's magnificent monument would have largely depended on his view of Wolsey, hostile or admiring. What it unequivocally illustrated to all contemporaries and to posterity was the cardinal's unprecedented combination of political and ecclesiastical power. It is surely for this reason that the monument did not survive his fall,[74] and it is a paradoxical testimony to its importance that its materials and its artist were re-employed by Henry VIII. Undoubtedly too, its size and expense prompted the king to commission an even grander and more costly monument himself.

It is frequently asserted that Wolsey's monument was intended to stand in the Lady Chapel of St George's Chapel, Windsor.[75] From February 1511 until his elevation to the episcopate as bishop of Lincoln in 1514, Wolsey held a canonry and prebend at St George's, where he would have seen the incomplete Lady Chapel begun by Henry VII and initially intended to house his own tomb and the shrine of Henry VI; it had been left unfinished once the king decided instead to erect a new chapel at Westminster Abbey.[76] Wolsey's influence has been adduced as the reason why the dean and chapter of Windsor entered into a contract with William Vertue for the completion of their Lady Chapel on 20 December 1511.[77]

[72] Cavendish, p. 182. Cavendish revealingly remarks of the ceremonies attached to Wolsey's receiving his cardinal's hat, 'I have not seen the lyke, unlesse it had byn at the coronacion of a myghti prince or kyng.'

[73] Perhaps, as in the Altoviti tomb and Soderini cenotaph, the decorative repertoire of the tomb included skulls and bones etc.; but these could hardly be said to have the same function as a *transi*. Cf. for Wolsey's 'worldly pompe incredible', William Roy's satire of Wolsey's procession, with two priests carrying large crosses and two secular men each holding a pillar, symbols of Wolsey's ecclesiastical and secular dignities (E. Arber (ed.), W. Roy and J. Barlowe, *Rede me and be nott wrothe, For I saye no thinge but troth* (London, 1871), p. 56). In the tomb project, the four pillars presumably stand for both secular and ecclesiastical power.

[74] Revealingly, Wolsey did not expect the king to return the whole monument: he doubtless hoped to salvage those portions which pertained directly to him and which could not simply be redeployed by the king.

[75] E.g. W. H. St. J. Hope, *Windsor Castle* (London, 1913), II, p. 482 and Mitchell, 'Works of Art from Rome', p. 191, n. 80 (inaccurately citing *LP*, I, 1506 and 4856 and misinterpreting the contents). It has been assumed that the wording of Benedetto's 1530 inventory proves that some of Wolsey's tomb was by then already assembled in the Lady Chapel at Windsor, but this is by no means clear: see above n. 22. Henry VIII's tomb was not moved to Windsor until 1565.

[76] *HKW*, III, pp. 210–22.

[77] Hope, *Windsor*, p. 482, there is no mention of Wolsey in the contract for the vault.

However, there is no firm evidence for this nor, apparently, for the claim that Wolsey's tomb was to be housed in the building. It is hard to believe that even Wolsey could have been granted a building conceived of as a royal shrine and burial chapel.[78] Wolsey did not leave a will and so it is difficult to know whether he had finally decided on the location for his tomb, which was probably still in Benedetto's workshop in 1530. The licence to found Cardinal College, Ipswich, in June 1528 seems to imply that Wolsey was to be buried in the college chapel,[79] but it is more likely that the tomb would have been placed either in his cathedral church, York Minster (in 1530 Wolsey certainly intended it as the location for as much of his tomb as he could salvage), or in the huge chapel projected for his Oxford college, Wolsey's greatest foundation.[80]

Cardinal College, Oxford, was certainly intended to house other work by Benedetto. Together with the list of components for Wolsey's tomb in Benedetto's inventory, there appear 'A chamynye of w(hi)t(e) marbull' and 'vj figures of clay of vij foote apece whiche sholde have s(er)ved for Oxforde'. Unfortunately, the marble fireplace seems to be lost but it may have resembled Benedetto's *Camino Gondi* of *c*. 1490–1501 or the *c*. 1514 *Camino Borgherini*: the sculptor's highly decorative style lent itself to such works, although it is likely that the English fireplace was less grand than its Florentine precursors. The six terracotta figures were, almost certainly, intended for the college's high altar, the commission for which had been mentioned by Benedetto in his letter of June 1529. In 1861 many pieces of smashed terracotta figure sculpture, including fragments of Pietro Torrigiano's high altar angels, were discovered in the filling of blocked up windows in Westminster Abbey: Mr John Larson of the Victoria and Albert Museum recently identified these fragments as sixteenth-century work.[81] It is possible that these fragments (plate 65) include pieces of Benedetto's figures, which were evidently in his Westminster workshop in 1530 and which would presumably have been taken over by the king, although as far as one can judge from the style of the fragments, they all seem consistent with Torrigiano's work. However, if pieces do belong to Benedetto's figures, their nineteenth-century location suggests that Henry commandeered them for use in Westminster Abbey, where they presumably were destroyed in the Commonwealth period.[82]

Mention of terracotta sculpture inevitably brings us to the best-known aspect

[78] Hardie, 'Wolsey', pp. 49–50 has demolished the edifice of conjecture that Wolsey was granted the chapel.

[79] Hardie, 'Wolsey', p. 50. *LP*, IV (ii) 4435, for the licence to found the Ipswich college and the mortmain licence 'for the erection of chantries and appointment of anniversaries and other prayers in the burial place of the said Cardinal'. Wolsey was actually buried in the so-called 'Tyrants' Sepulchre' at Leicester Abbey, where he rested in the company of Richard III (*LP*, IV (iii) 6757).

[80] For which, see J. Newman's essay in this volume.

[81] *Journal of the Royal Institute of British Architects*, 2 January 1890, p. 116. I am grateful to Mr Larson, Head of the Sculpture Conservation Section at the Victoria and Albert Museum, for showing me these fragments.

[82] For Puritan destructions at Westminster Abbey, see Perkins, *Westminster*, II, pp. 182ff.

of Wolsey's sculptural patronage: his employment of Giovanni da Maiano. The sculptor first appears in England in a letter of 18 June 1521 addressed to Wolsey, asking for the completion of payment for eight round images at Hampton Court.[83] These he had made, set in place, painted and gilded at £2 6s 8d each; he had also produced three narratives of Hercules at £4 each and was still owed £21 13s 4d. Although the stories of Hercules have disappeared, the Hampton Court roundels survive. They have caused a great deal of confusion because of the appearance of images from the same series of Caesars on the so-called 'Holbein gate' at Whitehall, constructed between 1530 and 1532 and demolished in August 1759 as part of a road-widening scheme.[84] George, duke of Cumberland, had intended to re-erect the gate in the Great Park at Windsor but nothing came of the project and the roundels seem to have been built into workmens' houses where two of them were seen in 1845 by Edward Jesse, Surveyor of the Royal Parks. He mistakenly thought they had been displaced from Hampton Court in Wren's time and they were subsequently set into the outer gate of the palace.[85] The eight roundels on the two inner gateways are themselves rather problematic: the four on Kent's gothick gateway have all, of course, been reset and the bust of Titus looks suspiciously eighteenth-century in style. The variation in colouring of the busts and their containing roundels would not have been noticeable when they were all painted (the bust of Augustus appears to have restored paintwork (plate 66)) but is surprising if they were all originally cast at the same time: the colour ranges from a brick red to a light limestone colour. Some of the surrounds (e.g. Vitellius and Augustus on the Anne Boleyn gateway) may even be stone. It is odd that these variations have never been highlighted and it would be helpful to have a detailed technical analysis of the roundels.

The Hampton Court terracotta roundels represent a cheap means of imitating the marble ones which appear on Cardinal Georges d'Amboise's Château Gaillon, and which themselves are usually said to be based on the decoration of the Certosa of Pavia.[86] At Hampton Court, the piecemeal application of such Renaissance forms superficially modernized an essentially traditional piece of

---

[83] Higgins, 'Sculptors', Appendix II. The busts are wrongly connected with the Victoria and Albert Museum glazed terracotta roundel by J. C. Robinson, *Italian Sculpture of the Middle Ages and Period of the Revival of Art* (London, 1862), p. 84.

[84] M. H. Cox and P. Norman (eds.), *Survey of London, XIV, St Margaret, Westminster III* (London, 1931), pp. 10–22 and Appendix A.

[85] H. S. Lewis and A. D. Wallace (eds.), *Horace Walpole's Correspondence with the Rev. William Cole*, II (London, 1937), pp. 176–8; *Gentleman's Magazine*, 25 (1846), 154; ibid., 25/2 (1846), 147; H. B. Wheatley, *London Past and Present: Its History, Associations and Traditions*, III (London, 1891), p. 513; J. T. Smith, *Antiquities of Westminster* (London, 1807), pp. 21–3; C. Harcourt-Smith, 'Three busts by Torrigiano (?)', *Old Furniture*, 5 (1928), 187–199; C. Beard, 'Torrigiano or da Maiano?', *Connoisseur*, 84 (1929), 77–86; the clearest analysis of the confusion in the literature between these roundels and the Torrigiano busts once housed in the gate is that of J. Pope-Hennessy, *Catalogue of Italian Sculpture in the Victoria and Albert Museum*, II (London, 1964), pp. 399–401.

[86] A. Blunt, *Art and Architecture in France 1500–1700* (Harmondsworth, 1980), p. 18 and p. 25.

architecture.[87] Wolsey's employment of Giovanni da Maiano to produce these medallions is the first known instance of their appearance in England. The importance this attaches to Wolsey's patronage may, though, simply be the result of an accident of documentary survival, for similar roundels can be seen at The Vyne (plate 67), in Hampshire, Hanworth and elsewhere.[88] The Vyne roundel, however, may have been moved by John Chute in the eighteenth century (it could even have come from the 'Holbein' gateway) rather than belonging to Lord Sandys's house: against this is the fact that The Vyne features, most conspicuously in the long gallery woodwork (plate 68) but also elsewhere in the decoration, a great deal of other Renaissance detail which certainly antedates 1528.[89] Conversely, the Hanworth roundels, which have themselves been thought to have been brought from the 'Holbein' gate, are instead doubtless to be identified with the 'antique heads' brought from Greenwich by Giovanni da Maiano and Antony Toto at the order of Henry VIII to modernize the house when he gave it (or, more correctly, Stephen Gardiner did) to Anne Boleyn in 1532.[90] The fact that it was thought desirable to bring these roundels to Hanworth indicates that they remained a popular form of decoration for at least a decade. It is frustrating, therefore, that it is at present uncertain whether Wolsey's use of them was innovative or itself conformed to a more widespread fashion.[91] There must once also have been a very large number of similar heads in more perishable materials such as papier-mâché, which Giovanni and his large workshop employed in 1527 for the antique heads used to decorate the Banqueting and Revels Houses at Greenwich.[92]

In 1845, during restoration of the Renaissance terracotta panel (plate 69) on the inner side of the clock tower at Hampton Court, it was discovered that Wolsey's arms had been cut away and replaced by those of Henry VIII, carved in stone, whilst the cardinal's hat 'was covered by a crown worked in wrought iron', a transformation analogous to the modifications which turned Anne Boleyn's

---

[87] J. Summerson, *Architecture in Britain 1530 to 1830* (Harmondsworth, 1953), ch. 1 and Howard, *Country House*, ch. 6.

[88] C. W. Chute, *A History of The Vyne in Hampshire* (Winchester, 1888); it appears in an eighteenth-century setting in the stone gallery underneath the famous long gallery. For the gallery, see also R. Coope, 'The "long gallery": its origins, development, use and decoration', *Architectural History*, 29 (1986), 50 and n. 74. I am currently embarking on a detailed study of this and the other roundels.

[89] Notably in the carving of the putti in the long gallery and chapel stalls: see W. R. D. Harrison and A. Chandos, *Illustrated Catalogue of Carvings: Oak Gallery, The Vyne* (Basingstoke, 1979). The putti are particularly remarkable, with their haloes slanted in perspective (plate 68).

[90] *HKW*, IV, p. 148; E. W. Ives, *Anne Boleyn* (Oxford, 1986), p. 193. See also *HKW*, IV, p. 104, for 'antique' heads – not necessarily of terracotta.

[91] From the second decade of the sixteenth century, such heads carved in stone or cast in terracotta, or in relief in panels, become an increasingly common form of decoration.

[92] S. Anglo, 'La Salle de Banquet et le théâtre construits à Greenwich pour les fêtes Franco-Anglaises de 1527', in J. Jacquot (ed.), *Le Lieu Théâtral à la Renaissance* (Paris, 1964), pp. 273–88; Anglo, *Spectacle, Pageantry, and early Tudor Policy* (Oxford, 1969), p. 214; *LP*, IV (ii) 3104; PRO, E36/227, fols. 2 and 24.

heraldic leopards into Jane Seymour's panthers by 'new makyng of the hedds and the taylls'.[93] The Hampton Court panel exhibits two naked, winged putti supporting between them Wolsey's arms, behind which his archiepiscopal cross stands beneath a cardinal's hat, flanked by thunderbolts. In the early nineteenth century, a lunette with Wolsey's monogram and the date 1525 (which had been covered by Henry's monogram) could be seen above the panel, whilst below it Wolsey's carved motto still survives (it had been covered by Henry's motto). The archiepiscopal cross and coat of arms are now entirely nineteenth-century work, but much else, including the classical columns and entablature, is original. Undoubtedly, the extremely high quality of this sculpture, as much as the classical architecture, proves that an Italian sculptor was responsible for it. If the date of 1525 is accurate, and if the conventional view is correct that Torrigiano left England before that date, Benedetto da Rovezzano and Giovanni da Maiano have to be considered as possible authors of the work; given the latter's earlier employment at the palace, he might seem the likelier candidate. However, the sturdy little figures demand comparison with their immediate models, those by Pietro Torrigiano at the east end of Henry VII and Queen Elizabeth's tomb; indeed, it seems certain that a model by Torrigiano was used by the sculptor responsible for the ensemble, for the relationship to Torrigiano's work is very striking.[94]

The pairs of draped angels (plate 70) at the entrance to the chapel of the palace, panels which are often ascribed to Wolsey's patronage, originated in a very different stylistic ambit.[95] The rather clumsy angels, evidently not the work of Italian artists, now support the painted arms of Henry VIII and Jane Seymour; those flanking the king's arms wear armoured breastplates, ornamented with winged cherub heads, birds and foliage. The style of these figures, apparently imitating French models, does not preclude a date in the mid or late 1520s, and the sole reference to them in the Hampton Court accounts, dating from July 1536 (when William Reynolds was paid for carving two crowns in freestone), appears to indicate the modification of existing panels. It is slightly surprising to find that this alteration had not taken place earlier and the carved royal mottoes on the

[93] *Gentleman's Magazine*, 24 (1845), 593–4 (it is unclear how the lunette was fitted underneath the window of the gateway); *HKW*, IV, p. 26.

[94] The terracotta panel is ascribed to Giovanni by Lees-Milne, *Tudor Renaissance*, p. 43, but the putti (the head of one, at least, is a restoration) reveal a deep debt to those of Torrigiano's Henry VII tomb base (Darr, thesis, p. 339), and the heads of the 1516 Dr Yonge tomb seraphs. Were it not for the (anyway rather problematic) date associated with the panel, one would have little hesitation in ascribing it to Torrigiano. Indeed, even if the date is correct, it is possible that the panel actually *is* a work by him. None of the works ascribed to Torrigiano in Spain certainly antedates 1526, the year in which his Westminster high altar was completed by Benedetto da Rovezzano, and the date of his departure may need reconsideration; alternatively, the work could have been executed at an earlier date and subsequently fixed into place at Hampton Court.

[95] *HKW*, IV, p. 135; G. D. Heath, *The Chapel Royal at Hampton Court*, Borough of Twickenham Local History Society, 42 (1979), p. 10. The chapel angels seem related to the sculpture of the Spencer tomb at Great Brington, Northants.

scrolls might also suggest that the panels only date from Henry's ownership of the palace.[96] Wolsey's employment, at Cardinal College, Oxford, of what must surely be native sculptors rather clumsily working in an Italianate idiom warns us against using stylistic quality as a criterion of attribution. The trio of naked putti on the oriel window of the show facade of Cardinal College, (plate 71), datable to 1526, with their background of crude ornament and savagely exuberant foliage forms, are closely related to 'Winchester school' works of the 1520s and show a much less sophisticated understanding of Renaissance forms than that exhibited in the tomb designed by Master John Lee for Bishop John Fisher at St John's College, Cambridge, and constructed between 1524 and 1532.[97] What is important, though, is that native sculptors were now attempting to copy Italian Renaissance putti, just as an English illuminator working in the mid fifteenth century for William Gray had tried to imitate the vine-stem style of his Italian models in some of Gray's Italian manuscripts.[98] Clearly, English sculptors were now required to provide Italianate sculpture as architectural decoration.[99]

At the Field of Cloth of Gold, in whose arrangements Wolsey was intimately concerned, the English temporary palace featured a large quantity of applied Renaissance detailing, perhaps most conspicuously on the Bacchus and Cupid fountains.[100] Although none is now visible *in situ* at Hampton Court, non-figural terracotta embellished with very similar 'antique' work seems once to

[96] It is difficult, though, to believe that the royal arms would have been carved with angelic, rather than heraldic supporters, even at the entrance to the chapel. The differentiation of angels with breastplates and simple garments for the king and queen would also be applicable for the king and Wolsey. The chapel was the last part of Wolsey's Hampton Court to be upgraded by Henry VIII; if Wolsey's arms had been represented here, they must either have been painted over or (if sculpted) effaced earlier in Henry's ownership of the palace: from 1530 to 1532 there are many references in the accounts to the affixing of Royal Arms and Beasts at Hampton Court (E. Law, *History of Hampton Court Palace in Tudor Times* (London, 1885), p. 124). The alterations in July 1536 could also be connected with the transformation of Anne Boleyn's arms into those of Jane Seymour. See also *HKW*, IV (ii), p. 135. For the chapel, see P. Curnow, 'The east window of the chapel at Hampton Court Palace', *Architectural History*, 27 (1984), 1–10.

[97] R. Willis and J. W. Clark, *The Architectural History of the University of Cambridge and of the Colleges of Cambridge and Eton* (Cambridge, 1886), II, pp. 282–3; the tomb is discussed by F. Woodman, *The Architectural History of King's College Chapel* (London, 1986), p. 206. At Christ Church itself, slightly later Italianate putti are found in the decoration of the Hall.

[98] *Duke Humfrey and English Humanism*, Catalogue of an Exhibition held in the Bodleian Library (Oxford, 1970), plate VI.

[99] After Henry took over the palace, Edmund More carved royal arms 'with severall bourders of antique worke' (Law, *Hampton Court*, p. 125) and by the 1530s, sculptors such as Richard Rydge were producing very high quality 'antique work' in designs probably drawn from continental woodcuts and engravings. See also A. J. Smith, 'The life and building activity of Richard Fox c. 1448–1528', unpublished PhD thesis, University of London 1989.

[100] S. Anglo, 'The Hampton Court painting of the Field of Cloth of Gold considered as an historical document', *Antiquaries Journal*, 46 (1966), 287–307; Anglo, *Spectacle*, chapter 4. For Wolsey's intimate involvement in the design of the palace and its ancillary buildings, see J. G. Nichols (ed.), *The Chronicle of Calais in the reigns of Henry VII and Henry VIII to the year 1540*, Camden Society 1846, pp. 77–85; *LP*, III (i) 825; J. G. Russell, *The Field of Cloth of Gold* (London, 1969).

have been very widely used by Wolsey.[101] In 1977, David Batchelor summarized the results of excavations in Lady Mornington's garden, an excavation intended to reveal the foundations of the Queen's Gallery, a two-storey building 180 feet long and 25 feet wide, built by Henry VIII between 1533 and 1535 and demolished by Wren in 1689–90 to make way for his Fountain Court. Close to the lowest level of the excavation, two pieces of terracotta were discovered (plate 72), pieces which Batchelor described as 'typical of the Wolsey period of the building'.[102] By this he must have meant to refer to a still unpublished excavation of June 1976 in the south range of Clock Court, which turned up a considerable amount of architectural terracotta decoration (plates 73, 74) reused as foundation material for a range generally considered to be amongst the later works carried out by Wolsey there. The earliest possible date for the terracottas would seem to be about 1514, when Wolsey acquired the lease of Hampton Court.[103] As Richard Morris has shown, these terracottas are intimately related to those at Sutton Place in Surrey, built by Sir Richard Weston after he had been granted the estate in 1521. The window mullions of Sutton Place are in an identical style to those excavated in Clock Court and are from the same workshop as those published in 1977.[104] The forms of the mouldings, as distinct from the repertoire of decorative forms employed to embellish them, are distinctively English.[105] This suggests either that Italian artists (or other European sculptors who had mastered the idiom) were supplied with templates and were responsible only for the decorative work[106] or that native craftsmen were, at this early date, studying the newly fashionable Renaissance designs, a point which would help explain the otherwise perplexing mixture of Gothic and Renaissance detailing. The excavations currently underway at Hampton Court may provide further evidence about the date and range of terracottas which Wolsey's building featured and help to clarify their relationship with those at Sutton Place and elsewhere. What already seems clear is that Renaissance designs may have been deployed on English domestic

---

[101] See, most recently, R. K. Morris, 'Windows in early Tudor country houses', in D. Williams (ed.), *Early Tudor England* (Woodbridge, 1988), pp. 125–38. For other terracotta decoration, see Howard, pp. 131–3 and S. J. Gunn and P. G. Lindley, 'Charles Brandon's Westhorpe: an early Tudor courtyard house in Suffolk', *Archaeological Journal*, 145 (1988), 272–89; see also *VCH Middlesex*, II, p. 375.

[102] D. Batchelor, 'Excavations at Hampton Court Palace', *Post-Medieval Archaeology*, 11 (1977), 36–49. For the correct dating of the Queen's Gallery, see Thurley, 'Henry VIII and the building of Hampton Court', 13–16.

[103] Law, *Hampton Court*, p. 16, citing BL, MS Claudius E vi, fol. 137. Law also notes that the site had been leased in 1505 to Giles Lord Daubeny, who appears to have engaged in building work there: see Simon Thurley's chapter. It was suggested at the conference that these terracottas might be linked with Daubeny's work rather than Wolsey's. This seems highly improbable given the appearance of the crossed-keys motif in the excavated fragments (plate 74), which links them to Wolsey beyond reasonable doubt.

[104] Morris, 'Windows', pp. 126–7.   [105] Ibid., p. 129.

[106] The reverse of this situation occurred in 1506, when English masons were supplied with template designs by Guido Mazzoni in the abortive project for a tomb for Henry VII.

architecture both much earlier and more widely than is generally thought. Wolsey's Hampton Court must have been amongst the earliest buildings to feature such terracottas and it is possible that this area of its decoration provided a stylistic model for later courtyard houses. What remains uncertain is why this form of decoration appears to have been so quickly abandoned at Hampton Court.

This outline of Wolsey's patronage of Renaissance sculpture emphasizes how little remains of all the great works which he funded: Giovanni da Maiano's terracotta roundels, the Clock Court panel, the reused sarcophagus from Wolsey's unfinished tomb and some architectural decoration at Christ Church Oxford, are the major survivals. But it was, perhaps, the very magnificence of Wolsey's patronage which ensured that, after his fall, it would be obliterated. However one views Wolsey's tomb, it is impossible to argue that it can be fitted comfortably into an English ecclesiastical tradition. It was designed and produced by the best Florentine sculptor available in England, to a brief which specified that it should surpass Henry VII's and Queen Elizabeth's monument in Westminster Abbey. By employing Italian sculptors, Wolsey both stressed the international scope of his patronage and helped to consolidate the new dominance of Renaissance stylistic norms in English sculpture. But it was the emphasis not so much on the tomb's style – innovative though it was – as on its scale and richness which separated Wolsey's tomb from all its predecessors as surely as Cardinal College surpassed its models.[107] A tomb conceived of as superior to any English king's, more splendid than any pope's, would not survive Wolsey's disgrace.[108] The fact that the king did not hesitate to use it as the nucleus of his own monument emphasizes that, however conventional the terms in which contemporary criticisms of Wolsey's pride were expressed, the causes of such criticism were real.[109] Wolsey's patronage was, above all, intended as a proclamation of his political and ecclesiastical importance. That it was clearly understood by his contemporaries in precisely these terms explains why so little was allowed to survive.

---

[107] *LP*, IV (ii) 4135 for Cromwell's comments on Cardinal College.

[108] See the comments of the French ambassadors to England, who were taken aback by the cardinal's overstated magnificence and the papal nuncio's comments on Wolsey's 'excessive pomp and great ostentation' (see above, p. 156).

[109] Cf. G. Walker, *John Skelton and the Politics of the 1520s* (Cambridge, 1988), pp. 161–8; Walker argues that 'Wolsey's activities were, in by far the greater part, necessitated by his pursuit of the Crown's interests and not by the personal appetites and desires which Skelton alleges.' The analysis of his tomb-project, however, suggests that in this instance at least, Wolsey's own pride and self-importance *were* exceptional. Wolsey may not have taken his candidacy for the papacy seriously (see above, p. 26), but the style of the tomb may have been redolent in his mind of a 'Romanitas' with appealing connotations.

CHAPTER 11

The fall of Wolsey

E. W. IVES

The fall of Thomas Wolsey is an event which has a precise date and an obvious explanation – or so it would appear.[1] On Wednesday 6 October the cardinal was in his seat at the council, on Saturday 9th he was indicted for praemunire and on Monday 18th he surrendered the great seal. A year later he was dead. The cause equally seems evident, what Mattingly described as a 'simultaneous catastrophe' to Wolsey's ecclesiastical and foreign policies, with the adjournment of the legatine court at Blackfriars on 31 July and the almost concurrent signing of the Franco-Imperial Peace of Cambrai, announcing to all his failure to achieve the annulment of Henry VIII's marriage to Catherine of Aragon.[2] As Shakespeare's comments so often do, the verdict of *Henry VIII* on the fall of Wolsey set the tone for future historians: 'When he falls, he falls like Lucifer, never to hope again.'[3]

It would, of course, be foolish to deny the significance of October, 1529. The dismissal and prosecution of Wolsey was a climactic event in English history, and not simply because it removed a figure of towering authority. Equally, the failure in royal policy at the end of July 1529 cannot be glossed over. It can hardly be imagined that the cardinal would have been discarded after achieving a favourable decision at the legatine court or if diplomatic finesse had put an end to Charles V's pressure on Rome.

History, however, is rarely uncomplicated, and the simple story of Wolsey's fall begs a number of important questions. In the first place, he had been under pressure for some months before Blackfriars and Cambrai. How did these months of severe struggle relate to those dramatic defeats? Secondly, why, after the cardinal's manifest failure to give the king what he wanted, did ten weeks elapse before he was indicted and ten days more before he lost office? And what of the further year before Wolsey became truly a target of Henry's vengeance when Walter Walsh, groom of the privy chamber, set out to arrest him in Yorkshire in November 1530 on a charge of high treason?[4]

[1] This essay elaborates and advances the argument put forward in E. W. Ives, *Anne Boleyn* (Oxford, 1986) (hereafter '*Anne Boleyn*').

[2] G. Mattingly, *Catherine of Aragon* (1950) (hereafter 'Mattingly'), p. 212. Works cited were published at London unless otherwise stated.

[3] *Henry VIII*, III, ii, 371–2.

[4] Cavendish, pp. 152–8.

Contemporary evidence certainly suggests that Wolsey's fall was less simple than it seems. The obvious starting point is the account which the cardinal's gentleman usher, George Cavendish, gives of the way in which his disgraced master's journey in October 1529 from the episcopal palace of York Place to internal exile at his house at Esher, was interrupted by an encounter at Putney with Henry Norris, chief gentleman of Henry VIII's privy chamber and keeper of the king's close stool.[5]

Norris had brought a message from Henry, telling Wolsey 'to be of good chere, for he was as myche in his highenes favour as ever he was', and to warrant this assurance he produced the king's private ring, always a proof of Henry VIII's personal intervention. 'And', said Norris,

> allthoughe the kyng hathe delt with you onkyndly as ye supposse he saythe that it is for no displeasure that he beryth you, but oonly to sattysfie more the myndes of some whiche he knowyth be not your frendes than for any indygnacion. And also ye knowe right well that he is able to recompence you with twyse as myche as your goodes amountithe vnto . . . Therfore Sir take pacience. And for my part I trust to se you in better estate than euer ye ware.

There ensued one of the more farcical moments of Tudor history. Wolsey scrambled from his mule and knelt in the mud, and the elegant Norris was forced to follow suit, imploring the cardinal all the while to believe his message. Wolsey then tried to take his cap off, but the strings jammed, so he had to tear it off before giving thanks to God and the king for such 'comfortable and joyfull newes'. The two then mounted, each somewhat grubby, and rode side by side for a distance before Norris departed with a personal gift of Wolsey's highly prized cross and a present for the king – no less than the cardinal's famous fool, Patch Williams.

Yet despite all this, Wolsey was not restored. Even as Norris spoke, process against the cardinal was continuing in the court of king's bench.[6] So what are we to make of the Putney episode? Cavendish, of course, was writing twenty-five years after the event and, though an eyewitness, was unlikely to have remembered Norris's words verbatim.[7] Yet he cannot have invented the production of something as talismanic as the king's ring, and that must dispose of the possibility that Norris was only a friend come to sympathize with Wolsey. Nor was the occasion unique. Ten days or so later, in the early hours of 2 November, Sir John Russell arrived soaking wet at Esher having ridden through the rain from Greenwich with a secret promise of urgently needed supplies for Wolsey, again authenticating his message by production of the

---

[5] Ibid., pp. 101–4.
[6] Wolsey had left York Place by 22 Oct. R. Scheurer (ed.), *Correspondance du Cardinal Jean du Bellay*, (Paris, 1969) (hereafter 'Du Bellay'), p. 112, on which date he made a formal surrender of his goods to the crown (*LP*, iv, 6017), but court process continued until judgement on 30 Oct. (J. A. Baker (ed.), *Reports of John Spelman*, Selden Soc. 93–4, 1977–8) (hereafter 'Spelman'), i, 190.
[7] Cavendish, pp. xxvi–xxvii.

king's ring.[8] But the following day saw the king at the opening of parliament listening as Thomas More abused Wolsey as 'rotten and fauty, . . . the great wether . . . of late fallen'.[9] Thus, at the very least, it must be accepted that the king was in secret and friendly communication with Wolsey at the very time that the cardinal was being prosecuted in Henry's name and publicly vilified in Henry's presence.

More's speech did, of course, describe Wolsey's correction as 'gentle' and we might follow those historians who see the king's action being influenced by long friendship and a desire to keep Wolsey available if required.[10] There was no effective attempt to replace him, and Scarpinello, the Milanese ambassador in London, tells us of Henry grumbling 'everyday I miss the cardinal of York more and more'.[11] Money is always a sure indicator of Henry VIII's real favour, and one may note that as well as the goods and chattels Russell promised, Wolsey was provided with a substantial sum in ready cash and restored to temporalties and a pension which left him still one of the richest men in England.[12] All this can mean only one thing – in 1529 Wolsey certainly did not fall like Lucifer. He had a remarkably soft landing.

I

Given that this was the case, many traditional views are necessarily called in question. What was the real significance of Blackfriars and Cambrai, and why the assault on Wolsey in October? New problems arise also. Why was it that a king who had so carefully not destroyed the cardinal failed to restore him to power when his new advisers proved wholly unable to solve his matrimonial problem? And what was it, four months after his loss of office, which made it necessary to rusticate the cardinal in February/March 1530, and why the ultimate charge of high treason?

The problems are evident, but the story recorded by Cavendish itself gives a clue to the riddles of Wolsey's fall. In explaining to Wolsey the king's actions against him, Norris said:

> it is for no displeasure that he beryth you, but oonly to sattysfie more the myndes of some whiche he knowyth be not your frendes

'To satisfy some he knoweth be not your friends' – in other words, what the king had done was in part a response to third parties, to what would now be described as the political circles of the day.

[8] Ibid., pp. 110–12. Cavendish states that Russell arrived about midnight on All Hallows Day (1 Nov.) and left so as to be back at court by dawn on 2 Nov.

[9] Hall, p. 764.

[10] E.g. J. S. Brewer, *The Reign of Henry VIII* (1884) (hereafter 'Brewer'), II, 386–7; Pollard, pp. 262–3; J. J. Scarisbrick, *Henry VIII* (1968) (hereafter 'Scarisbrick'), pp. 235–40; G. R. Elton, *Reform and Reformation* (1977) (hereafter 'Elton, *Reform*'), p. 113.

[11] *CSPV 1527–33*, 637.   [12] Pollard, p. 253; see below n. 135.

Historians of previous generations attached a relatively low importance to politics in Tudor England. Their emphasis was on rulers who worked through trusted ministers to execute royal policy within constitutional parameters; successful kingship was a matter of dominating and controlling naturally contentious and centrifugal power groups in the community; danger arose from a failure of policy or control and from external pressure. Hence Pollard interpreted Henry VIII's leniency towards Wolsey in 1529 as a move to keep him 'in view as a possible alternative' to the new minister, Norfolk, and 'to hold the balance between opposing parties'.[13]

Today, however, it is clear that politics was at the heart of monarchy and government in sixteenth-century England, and of nothing was this more true than the career of Thomas Wolsey. It was political and courtly skill which brought him to power, as Polydore Vergil makes clear; Polydore, of course, disliked the cardinal, but he had been close to those involved and was writing demonstrably within twenty years of the events – indeed, he claimed he wrote concurrently.[14] It was these qualities, too, which created the very special relationship with Henry VIII which kept Wolsey in power, and throughout his fifteen-year domination of English affairs, politics were never far away. The years 1515, 1516 and 1517 saw Wolsey overcoming substantial opposition from various quarters, while in 1519, the ripples from the affair of the 'minions' went a good deal wider than is often realized.[15] As for 1520, this was the year of the Field of Cloth of Gold, a celebration intended almost as much to demonstrate the political clout of Thomas Wolsey as the European standing of Henry VIII.[16]

Attempts have, it is true, been made to distance Wolsey from the next great crisis, the destruction of Buckingham, but the weight of contemporary opinion is in the opposite direction.[17] Recent work has sought to cast similar doubt on the

---

[13] Pollard, pp. 262–3.

[14] Polydore Vergil, *Anglica Historia, 1485–1537*, ed. D. Hay (Camden Soc. 4 ser. 74, 1950) (hereafter, 'Vergil'), pp. xx, 194–8; cf. Richard Fox, *Letters, 1486–1527*, ed. P. S. and H. M. Allen (Oxford, 1929), pp. 52–5. Cavendish, pp. 11–12 also stresses the importance of Wolsey's courtly skills.

[15] *Anne Boleyn*, pp. 15–17; G. W. Bernard, *The Power of the Early-Tudor Nobility* (Brighton, 1985) (hereafter 'Bernard, *Nobility*'), pp. 11–26; A. Ogle, *The Tragedy of the Lollards Tower* (Oxford, 1949), pp. 114–56; D. Starkey, *The Reign of Henry VIII: Personalities and Politics* (1985) (hereafter 'Starkey'), pp. 73–4; see below also n. 74.

[16] The climax of the Field of Cloth of Gold was the high mass sung by Wolsey on 23 June. J. G. Russell, *The Field of Cloth of Gold* (1969), pp. 171–7.

[17] C. Rawcliffe, *The Staffords, Earls of Stafford and Dukes of Buckingham, 1394–1521* (Cambridge, 1978), p. 44; Bernard, *Nobility*, pp. 14, 199–200 and the sources cited at p. 215. Cf. Vergil, pp. 264–5, 272–80; Pollard, p. 316 (for Wolsey's own comment); H. Miller, *Henry VIII and the English Nobility* (Oxford, 1986) (hereafter 'Miller'), pp. 49–51 (especially for the comment of Buckingham's son); M. Levine, 'The Fall of Edward, duke of Buckingham', in A. J. Slavin (ed.), *Tudor Men and Institutions* (Baton Rouge, 1972), pp. 43–5. B. Harris, *Edward Stafford, Third Duke of Buckingham, 1478–1521* (Stanford, 1986), pp. 203–6 is sceptical of the contemporary view on grounds of the hostility of the reporters (a non-sequitur) and the fact that the duke did not threaten Wolsey, but then adduces the reports of foreign ambassadors that Stafford was plotting against Wolsey. The duke's own incautious remarks make it certain that he fantasized about some kind of action if he could secure

suggestion that the affair of the Amicable Grant in 1525 was characterized by
tension between the cardinal and the dukes of Norfolk and Suffolk.[18] Admittedly
the surviving correspondence does not support the idea of an opportunistic
attempt to exploit the crisis to unseat Wolsey, still less any calculated aristocratic
plot; equally unlikely is the suggestion that the dukes dragged their feet over
enforcing royal policies in their home territories in order to embarrass the
minister. But it nevertheless seems clear that Norfolk and Suffolk were determined that blame should not rest on their shoulders, and that it was their united
opposition which forced the minister to accept political defeat and withdraw the
grant.[19] Politics changes day by day, and it involves programmes as well as
personalities; there is no contradiction between vigorous initial attempts to
implement a policy and growing doubts about it, leading to a move to force its
instigator to back down.

Whatever the truth about the events of the spring of 1525, the following winter
certainly saw Wolsey deeply involved in political manoeuvre. The issue was the
reform of the royal household, and the minister used the opportunity to attempt
to curb the potential political influence of the privy chamber.[20] While on embassy
to France eighteen months later, Wolsey felt even more threatened by what might
be happening in his absence, as his letters to the king – embarrassing to read even
after five centuries – make amply clear.[21]

This story of a crisis every year or two during Wolsey's period in office could be
augmented with several minor episodes. Some of it we may dismiss as Wolsey's
own imagination, the product of his well-attested inferiority complex. In other
cases we may conclude that the trouble was real but stirred up by Wolsey himself
– whether by the abuse of royal power to pay off old personal scores or by private
vindictiveness – as in his treatment of Henry Standish and Sir Robert Sheffield,
the neutralizing of the probably harmless Pace and the selective prosecution of
alleged offenders against the enclosure legislation.[22] But, if nothing else, all this
was evidence of Wolsey's conviction that political power had to be fought for and
defended vigilantly, and, it is hard not to conclude that his belief was grounded
in reality, not paranoia.

Thomas Wolsey, therefore, had been a politician and a courtier through all his
years in public life. His fall, too, must be seen in that same context. The story
began, according to Cavendish, some time before the Battle of Pavia (February,

allies. To argue for Wolsey's involvement in Buckingham's fall is not to imply that he had a considered policy to destroy the nobility, any more than Henry VIII did.

[18] G. W. Bernard, *War, Taxation and Rebellion in Early Tudor England* (Brighton, 1986), pp. 76–92.

[19] Note especially the letters of 12 and 17 May, PRO, SP1/34, fols. 196–7, 209–10 (*LP*, IV, 1329, 1343).

[20] Starkey, pp. 86–9.   [21] *StP*, i, 267, 278–9 (*LP*, IV, 3382, 3423).

[22] J. A. Guy, *The Cardinal's Court* (Hassocks, 1977) (hereafter 'Guy, *Court*'), pp. 76–8; M. Dowling,
Humanism in the Age of Henry VIII (Beckenham, 1986), pp. 168–9; G. Walker, *John Skelton and the
Politics of the 1520s* (Cambridge, 1988) (hereafter 'Walker, *Skelton*'), pp. 76–8; J. J. Scarisbrick,
'Cardinal Wolsey and the Common Weal', in E. W. Ives *et al.* (eds.), *Wealth and Power in Tudor
England* (1978), pp. 63–7.

1525), when a clique of nobles seized on Anne Boleyn as 'a suffycyent and an apte instrument to bryng . . . hyme owt of the kynges highe fauour and them in to more auctorytie of rewle and cyvell gouernance'.[23] In the event they drew back having failed to put together a convincing-enough case to disrupt 'thespecyall fauour that the kyng bare to the cardynall'. In 1527, however, there was another opportunity when Wolsey's absence in France left the field open 'to deprave hyme so vnto the kyng in his absence that he shold be rather in his hyghe displeasure than in his accustomed fauour'.[24]

Although Cavendish had a good nose and memory for political nuances, he must, in this case, be both premature and condensed in his chronology. Research has yet to demonstrate awareness of Henry's involvement with Anne in any contemporary source before the summer of 1527, although one of the king's own letters allows us to project his interest back to the spring of 1526.[25] Cavendish, of course, may be correct in saying that there were noble grumblings against the cardinal before Pavia, but if so, these can have had nothing to do with Anne and were no more than a further episode in the long saga of such incidents. As for Cavendish's suggestion that the attack revived in 1527, the demonstrable anxiety which Wolsey exhibited lasted only as long as the cardinal was abroad. Back in England he quickly recovered his old dominance with a huge court gala to mark Henry VIII's election to the French knightly order of St Michael and a grand star chamber meeting to announce his other diplomatic triumphs to 'the lordes spirituall and temporal of the kynges counsail, and the Maior and Aldermen of the citie of London and the iudges of the law, and all the Iustices of peace of all shyres then beyng at Westminster'.[26] As for 1528, this turned out to be – at least on the central problem of the divorce – a year of marked success for the cardinal, with the arrival in England at the end of September of Cardinal Campeggio, armed with greater powers from the pope than anyone could have expected. A final resolution to the king's marital difficulty now seemed within grasp and the evidence indicates that Henry and Anne were united in their confidence in the man who had worked the miracle.[27]

What changed matters decisively was that Anne Boleyn became convinced – not later than the middle of January – that Wolsey was, in fact, not to be trusted, that he was stringing out the divorce proceedings, no doubt in the hope that Henry would tire of her.[28] Anne, after all, had grown up through the court and could recognize the manipulation and calculation involved in office much better than Henry, who always tended to believe in a simple world where the king spoke and it was done – hence his tendency to see argument and contradiction as conspiracy.

Anne Boleyn's break with Thomas Wolsey marked the start of the cardinal's

[23] Cavendish, pp. 35–6. [24] Ibid., p. 44. [25] *Anne Boleyn*, pp. 101–2, 107–9.
[26] Ibid., p. 132; Hall, pp. 733–5.
[27] *Anne Boleyn*, pp. 132–5. [28] Ibid., pp. 136–7.

downward slide not merely because it was the end to a personal relationship. Anne's reaction went much further. Since Wolsey would not free the king to marry again, she determined to find allies who would join her to achieve what Henry and she wanted. Thus, as Cavendish suggests, she made common cause with others offended by the cardinal's monopoly of authority, the chief of whom were her father, her uncle the duke of Norfolk, and the duke of Suffolk, and by doing so she created the best possibility in a decade for a change of power.[29] What had for so long proved an unassailable partnership of king and minister (which the wise resigned themselves to accept), was now subverted by someone who possessed a novel, uniquely intimate and unchallengeable relationship with the king, and who wanted the cardinal out of the way. The point was a commonplace of the time, but it was particularly well put by the vice-chamberlain, Sir John Gage; 'my lorde his enemyes and hinderers', he was reported to have said, 'have had tyme with the king before his frendes'.[30]

So much for the starting date of Wolsey's troubles. The next problem is to explain the way Wolsey responded, or more properly failed to respond. Why did the old professional begin to lose first one round and then another? One answer is obvious. The king's matrimonial problem was insoluble, given that Campeggio would countenance no annulment of the Aragonese marriage on the terms Henry wanted, and that Henry, invincible in the conviction of divine inspiration, angrily refused all advice to change his plea. All Wolsey could do, as Campeggio reported, was to 'shrug his shoulders and say that the only remedy is to satisfy the king's wish in some way or other and let it stand for what it is worth'.[31]

There was, however, another reason for Wolsey's inability to defend himself as of old, and that became clear when Henry, convinced at last that the pope would not make further concessions in advance of the legatine hearing, decided to go to trial with all possible speed.[32] Wolsey concurred, in the confidence that the impending European peace conference would wait for him, but when it would not, he was placed in a hopeless position. The king, obsessed with the justice of his claim, believed that Blackfriars must have the highest priority; Wolsey, knowing the dubious justification of the claim in law and the opportunities inherent in a grand European peace negotiation, believed that he should be released to go to Cambrai. Inevitably, Henry's order of priorities prevailed, and Wolsey had to devote himself to the trial – thereby discarding the potential ace of England's diplomatic value to the Emperor and to Francis I, in favour of an outside gamble on success at the legatine hearing. In other words, what undermined his position so gravely was not the failure to secure a decision at the Blackfriars hearing so much as being held there while real opportunities at

---

[29] Cavendish, pp. 35–6; CSPS 1527–9, pp. 885–6.

[30] BL, Cott. Tit.B I, fo. 375 (LP, IV, 6112). The report continued: 'Neuertheles he [Gage] trustith that, God willyng, they shalbe preuented in suche wise that their purpose shall take small effect.'

[31] Brewer, II, 486.   [32] For the following see Anne Boleyn, pp. 139–40, 144–5.

Cambrai went begging. Henry VIII, by insisting that litigation must come before negotiation, robbed himself and his minister of any real chance of victory.

The blame for Blackfriars and Cambrai thus belonged more to Henry than to Wolsey, but it was Wolsey who would pay the penalty – or so Catherine of Aragon and many others expected and so most historians have thought.[33] Pollard roundly declared, 'Wolsey's power was gone'.[34] But what exactly did Pollard and those who have thought likewise imagine happened to the cardinal at the end of July 1529? Loss of office? This, notoriously, did not occur. Exclusion from public affairs? Correspondence between Henry and Wolsey after Blackfriars shows no sign of strain: Henry expresses recognition and approval of Wolsey's efforts; as late as 28 August Henry sought prior confidential advice from the cardinal before broaching diplomatic matters to the council.[35] As for the king's alleged firmness in putting an end to Wolsey's despairing attempt to subvert the calling of parliament, both the attempt and the firm response are inventions of the historian.[36]

Was Wolsey, perhaps, excluded from the king's presence? Geoffrey Elton follows Pollard's hint and says that Henry 'ostentatiously refused to visit the cardinal's house', but reading this significance into the king's itinerary in August 1529 is wholly unjustified.[37] Henry had originally accepted Wolsey's invitation to visit The More, but on learning that the sweat had broken out at Rickmansworth announced that:

> therfor his Highnes will not goo thither, but in stede of that goo to Titennehanger [another of Wolsey's houses], and take such chere of your Grace there as he shulde have had at the More.[38]

Tyttenhanger was only three miles from St Alban's where the king knew the minister would base his own household, and Wolsey's 'cheer' certainly included attending himself to entertain the king.[39] As for Wolsey's enemies, they most

---

[33] *CSPS 1529–30*, p. 133; *Anne Boleyn*, p. 142.   [34] Pollard, p. 234.   [35] See below, pp. 300–1.

[36] Gardiner's letter (PRO, sp1/55, fols. 188–9 (*LP*, iv, 5993)) dated 'Windsor, Wednesday', asking Wolsey to send the writs for the elections in Notts and Derbys which the king intended to send out via the duke of Norfolk, and also those for Bucks, Beds, Hants and Southampton, was not a late measure to force a recalcitrant chancellor to put in motion the election of MPs (*pace* Elton, *Reform*, p. 111 following Pollard, pp. 241–2). Although calendared under October 1529, the letter can be associated with PRO, sp1/55, fols. 43–4 (*LP*, iv, 5831) of 6 August and internally dated as 18 August. Its purpose was evidently to secure the election of royal nominees – at least nine of the twelve MPs returned for the relevant constituencies held royal office (most in the household) or were connected with Wolsey or Anne Boleyn. S. T. Bindoff (ed.), *The House of Commons, 1509–1558* (1982) (hereafter 'Commons'), I, 293, 562–3, 666–7; II, 43, 194–5, 314–5, 538–9, 568–70, 602–4, 651–2; III, 72–5, 268–9.

[37] Elton, *Reform*, p. 111.

[38] H. Ellis, *Original Letters* (series 1: 1824; series 2: 1827; series 3: 1846) (hereafter 'Ellis, *Letters*'), III, i, 345 (*LP*, iv, 5825).

[39] N. Samman, 'The Henrician court during Cardinal Wolsey's ascendancy, *c.* 1514 to 1529', PhD Wales (1989) (hereafter 'Samman'), p. 386 citing PRO, sp1/55, fols. 96–7 (*LP*, iv, 5886), and ibid., iv, 5906 (16). Samman has established that, contrary to what is normally stated (e.g. *Anne Boleyn*,

definitely did not sweep into power that summer. They were certainly and, as we shall see, significantly with the king, but they were in the saddle only in the hunting field. In fact, very few of the supposedly fatal consequences of Black-friars and Cambrai survive careful scrutiny, nothing more, perhaps, than a dent in Wolsey's reputation for omnipotence and a willingness on Henry's part to listen to those other voices around him, and that was a situation by no means beyond recovery – and perhaps not as unusual as historians have imagined.[40]

Then what had happened to Anne Boleyn and her allies? The answer is that in June and July 1529 they had put together a carefully prepared attempt at a coup against Wolsey. This envisaged the sudden arrest of the cardinal and his agents, the seizure and scrutiny of all their papers, a rigorous interrogation of the suspects, and the calling of parliament to deal with the malefactors – no doubt by attainder – and to put through a programme of reform. The defeat at Blackfriars seemed the opportune moment to strike, and they launched the coup immedi-ately – only to find Henry unwilling to throw Wolsey to their mercy, and Wolsey adept enough to bribe his way out of trouble. Their sole success was to persuade Henry to call parliament for November.[41] Wolsey, therefore, far from being destroyed after the reverse at Blackfriars, was able to win a defensive victory.

This is revisionism with a vengeance, and clearly needs to be demonstrated in some detail. The decision to call a parliament is readily substantiated. The relevant instructions were entered on the close roll on 9 August, but the decision had certainly been made by 6 August and probably before Henry left Greenwich in the first few days of the month.[42] As for the proposed coup, the detailed plans are to be found in papers confiscated from Thomas Lord Darcy in 1537, after the Pilgrimage of Grace.[43] These are easily dismissed as the random jottings of a man with a grievance – which Darcy certainly was. Yet although they are not the work of a professional draftsman, they amount to a practical political plan to get rid of the cardinal, in sharp contrast to the common order of complaint against him. John Guy has drawn attention to the parliamentary programme which is included, but there is more, for example a detailed dossier of Wolsey's misdeeds, with notes for the investigators and texts of proclamations ready to be issued inviting more complaints from the country at large.[44] The planning is suggest-

---

p. 143), Henry and Wolsey did meet from time to time during a summer progress. Gairdner drew attention to the story told by Nicholas Sander (1585) that during the meeting at Tyttenhanger, the issue of discussion was royal policy in the face of the revocation of the divorce suit to Rome: J. Gairdner, 'The Fall of Cardinal Wolsey', *Transactions of the Royal Historical Society*, n.s. 13 (1899) (hereafter 'Gairdner'), pp. 78–81.

[40] Samman argues persuasively that Wolsey never enjoyed exclusive access to the king.

[41] The extent of this success must not be exaggerated. The calling of a parliament in 1529 or 1530 was, statistically, a high probability. See also n. 65.

[42] PRO, sp1/55, fols. 43–4 (*LP*, IV, 5831), and ibid., IV, 5837.   [43] See below, note 54.

[44] J. A. Guy, *The Public Career of Sir Thomas More* (Brighton, 1980) (hereafter 'Guy, *More*'), pp. 106–7; 206–7. But, *pace* p. 106 n. 56, the fol. edited at pp. 206–7 is not 'quite separate' from the rest of the text, see below note 54 (1).

ively like the successful coup against Empson and Dudley in 1509, and the main body of the material was in being at the start of July 1529.[45]

One man's planning does not, however, make a coup. What evidence is there of actual steps being taken to force Wolsey out of office at the end of July 1529? The answer is to be found in a few strangely neglected sentences in Hall's Chronicle. What he says is detailed and clear. When, after the failure of the legatine hearing,

> the nobles and prelates perceiued that the kings fauor was from the Cardinal sore minished, euery man of the Kynges Counsaill, beganne to laye to him suche offences, as they knewe by hym, and all their accusacions were written in a boke, and all their handes set to it, to the number of thirtie and foure, which boke they presented to the kyng. When the kyng saw the boke, he marueiled not a litle, for by the Articles conteigned in thesame, he euidently perceiued the high pride and couetousnes of the Cardinal, and saw openly with what dissimulacion and clokyng he had handeled the kynges causes: how he with faire liyng woordes, had blynded and defrauded the kyng, most vntruly, whiche accusacions sore moued the kyng against hym, yet he kepte it close for a time, and so the Kyng rode on his progresse with the Quene to Woodstocke.[46]

By the start of July 1529, therefore, Thomas Darcy had a strategy and a list of complaints against Wolsey ready prepared, and at the end of the month, a book of articles against Wolsey was put to Henry and Henry gave orders to summon a parliament. These are suggestive concurrences, but to make further progress it is necessary to establish the nature of the book of articles described by Hall. The document itself has not yet been identified and the probability must be that it has not survived. Hall, however, tells us something more about it, a few pages later in his account:

> Duryng this Parliament was brought doune to the commons, the boke of articles whiche the Lordes had put to the kyng agaynst the Cardinall, the chief articles were these. [nine items are specified] ... These Articles with many more, red in the common house, and signed with the Cardinalles hande, was confessed by him, & ther was shewed a writyng sealed with his Seale, by the whiche he gaue to the kyng all his mouables and vnmouables.[47]

This is a vital clue, for the text of a petition against Wolsey which substantially corresponds to the detail of Hall's account is extant, thanks to transcriptions

---

[45] See below note 54.

[46] Hall, pp. 758–9. This corrects the reading in *Anne Boleyn*, p. 142 where 'to the number of thirtie and foure' is taken to refer to 'handes' rather than 'accusacions'. The syntax is typically convoluted and by itself ambiguous, although if Hall had intended 'thirtie and foure' to indicate the number of counsellors, the figure might more naturally have come after 'every man of the Kynges Counsaill'. However the discussion set out below (pp. 308–9, 311) makes it clear that fewer than seventeen counsellors signed and that Hall must, therefore, have been referring to the charges. For thirty-four counsellors to sign a petition would certainly be exceptional.

[47] Hall, pp. 767–8.

published by Edward Coke and Lord Herbert of Cherbury in 1644 and 1649 respectively.[48]

The petition is dated 1 December but had, despite its date, been in circulation for several weeks as is independently corroborated in the correspondence of the French ambassador, Jean du Bellay. In a letter to the duc de Montmorency dated 22 October, the envoy set out what he knew of the charges against the cardinal.

> [There are] allegations [which] concern the peculations he has engaged in, but by themselves these are no hanging matter. They accuse him of high treason on the ground that he has retained the post of legate for more than a decade, contrary to the laws of the land; because at Amiens he agreed to include the duke of Ferrara in the League without the king's consent, and gave the king [Francis I] an obligation in his own hand, again without the king's authority; and furthermore because he declared war on the emperor against his [Henry's] wishes. They claim that even the least of these offences will cost him his head.

Although the fourth of the 'capital' charges listed here is not specifically made in the petition produced in parliament, the first three correspond precisely with its three opening items (but in the order 1,3,2) and establish beyond doubt that an earlier version did lie behind the December text.[49] Furthermore, since Du Bellay's letter was written immediately after Wolsey's loss of the great seal, the interval between the July 'articles' and this anticipation of the December petition is reduced to two and a half months – a circumstance which, it may be felt, would make it actually improbable for the one not to be based on the other.

Du Bellay's letter of 22 October thus provides good ground for believing Hall's

---

[48] Edward Coke, *The Fourth Part of the Institutes of the Laws of England* (1797) (hereafter 'Coke'), pp. 88–95; Edward Herbert, Lord Herbert of Cherbury, *The History of England under Henry VIII* (1870) (hereafter 'Herbert'), pp. 408–17. Herbert is the source for the version in William Cobbett (ed.), *A Complete Collection of State Trials* (1809), I, 371–9. For the differences between Coke and Herbert, see below nn. 50, 103. *Commons*, II, 143, following R. E. Brock, 'The courtier in early Tudor society', PhD London (1964), p. 56, refers to additional signatures to parts of the petition, so implying the existence of another text (apparently ms). The footnote in the thesis (and the accompanying quotation) is, however, to *LP*, IV, 6075, which is a summary of the Herbert text in the 1706 edition. I have been unable to verify any alternative source for the data presented by Brock. BL Cott.Vesp.F ix, fols. 175–7v. is a partial ms copy from para. 28 to the end (early eighteenth-century?), which does not derive from the printed texts, but confirms them. I have been unable to examine the copy at Holkham (Historical Mss Commission (hereafter 'HMC'), *9th Report* (1883–4), p. 365), which could conceivably be the text which Coke used.

[49] Du Bellay, p. 112. 'Les poinctz ou l'on le cherche sont les pilleries qu'il a faictes, mais tout cela ne le feroit mourir. Ilz prennent pour lese-majesté qu'il ayt guardé la legation plus de dix ans contre les loix du pays; qu'estant a Amyens, il accorda de mectre le duc de Ferrare en la Ligue sans le seau du Roy et qu'il bailla au Roy (Francis I) une cedule obligatoire de sa main sans le commandement pareillement dudict sieur; et qu'encores depuys, il feist intimer la guerre a l'Empereur contre son intention. Le maindre de ces poinctz, comme ilz pretendent, luy faict perdre la teste.' (I am grateful for the help of R. J. Knecht in elucidating Du Bellay's despatches.) The December petition explains that the 'obligation' bound Francis to accept Wolsey's arbitration in any dispute with the pope over the treaty he had arranged between them. The charge of declaring war on Charles V referred to the defiance of the emperor at Burgos in January 1528. Although alluded to by Norfolk when speaking to Chapuys in October 1529 and mentioned specifically in March 1530, it was omitted in the petition, unless it was the inspiration of para. 12 which alleged unapproved communication with ambassadors. *CSPS, 1529–30*, pp. 293, 486; Pollard, pp. 158–9 and 158 n. 4; Scarisbrick, p. 199.

story that the parliamentary complaints in December derived from the July 'articles' and an important corollary follows: something of the contents of the earlier 'boke' should be recoverable from the later 'petition'. Hall's account implies that the two were identical, but this cannot be wholly true. The versions of the complaints transcribed for Coke and Herbert contain forty-four articles, where Hall's original contained thirty-four, although this could be explained by the evident fact that the seventeenth-century transcribers were using a garbled version or versions.[50] Furthermore, the text shows signs of development between July and December: rewriting is demonstrable in the preface; the date of the subscription, 1 December, is an obvious change; the name of Thomas More, signing first as chancellor, must be a novelty.[51]

There are also what seem to be anachronistic survivals from the earlier text – such as pointing out that by preventing rights of presentation the cardinal 'is in danger to your grace of forfeiture of his lands and goods, and his body at your pleasure', and the final demand that Henry 'set such order and direction upon the said lord cardinal as may be to the terrible example of others', despite Wolsey's surrender in October to the full rigour of the penalties of praemunire.[52] One may further observe that according to Hall, the text shown to the commons had, in contrast to the surviving version, been countersigned by Wolsey, and included the important charge, omitted in the surviving text, that the cardinal had taken the great seal with him to Flanders.[53] Thus one must suspect that there are omissions as well as confusions and elaborations in what is now extant, but these are in no way sufficient to destroy Hall's testimony that the articles of July and the petition of December 1529 were in essence the same.

To link the July 'boke' with that sent to the commons in December is, of course, to connect the abortive challenge to the cardinal after Blackfriars with the successful attack on him later in the year. Can the chain be made complete by establishing a link with the draft plans of Thomas Darcy? Darcy's criticisms cover the same ground as, and are strikingly similar to those of the December 'petition'.[54] The assessment of Wolsey is the same: specific allegations that he showed disrespect to the king; that he abused the monasteries, especially over the matter of

---

50 It is, of course, possible that the figure '34' instead of '44' is a crude error by Hall's editor or printer. There is some indication that Herbert saw Coke's text, for Coke, p. 88 justified printing the charges 'the rather for that in our Chronicles they are very untruly rehearsed', and Herbert, p. 408 claimed to print 'the rather for that our vulgar chronicles misreport them'. However Herbert is not dependent on Coke or vice versa. Each claimed to have used the original and reliance on a third text/texts is demonstrable since each version has significant passages with an obviously correct reading (Coke: paras. 4, 9, 27, 41, 42; Herbert: preface and paras. 9, 41, 43). Herbert, however, has fewer errors overall. That the text/texts being copied were already garbled is clear from the fact that para. 19 begins by refering to the contents of para. 29.

51 The preface refers to 'the lord cardinall of York, lately your graces chancelour': Coke, p. 88.

52 Para. 7 and conclusion: Coke, pp. 90, 95.

53 Hall, pp. 767–8.

54 The Darcy material against Wolsey consists of certainly six items. (1) PRO, sp1/54, fols. 234–41 (*LP*, IV, 5749(1)): 4 sheets folded into a gathering of 8 folios, containing articles against the cardinal under various headings: Darcy's hand; fol. 234 is title page and carries the date 1 July, 1529; material

the small houses he dissolved; that he exploited the fiscal possibilities of his church position; and that as chancellor, he interfered with the common law. There are verbal echoes too – in Darcy's draft we find: Wolsey's 'great orgull and pridde and insatial cuvetusnes', and in the articles: his 'high, orgallous and insatiable mind'.[55] Two charges occur in the same detail in each text – that the cardinal appropriated the goods of deceased church dignitaries (who are named), and that he retained most of the income due from the benefices held by his son, Thomas Wynter.[56] Not all the complaints in the December text appeared in Darcy's work in July, but the closeness of the documents is such as to suggest that the one was very plausibly a basis for the other.[57]

runs continuously; marked up for a scribe; final verso, fol. 241, is blank. (2) SP1/54, fol. 242 (LP, IV, 5749(2)): single sheet containing further articles; Darcy's hand; no date or title. (3) SP1/54, fol. 243 (LP, IV, 5749(3)i): paper lengthwise containing draft proclamation re Wolsey's offences; Darcy's hand. (4) SP1/54, fol. 243v (LP, IV, 5749(3)ii): scribal copy of a further draft proclamation re Wolsey's offences. (5) SP1/122, fols. 48v–57 (LP, XII (ii) 186(38)i): 10 sheets lengthwise containing a petition complaining of the prominence of clerics on the council of the North (a role promoted by Wolsey: R. B. Smith, Land and Politics in the England of Henry VIII (Oxford, 1970), pp. 153–5); scribal hand; corrections by Darcy. (6) SP1/122, fols. 58–9 (LP, XII (ii) 186(38)ii): preliminary draft of 5; Darcy's hand. Two further items may also belong to the group. (7) E314/82/5(i): single sheet containing 'articuls for the k agaynst the c'; scribal hand. (8) ibid., 5(ii), single sheet containing text of (7) in Latin; same hand. 7 and 8 are on paper with the same watermark as 4 and 5, in a hand which may be that of 4 (but not 5), indicate names by initials (a Darcy habit), and come from a collection where other Darcy material is to be found. I am indebted to Dr S. J. Gunn for drawing my attention to 7 and 8, and to Dr Richard Hoyle for discussing the comparison of the documents. 7 and 8 contain four charges: (a) misuse of money levied by the crown for defence and the recovery of France; (b) securing papal bulls to the prejudice of the king who 'by the auctorite of the church . . . is a person mixt in gevyng . . . aswell secular benefices as regular', so setting a precedent for future legatine and papal claims; (c) coining of bullion etc. in 'much gretter summys than it besemys any oon prelate' (£7,000); (d) 'Also that ye, C[ardinal], intromyt yourself with nigromancy which is prohibit by the laws of God, and to the occupiers of the sane gif your cownsayll, ayde, and help, and so fauour them that they be not nor haue not beyn correct[ed] and ponysshed. And ferthermore, saye susspeciously and agaynst the law of God that ye wast no tyme in idilnesse but the tyme of masse, aswell the Sundays as oder, in contempt of the laws and [de]keys of the church'. 7 and 8 frequently drop into direct speech and may be an attempt at preparing an indictment to be read out in court, with the Latin version then being entered for the record.

[55] cf. PRO, SP1/54, fol. 237v (LP, IV, 5749 at p. 2551) with Coke, p. 89.

[56] cf. PRO, SP1/54, fol. 234v (LP, IV, 5749 at p. 2548) (listing Bishop (William) Smith of Lincoln, Archbishop (Thomas) Savage, (Cardinal Christopher) Bainbridge, (Thomas) Dalby (archdeacon of Richmond), (Mr Robert) Toneys, Bishop (Thomas Ruthal) of Durham, Bishop (Richard Fox) of Winchester) with para. 30: Coke, p. 92 (which omits Bainbridge) – see also SP1/54, fols. 237v, 239 (LP, IV, 5749 at pp. 2551, 2552). For Winter, cf. para 27: Coke, p. 91+, with SP1/54, fol. 239 (LP, IV, 5749 at p. 2552). Cf. also SP1/54, fol. 238v (LP, IV, 5749 at p. 2552): 'The surmysses whye the said housses wer pulled dowen, made to the poppe for the awctorites', with paras. 19 and 29; Coke, pp. 91–2.

[57] Darcy may also have prepared material for the October attack on Wolsey, as well as that in July. MSS (7) and (8) (note 54 above) presume an indictment and so probably fit with the later date; MSS (5) and (6) purport to be a response to a call from the king and the 'Chauncellour & Speker of the high Court of Parliament' to submit grievances, and could have been prepared in the expectation that More would issue such an invitation in his speech of 3 November. On the other hand, the reference could be to Darcy's draft petitions inviting the submission of grievances (MSS 3 and 4) which speak of Wolsey as still in office and are probably, therefore, part of the July plan.

If this was the case, then something more can be established about the attempted coup in July. The December petition begins with the central charge that Wolsey had offended against the statute of praemunire – which may seem hardly surprising, given the king's bench action against the cardinal in October. Darcy's memoranda, however, show that in July he was already aware that the minister's Achilles heel might be his vulnerability to an accusation of praemunire.

> Then [i.e. 'at his entere to awctorite'] none of hygh or low degre durst enter in to the danger of the premenire but that for exampull of vtthers they were punisshed accordyngly, & also by him; & how many tymes he haith therein offended in giffynge of promocions by prevencion & facalties & vttheres that he gaffe them to accordyngly may appere by matter of record.[58]

This is a highly significant comment, for the burden of the information which the attorney-general would lay against Wolsey in king's bench in the following October would be precisely that he had used his legatine authority to prevent a presentation by the prior of Lewes.[59] Admittedly this was only one of the allegations made against Wolsey by Darcy, but later he returned to the theme and noted the need:

> to lern whatt cavsses & matter is within the premenire stattutes & subuersion of lawes, & for that to see who haith sufferd & when & how therefor, after presidenttes & records yn tymes past.[60]

Clearly, by late July 1529, Darcy had already recognized that Wolsey was open to a charge of praemunire.

Given Thomas Darcy's evident interest and the prominence of the offence in the December 'petition', it is reasonable to suppose that the intervening book of articles submitted to the king in late July also included the charge of praemunire. In other words, breaching the antipapal statutes of the fourteenth century was not a convenient accusation thought up after a decision in October to destroy the minister, it was, from the outset, a vital weapon in the campaign against him. That would certainly square with what is known about the active use of the writ in the early sixteenth century – not least against Wolsey himself in 1521.[61] It is, admittedly, very likely that before Wolsey acknowledged the December text of the complaints against him, the nature of praemunire had been further explored by the king's lawyers as Darcy had suggested: explored and elaborated, for the offence as defined in the confession – not merely using the legatine authority but obtaining it from the pope in the first place – was only enunciated judicially in the summer of 1530, following a series of praemunire cases in king's bench arising out of Wolsey's own submission.[62] But niceties of legal doctrine apart, it is

---

[58] PRO, sp1/54, fol. 237v (*LP*, iv, 5749 at p. 2551).   [59] Spelman, i, 190.
[60] PRO, sp1/54, fol. 239 (*LP*, iv, 5749 at p. 2552).
[61] Spelman, ii, 68.
[62] Ibid., i, 190–1; ii, 69. This reading of Wolsey's offence was specifically denied by Pollard (pp. 245–7).

evident that Wolsey's critics were well aware in July 1529 that his position and behaviour as legate had exposed him to the praemunire laws.

How, then, did Wolsey escape in July 1529? The suggestion advanced above is that he bought his way out of trouble. The evidence here is a letter from court, written by the king's secretary, Stephen Gardiner, on Sunday 1 August. This reveals that the cardinal had, the previous evening, released a large sum to the king, perhaps £1,200, which was outstanding as his last half year's income as bishop of Durham, a see which he had surrendered in February in favour of Winchester.[63] The actual beneficiary was not Henry but none other than Lord Rochford, Anne Boleyn's father, to whom the king had awarded the *sede vacante* income of the see, and Wolsey also offered Rochford every assistance to expedite payment. It was a shrewd move, given the notorious avarice of Anne's father, and with Henry expressing pleasure at Wolsey's generosity it was clearly not opportune for the cardinal's enemies to press the attack on him any further.[64] The articles of complaint went into cold storage, and the only item which survived from Darcy's carefully articulated plans was the decision to call a parliament.[65]

The failure of the attempt to bring Wolsey down in late July 1529 helps to explain the minister's survival after receiving supposedly mortal blows at Blackfriars and Cambrai. At the same time it raises a further question. What was it turned the king's refusal to contemplate a praemunire charge in July into approval for such a charge in October?

A score of surviving letters and drafts make the story clear.[66] Wolsey, as has already been noted, continued to manage English diplomacy during the month of August. The main topic was the implementation of the Peace of Cambrai, in which England had been given a late face-saving mention, largely because of the loans Henry had made to Charles V and particularly to Francis I to pay off his ransom. Wolsey (with Henry VIII's approval) sought to exploit this to regain some diplomatic influence in Europe and therefore raised a series of objections to the process of ratifying the peace. French support, however, was of vital interest to Henry if he was to secure his divorce, and late in August the cardinal's policy and the king's interest came into conflict.

This was quite unexpected and followed the request from Henry VIII on 28

---

[63] PRO, sp1/55, fols. 25–6 (*LP*, iv, 5816).

[64] *Anne Boleyn*, pp. 6–7. Henry's reaction is mentioned in Gardiner's letter. Rochford tried to get Wolsey to pay over the sum directly, thus avoiding the delay and risk in collecting it himself.

[65] Darcy's complaint about the taking of bonds by Richmond's council seems also to have been conceded: R. R. Reid, *The King's Council in the North* (1921), pp. 110–12; *LP*, iv, 5815 (26). I owe this reference, confirming Hall's chronology, to Dr S. J. Gunn.

[66] For the following see *Anne Boleyn*, pp. 142–7. The apparent sequence from the arrival of the French ambassador (26 Aug.: *LP*, iv, 5911) to (?) 12 Sept. is: ibid., iv, 5885, 5875, 5879 and 5880, 5881(i), 5884, 5881(ii), 5882, 5885, 5890, 5893, 5894, 5918, 5883, 5923, 5925, 5928, 5936.

August for private advice from Wolsey, before he discussed with his council and the French ambassadors the demands which Francis I was making concerning the Treaty of Madrid.[67] Wolsey's reply made a good deal of the dangers arising from the apparently open-ended nature of England's military commitment in the treaty, and he went on to imply bad faith on the part of the French for omitting a qualification which he had himself negotiated at Amiens in August 1527. His assessment aroused Henry's sense of ill usage when, after a day's hunting, the king saw Wolsey's letter late on Monday, 30 August. However, he instructed Rochford and Gardiner to brief him in more detail the next day, and after further consideration with them, decided that Wolsey had it wrong and the minister's recommendations were ignored. Wolsey hit back at Gardiner with his usual fury towards anyone who dared to obstruct his advice to the king, and Gardiner replied with firm common sense:

> If your grace had been here and seen howe the kinges highnes toke it, [you] wold rather haue studied howe by sume benigne interpretacion to haue made the best of that which is past remedye thenne to haue persysted in the blamyng of non obseruation of couenauntes on the French partie.[68]

He also made clear that Wolsey was suspected of trying to stir Henry against the French, and although the cardinal replied denying this with fulsome expressions of his indebtedness to Gardiner, concurrently the French ambassador was writing home to say that the English had withdrawn all their queries, that Norfolk, Suffolk and Rochford were in high favour, and that Wolsey was on the way out.

The cardinal countered by requesting an emergency interview with the king to impart information too delicate for paper. Henry, however, insisted on some prior indication of the subject to be discussed, and the meeting took place only after a week's delay and in the full blaze of court publicity at the departure of Campeggio.[69] The story of that meeting at Grafton has often been told, usually following Cavendish's report that Suffolk denied the cardinal over-night lodgings so that despite an excellent interview with Henry on the evening of his arrival, Wolsey returned the next day too late to prevent Anne Boleyn carrying the king off on an impromptu picnic. This is a tale which obviously ought to be true but in fact it does not coincide with the earliest evidence. This shows that Henry spent the morning in council with Wolsey, and that after the king left, the session continued until nightfall. Wolsey, therefore, may well have won some ground back at Grafton, but if so it was not enough. Twenty days later he was indicted.

---

[67] *StP*, i, 337–8 (*LP*, IV, 5875).   [68] PRO, SP1/55, fol. 120 (*LP*, IV, 5918).

[69] *Anne Boleyn*, pp. 147–50. Since Gardiner acknowledged Wolsey's letter and requested these further details on 12 September, it is evident that (*pace* ibid., pp. 147–8 and n. 74), Wolsey cannot have seen Henry before the meeting at Grafton.

II

The reassessment advanced in this paper thus far has deliberately been confined to establishing what happened. It has suggested that the final pressure on Wolsey only began in January 1529 as a consequence of Anne Boleyn's turning against him; that it was Henry VIII's own policies which faced his minister with the impossibility of the Blackfriars hearing and ruled out diplomatic manoeuvre, Wolsey's strongest suit; that a carefully worked-out attack which focused on his vulnerability to praemunire was launched against the minister at the end of July, but that he was able to block it; and that it was a month later before the king lost confidence in him – and that as a result of the cardinal's miscalculation of the diplomatic priorities. What remains is the question, 'Why?', and to to pursue that question it is necessary to place the episode in the perspective of Tudor realities, most particularly faction.

Revisionist voices have of late been raised against the suggestion that 'faction' is a helpful concept for the understanding of Tudor society and Tudor politics.[70] At a human level the objection is understandable – historians, like everyone else, are tempted to react against something which threatens to become a new orthodoxy, and the more so if – as is all-too-frequently the case with 'faction' – the orthodoxy is proclaimed prematurely, simplistically and with too little thought. But historians are, nevertheless, obliged to take evidence seriously. Hypotheses which do not may be more interesting, but only those which grapple with the record as it actually exists are entitled to consideration. Thus, if Thomas Wyatt writes about the pressures and choices implicit in the life of the courtier, he must be taken seriously.[71] When all the ambassadors in London report to their governments in 1529 that powerful groups were plotting against Wolsey, that must be taken seriously.[72] 'Faction' is a phenomenon which cannot be ignored by historians of the sixteenth century, because at the time, both Englishmen and strangers alike took it for granted.

It is important, moreover, to recognize the real issue which the hypothesis of faction attempts to address. It is this. How and in what form did political activity operate in the Tudor monarchy? Was the fall of Wolsey an example, in Harold Wilson's words, of the minister being 'blown off course', or was there a thread, a shape, a pattern to it all? And if that was so, what was that shape? The case argued by this author in 1972, following earlier essays by Neale and Elton, was for 'the pervasiveness of faction in court life and the primacy of faction in Tudor politics' and a convincing alternative hypothesis has yet to be advanced.[73] The

---

[70] e.g. Bernard, *Nobility*, p. 206; Walker, *Skelton* especially pp. 183–4, and below at n. 74.

[71] Thomas Wyatt, *Collected Poems*, ed. J. Daadler (Oxford, 1975), nos. cv–cvii, pp. 100–12.

[72] *Anne Boleyn*, pp. 136–7.

[73] E. W. Ives, 'Faction at the Court of Henry VIII: the Fall of Anne Boleyn', *History*, 57 (1972) (hereafter 'Ives, *History*'), 186. Cf. J. E. Neale, 'The Elizabethan Political Scene', *Proceedings of the British Academy*, 34 (1948), 97–117; G. R. Elton, 'Thomas Cromwell's Decline and Fall', *Cambridge Historical Journal*, 10 (1951), 150–85.

onus is on anyone who is sceptical about faction to propose – and demonstrate – a different articulation in Tudor politics.[74]

It is equally important, however, not to go to the other extreme. 'Faction' is not a universal and all-sufficient explanation for every problem in Tudor history. Suggestions that Wolsey's fall was 'nothing but faction' would be puerile. The events of 1529 were shaped by a variety of factors ranging from Italian ecclesiastical politics and the interplay of European diplomacy, through the niceties of canon law and theology, to the personalities and relationships of the leading protagonists. To argue a role for faction is not to deny all this. It is, rather, to suggest that the interplay of these factors was significantly affected by political alignments in the court and beyond. Faction, in other words, helped to determine the terrain on which the cardinal fought his last political battles. But there can be neither time nor patience for sterile discussions of Tudor politics in reductionist terms – either 'faction is everything' or 'faction is nothing'. A decade and a half ago I wrote that:

> the chronicle of the court of Henry VIII will always resemble more a jig-saw with pieces missing than an integrated pattern. But . . . to re-arrange the jig-saw with a cautious eye on the notion of faction is an illuminating exercise.[75]

There seems no good ground to alter that opinion.

The significance of faction is forced into any discussion of the fall of Wolsey – if for no other reason – by the need to explain the motivation of the king. What is clear throughout the story is how loath Henry VIII was to abandon Thomas Wolsey, and how cushioned was the impact of his wrath when he at last decided to drop him.[76] A year later the Milanese ambassador reported the popular gossip that the cardinal's arrest at Cawood reflected the regret of his rivals at previously 'having made him fall on a feather bed', but one can have little doubt that this had not been from good will but because they had been unable to motivate Henry to greater rigour.[77] The burst of royal distrust which did result in the dismissal of the minister came very late, was short-lived, and within a few weeks the king was secretly back-tracking. Henry evidently abandoned Wolsey only under pressure. The question is, pressure from whom?

One obvious answer is Anne Boleyn. She took the lead against Wolsey – and

---

[74] Of the critics, G. W. Bernard, 'Politics and Government in Tudor England', *Historical Journal*, 31 (1988), 159–82 offers rhetorical questions and assertions. G. Walker, 'The "Expulsion of the Minions" of 1519, Reconsidered', *Historical Journal*, 32 (1989), 1–16 does advance a serious alternative hypothesis – that of conciliar action. This, however, would only dispose of the notion of faction on the reductionist assumption that the choice is *either* Wolsey *or* the council (see also Walker, *Skelton*, pp. 177–9). Given that the evidence indicates that Wolsey dominated the council (cf. the December petition paras 9, 10, 11, 12, 15: Coke, pp. 90–1; John Skelton, 'Why come ye nat to courte', lines 181–9 and Guy, *Court*, pp. 29–30), one would expect counsellors and minister to tell the same tale, as Samman demonstrates. For P. Gwyn, see below n. 86.

[75] Ives, *History*, pp. 186–7. For comments on the dangers of an exclusively factional interpretation, see G. R. Elton, 'Tudor Government', *Historical Journal*, 31 (1988), 425–34.

[76] See above pp. 288, 293–4 and below at n. 135. [77] *CSPM*, 832.

pursued him relentlessly. It was her privileged position which did the vital damage to the king's confidence in him, and when the episode was over, she was the real victor.[78] The view of older historians that her influence was only incidental to the story is wholly unconvincing; without her involvement, Wolsey would probably have survived in 1529 as he so often had before. Yet although Anne Boleyn must be central to any explanation of the fall of Wolsey, she is not in herself a sufficient explanation. Much more than a catalyst, Anne was, nevertheless, only one element in the equation.

What contemporary observers also point to is an alignment against Wolsey of 'diuers of the great estates and lordes of the Councell', including the dukes of Norfolk and Suffolk and Lord Rochford. This is how Cavendish remembered the situation, but it is also the way in which the imperial ambassador saw it at the time, and it was he who noticed the junction between this group and Anne Boleyn.[79] As for the French ambassador, Jean du Bellay, he wrote of 'Norfolk and his gang'.[80] Norfolk, Suffolk and Rochford were active against the minister before Blackfriars, and it was Suffolk who made the famous protest at the trial: 'By the Masse, now I see the olde sawe is true, that there was neuer Legate nor Cardinall, that did good in England.'[81] The trio was prominent at court in August, and the three of them emerged as the leading public figures once the cardinal had been dismissed.[82] Also associated with them was Thomas Darcy who put the detail into the July plot. Another was Francis Bryan whose reports from abroad kept up a nice line in implication against Wolsey, while Stephen Gardiner had established relations with Anne Boleyn several months before becoming the king's secretary.[83]

A recent study has, it is true, argued that Charles Brandon's hostility to Wolsey was limited, and was less a matter of hunting with the factional pack than loyally shadowing the king's own disenchantment with the minister.[84] This suggestion might persuade, if the failure of the legatine court really was the decisive point in the king's turning against the cardinal; the evident signs of Suffolk's beginning to act against Wolsey earlier in the year would then be merely perceptive anticipations of his master's mind. But if, as has been argued above, Henry became disenchanted with Wolsey only in September, the suggestion that Suffolk was following the royal lead would not account for the duke's behaviour towards Wolsey over the previous nine months. Du Bellay was certainly in no doubt about

---

[78] *Anne Boleyn*, pp. 143, 150–1.
[79] Cavendish, pp. 35–6, 43–4; *CSPS*, 1527–9, pp. 885–6; for the following see also *Anne Boleyn*, pp. 136–7, 140–3.
[80] V.-L. Bourrilly, P. de Vaissière, (eds.), *Ambassades en Angleterre de Jean du Bellay* (Paris, 1905), no. 188 at p. 543.
[81] Hall, p. 758; Cavendish, p. 90; *CSPS*, 1529–30, pp. 235–6.   [82] *Anne Boleyn*, p. 151.
[83] Ibid., pp. 128, 136–8.
[84] S. J. Gunn, *Charles Brandon, Duke of Suffolk* (Oxford, 1988), (hereafter, 'Gunn, *Brandon*'), pp. 106–14.

Suffolk's position. At the end of June he warned Montmorency that 'it was as a member of the Anne Boleyn camp that the duke of Suffolk came to see you'.[85]

Another objection to explaining Wolsey's fall at least partially in terms of faction, is that the motive of Wolsey's enemies is not plausible.[86] Plainly, few people were capable of, still fewer interested in, taking on the work load which so fascinated Wolsey, so why should Norfolk or any of the others have wanted to oust him from office? The answer is that what was at issue was not the duties of the minister but his status. Wolsey's commanding position devalued the other figures at court. Boleyn, who had been squeezed out of household office by the cardinal, undoubtedly saw his daughter as a means to recover and increase his own standing with the king; Norfolk, who had never yet achieved the status in England of the duc de Montmorency in France, seems to have expected a similar benefit.[87] What was at stake for Darcy was not only the settling of a personal grudge but the recovery of an authority and a reputation blighted by the cardinal.[88] As for Gardiner, any loss of royal favour by Wolsey would be his great opportunity, while Suffolk had visions of great state office and a chance to be co-leader of a new regime.[89] For Anne, of course, a crown beckoned.

From New Year 1529, one can see these people chipping away at Wolsey's position, and although their direct assault in July was blocked, their presence at court during the summer, and particularly that of Anne Boleyn, was an enormous advantage. Rochford's attendance as chaperon for his daughter almost gave him the status of counsellor in residence and he, assisted by Gardiner, seems to have been behind the crucial reversal of diplomatic policy on 31 August. This was clearly a deliberate blow directed at Wolsey as well as a bid to have Rochford's own diplomatic expertise recognized, and it was followed by stalling on the cardinal's request for access to the king's presence. Here we have all the classic ingredients of faction: an alliance whose target was an individual, which operated by seeking to put pressure on the ruler, and which sought to exploit the mechanisms of the court.

It is at this point that the 'boke of articles' has more to tell us. As has been seen, some at least of the complaints which appear in the December petition and can be presumed to have featured in the original 'boke' were known to Jean du Bellay by 22 October. It is, however, curious that the offences which he described do not correspond with the accusations which had been put to Wolsey in king's bench a fortnight before – and which the minister confessed the very day the ambassador's letter was despatched.[90] Du Bellay, that is, knew that Wolsey had been accused, but was informed in detail about the wrong charges!

[85] Du Bellay, p. 58. 'C'estoyt de la menee de Anne Boleyn que le duc de Suffolk estoyt allé vers vous.'
[86] e.g. P. J. Gwyn, *The King's Cardinal* (1990), p. 570.
[87] *Anne Boleyn*, pp. 125, 131; Guy, *More*, pp. 97–8.
[88] PRO, sp1/55, fol. 241 (*LP*, iv, 5749 at p. 2554).
[89] Guy, *More*, pp. 32–3, 107, 109, 115–18, but cf. Gunn, *Brandon*, pp. 112–17.
[90] Du Bellay, p. 112; *LP*, iv, 6017, 6035; Spelman, i, 190.

A possible explanation of this discrepancy is suggested by the ambassador's observation that Wolsey had been offered the choice between answering to the king or to parliament and that he had chosen the former.[91] As 'answering to the king' clearly meant facing the charges brought in king's bench (about which Du Bellay knew nothing), the likelihood must be that the accusations which the ambassador had been told about were those threatened by the alternative, 'answering to parliament'. It is also possible to hazard the guess that Du Bellay obtained the information in his letter of 22 October from the formal announcement Norfolk had made three days before in star chamber, about Wolsey's 'diuerse and sondery offences'.[92]

The obvious inference to draw from this is that in late October 1529, the July articles were again being used to publicize the option of proceeding against the minister in parliament. But why? Continued promotion of that option would appear to be a pointless contradiction of the decision taken ten days previously to prosecute Wolsey at common law. It might of course, be argued that what the crown wanted was to force Wolsey's surrender in king's bench, and that talk about attainder was nothing more than psychological pressure. This, however, seems unlikely since the same charges would be pressed again in the December petition, despite the fact that by then Wolsey had been restored to royal protection.[93] A more probable explanation for such a divergent strategy being persisted with, is that the alternatives offered to Wolsey represent rival policies for dealing with the minister which were in contention in court and council. One, envisaging an act of attainder was based on Lord Darcy's careful work towards such a measure, and had already been promoted by Anne Boleyn's allies in July. The other was more moderate – prosecution in king's bench – and this was the course eventually adopted.

The choice of that course is readily explained by a factor which we have seen was operative throughout Wolsey's fall: Henry VIII's wish to avoid extreme action against him. A prosecution under the praemunire statutes was the minimum the king could do, given the evidence, and it had the added advantage of weakening the campaign for a parliamentary attainder by giving Wolsey the opportunity to make a personal surrender to Henry, twelve days before the parliamentary session began. Certainly, such an explanation would fit with the evidence we have in Hall's *Chronicle*. In the first place, Hall had no doubt that the decision to prosecute was a response by the king to a demand from the council for action. His version is that 'all the lordes and other the kynges counsaill' were absent from the opening of the Michaelmas law term on 9 October, having:

> gone to Wynsore to the Kyng, where they enformed the Kyng that all thynges that he [Wolsey] had done almoste, by his power Legantyne, were in the case of the premunire and prouision: and that the Cardinall had forfected, all his landes,

---

[91] Du Bellay, p. 112.   [92] Hall, p. 760.

[93] On 18 Nov.: Thomas Rymer, *Foedera* (1704–35) (hereafter 'Rymer'), xiv, 351 (*LP*, iv, 6059).

tenementes, goodes and catelles to the kyng: wherefore the kyng willyng to ordre him accordyng to the ordre of his lawes, caused his attorney Cristopher Hales to sue out a Writte of Premunire against hym.[94]

A Chapuys letter indicates that the council was with Wolsey at Westminster until 6 October, and since time would have been needed to prepare the indictment (which was entered on 9 October), the confrontation with Henry should probably be placed on either the 7th or early on the 8th.[95] Hall's account also picks up the point that the king's decision was to proceed 'accordyng to the ordre of his lawes', almost as though to imply that an alternative procedure was on offer – and it must be remembered that Hall was fully cognizant of the July campaign.

The 'boke of articles' may, thus, represent the option the king rejected in the attack on Wolsey. If so, it would certainly provide a convincing explanation for Norfolk's continuing to canvas the complaints, despite the indictment of the cardinal in king's bench. Royal leniency spelled danger for the duke and the rest of the Boleyn faction, and it was clearly imminent – Wolsey, in fact, would be pardoned secretly and by word of mouth on 2 November.[96] The more currency, therefore, which could be given to the articles, the more difficult it would be to make that leniency public. Pressure was the name of the game, but pressure on Henry, not Wolsey.

This reading would also suggest an explanation for the 'very unpleasant language' Thomas More used against Wolsey at the opening of parliament, which his apologists find it hard to swallow, and which, as we have already seen, appears to contradict the concurrent private signals being made to the former minister by the king.[97] However, once it is recognized that Henry was under pressure from Anne and her allies to abandon his lenient treatment of Wolsey, it becomes easy to see how he needed the issue of the cardinal to be put to parliament at the start of the session in a way which would discourage further agitation. More's speech did exactly that. Darcy had anticipated a speech inviting

[94] Hall, p. 760. Pollard, p. 242 and n. 3 understands 'were gone' to mean that the counsellors went to Windsor on 9 October, following a rapid visit to London by the king on 8 October – quoting, for the latter, Du Bellay's letter of 12 October to Francis I (*LP*, IV, 6022; cf. Du Bellay, pp. 97–101; Samman, p. 386 concurs). However, comparison of this letter with the previous one (Du Bellay, pp. 91–4) and the letter of Chapuys of 8 October (*CSPS*, *1529–30*, pp. 276–9) suggests that any royal visit must antedate Du Bellay's first interview with the council on 3 October. This would indicate Hall to mean that the counsellors 'were away at', not 'went to' Windsor on 9 October.

[95] The council was busy at Westminster each day from 3 October, up to and including the morning of 6 October when it met Chapuys. If Henry's visit is redated (as n. 94 above), room is left for the delegation Hall describes to go to Windsor on 6 or 7 October and for the indictment to be drawn in time to be preferred in king's bench on 9 October.

[96] Wolsey's letter of 2 Nov. (*StP*, I, 348–9 (*LP*, IV, 6024) dated by association with Russell's visit – see above n. 8) asks 'that as sone as yt shal seme to your petyfull hart and to stand with Your Gracys honor, yt may opynly be knowen to my poore frendes and servanttes that Your Hyghnes hath forgeven me myn offence and tresspace, and delivryd me from the daunger of your lawys'. The inference must be that this news had been brought by Russell.

[97] See Gairdner, p. 90 for the comment.

complaints against the previous regime – he had them ready.[98] Instead, More began with the required denunciation of Wolsey's offences, then announced that he had already been gently corrected, and ended by consigning the cardinal to insignificance as no more than a dire warning to others.[99] Thomas More, one may suggest, was deliberately and on instructions, setting out to forestall an attack on the cardinal. Far from it being an example of political time-serving which stabbed in the back a man he had worked with for a decade, still less a contradiction of the king's secret wishes, the speech of the new chancellor was of a piece with the comfort and assistance which Henry was sending to the old. As Chapuys would report:

> from the beginning [the king] determined not to lay this case before parliament, because had it decided against the cardinal, he could not, in face of such a decision, have pardoned him as he intended to do.[100]

If this reading of More's purpose is correct, his speech was certainly a success. No hue and cry was raised against the disgraced cardinal, and parliament instead got down to business.[101] Only when the session was drawing towards a close was there a brief revival of interest in Wolsey's offences and the introduction into the commons of the text of the complaints against him.[102] How and why this final flurry?

As has been noted, this, the surviving text, took the form of a petition to Henry VIII dated 1 December. It has seventeen signatories: the chancellor, twelve lay peers, two courtiers who were MPs, and two judges.[103] Geoffrey Elton, despite the poor representation of the commons, describes the petition as the work of a committee of both houses. Its purpose, he suggests, was to set in motion the act of attainder against the cardinal – a view which necessarily leads him to reject Hall's statement that the document arrived in the commons already counter-signed by Wolsey.[104] Pollard, accepting Hall's statement on that point, rejected the notion that the petition was directed towards securing an act of attainder, but he too saw it as the work of a committee of both houses (as did S. T. Bindoff).[105] S. E. Lehmberg, recognizing the balance of the signatories, ascribes the petition to a committee of the upper house (although he thereby fails to account for the presence of the two MPs). In his view the document was not intended to secure

---

[98] See above n. 47.   [99] Guy, *More*, pp. 113–14.

[100] Charles V, *Correspondence of . . .*, ed. W. Bradford (1850) (hereafter 'Bradford'), p. 306.

[101] Lehmberg, p. 81.   [102] See above, n. 47.

[103] See above, n. 48. The signatories were: More (chancellor), Norfolk and Suffolk (dukes), Dorset and Exeter (marquesses), Oxford, Northumberland, Shrewsbury (earls), FitzWalter, Rochford, Darcy, Mountjoy, Sandys (barons), William Fitzwilliam (treasurer of the household), Henry Guildford (comptroller), John Fitzjames (CJKB) and Antony Fitzherbert (JCP) (Coke, p. 95), i.e. in order of precedence. The 6th to 9th places in Herbert (p. 417) read: 'Shrewsbury, Fitzwalter, Oxford and Northumberland'. BL, Cott.Vesp.F ix, fol. 177v agrees with Coke but lays out the names in a way which clearly follows a lost MS rather than Coke, and makes it possible to see why Herbert read the list in the wrong order.

[104] Elton, *Reform*, pp. 112–13.   [105] Pollard, pp. 258, 261–2; *Commons*, II, 264.

action against the cardinal but 'to record Wolsey's misdeeds and to impress upon Henry the strength of the feeling against him'.[106]

The evident difficulty indicated by these various assessments arises from a general assumption that when Hall wrote: 'Duryng this Parliament was brought doune to the comons, the boke of articles whiche the Lordes had put to the kyng agaynste the Cardinall', he meant that the petition came down from the house of lords to the house of commons.[107] What is clear, however, is that Hall intended no more than a reference back to the complaints submitted to the king in late July: 'the Lordes' does not mean the upper house, but what were earlier described as 'the nobles and prelates . . . euery man of the Kynges Counsaill'.[108] Among the commentators, only Edward Coke seems to have recognized that the petition originated outside parliament.[109] What we have are the July articles in a new guise and there is no need to invent an unevenly constituted, vaguely purposed and manifestly abortive parliamentary committee to produce it, or to doubt Wolsey's signature on the text (which Hall almost certainly handled).

Given that the December petition was not part of a parliamentary process, why was it introduced into the commons? The possible answers depend on whether the document should be construed primarily as a petition or primarily as a confession. Hall's evidence suggests the latter, for he is quite specific that the document was introduced in the house after it had been acknowledged by Wolsey. In other words, what had begun as a petition had been turned into a confession before it reached the commons. Lehmberg, therefore, might appear to be correct in his suggestion that 'the petition was sent down only to inform the Commons and to demonstrate that all necessary action against Wolsey had been taken'.[110]

On the other hand, Lehmberg's hypothesis does not explain why the December text was framed as a petition to Henry VIII in the first place, or why it included the demand – overtaken by the surrender of the cardinal in October – that steps should be taken to ensure that Wolsey:

> be so provided for, that he never have any power, jurisdiction, or authority, hereafter to trouble, vex, and impoverish the commonwealth of this your realm, as he hath done heretofore, to the great hurt and damage of every man almost, high and low.[111]

Cavendish's somewhat garbled recollection was that the complaints were entered with attainder in mind, and that this was blocked by Cromwell's eloquence.[112] That, however, cannot be the case. First there is the difficulty that it would mean that More signed a document directly contradicting the king's known wish for moderation. Even more insuperable is the fact of Wolsey's own

---

[106] Lehmberg, pp. 102–3.   [107] Hall, p. 767.   [108] Ibid., p. 759.
[109] Coke, p. 88 makes no reference to parliament and attributes the petition to 'the lords and others of (Henry VIII's) privy councell and . . . two of the principall judges'.
[110] Lehmberg, pp. 103–4.   [111] Coke, p. 95.   [112] Cavendish, pp. 112–13.

signature: it is an inept attempt at attainder which is compromised, before it is launched, by a full confession by the accused!

To reconcile the extra-parliamentary nature of the petition with its arrival in parliament as a confession, it is necessary to look to what was going on outside the two houses, and once more to the behaviour of those whom Henry recognized 'were not Wolsey's friends'. The documentation is scrappy, a good deal of it is mutilated and most undated, but the outline is clear.

Wolsey's submission to the king, though abject and total, had not been made without guarantees, in particular from Norfolk and Suffolk.[113] He seems to have been completely convinced that he was surrendering only his temporal possessions:

> As God be my judge, I nevyr thowgth and [so I was assured] at the makyng of my submyssyon, to depart [from any of my pro]motions . . . these nobyll men dyd other wyse promyse, on ther honors, to me, opon trust whereof I made the fynale gyft of myn hole estat.[114]

What he experienced, however, was 'dayly alteration' and continual pressure.[115] Throughout the time parliament was in session his future was in doubt; letters passed, judges visited, the duke of Norfolk arrived without warning and in the course of this, the 'petition' was forced on his attention.[116]

What his enemies still wanted, of course, was security against a Wolsey come-back – action to make certain that 'he be so provided for, that he never have any power . . . hereafter to trouble', perhaps, as was claimed, 'the common-wealth', but most certainly them themselves. The delay and the steady erosion of what he had thought saved from the wreck drove Wolsey to distraction, and only when he had confessed his guilt was any progress made on his case.[117] It would indeed seem very reasonable to conjecture that although the October attempt at attainder had failed, the complaints and the threat they carried were revived in December to extort a confession from Wolsey as the price he had to pay to secure a resolution of his problems – much though he might protest his innocence in private.[118] In October 1529 the object had been to obstruct Henry's leniency by publicizing what Wolsey was accused of having done. In December the objective was the same, the technique slightly different: extorting a confession which advertised what Wolsey himself admitted he had done. Such a confession did not merely humiliate. As Chapuys recognized, the one thing which no desire by Henry to restore his old friend to power could over-ride was a condemnation in parliament.[119] Forcing Wolsey to admit a range of offences against the crown

---

[113] *StP*, I, 352, 355 (*LP*, IV, 6098, 6181); Ellis, *Letters*, 1, ii, 7–9, 10–13.
[114] *StP*, I, 355–6 (*LP*, IV, 6181).
[115] Ibid., I, 350–2, 357 (*LP*, IV, 6114, 6226, 6263).
[116] Ibid., I, 350–2, 354 (*LP*, IV, 6114, 6204, 6263); Cavendish, pp. 113–20.
[117] HMC, *Mss of the Marquis of Bath* (1904–8), II, 5.   [118] *StP*, I, 354 (*LP*, IV, 6204).
[119] See the comment of Chapuys at n. 100.

much wider than anything he had confessed at common law, and drawing that admission to the attention of the commons, was as near as his enemies could get to such a formal parliamentary censure.

As well as suggesting something of the manoeuvres behind Wolsey's surrender and house arrest, the December text of the 'boke of articles' sheds some further light on the nature of faction in Wolsey's fall. If the December text is, as has been argued, a revival of the October complaints and related through them to the July attack on Wolsey, the possibility must be that the list of the December signatories is the list of the faction which for at least six months had been trying to bring the cardinal down. The signatures of Norfolk, Suffolk, Rochford and Darcy would certainly suggest this. The list, however, also includes several supporters of the existing queen who were deeply hostile to any idea that Anne should succeed Catherine, and who had, as far as is known, no link with Norfolk and his other allies in July 1529.[120] In the case of another signatory, William Fitzwilliam, there is positive evidence against his involvement in the attempted coup. Not only had he for nearly a decade been Wolsey's staunchest ally at court, but on 1 August it was Fitzwilliam who presented Wolsey's offer to Henry of accommodation at The More during the forthcoming progress.[121] The conclusion must, therefore, be that the December list is an aggregate of the faction which had failed in July and other groups and individuals who had joined subsequently. Indeed, it seems safe to conclude that they had done so by October, because the council meeting of 19 October which was called to publicize Wolsey's offences (and is the likeliest source of Du Bellay's information on the 22nd), was attended by precisely the same twelve peers who would sign the petition in December.[122]

For the attack on Wolsey in October 1529 to be recognized as the work of a coalition is to place the episode as yet another example of what may be termed the phenomenon of 'grand faction' in Tudor England – the coming together of disparate groups and individuals to pursue one single objective, in this case the removal of the minister from power.[123] Supporters of Anne and Catherine may seem strange bedfellows, but the adherence of the latter is readily explicable by their offence at Wolsey's continuing attempts to undermine her success at Blackfriars and, perhaps, by concern at his alleged softness towards heresy. Certainly someone thought it worthwhile to include in the complaints against Wolsey a reference to his role in obstructing the repression of heresy at Cambridge in 1523.[124] Fear of Lutheran infection would, of itself, have provided a ready link with Norfolk's ally, Darcy, while another signatory, Henry Guildford, although personally committed to the king, was also deeply offended at the way

[120] E.g. Exeter (see *Anne Boleyn*, p. 125); Mountjoy (see Mattingly, pp. 102, 264); Sandys (see *CSPS, 1534–5*, p. 375); Shrewsbury (see *CSPS, 1529–30*, pp. 804–5; Bernard, *Nobility*, p. 50).
[121] PRO, sp1/55, fols. 27–8 (*LP*, IV, 5817).   [122] Miller, p. 111.   [123] Ives, *History*, pp. 179–80.
[124] para. 43: Coke, p. 94. The events referred to can only have taken place in the parliament of 1523.

Catherine had been treated.[125] He had private grievances, too, as well as being familiar, in his capacity as comptroller of the household, with the hostility of the lesser court officers to Wolsey's interference – something which also explains Fitzwilliam's desertion of the minister at long last.[126] The signature of Sir John Fitzjames, chief justice of England, can be similarly accounted for as representing the dislike of the common-law judges for the cardinal's supposedly over-free use of chancery injunctions, although the grievance of Anthony Fitzherbert, the other judge who signed, appears in detail as one of the actual articles of complaint.[127]

The October attack on Wolsey was thus a characteristic instance of Tudor grand faction such as is seen next in the destruction of Anne Boleyn, and it was typically brief.[128] Very probably these last minute adherents joined the wolf pack only towards the end of September when it appeared that the king was at last willing to act against the cardinal, and once the cardinal was out of the way, there was nothing to keep the alliance together, certainly not supporters of both Catherine and Anne. Even the faction which had attempted the July coup did not stay of one mind for long, and by 1531 there were wide rifts between Norfolk, Suffolk, Rochford and Darcy.[129] That this was the case should cause no more surprise than the collapse of the larger grouping. Factional alignments pursued objectives expressed in terms of people, and once those objectives had been realized, new imperatives inevitably began to operate. Ironically, the point would be demonstrated most forcibly by the one group among Wolsey's October critics which did exhibit some continuity, the supporters of Catherine. Traceable back to the reign of Henry VII, it would effectively be destroyed by the attack on the Courtenay and Pole families in 1538, precisely because it had not adjusted to new circumstances.[130]

The fall of Wolsey confirms, therefore, that in seeking to understand Tudor faction we are dealing with a phenomenon which is varied, subtle and changing. But in this, faction only reflected what it was – and what makes it quicksilver to understand – the expression of the organic relationships which radiate from the individual: in the vertical plane with superiors and inferiors; horizontally with equals – both individuals and in groups – on different bearings and at varying ranges; relationships which mature and decay over time; and all influenced by stability or change in the overall environment. A helpful analogy is the operation of British politics, two and three centuries later, before the age of mass parties. Faction is dynamic and fluid, not a thing of structures, but one ignores it at one's peril.

[125] *CSPS, 1531–3*, pp. 175–7.   [126] *Commons*, II, 143, 264; paras. 33–36, 39; Coke, pp. 92–3.
[127] E. W. Ives, *The Common Lawyers of Pre-Reformation England* (Cambridge, 1983), p. 219; paras. 20, 21, 31: Coke, pp. 91+, 91.
[128] *Anne Boleyn*, pp. 337, 346–9, 355–7, 413–15; E. W. Ives, *Faction in Tudor England* (2nd ed. 1986), pp. 17–18.
[129] *Anne Boleyn*, pp. 170–7.   [130] Ibid., pp. 124–5, 415–16; Elton, *Reform*, pp. 279–81.

III

With his pardon at last granted, Wolsey still had some months of life left, but history traditionally accords him little further attention. Yet the events of those final months serve, even in brief, as a revealing coda to the story of the cardinal's fall, restating the theme of 1529 and then, in the end, inverting it.

Wolsey's reaction to the loss of office certainly confirmed where his priorities lay. In a frantic assault on the court, he showered promises on his former supporters and largesse on his enemies.[131] He targeted Anne Boleyn in particular; 'attaining her favour' was 'the only help and remedy'.[132] He did everything he could to remain in proximity to the king. Esher, or even better Richmond, would be his Colombey-les-Deux-Eglises.[133]

The faction which had supplanted him continued to be terrified at the possibility of his recovery. Anne was unyielding in her insistence that Henry keep his promise not to see Wolsey, but in February 1530, Russell reported to Chapuys a telling conversation he had had about the cardinal's future with a very worried Norfolk.[134] Hence it was that pressure on Wolsey was not relaxed for an instant, despite the 'resolution' of his position and the open royal pardon which had followed.[135] Eventually the faction attempted to distance Wolsey from the court by forcing him to move to Yorkshire, but even so, Henry maintained his links with the cardinal, supplying funds, writing on Wolsey's behalf to require 'the favourable and loving assistance of the noblemen and others in those parts', and making remarks which kept the cardinal's hope alive.[136]

The departure for Yorkshire seems, however, to have coincided with a decisive shift in Wolsey's thinking. Faced by the realization that he would not be able to return to power in the immediate future, he crossed the line from legitimate Tudor politics to high treason, and began to plot with unfriendly or potentially unfriendly foreign powers to force his way back into office. Why he rejected the wiser course of waiting until his rivals demonstrated their ineffectiveness is not clear. Perhaps it was the move away from the familiar ambit of the court which produced such desperation, or perhaps he had become convinced that only

---

[131] *Anne Boleyn*, pp. 157–9; *CSPS*, 1529–30, pp. 468–9; Ellis, *Letters*, I (ii), 12–13; *StP*, I, 351–2, 355 (*LP*, IV, 6181).

[132] *StP*, I, 352.

[133] According to Cavendish (pp. 123–4), Wolsey moved from Esher to Richmond in early February, 1530.

[134] Bradford, pp. 309–10.

[135] *LP*, IV, 6213, 6214, 6220. The persistence of royal favour to Wolsey is evident in the fact that in the end he did not (*pace* common opinion) forfeit the see of Winchester and the abbey of St Albans. What he surrendered was *control*, against compensation of a pension of 1000 marks from Winchester: Rymer, *Foedera*, XIV, 371; PRO, SP1/57, fols. 4–15 (*LP*, IV, 6220). The indenture was very similar to ones entered into by nobles incurring royal disfavour and the expectation of such documents was that they might be cancelled after a period of good behaviour.

[136] Pollard, pp. 273–5; Ellis, *Letters*, I (ii), 173.

tough action would break the hold which Anne Boleyn had over Henry.[137] Whatever the explanation, before Easter Wolsey had opened negotiations with Francis I and Charles V, and soon afterwards with Catherine of Aragon and the pope.[138] By August he was communicating daily with Chapuys, using his physician Dr Augustine ('Agostino') to pass the messages.[139] Augustine (who throughout his career doubled as medical man and professional secret agent) was also the link with France.[140]

Of these overtures, undoubtedly the more dangerous were those to Catherine, the emperor and the pope which were directed at securing an order from Rome for Henry and Anne to separate.[141] What, however, brought the cardinal down seems to have been discovery of his communications with France.[142] Their exact nature is so far obscure. Since the English government was desperate to maintain relationships with its most vital ally, it responded to the discovery of Wolsey's plans with a news embargo, until confessions by the arrested Augustine made it possible to issue a suitably edited version blaming the pope and whitewashing the behaviour of the French envoy.[143] But the fact that this had to be done shows

[137] Cf. the tone of Wolsey's letter to Henry on arrival in the diocese of York in April 1530: PRO, SP1/57, fols. 78–9 (LP, IV, 6344).

[138] Ibid., IV, 6273, 6307; CSPS, 1529–30, pp. 468, 476, 485, 514, 600–1, 619.   [139] Ibid., p. 692.

[140] Ibid., p. 448; CSPV, 1527–33, 637. For Augustine, see E. A. Hammond, 'Doctor Augustine, physician to Cardinal Wolsey and King Henry VIII', Medical History, 19 (1975) (hereafter 'Hammond'), 215–49. Chapuys considered medical men especially suitable as agents 'because they can come and go to all places without suspicion': ibid., 19, 235.

[141] CSPS, 1529–30, pp. 819–20. According to the report of Augustine's confession (see below n. 144), by Vaux, the French ambassador, as told by the Venetian envoy to Chapuys, Wolsey expected that this would lead to a papal interdict, 'pensant par ce moyen que tout le Royaulme se mutineroit contre les Gouvernemens, et que en tel trouble jl rempoigneroit le manyement' (Bradford, pp. 325–6). Pollard (pp. 296–7) precised the calendar version (CSPS, 1529–30, p. 820) as: 'he hoped to cause a rising throughout the country and in the midst of the confusion seize again the reins of government', and deemed the charge 'highly improbable'. The passage becomes entirely credible (though optimistic) if translated in the passive and without introducing the anachronistic institutional term, 'the government', e.g. 'thinking by this means the whole realm would rise up against the [current] policies and that in the [ensuing] trouble he would again grasp the management of affairs'.

[142] LP, IV, 6720; CSPS, 1529–30, pp. 804–5. The suggestion is advanced in Anne Boleyn, pp. 157–9 that the French might deliberately have 'shopped' Wolsey, in which case the cover-up (see below n. 143) was collusive. For the English political dimension of Wolsey's fall and the continued pressure from his enemies, see ibid., pp. 157–9. The importance of the latter is accentuated by Henry's continued reluctance to destroy Wolsey (ibid., p. 158). The assurances made to Wolsey after his arrest by Shrewsbury and Kingston repeat those of Norris and Russell the year before (Cavendish, pp. 164–5, 172 and above pp. 287–8).

[143] L. R. Gardiner, 'Further news of Cardinal Wolsey's end, November–December, 1530', Bulletin of the Institute of Historical Research, 57 (1984), 99–107; StP, VII, 211–13 (LP, IV, 6733); CSPV, 1527–33, 632. The copy of the 'confession' put to (? agreed with) Vaux, the French ambassador and sent to inform Francis I is even more suspect than Gardiner suggests (pp. 103–4). It was in the hand of Augustine, but purported to be 'a certen clause translated out of Latine and into Englishe' which Wolsey had asked Augustine to write out and send to Vaux (and which he claimed he had not done). One is forced to ask (a) who wrote the original Latin? (b) if the inference was 'Wolsey' who needed an amanuensis in order to conceal his own hand, why was not the original produced? (c)

that there was a good deal to hide, and we may note that Norfolk took over Augustine as his agent to Charles V.[144]

So Wolsey fell for the last time, an object lesson in the ways of Tudor politics. Stripped of office by factional assault, the hope of renewed royal favour blocked, he had become the victim of the high risk alternative which faced all who could neither break down nor break into the court circle. If the accepted mechanisms for persuading the king were closed, forcing him to listen was the only way. Faction drove Wolsey from office, and faction drove him into high treason.

why was not a copy of that Latin text prepared for Vaux rather than a translation? (d) why was the translation made into English and not French? The suspicion must be that the text was never other than in English, and was a fiction given some credibility by being written out in the hand of a known secret agent.

[144] *Anne Boleyn*, p. 159 n. 25; Hammond, pp. 225–6. n.b. also Augustine's recognizance in £100 to keep secret his depositions about Wolsey: PRO, sp1/58, fol. 215 (*LP*, iv, 6763).

Index

Places in England are given in their sixteenth-century counties. Dates after titles are those at which the individual concerned inherited or was granted them.